Generational Politics in the United States

Generational Politics in the United States

From the Silents to Gen Z and Beyond

Sally Friedman and David Schultz, Editors

UNIVERSITY OF MICHIGAN PRESS

Ann Arbor

For questions or permissions, please contact um.press.perms@umich.edu

Published in the United States of America by the
University of Michigan Press
Manufactured in the United States of America
Printed on acid-free paper
First published June 2024

A CIP catalog record for this book is available from the British Library.

Library of Congress Cataloging-in-Publication Data

Names: Friedman, Sally, 1950– editor. | Schultz, David A. (David Andrew), 1958– editor. |
    Michigan Publishing (University of Michigan), publisher.
Title: Generational politics in the United States : from the Silents to Gen Z and beyond / Sally
    Friedman and Davy Schultz, Editors.
Description: Ann Arbor : University of Michigan Press, 2024. | Includes bibliographical references
    and index.
Identifiers: LCCN 2024000456 (print) | LCCN 2024000457 (ebook) | ISBN 9780472076765
    (hardback) | ISBN 9780472056767 (paperback) | ISBN 9780472904440 (ebook other)
Subjects: LCSH: Generations—Political aspects—United States. | Generation Y—Political activity—
    United States. | Generation Z—Political activity—United States. | United States—Politics and
    government—21st century. | BISAC: POLITICAL SCIENCE / Civics & Citizenship |
    POLITICAL SCIENCE / American Government / General
Classification: LCC JK275 .P46 2024 (print) | LCC JK275 (ebook) | DDC 320.973—dc23/
    eng/20240214
LC record available at https://lccn.loc.gov/2024000456
LC ebook record available at https://lccn.loc.gov/2024000457

DOI: https://doi.org/10.3998/mpub.11621506

The University of Michigan Press's open access publishing program is made possible thanks to
additional funding from the University of Michigan Office of the Provost and the generous support
of contributing libraries.

Cover illustration courtesy iStock.com / frimages

To Roberta Sigel and Herbert Weisberg,
our graduate school professors, with thanks.

Contents

Acknowledgments ix

Introduction: Generations in American Politics 1
 David Schultz and Sally Friedman

Part I: Foundations

1 | Generations, Politics, and the Practice of Political Science 11
 David Schultz

2 | Generational Change in Partisanship:
 An Age-Period-Cohort Accounting 34
 Laura Stoker

3 | Collective Memory and the Pandemic Emergence of
 Generation Z 85
 Scott L. McLean

Part II: Attitudes and Opinions

4 | Generational Divides, Changing Times, or Aging?
 Examining Immigration Opinion in the U.S., 2004–2018 117
 Jeffrey C. Dixon, Andrew S. Fullerton, and Victoria E. Nash

5 | Generational Attitudes toward Drug Policies in the
 United States 139
 Leah Hutton Blumenfeld

6 | Gender and the Generations: You Haven't Come a
 Long Way Yet, Baby 162
 Whitney Ross Manzo and David B. McLennan

7 | What American Heroism Teaches Us about Generations
and Politics   182
Bruce Peabody

Part III: Participation and Political Engagement

8 | "The Times They Are a Changin'": Generational Comparisons
of the Civil Rights Movement with the Current-Day
Climate Movement   213
Robin Boyle-Laisure

9 | Building Youthful Habits of Voting   238
Niall Guy Michelsen

10 | Presidential Candidates on Campus and Civic Engagement
among College Students: Mobilizing a New Generation   260
Kenneth W. Moffett and Laurie L. Rice

Part IV: Impact

11 | Millennial Generation Political Engagement—Democratically
Motivated or Disenchanted? Insights from the 2020 Election   299
Ashley D. Ross and Stella M. Rouse

12 | Generational Shifts Change Politics in Florida   328
Susan A. MacManus and Anthony A. Cilluffo

13 | How They Govern: Do Millennial Mayors Bring a
Generational Perspective to Their Activities?   355
Sally Friedman, Michael A. Armato, and Emily R. Matott

14 | The Language of Representation: How Millennial and Non-
Millennial Legislators Present Themselves to Constituents   385
Sally Friedman, Emily R. Matott, and Andrew McMahon

Contributors   419

Index   425

Digital materials related to this title can be found on
the Fulcrum platform via the following citable URL:
https://doi.org/10.3998/mpub.11621506

Acknowledgments

First and foremost, and most immediately, we would like to acknowledge a terrific group of contributors. Collectively, the variety of the topics included helps us appreciate the impact of generations and generational research. To a person, these contributors were the utmost in professionalism. Everyone worked in a timely manner, was responsive to feedback, and expressed excitement to be part of the project. The contributors truly made our job as editors easy, and they proved to be simply a group of good people.

We would also like to thank some very thoughtful reviewers for their time and extremely helpful comments.

Additionally, we appreciate the support of colleagues, students, and friends. In the context of this project, Sally would particularly like to thank colleagues Peter Breiner, Michael Malbin, Brian Greenhill and Anne Hildreth (professor emeritus). We thank graduate students, including Amalini Fernando, Grace Kwiatkowski, Sam Eisenkraft, Farzin Shargh, and several iterations of students including the Albany pos250 critical thinking class. In the latest iteration, students even drew pictures representing their conceptions of their own and earlier generations. Surprise, every one of the pictures of the current generation included someone using a cell phone!

Here, the contribution of graduate student Emily Matott (Albany) stands out, in addition to being a coauthor on two chapters (13 and 14) of this book. Always with good humor, Emily did an incredible amount of work, writing her chapters, proofreading, and editing. From virtually the beginning, she was a big part of the process.

David thanks his students who have taken his Generations class and also the many community groups whom he presented to over the years discussing the concept of generational change. He also thanks Roberta Sigel, one of his professors at Rutgers University, for introducing him to the topic of political socialization. She, along with Mary Hanna, his first political science professor at Binghamton University, were major influences in stimulating David's views on political learning.

Sally also thanks Professors Herb Weisberg and Richard Niemi, as well as friends and family Dan and Irene Friedman, Carol Young, John Masker, Christine Bird, Steve Livingston, Brian White, Karyn Kalita, and of course Provada, the most patient (and sometimes most stubborn) guide dog ever.

Finally, we would like to thank the editorial staff at the University of Michigan, particularly Elizabeth Demers, Haley Winkle, Kevin Rennells, and John Raymond as well as the many other folks who assisted. The process of putting any book together is a difficult one under any circumstances but particularly one this size and with this many authors.

Thanks everyone.

Introduction

Generations in American Politics

David Schultz and Sally Friedman

[handwritten: Study of generations → "understudied"]

As the Beatles sang in the song "Revolution", "You say you want a revolution / Well, you know / we all want to change the world." Every generation likes to think it is unique. Every generation labels itself in certain ways and is similarly characterized by others. Images and stereotypes of generations abound in popular culture, and a number of academic disciplines (including sociology, business, and marketing, see chapter 1) similarly engage.

But let's dig beneath the stereotypes. As a potentially important concept with the possibility to be relevant for many tried-and-true aspects of American politics, the impact of generations has been notably understudied in political science. Other demographics, including race, class, and gender, rightly receive considerable attention, but the study of generations lags behind.

The chapters in this volume focus attention on a wide range of topics, showing the utility of a generational lens. Topics range, for example, from generational changes in drug policy (Blumenfeld, chap. 5), presidential visits to college campuses (Moffett and Rice, chap. 10), and the activities of millennial mayors (Friedman, Armato, and Matott, chap. 13). Each chapter contributes to a broader discussion of key themes in American politics, telling an important story in its own right. Taken together, the chapters cover a diversity of subject matter, suggesting the potential impact for generations in a wide variety of contexts. The chapters also employ a wide variety of methodological tools, ranging from historical and qualitative to quite sophisticated quantitative analyses. Additionally, a focus on generations reminds us, as political scientists, to engage with some intriguing concepts: political socialization and formative experiences, the actual and perceived impact of historical events, and the linkages of generations to alternative causal mechanisms.

A In this regard, the authors in this book seek to isolate and define what it means to be a generation and how it contrasts to age as a variable. The authors seek to clarify, as Bobby Duffy (2021) recently pointed out when generations or generational change are discussed, the differences between three different phenomena that are often confused or conflated: (1) period effects or exposure of all of society to some major event; (2) life cycle effects or attitudinal changes as individuals age; and (3) cohort effects or the development of different attitudes for those of different ages because of socialization. Sorting out the three and understanding how they are part of or distinct from generational effects is *goal of book* one goal of this book. In effect, we ask, Do generations matter? The conclusion of the book is yes, but often in subtle ways, and often the effects come in interaction with other variables.

As has been referenced above, the first chapters of the book highlight fundamental concepts, including some of the conceptual and methodological issues inherent in the study of generations. In chapter 1, "Generations, Politics, and Political Science," David Schultz introduces the reader to the classic study on generations by Karl Mannheim *Ch 1* (1926). His chapter sorts through the substantive and methodological debates central to generational studies, setting the stage for subsequent chapters and authors who seek to answer the questions he poses. In the process, he identifies the five generations—Silents (1925–45); *5 generations* Baby Boomers (1946–64); Gen X (1965–80); Millennials (1981–95); and Gen Z (1996–2013)—that are the primary focus of the book. These generations are preceded by the Greatest or World War II generation (1900–1924) and followed by the Alphas (2014–?).

In chapter 2, "Generational Change in Partisanship: An Age-Period-Cohort Accounting," Laura Stoker lays out what is likely the most sophisticated methodological tool employed in generational analysis: *Ch 2* the age-period-cohort (APC) model. Providing a detailed explanation of complex methodological material, Stoker applies the model to key variables in political behavior: trends in party identification, in the number of citizens who identify as independents, and in affective polarization. As do other chapters in the book, findings present a nuanced picture. Generations and generational replacement matter, but so do age and period effects as well as simple shifts in the nation's demographics.

In chapter 3, "Collective Memory and the Pandemic Emergence of Generation Z," Scott McLean returns to the underpinnings of generational theory in a different way: "My argument is that political scientists should build beyond their analyses of age cohorts and focus on ways to account for the role of nationally traumatic and triumphal events in shaping the political concerns and collective memories of emerging generations." McLean adds that "rather than reflexively presuming that age cohorts are identical to generations, or that whatever events occur in a cohort's political 'coming of age,' are always generation-defining, political scientists should delve deeper into the events themselves, and attempt to trace how the experiences translate into political behavior across time." Do members of a specific age-cohort consciously think of themselves as a generation? Which "defining" events, in the long run, will make a difference? In the process, McLean delves deeply into the events that have the potential to make a difference for the Gen Z cohort and explores what we know about their behavior so far.

Ch 3

Acknowledging some overlap, we organize subsequent material into three parts: part II of the book focuses on attitudes and opinions, part III emphasizes the political engagement of young people, and part IV focuses broadly on potential impact as we examine generational change. Taken together, the chapters are indicative of the variety of attitudes that could be impacted by generational differences.

In chapter 4, "Generational Divides, Changing Times, or Aging? Examining Immigration Opinion in the U.S., 2004–2018," Jeffrey Dixon, Andrew Fullerton, and Victoria Nash qualify the idea that Millennials, because of their liberal politics, are more supportive of a more welcoming immigration policy. Conducting an APC analysis using data from the General Social Survey, the authors find bivariate relationships between generation and immigration attitudes (the Millennial cohort is more supportive and less opposed), but with a number of control variables taken into account, "these results indicate that Millennial cohorts are more supportive of immigration, but it appears to be due to the fact that they are younger on average or experiencing key life events during a more liberal time period, or both."

Ch 4

In a different policy area, chapter 5, "Generational Attitudes toward Drug Policies in the United States" by Leah Hutton Blumenfeld begins by noting the significant increases in public support for the legaliza-

Ch 5

tion of marijuana, a trend generally understood as indicating stronger support among younger generations. Interestingly, Hutton Blumenfeld argues that the picture is not so unidirectional: "Change is not necessarily a result of generational replacement but can also be explained by changing attitudes within and across generations."

In chapter 6, "Gender and the Generations: You Haven't Come a Long Way Yet, Baby," Whitney Ross Manzo and David McLennan turn our attention to the state of women's representation as elected leaders. Theories of socialization would lead us to expect attitudes toward women leaders would become more favorable over time, but as the chapter title indicates, examination of a variety of political attitudes shows a more complex and not-always favorable picture. Findings based on Meredith polls from 2016 and 2018 (North Carolina) show a complex set of interactions between generations, gender, and the nature of the attitudes under study. Some positives notwithstanding, "all generations were united in the belief that 'Americans aren't ready' to elect a woman." Gen Z men thought that women "aren't tough enough for politics" and, especially on the Republican side, were more likely to have preferences for male leaders. Moving toward the future, because Gen Z men did favor ideas about general equality, the authors suggest: "groups interested in more representation of women in politics might do better to advocate for laws and policies that benefit women rather than putting the emphasis on electing them to office."

From a different perspective and stepping beyond attitudes on particular issues, in chapter 7, "What American Heroism Teaches Us about Generations and Politics," Bruce Peabody reminds us that generations can have an impact on our symbols and, more deeply, on our values. In particular, "heroes may serve as an emblem of unity in a society" and an "important cultural marker of a nation's purported union around key values, symbols, and icons." His study asked respondents to evaluate a list of past and contemporary individuals who have been classified as heroes, as well as the traits different generations thought were "heroic." While the author finds notable generational differences, he also finds current levels of party polarization have gone so far as to even infuse these on-the-surface not-necessarily political results with identifiers of the two major political parties.

In part III, we turn to a focus on civic engagement/mobilization. The attitudes of particular generations matter, but how do individuals translate these attitudes into political participation? How do we get people of the younger generations more involved? Have their patterns of involvement changed over time? In what ways does their involvement make a difference?

In chapter 8, "'The Times They Are a Changin': Generational Comparisons of the Civil Rights Movement with the Current-Day Climate Movement," Robin Boyle-Laisure asks us to take a historical look at the role young people have played in important social movements. She employs a comparison between the civil rights movement of the 1960s and the current climate movement. The author's focus reminds us of the key roles—organizing activities on college campuses, taking the lead in protest activity, and generally publicizing the importance of key issues—young people have played in each. Additionally, Boyle-Laisure suggests that leaders of both movements have invoked the concerns of young people by pointing up the need to make the lives of the next generations better. Finally, even in an age of advancing technology, Boyle-Laisure harkens back to the importance of personal networks as a key tool that could further aid the modern-day climate movement.

But how do we get young people even more involved, particularly in more conventional modes of participation? With a focus on voting, the next two chapters tackle this question, suggesting very different possibilities.

In chapter 9, Niall Michelsen makes the case for "Building Youthful Habits of Voting." Conceptualizing costs, distractions, and resources of young people at the age of their first vote, he argues the more we start early, the easier we're making it for individuals to want to get in the game. From that perspective, 16 year olds incur fewer costs and have fewer distractions (they're not dealing with transitions to college, jobs, or family). Also, they're more likely to have the stability of living in their home environments and to piggyback on material learned in civics classes, particularly if they subsequently choose not to attend college. In short, we need to start building habits of voting early, and in Michelsen's view, we need to do so by lowering the voting age to 16.

In chapter 10, "Presidential Candidates on Campus and Civic Engagement among College Students," Kenneth Moffett and Laurie Rice turn to another route to enhancing civic engagement by demonstrating the impact presidential candidates can have by visiting college campuses. After arguing that presidential candidate visits can make a difference, the authors examine the impact Senator Bernie Sanders' visit had on one campus. Attending and volunteering at the Sanders' rally yielded higher probabilities of voting in the 2016 primaries and persisted into the general election.

Part IV focuses broadly on the potential impacts of generational change. In chapter 11, "Millennial Generation Political Engagement—Democratically Motivated or Disenchanted? Insights from the 2020 Election," Ashley Ross and Stella Rouse focus on two snapshots of Millennials (2016 and 2020), comparing a number of attitudes. Even as findings demonstrate what the authors label a "Millennial persona" they also find notable differences among racial and ethnic subgroups, and, in some instances, Millennials don't differ much from older cohorts. In the end, depending on the unfolding of events, the authors simultaneously point to possibilities for both disenchantment and continuing engagement.

In chapter 12, "Generational Shifts Change Politics in Florida," Susan MacManus and Anthony Cilluffo focus on the politics of a key battleground state. The chapter argues that the description of Florida as dominated by elderly voters is too simplistic. Demographic shifts (toward a more diverse population, including a significant rise in the number of non-Hispanic whites) along with shifts in the generational balance have combined to impact changes in party identification (younger generations are more likely to vote Democratic or express no party affiliation), thus impacting campaign strategies and voting behavior.

But what of Millennials who have actually come to hold positions of political power? In the final two chapters, Sally Friedman and her colleagues turn our attention to Millennials and governing. In chapter 13, "How They Govern: Do Millennial Mayors Bring a Generational Perspective to Their Activities?," Friedman, Michael Armato, and Emily Matott report on a qualitative analysis of the activities of four similarly situated (as matched by census data) pairs of mayors, one a Millennial and one an older mayor. Compared to their non-Millennial counterparts, the Millennial mayors were more likely to combine traditional economic development with social justice concerns, and they were more likely to reach out to Millennials. Yet some of the non-Millennial mayors engaged in the same kinds of activities as did the Millennials; other characteristics of the mayors mattered; and the needs and character of each city conditioned the activities of all mayors. The authors conclude with a "qualified yes" when thinking through the ways in which Millennial status made a difference in governing.

The conclusions are similar through an examination of Millennial (compared to non-Millennial) members of Congress, both groups elected as new members in 2018. In chapter 14, "The Language of Representation: How Millennial and Non-Millennial Legislators Present Themselves to Constituents," Friedman and her colleagues, Emily Matott and Andrew McMahon, use the latest in content analysis, web scraping technology, to examine several data sets prominent in the literature on Congress to test hypotheses about whether Millennial legislators focused on different topics as they presented themselves to constituents. Taking partisanship into account and recognizing that numerous additional influences impact legislative behavior, the findings again indicate a qualified yes.

h14

If one thinks that the purpose of political science is to describe, explain, and then predict political phenomena, the chapters in this volume have gone a long way in securing the first two goals. We have learned a lot about what a generational effect is and is not. It is of course difficult to make firm predictions for the future. Will generational shifts lead to new or redefined political parties? Will that change voting and policy preferences? Will the current political polarization be broken or changed as a result of a generational shift? There is evidence for many of these claims. Yet this volume is not meant to be the final voice on generational politics. It is a call for others also to take generations seriously, applying perhaps the same tools of analysis and asking the same questions that would be asked of other political variables, constructs, and phenomena. Our hope is that we can wrest generations from the domain of pop culture and lend to its analysis the type of empirical work that is characteristic of what good political science can do.

what could happen in the future

NOTE

As examination of the following chapters will show, there are several different dates referring to the work of Karl Mannheim. The discrepancies in Mannheim's citations are due to different versions of the German to English translation. Authors also have somewhat different delineations of the varying generations studied.

REFERENCES

Duffy, Bobby. 2021. *The Generations Myth: Why When You're Born Matters Less Than You Think*. New York: Basic Books.

Mannheim, Karl. (1926) 1952. *Essays on the Sociology of Knowledge*. London: Routledge and Kegan Paul.

Part I

Foundations

[handwritten: classic study on generations → Karl Mannheim]

[handwritten: ☆5 generations of primary focus]

1 | Generations, Politics, and the Practice of Political Science

David Schultz

[handwritten: preceded by WWII/ greatest generation, followed by Alphas]

What is a generation, and what role does this concept have in the study of American politics? How do we separate out differences in political attitudes and behavior among individuals depending on when they were born, their age, or how they were socialized? The challenge for generational studies in political science is sorting these phenomena out.

There is no doubt that, in popular culture, business, and in other academic fields, generations as a concept is an important and often talked about term. Perhaps awareness of generations as a concept started many decades ago with the arrival of the Baby Boomers in the 1960s who somewhat self-consciously and noisily distinguished themselves from their parents. The Boomers came of age with the rise of television and rock and roll and, at least for one segment of that generation, were defined by the Vietnam War, Rachel Carson's *Silent Spring* ([1962] 2002) and Earth Day, or Betty Friedan and the *Feminine Mystique* (1963). To the dismay of Millennials and other later generations, they continue to recount where they were when JFK (President John F. Kennedy) was assassinated and reminisce over seeing the Beatles on the *Ed Sullivan Show* on February 9, 1964. The Beatles' "Revolution" or the Who's "Talking about My Generation" are their songs. The Baby Boomers self-consciously and collectively defined themselves as a new generation seeking to remake the world in their image. Since then, later generations have been defined or defined themselves in relation to them.

[handwritten margin note: Baby Boomers 1946–64]

But in recent years business and pop culture have made a lot of noise about generations, emphasizing the difference in work habits for each and why it is important to know these differences as part of lead-

[handwritten: diff work habits of generations]

ership or to promote recruitment or increase sales (Lancaster and Stillman 2003; Stillman and Stillman 2017; Zemke, Raines, and Filipczak 2000; Ritchie 2008). On a different level, generational issues have been the source of what might be called ranting behavior. Boomers were noted for not liking Millennials and the latter blamed the former for all types of social ills (Gibney 2017).

Finally, in many academic fields the concept of generations has occupied a prominent role. Business, marketing, and human resources management have talked about generations as a concept for years. There is a rich body of sociological literature that has long thought about generations as an important concept or variable of analysis. Some of this generational analysis, especially with the arrival in 1991 of William Strauss and Neil Howe's *Generations: The History of America's Future, 1584 to 2069*, has facilitated the transformation of the academic concept of generations into something more mainstream and part of pop culture. Across a range of areas of everyday life, pop culture, and academic disciplines, generations as a tool of inquiry and object of curiosity has become more established.

Generational analysis in the field of political science has received sporadic attention. At either the individual, or micro level, such as with voting, the meso or political party or interest group level, or at the macro or nation-state level, variables such as race, class, or gender are staples (Lewis-Beck et al. 2008; Nownes 2012; Hershey 2017; Weisband and Thomas 2015; Art and Jervis 2016; Lukes 2006; Bendix 1974). The point here is that in political science there is a clear stock of variables that both serve as objects of inquiry and tools of analysis, yet generation is not generally one of them.

Pick up a copy of almost any basic American politics textbook. Race, class, socioeconomic status, gender, region, and religion are typically discussed and described as the points of cleavage for political consensus and disagreement (Bond and Smith 2013; Greenberg and Page 2011). One will also see in many political science books discussions of age and cohort. Surprisingly, missing from so much analysis is a discussion of generations. Examination of the *American Political Science Review* article and book review titles from 1987 to 2020 found seven uses of the word "generation." The *American Journal of Political Science* had two from 2007 to 2017, and the *Journal of Politics* had six from 1983 to 2020. *Polity, PSNow, Perspectives on Politics*, and *Political Science Quarterly* had none. By comparison, from 1985 to 2020 the *American Political Science Review* had 34 titles or book reviews with the word "race" in it,

23 with the word "gender," and 34 with "religion." Generation appears as a less frequent variable or topic for analysis.

Is a political science of generations possible? Are generations as an object of inquiry and tool of analysis useful as something worthy of political description, explanation, and prediction? An emerging body of political science research on attitudinal differences suggests yes (Cahn and Cahn 2016; Taylor 2015; Rouse and Ross 2018). Other works, such as Morton Ender, David Rohall, and Michael Matthews's *The Millennial Generation and National Defense* (2014), compare the views of college students attending military institutions of higher learning to students at civilian colleges with respect to concerns about the role of the military and national defense. Several works explore the political participation of young people (Hancock 2011; Lawless and Fox 2015; Shames 2017) and Brent Steele and Jonathan Acuff have written *Theory and Application of the "Generation" in International Relations* (2012). Desante and Smith (2020) have looked at how racial attitudes are playing across generations, testing the claim that the Millennials are a postracial generation. Their conclusion is that at least for white Caucasian Millennials, their attitudes are not necessarily much different than those of previous generations, even if they no longer share the overt type of racism or attitudes that previous generations held. The Pew Research Center, although not exclusively staffed by political scientists, has done a lot to explore political attitudes across generations, seeking to document differences in American public opinion over time and what it means for political change.

The purpose here is not to undertake a full-blown literature review. It is sufficient to say that even if sociologists and other related academic fields have looked at generations as a concept, political scientists have not devoted as much attention to it as they should.

Asking why generations are understudied is an interesting question and would make for terrific speculation. Instead of dwelling on that question the focus here is more methodological and substantive. What would it mean to study a generation? How is the concept related to other variables? Is it a structural variable? What does a focus on generations do in terms of describing, explaining, and predicting American political behavior? How do we determine if differences across generations are the product of period, life cycle, or cohort effects? What can we learn about politics that we do not otherwise know if generations were to become a substantive variable for analysis? These are many if not all of the questions one needs to ask. In effect, what do we mean by a generational study of American politics?

The Discovery of Generations

What is the concept of generations and where did it as an idea originate?

First, there is no question that academics including political scientists have used the word "generations" for many years. Key (1955), Sundquist (1973), and Burnham (1970) employed the term in relation to describing critical elections and how and why party compositions and loyalties change over time. One generation or cohort of people pass away and are replaced by a different one who may have different interests or views on the world, including politics. Others such as Abramson (1975, 1979, 1983) and Converse (1976) described how a change in generations led to shifts in voting patterns. Jervis (2017) discusses generations in terms of how social-psychological forces and events influence individual actors in their judgments regarding international politics. The discussion in these works seems to use generations interchangeably with the concept of cohort to describe the political change or phenomena they were addressing. In addition, generations as a distinct concept of study or object of inquiry was not something their works focused on. Stoker (2014) pointed out that the use of the concept of generations seems to gyrate between the idea of lineage generation and political generation. Delli Carpini (1989) has made the same point.

While there are clear psychological roots to the concept of generations (Freud 1964; Erikson 1968; Piaget 1967; and Kohlberg 1968), the sociological use of the term has a distinct origin. Delli Carpini (1989) locates the origin of the concept in two sources. The first is with Giuseppe Ferrari (1874, 8–9) who saw at approximately 30-year intervals a changeover in individuals who left their imprint on politics. Specifically, one generation or group of people aged out, only to be replaced by another group who brought their views to politics. Ferrari's periodic influence on politics simply seemed to assume that the coming and going of a group of people of the same age would foster change. Left unanswered in his theory were several questions. First, how are the beliefs acquired for each generation? Second, how wide or broad is a generation? By that, is a generation a group of people born within one, five, or ten years of one another? Third, is each generation unique or how does age connect to generation? By that, as each generation ages does it produce a similar pattern of political orientations shared by others from a previous generation at the same age?

Ferrari and others who became part of the French positivist wing of generational analysis linked life cycle or aging and age-cohort to their theory. Generational change was tied to what they saw as ultimately an individualistic characteristic of all of us in terms of simply growing older. This is a developmental psychological theory. Simply being born around the same age was enough to qualify as a generational cohort and therefore political or social change occurred with a somewhat group aging or life cycle process. Missing from this theory was an idea of a collective consciousness or self-awareness that a group was part of a generation. Again, merely being born at approximately the same time made one part of a generation. This use of generations seems closer to contemporary pop culture or marketing references to the term, which simply lump together a group of people born between certain dates and call them a generation. This is more of a cohort analysis (Babbie 2013, 107; Baker 1999, 93).

Perhaps the most influential model for the concept of generations is Karl Mannheim's "The Sociological Problem of Generations" (1928). Mannheim seeks to develop a meaningful, formal theory of generations for sociologists, yet he notes how the term lacks clear definition. The problem for him is that a group of people simply born at the same time do not constitute a generation. This is just a group, but it does not have necessary interrelationships or connections (1928, 194). Mannheim wishes to distinguish what he calls concrete groups from other groups, such as families, which he defines as a union of a number of individuals through naturally developed or consciously willed ties (165). Mere similarity of location in age or time is not enough to define a generation. Biological location, such as being born together or near one another in time, is important but not enough (167). For example, twins separated at birth and raised separately may be biologically related but not part of the same family. Class is an objective fact, but class consciousness or awareness that one is grouped together with others is a different issue. People born in China and Europe in 1800 may not form a generation even if they are of the same age cohort. Contrary to Ferrari, merely being born approximately at the same time is not enough to form a generation. Some type of consciousness or self-awareness is also needed on top of location in order to form a generation (168–70).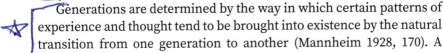

Generations are determined by the way in which certain patterns of experience and thought tend to be brought into existence by the natural transition from one generation to another (Mannheim 1928, 170). A generational theory of change is marked by five characteristics: new participants in the cultural process are emerging; former participants are constantly exiting; members of any one generation can participate only in a temporally limited section of the historical process; generations transmit the accumulated cultural heritage; and generational change is continuous. For Mannheim, there is a constant stream of new cohorts and age groups that bring with them fresh contact of new life with old. Fresh contacts are a product of shifts in historical and social situations. Part of consciousness of a generation is the interface of generations with one another to develop a consciousness of self (172). How do generations move then from a merely formal concept to an actual bonding (182)? Something is required to disturb a cohort, perhaps some event, that triggers a cohort into becoming a generation with self-awareness that they are bonded together with collective impulses that are distinct from those who come before and after them (182–84). Some triggering action is required to do this (191), and this occurs at some formative point in time for individuals, specifically adolescence.

For Mannheim, a generation is something more than similarity in a position in the world, such as the proletariat vis-à-vis the bourgeoisie. It requires generational consciousness much like Marxists discussed class consciousness. For Mannheim, one can have a group of people born and socialized at the same time but remain merely a cohort. Something occurs that collectively transforms those in the same age cohort and location into becoming aware of their generation. They thus are self-aware of how they stand in relation to those before and after them. They acquire cultural knowledge from a previous generation and pass it one to the next, but in doing so they interpret it through their experiences and perspectives.

Unlike Ferrari or those similar to him, Mannheim does not see generations as individualistic and as a natural product of aging or the life cycle process. It is a collective transmittal process that changes or builds upon inherited information. It is a process that is both derivative and new in terms of the knowledge and awareness that each generation possesses.

The Methodological Issues in Generational Studies

Mannheim and Ferrari offer competing but incomplete models or theories about generations. Subsequent academics have developed the concept more fully. Perhaps the most famous is William Strauss and Neil Howe, *Generations: The History of America's Future, 1584 to 2069* (1991). They define a generation as a cohort group whose length approximates the span of a phase of life and whose boundaries are fixed by peer personality (60). Their generational model is in two stages. First, they argue that "decisive" events will affect people differently based on their stage in life (61), which they define as youth, rising adulthood, midlife, and elderhood. These decisive events create distinct cohort groups of about twenty-two years in length. These events form a peer group defined by a common age location, beliefs, and behavior (64). At some point in rising adulthood the defining event is experienced collectively by members of the cohort, forming this sense of peer membership or generational consciousness.

Stage 1 *Stages of life*

The second stage occurs approximately twenty years later. Here is when the previous cohort has begun to exit, replaced by a new one that is now in a position to act on their views and perspectives. Thus, stage one, generational consciousness, is formed in early adulthood, and stage two occurs in the 40s to 50s age range when one can act on the worldview. In this model, a previous generation nurtures the next, and the new generation does the same for its children. Thus, each generation has an impact in molding the next—a form of socialization.

Stage 2

But in addition to this basically two-stage model of learning and then acting on a generational consciousness, Strauss and Howe add some additional features that build upon what is essentially Mannheim's model. One, generations have to been understood historically in relationship to one another. Each generation has to be understood in terms of when it was born and located in time to previous generations. Two, multiple generations exist at the same time and therefore for any rising generation it is uniquely located around a different mix of generations. Three, the cycle of generations repeats itself over time. Thus, in their book they argue that American history is defined by repeating patterns of four generational cycles, creating almost a spiral over time that includes a repeat of past generational attitudes merged with new historical facts to produce a unique generational ethos.

The model is fascinating but it leaves a lot unanswered. We do not know what a triggering event is that helps form a generational consciousness and why some events serve that purpose and others do not. Additionally, there is a problem of still identifying the exact age when one is imprinted. The book suggests before young adulthood, but the authors are quick to dismiss fixed ages (62) and suggest that it is open.

Issues w/ theories of generation

Thus, while 22 years in length is suggested as an age range marking a generation, and something happens within those segments of time to form a peer personality, Strauss and Howe fail to be more specific. Why are those ages 22 and 44 of different generations while those only 18 years apart are not? Perhaps generational lengths could be longer or shorter.

Another problem with the Strauss and Howe model is that despite arguing that some event or crisis needs to trigger a generational aware-ness, their text seems to imply that generations are inevitable. They list a constant supply of successive generations in American history and project the same into the future. There is also a problem of examining how generations correlate with other variables such as race, class, and gender. How do we account for variations within a generation regard-ing attitudes? Finally, there is the woodenness of the model. Friedrich Engels was accused of transforming Karl Marx's dialectical material-ism (a tool of analysis) into historical materialism, or a theory of his-tory and prediction (Benjamin 1978). There was a sense of determin-ism in the model, suggesting perhaps the communist revolution was inevitable. Strauss and Howe's model does the same. It is not simply identifying past generations but predicting an inevitability.

The purpose in highlighting Strauss and Howe and Mannheim is to point to some basic questions any theory or concept of generations must have for any social science field, let alone for its application in political science and for politics. Is a generation simply a cohort of approximately the same age? If not, what type of events trigger the forming of a collective mentality? When does that trigger occur? If it occurs in adolescence, what do we mean by that term at a time when psychologists differ on its meaning or boundaries? How or can we define clear cutoffs regarding one generation as opposed to others? Generations do not end all at once, so how do we factor gradualism or generational replacement into a theory? Is it possible that generational replacement for each generation is slow at first, accelerating as more of them age out at the same time? All these are methodological ques-tions that potentially impact substantive conclusions about genera-tional change and differences.

How do we account for differences within a generation in terms of how people across race, class, gender, region, and religion might per-ceive a triggering event differently? Could there be different triggers for different groups? How do we account for intersectionality? Addi-tionally, Strauss and Howe's model still does not clearly account for age

how does age of technology effect gen?

and sorting it out from generation. Updating their book to the present with people living even longer, it is possible to have more than four generations occurring simultaneously? Also, with social media and other advances in technology, can a generation have a broader geographic or international sweep or form more rapidly or quickly than others? In their subsequent books (Strauss and Howe 1997; Howe and Strauss 2000) they make minor refinements to the arguments presented in *Generations*. In both they define a generation as a society-wide peer group, born over a period roughly the same length and passage from youth to adulthood, who collectively possess a common persona (Strauss and Howe 1997, 6; Howe and Strauss 2000, 40). However, there are some basic problems and unanswered questions found in *Generations* that persist in their newer works.

Most fundamentally, the central problem in generational studies, as noted in the introduction, is sorting out three questions or issues. Duffy (2021) argues that differences across generations need to untangle (1) period effects or exposure of all of society to some major event; (2) life cycle effects or attitudinal changes as individuals age; and (3) cohort effects or the development of different attitudes for those of different ages because of socialization. If we are going to argue that generations matter then determining if attitudes vary because of period, life cycle, or cohort effects is critical. As we shall see in this book, Laura Stoker (chap. 2) seeks methodologically to craft a theory to sort out the three issues, with other chapters offering a variety of studies and conclusions that also address the questions posed in this chapter.

Meet the Generations

One way to define a generation is simply by birth year. This is the Ferrari approach. How long should a generation be and when does it begin and end? Drawing upon the Mannheim and Ferrari classifications, perhaps a generation is marked by a period of between 20 and 30 years. That period roughly corresponds to a cycle of birth to adulthood. Second, a generation in terms of when it begins and ends is a product of historical time markers. Perhaps major events, such as major wars, technology (the rise of television or the internet), economic crises, or other cultural landmarks define the beginning or end of a generation.

There is significant debate surrounding the dating and naming of generations. We need not engage in the details of the debate, but it is

TABLE 1.1. Recent Generations in U.S. Politics

Generation	Birth Years
Greatest	1900–1924
Silent	1925–1945
Baby Boom	1946–1960
Gen X	1961–1981
Millennial	1982–1995
Gen Z	1996–2013
Alpha	2014–

Source: Pew Research Center.

worth noting the controversy regarding the exact dates that begin and cut off generations (Strauss and Howe 1991, 96; Lancaster and Stillman 2003, 21–29; Stillman and Stillman 2017, 1; Pew Research Center 2018; Dimock 2019; Pinsker 2020; Dalton 2009, 9; Rouse and Ross 2018, 1; Taylor 2015; Zukin et al. 2006, 14–15). For our purposes, generations shall be defined approximately according to the time parameters in table 1.1.

Dispute over generational breakpoints point to several problems. First, researchers are not in agreement in terms of the markers of when generations begin and end (MacManus 1995, 18–23). MacManus (1995) and Glenn (1972) contend that clarity in terms of when generations begin and end is critical if we wish to sort out the effect that life cycle changes have in terms of assessing what independent value generations have and how we separate out period, life cycle, and cohort effects (Stoker 2014).

Second, another problem with these different boundaries is a demographic issue. Over time America has become racially more diverse and has also changed in other ways, such as becoming less religious. Depending on when or where researchers draw generational lines, one gets larger or smaller cohorts with different demographics and also with potentially different political attitudes. But methodologically, whether one ascribes to Ferrari or Mannheim, it is not possible to settle the cutoff issues for generational markers but it is important to note the controversy.

Third, assuming there are important events, period, or cohort factors that explain generations, what are the defining adolescent coming of age factors that influenced each generation? Table 1.2 breaks them down. We can see that for each generation there were defining or com-

TABLE 1.2. Defining Events for Generations

Greatest (1900–1924)	Silent (1925–45)	Baby Boomer (1946–60)	Gen X (1961–81)	Millennial (1982–95)	Gen Z (1996–2013)	Alpha (2014–)
World War I	Pearl Harbor	Cold War	Nixon/Watergate	End of Cold War	Parkland Shootings	
Great Depression	World War II	JFK Assassination	Ronald Reagan	9/11 terrorist attacks	Great Recession	
Pearl Harbor	Korean War	Nixon/Watergate	Columbine	Sandy Hook/Parkland Shootings	Obama Election	
World War II	Cold War	Civil Rights Movement	End of the Cold War	Great Recession	Sandy Hook/Parkland Shootings	
Prohibition		Vietnam	Gulf War	Obama Election	Tech Revolution	
		MLK Assassination	Oklahoma City Bombing	Tech Revolution	Trump Presidency	
		Landing on the Moon	Roe v Wade	Trump Presidency	Overturning Roe v Wade	
		Roe v Wade		Overturning Roe v Wade	Gay rights Movement	
				Gay Rights Movement		

ing of age events that presumably affected them collectively and distinctly. Yes, all those living at the time did experience the attack on Pearl Harbor, the JFK assassination, Watergate, the Columbine shooting, or the Sandy Hook massacre, but those at the same age might have uniquely experienced these events at a formative stage, impacting their worldview and fusing a sense of collective identity. Identifying these coming-of-age events and showing a unique generational and coming of age impact is critical to generational studies.

Fourth, we also need to understand how across-generation demographics vary. Over the course of the last several generations the demographics of America has changed. We have become a far less white Caucasian Christian society and more one that is racially mixed, less Christian, more secular, and with a greater percentage of immigrants. Demographics may not be political destiny when it comes to success in campaigns and elections, but demographics do matter in terms of political attitudes. We need to understand something about how changing demographics impact generational politics or change. Table 1.3 looks at some of this relevant demographic information, indicating the changing racial composition over time. Note how in moving from the Greatest and Silent generations to Gen Z that each generation is becoming more racially and ethnically diverse. Pew notes that nearly half of Gen Z are racial or ethnic minorities (Fry and Parker 2018).

Generational change is not all or nothing. Generations gradually rise and then fall in terms of population size and engagement as other generations do the same. We need to assess generational influence relative to other generations. Table 1.4 looks at the maximum population size for

[handwritten margin notes: inc. in diversity / decline in religion]

TABLE 1.3. Race and Ethnicity Distribution of the U.S. Population by Generation, 2018 (%)

	Gen Z and younger	Millennial	Gen X	Boomer	Silent and Greatest
White	23	20	20	26	10
Asian	25	27	23	19	6
Black	31	24	20	20	5
Native Hawaiian/ Pacific Islander	31	27	21	17	4
American Indian/ Alaska Native	32	24	19	20	5
Hispanic	38	25	21	13	4
Two or more races	53	22	13	10	3

Source: Data from Statista, "Distribution of the race and ethnicity of the United States population in 2018, by generation," available at https://www.statista.com/statistics/206969/race-and-ethnicity-in-the-us-by-generation/

TABLE 1.4. Generational Population Estimates

Generation	Birth Years	Peak Population Estimate	Current Population estimate (2021)
Greatest	1900–1924	45 M	70,000–90,000
Silent	1925–1945	55 M	23,000,000
Baby Boom	1946–1960	78.8 M	71,600,000
Gen X	1961–1981	64.6 M	65,200,000
Millennial	1982–1995	76.2 M	72,100,000
Gen Z	1996–2013	68.6 M	68,600,000
Alpha	2014–	?	27,800,000

Source: Data from U.S. Census Bureau 2019 Census Projections; Pew Research Center; and Statistica.

TABLE 1.5. Percentage of Each Generation Expressing No Religious Affiliation in 2021

Silent	18%
Baby Boomer	26%
Gen X	36%
Millennial	45%
Gen Z	48%

Source: Data from Burge (2021), "Gen Z and Religion in 2021."

each generation and then at its status most recently. What we find, for example, is that while for nearly 30 years the Boomers were the largest cohort, they are now waning compared to the Millennials and Gen Z who are ascendent in terms of potential political strength. In fact, as of 2018, Millennials and Gen Z outnumber Boomers (Andrews 2016).

Finally, table 1.5 looks at religious affiliation across generations. It finds that each generation has become less religiously affiliated, perhaps more secular and less traditionally Christian. The demographics of each successive generation reveal an America that is more racially and ethnically diverse and less religious (or Christian). Additionally, other studies point to how the current Gen Z is more dominated by immigrants compared to the early ones examined here (Fry and Parker 2018). In effect, across-generation demographics are changing. The task of generational analysis in political science is to determine what impact such changes have on political attitudes and behavior. Any study of generations must account for or control for these demographic changes.

Political Science, Generations, and Political Socialization

The starting point of political science examining the concept of generations begins with the concept of political socialization.

Until the 1960s little political science research was undertaken on how individuals acquire political attitudes and how those attitudes change. In developmental psychology the assumption was that a lot of preliminary learning came from one's parents (Kohlberg 1968; Piaget 1967). Initial values were learned from and imparted from parents who passed them on to their children. At some point in adolescence children begin to break away from parents, form their own identity, and begin to become more socially aware, affected by the attitudes and views of their friends. Learning does not stop, but new forces become more important, and as individuals mature into adulthood they adopt a set of beliefs and ideas that help form their identity and personal worldview. Moreover, there was a common perception that as one aged, one's values changed (Abramson 1975, 1979, 1983; Desilver 2014; MacManus 1995; Williamson, Evans, and Powell 1982). One way to capture that belief was with the famous quote of François Guizot, who declared "not to be a republican at 20 is proof of want of heart; to be one at 30 is proof of want of head." Parental influence formed early values; the aging process made us more conservative. While these are interesting assumptions, there is little evidence to back up these claims. Generations as a concept referred to the passing of information from parents to children. As Stoker describes it, generation was a lineage term involving kinship and natural lines of descent (Stoker 2014, 378). One generation raises the next, and in the process educates and socializes the latter.

In the 1960s the political science profession turned to the study and measurement of political attitudes, their acquisition from parents or other sources, and how they translated into behavior. Roberta A. Sigel (1970, 1981, 1989) was one scholar who studied this. However, there were many others who examined various aspects of political socialization in terms of how schools, work, and peer groups, among other sources, contributed to political learning and socialization (Hyman 1959; Goodman 1958; Lipset and Wolin 1965; Davies 1965; Lane 1959; Greenstein 1965; Frenkel-Brunswik et al. 1950; Lawson 1963; Ziblatt 1965; Bronfenbrenner 1967; Edelstein 1962; Jennings and Zeigler 1970; LeVine 1960; Howard 1966; Banfield 1958; Lafferty 1989; Lovell and Stiehm 1989; Morris, Hatchet, and Brown 1989; Carroll 1989; Horowitz 1989).

Political Learning as individualistic

What researchers were left with were models that emphasized early childhood political learning that suggested lifelong fixed values, versus a model that looked at continuous change and learning. Yet in both cases the models were individualistic. Individuals had their own unique learning and socialization experiences that defined their own values, even if at times one collectively attended the same religious institution or was in the same school as others. Political learning was mostly seen as individualistic, and little thought was given to how a group of people of the same age or same point in time learned and acted on values. Socialization might vary by race, class, or gender, but there was not a generational notion of political learning and socialization in terms of a new group of individuals linked by age possessing a distinct set of political values.

However, political scientists did discover adolescence and the childhood roots of political behavior. Perhaps inspired by psychological biographies such as Erik Erikson's *Young Man Luther* ([1958] 1993), one could understand something about presidents by looking back to their youth. James David Barber's *Presidential Character* ([1972] 2009) is one example of that. Barber sought to construct a means to describe and categorize presidents, partly as a predictive tool to assess possible performance before they are elected. The basic problem faced when selecting presidents is to make an accurate guess about what type of president the candidate will be.

However, Barber did not employ a generational aspect or category in his assessment of presidential character. Each president has a unique biography, and it is not the product of something more social or collective, such as a group set of experiences as being white, male, or of a particular religion. Thus, like other political scientists of his time, and even much to this day, generations as a concept was generally ignored or given a lower status when compared to other staple collective variables such as race, socioeconomic status, gender, religion, or region.

The field of political science has not totally ignored the concept of generations. What do political scientists mean when they refer to generations? Delli Carpini (1989, 42) described a generation as

an age cohort whose values, attitudes, opinions, and/or behaviors have been shaped in relatively stable and unique ways by history. Generations react to specific historical circumstances in unique ways because different age cohorts tend to experience

polysci definition of generations

different aspects of that history, and because different age cohorts, due to their relative location in the life cycle, tend to interpret the same historical experiences in different ways.

Delli Carpini's discussion of the complexity of generational research remains arguably one of the most astute to this day. He raised questions about defining a generation, separating or isolating it and its effects from aging and other variables. He queried about whether value and attitude changes across generations could be ascribed to and located in other causes, such as race, gender, or life cycle effects. He described how the size of a generation, its demographic diversity, and rate of cohort replacement impact issues such as political change or the rate of political change. Finally, he speculated on the segmentation of generational time units and how inclusive the generation is. Overall, his methodological critique of generational studies remains cogent to this day, with future political science research needing to address these issues.

Other political scientists undertaking generational analysis have also sought to address these issues. Rouse and Ross (2018, 23) declare that "what forms generational identity is contingent on life cycle as well as the events that take place that shape shared beliefs and values." They see every generation as having its own personality or identity (4), with age shaping the way events are shared as a group (23). Their approach has been to work from pregiven generational categories and to then see if there are valid differences in them, finding that there are. Finding validity in these distinctions, it would be interesting to test or investigate how generational attitudes change with the age of a cohort and also with its aging or life cycle.

Taylor (2015, 16) describes generations as one of the many "tribes" dividing America. Noting his debt to Mannheim and Strauss and Howe (64), he sees generational difference as the product of life cycle, period, and cohort effects, and he suggests that over time the demographic changes will benefit Democratic Party politics (22). Zukin et al. (2006, 11) declare that the "generational perspective is a product of many influences, based in part upon what has been learned through informal and formal education, . . . key events that occur while one is coming of age; longer term trends that lead to changes in circumstances from previous generations." The limited political science research thus far draws upon birth year, cohort, and, in some cases, the defining belief or consciousness raising or self-awareness aspect for defining a generation. But as noted above, what's not clear is the basis for the classification—is it categorical or empirical? Political science research going forward must address this issue.

Political science research needs also to apply its traditional tools of analysis to generational studies. Good empirical science literature will not simply undertake blanket analysis of gender, race, or religion, for example, without also qualifying the research to point out that not everyone who is African American or female holds the same views, even within a generational cohort. There are differences in attitudes and behavior within each group. The same is the case with generations. Desante and Smith (2020), for example, undertake a very detailed and rich study of Millennial Caucasians (especially male), finding that their views on race are more similar to previous generations and clearly different from Millennials of color. Their research thus looks at generations as one of several variables and it seeks to understand how it interacts with race and gender, as well as many of the other variables that political science considers important.

Conclusion: Toward a Political Science Theory of Generations

A political science theory of generations is important and it would contribute to our understanding of politics. Yet there are many issues that need to be addressed if one is to place the study of the topic on a firmer footing.

The first is simply a clear definition of what a generation is. We have many conceptions of the concept, but no agreed upon meaning. The issues are with what qualifies as a generation and with defining its period and what counts for differences across generations. Is a generation a dependent or independent variable? Is the concept pregiven or do we define generations empirically? Are generations simply age cohorts, as Ferrari suggested, or are they age cohorts plus consciousness, as argued by Mannheim? Is it a kinship and lineage concept, or does it have a distinct political meaning? If the latter, what counts as markers or evidence for the creation of generational self-awareness and how broad and deep does it have to be? There is then the need to sort out other variables and how they relate to generations, as well as to separate it from other factors that can explain political change.

Generational studies need to build on previous research. For example, Roberta Sigel's work on political socialization and the political engagement of adolescents did not address generational change. Is it possible to amend her theory to add a component that factors in a value regarding how cognition or affect varies across time? Or can her theory of socialization be used as a tool for understanding generational change? One could build in differences in generational attitudes on issues as ways to measure change. One way would be to quantify the rate and degree of generational change as a way to hypothesize how socialization changes over time. If political socialization is so powerful, how do we account for changes across generations when the presumption should be that attitudes carry from parent to child?

In terms of what to study, what should political science look at as evidence of generational change or difference? Should the focus be on individual voting or other political behavior? Should it include leadership style, party composition, or agenda setting? These are all possibilities. Research also needs to be attentive to how the variable generations intersects or is controlled with other variables that might offer richer senses of how the latter affect generational change in terms of depth and breadth. There may be a generational effect, but how does it vary by race, class, gender, region, and religion? Furthermore, is there a way to identify and measure defining events that each generation experiences and sort out how they affected one generation compared to another? Holding constant age might yield more information on a generational effect. At the same time, generation is a form of cohort but also within generations there are different cohorts. Looking at ways to both hold constant cohort and segment generations would yield important knowledge that would help sort out real generational effects. The same would be true for long-term longitudinal studies of specific cohorts from the same generation to see the effects of aging, race, gender and so forth.

Finally, generations have been hinted at in terms of their impact for international politics and critical realignments. These areas of research could be developed more fully, as well as placing generations in a comparative context. What we do not know is the degree, for example, to which generational shifts affect party composition and voting patterns, perhaps contributing party critical realignments and change. Has the rise of social media transformed the way generations are formed? Is there a global generation influence or way of thinking? If we could calculate the rate of generational change over time it might suggest a way to measure or predict, for example, aggregate shifts in public opinion over time and how and whether learning as an adult, as Roberta Sigel suggested, alters or affects socialization patterns acquired as adolescents.

Overall, there is potentially much to be learned about generations and how as a concept it connects to American politics, change, and the other critical concepts that are already staples of political science analysis. The task of the remaining chapters in this book is to begin to sort out these questions and turn generational studies into a study of empirical political science.

REFERENCES

Abramson, P. R. 1975. *Generational Change in American Politics*. Lexington, MA: Heath.

Abramson, P. R. 1979. "Developing Party Identification: A Further Examination of Life Cycle, Generational, and Period Effects." *American Journal of Political Science* 23 (February): 78–96.

Abramson, P. R. 1983. *Political Attitudes in America*. San Francisco: W. H. Freeman.

Allison, G. T. 1971. *Essence of Decision: Explaining the Cuban Missile Crisis*. Boston: Little, Brown.

Andrews, T. M. 2016. "It's Official: Millennials Have Surpassed Baby Boomers to Become America's Largest Living Generation." *Washington Post*, April 26, A1.

Art, R. J., and R. Jervis. 2016. *International Politics: Enduring Concepts and Contemporary Issues*. New York: Pearson.

Babbie, E. 2013. *The Practice of Social Research*. Belmont, CA: Wadsworth.

Baker, T. L. 1999. *Doing Social Research*. New York: McGraw-Hill.

Banfield, E. C. 1958. *The Moral Basis of Backward Societies*. New York: Free Press.

Barber, J. D. 2009. *Presidential Character: Predicting Performance in the White House*. New York: Routledge.

Bendix, R. 1974. "Inequality and Social Structure: A Comparison of Marx and Weber." *American Sociological Review* 39 (2): 149–61.

Benjamin, W. 1978. "Theses on the Philosophy of History." In *Illuminations*, translated by Harry Zohn, 253–64. New York, Schocken Books.

Bolland, E. and C. Lopes. 2014. *Generations and Work*. London: Palgrave Macmillan.

Bond, J. R., and K. B. Smith. 2013. *Analyzing American Democracy: Politics and Political Science*. New York: Routledge.

Bristow, J. 2016. *The Sociology of Generations*. London: Palgrave Macmillan.

Bronfenbrenner, U. 1967. "Response to Pressure from Peers versus Adults among Soviet and American School Children." *International Journal of Psychology* 2 (3): 199–207.

Burge, Ryan P. 2021. "Gen Z and Religion in 2021." Available at https://religioninpublic.blog/2022/06/15/gen-z-and-religion-in-2021/

Burnham, W. D. 1970. *Critical Elections and the Mainspring of American Politics*. New York: W. W. Norton.

Cahn, D., and J. Cahn. 2016. *When Millennials Rule: The Reshaping of America*. Brentwood, TN: Post Hill Press.

Carroll, S. J. 1989. "Gender Politics and the Socializing Impact of the Women's Movement." In *Political Learning in Adulthood: A Sourcebook of Theory and Research*, edited by Roberta S. Sigel, 306–39. Chicago: University of Chicago Press.

Carson, R. (1962) 2002. *Silent Spring*. New York: Houghton Mifflin.

Converse, P. E. 1976. *The Dynamics of Party Support: Cohort-Analyzing Party Identification*. Beverly Hills, CA: Sage.

Dalton, R. J. 2009. *The Good Citizen: How a Younger Generation Is Reshaping American Politics*, Thousand Oaks, CA: CQ Press.

Davies, J. C. 1965. "The Family's Role in Political Socialization." *Annals of the American Academy of Political and Social Science* 361 (2): 11–19.

Delli Carpini, M. 1989. "Age and History: Generations and Sociopolitical Change." In *Political Learning in Adulthood: A Sourcebook of Theory and Research*, edited by Roberta S. Sigel, 11–55. Chicago: University of Chicago Press.

Desante, C. D., and C. W. Smith. 2020. *Racial Stasis: The Millennial Generation and the Stagnation of Racial Attitudes in American Politics*. Chicago: University of Chicago Press.

Desilver, D. 2014. "The Politics of American Generations: How Age Affects Attitudes and Voting Behavior," Pew Research Center, July 9. https://www.pewresearch .org/fact-tank/2014/07/09/the-politics-of-american-generations-how-age-affects -attitudes-and-voting-behavior/

Dimock, M. 2019. "Defining Generations: Where Millennials End and Generation Z Begins." Pew Research Center, January 17. https://www.pewresearch.org/fact-ta nk/2019/01/17/where-millennials-end-and-generation-z-begins/

Doherty, C. 2017. "The Generational Gap in American Politics." Washington, DC: Pew Research Center.

Duffy, B. 2021. *The Generations Myth: Why When You're Born Matters Less Than You Think*. New York: Basic Books.

Edelstein, A. S. 1962. "Since Bennington: Evidence of Change in Student Political Behavior." *Public Opinion Quarterly* 26(4): 564–77.

Ender, Morton G., David E. Rohall, and Michael D. Matthews. 2014. *The Millennial Generation and National Defense*. London: Palgrave Macmillan.

Erikson, E. H. 1968. *Identity, Youth and Crisis*. New York: W.W. Norton.

Erikson, E. H. (1958) 1993. *Young Man Luther: A Study in Psychoanalysis and History*. New York: W.W. Norton.

Ferrari, G. E. 1874. *Teoria dei Periodi Politici*. Milan: Hoepli.

Frenkel-Brunswik, E., T. W. Adorno, D. J. Levinson, and N. Sanford. 1950. *The Authoritarian Personality*. New York: Harper.

Freud, S. 1964. *New Introductory Lectures on Psychoanalysis*. Translated by James Strachey. New York: W.W. Norton.

Friedan, B. 1963. *The Feminine Mystique*. New York: W.W. Norton.

Fry, R., and K. Parker. 2018. "Early Benchmarks Show 'Post-Millennials' on Track to Be Most Diverse, Best-Educated Generation Yet." Washington, DC: Pew Research Center.

Gibney, B. C. 2017. *A Generation of Sociopaths: How the Baby Boomers Betrayed America*. New York: Hatchette Books.

Glenn, N. D. 1972. "Sources of the Shift to Political Independence: Some Evidence from a Cohort Analysis." *Social Science Quarterly* 53:494–519.

Glenn, N. D. 1976. "Cohort Analysts' Futile Quest: Statistical Attempts to Separate Age, Period, and Cohort Effects." *American Sociological Review* 41: 900–904.

Goldstein, L. J., and D. Schultz. 2015. *Conceptual Tension: Essays on Kinship, Politics, and Individualism*. Lanham, MD: Lexington Books.

Goodman M. E. 1958. "Emergent Citizenship: A Study of Relevant Values in Four-Year-Olds." *Childhood Education* 35: 248–51.

Greenberg, E. S., and B. Page. 2011. *The Struggle for Democracy*. New York: Pearson.

Greenblatt, A. 2015. "Millennial Generation." *CQ Researcher* 25: 553–76.

Greenstein, F. I. 1965. "Personality and Political Socialization: The Theories of Authoritarian and Democratic Character." *Annals of the American Academy of Political and Social Science* 361 (1): 81–95.

Hais, M. D., and M. Winograd. 2011. *Millennial Momentum: How a New Generation is Making America*. New Brunswick, NJ: Rutgers University Press.

Hancock, A. 2011. *Solidarity Politics for Millennials*. New York: Palgrave Macmillan.

Hershey, M. R. 2017. *Party Politics in America*. New York: Routledge.

Horowitz, I. L. 1989. "The Texture of Terrorism: Socialization, Routinization, and Integration." In *Political Learning in Adulthood: A Sourcebook of Theory and Research*, edited by Roberta S. Sigel, 386–414. Chicago: University of Chicago Press.

Howard, J. R. 1966. "The Making of a Black Muslim." *Transaction* 4: 15–21.

Howe, N., and W. Strauss. 2000. *Millennials Rising: The Next Great Generation*. New York: Vintage.

Hyman, H. 1959. *Political Socialization: A Study in the Psychology of Political Behavior*. Glencoe, IL: Free Press.

Isaak, A. C. 1985. *Scope and Methods of Political Science*. Pacific Grove, CA: Brooks/Cole.

Jennings, M. K., and H. Zeigler. 1970. In *Learning about Politics: A Reader in Political Socialization*, edited by Roberta S. Sigel, 434–53. New York: Random House.

Jervis, R. 2017. *Perception and Misperception in International Politics*. Princeton: Princeton University Press.

Kellstedt, P. M., and G. D. Whitten. 2013. *The Fundamentals of Political Science Research*. New York: Cambridge.

Key, V. O., Jr. 1955. "A Theory of Critical Elections." *Journal of Politics* 17: 3–18.

Kohlberg, L. 1968. "Moral Development." In *The International Encyclopedia of the Social Sciences*. New York: Macmillan.

Lafferty, W. M. 1989. "Work as a Source of Political Learning among Wage Laborers and Lower-Level Employees." In *Political Learning in Adulthood: A Sourcebook of Theory and Research*, edited by Roberta S. Sigel, 102–42. Chicago: University of Chicago Press.

Lancaster, L. C., and D. Stillman. 2003. *When Generations Collide: Who They Are. Why They Clash. How to Solve the Generational Puzzle at Work*. New York: Harper Business.

Lancaster, L. C., and D. Stillman. 2010. *The M-Factor: How the Millennial Generation Is Rocking the Workplace*. New York: Harper Business.

Lane, R. E. 1959. "Fathers and Sons: Foundations of Political Belief." *American Political Science Review* 24: 502–11.

Lawless, J. L., and R. L. Fox. 2015. *Running from Office: Why Young People Are Turned Off to Politics.* Oxford: Oxford University Press.

Lawson, E. D. 1963. "Development of Patriotism in Children—A Second Look." *Journal of Psychology* 55: 279–86.

LeVine, R. A. 1960. "The Internalization of Political Values in Stateless Societies," *Human Organization* 19: 51–58.

Lewis-Beck, M. S., W. G. Jacoby, H. Norpoth, and H. F. Weisberg. 2008. *The American Voter Revisited.* Ann Arbor: University of Michigan Press.

Lipset, S. M., and S. S. Wolin. 1965. *The Berkeley Student Revolt.* New York: Doubleday & Company.

Lovell, J. P., and J. H. Stiehm. 1989. "Military Service and Political Socialization." In *Political Learning in Adulthood: A Sourcebook of Theory and Research,* edited by Roberta S. Sigel, 172–202. Chicago: University of Chicago Press.

Lukes, S. 2006. *Individualism.* Lanham, MD: ECPR Press.

Mannheim, K. (1928) 2009. "The Sociological Problem of Generations." Copy available at https://1989after1989.exeter.ac.uk/wp-content/uploads/2014/03/01_The_Sociological_Problem.pdf

MacManus, S. 1995. *Young v. Old: Generational Combat in the 21st Century.* Boulder: Westview Press.

Morris, D., S. J. Hatchett, and R. E. Brown. 1989. "The Civil Rights Movement and Political Socialization." In *Political Learning in Adulthood: A Sourcebook of Theory and Research,* edited by Roberta S. Sigel, 272–305. Chicago: University of Chicago Press.

Nownes, A. J. 2012. *Interest Groups in American Politics: Pressure and Power.* New York: Routledge.

Pew Research Center. 2018. "The Generations Defined." https://www.pewresearch.org/st_18-02-27_generations_defined/

Piaget, J. 1967. *Six Psychological Studies.* New York: Random House.

Pinsker, J. 2020. "Oh No, They've Come Up with Another Generation Label: How Much Do Members of 'Generation Alpha,' or Any Generation, Really Have in Common?" *Atlantic,* February. https://www.theatlantic.com/family/archive/2020/02/generation-after-gen-z-named-alpha/606862/

Ritchie, K. 2008. *Marketing to Generation X.* New York: Lexington Books.

Rouse, S. M., and A. D. Ross. 2018. *The Politics of Millennials: Political Beliefs and Policy Preferences of America's Most Diverse Generation.* Ann Arbor: University of Michigan Press.

Schultz, D. 2018. "Parkland and the Political Coming of Generation Z." *The Hill,* May 23.

Shames, S. L. 2017. *Out of the Running: Why Millennials Reject Political Careers and Why It Matters.* New York: NYU Press.

Sigel, R. S. 1970. *Learning about Politics: A Reader in Political Socialization.* New York: Random House.

Sigel, R. S. 1989. *Political Learning in Adulthood: A Sourcebook of Theory and Research.* Chicago: University of Chicago Press.

Sigel, R. S., and M. B. Hoskin. 1981. *The Political Involvement of Adolescents.* New Brunswick, NJ: Rutgers University Press.

Statista. "Distribution of the race and ethnicity of the United States population in 2018, by generation." Available at https://www.statista.com/statistics/206969/race -and-ethnicity-in-the-us-by-generation/

Steele, B. J., and J. M. Acuff. 2012. *Theory and Application of the "Generation" in International Relations and Politics*. London: Palgrave Macmillan.

Stillman, D., and J. Stillman. 2017. *Gen Z @ Work: How the Next Generation Is Transforming the Workplace*. New York: HarperBusiness.

Stoker, L. 2014. "Reflections on the Study of Generations in Politics." *Forum* 12 (4): 377–96.

Strauss, W., and N. Howe. 1991. *Generations: The History of America's Future, 1584 to 2069*. New York: Quill.

Strauss, W., and N. Howe. 1997. *The Fourth Turning: An American Prophecy*. New York: Broadway Books.

Sundquist, J. L. 1973. *The Dynamics of the Party System*. Washington, DC: Brookings Institution.

Taylor, P. 2015. *The Next America*. New York: Public Affairs.

Twenge, J. M. 2017. *iGen: Why Today's Super-Connected Kids Are Growing Up Less Rebellious, More Tolerant, Less Happy—and Completely Unprepared for Adulthood—and What That Means*. New York: Atria Books.

Weisband, E., and C. I. Thomas. 2015. *Political Culture and the Making of Modern Nation-States*. New York: Routledge.

Williamson, J. B., L. Evans, and L. Powell. 1982. *The Politics of Aging: Power and Policy*. Springfield, IL: Charles E. Thomas.

Zemke, Ron, Claire Raines, and Bob Filipczak. 2000. *Generations at Work: Managing the Clash of Veterans, Boomers, Xers, and Nexters in Your Workplace*. New York: AMACOM.

Ziblatt, D. 1965. "High School Extracurricular Activities and Political Socialization." *ANNALS of the American Academy of Political and Social Science* 361 (1): 21–31.

Zukin, C., S. Keeter, M. Andolina, K. Jenkins, and M. X. Delli Carpini. 2006. *A New Engagement? Political Participation, Civic Life, and the Changing American Citizen*. New York: Oxford University Press.

2 | Generational Change in Partisanship

An Age-Period-Cohort Accounting

Laura Stoker

In the 1964 presidential election, Lyndon Johnson trounced Barry Goldwater, earning 61.1 percent of the popular vote and carrying 44 states. Democrats picked up seats in both the House and the Senate, ending up with 68 percent of the seats in each chamber. Though a strong performance by the Democrats, it also marked the continuation of a pattern in which they prevailed over the Republicans.[1] The dominant position of the Democrats was also evident in national survey data, which showed them holding a two to one edge in the percentage of party identifiers.

Over the ensuing years, however, the Democrats' edge over the Republicans dwindled, ushering in a period of volatility in the party holding the presidency and majorities in Congress, and of parity in the balance of party identifiers. According to the American National Election Studies (ANES), the Democrats' 67–33 percent advantage in identifiers as of 1964 declined to 62–39 percent by 1980, to 57–43 percent by 1992, and to 51–49 percent by 2016. This development drew a great deal of attention from scholars writing in the 1980s and 1990s, who argued that a slow-moving or secular realignment was underway, especially in the South, fueled by generational and demographic change (e.g., Alwin 1998; Abramowitz and Saunders 1998; Carmines and Stimson 1989; Miller 1992; Norpoth 1987).

Alongside this partisan realignment came another attention-grabbing development: "partisan dealignment"—a growth in the percentage of citizens claiming to be Independent rather than party-affiliated. Here the changes were front-loaded, with the percentage of

Independents climbing by 13 points between 1964 and 1972 (from 23% to 36%) though also drifting upward in later years. This prompted research into the causes of the rise and the differences between those who identify as Independent but lean toward one of the parties from both weak party identifiers and pure Independents (e.g., Abramson 1976, 1979; Craig 1985; Keith et al. 1992; Knoke and Hout 1974; Norpoth and Rusk 1982; Stanga and Sheffield 1987; Wattenberg 1981). Research established that while the entrance of the Baby Boomers may have exacerbated the early surge, the turn toward registering as Independent was evident across all age and demographic groups (Knoke and Hout 1974; Norpoth and Rusk 1982). It also taught us that the "Independent" and "partisan dealignment" labels are misleading if not misnomers, because most Independents are "leaners" who look like partisans in their candidate evaluations and voting behavior (Keith et al. 1992; Klar and Krupnikov 2016; Petrocik 2009), even if distinctive in other ways, for example in their heightened distrust of government (Pew Research Center 2010, 2019).

The 1980s then ushered in a third major development: partisan polarization within the electorate. Since then, issue positions, social identities, and ideological affiliations have become increasingly aligned with party identification and increasingly different between Democratic and Republican identifiers (Abramowitz 2013; Fiorina 2017; Levendusky 2009; Mason 2015, 2016), which has brought a rise in party-line voting (Abramowitz and Webster 2018; Bafumi and Shapiro 2009; Bartels 2000; Hetherington 2001). More ominously, Democrats and Republicans have increasingly come to express antipathy toward the other party and its members; that is, "negative partisanship" or "affective polarization" has been on the rise (Abramowitz and Webster 2016; Iyengar and Westwood 2015; Iyengar et al. 2019). There is some evidence that generational change has been fueling the greater alignment of party identification with ideology and issue attitudes (Stoker and Jennings 2008), but no research considering whether generational differences also lie beneath the growth in affective polarization.

The objective of this chapter is to revisit these developments with the benefit of 50 years of survey data and an approach designed to identify the extent to which they have been driven by generational replacement. This analysis will update and extend our understanding of how generational dynamics shaped the partisan realignment and the growth of Independents, inasmuch as most of the research on these topics is decades old.[2] It breaks new ground in addressing whether the growing affective polarization has been fueled by generational change.

The analysis combines an individual-level and a macro-level focus. At the individual level, a primary goal is to identify the effects of generation—that is, effects associated with the year of birth and eventual entry into the electorate—on the likelihood of identifying as a Republican vs. a Democrat, on identifying as an Independent rather than as a partisan, and on Democrats' and Republicans' in-party and out-party evaluations. The macro-level focus turns to explain the trends themselves—the erosion of Democratic dominance in the balance of party identifiers both inside and outside of the South, the growth in Independent identification, and the rise of affective polarization. Here the question is the extent to which these developments can be attributed to generational replacement as opposed to the aging of the population, other shifts in its demographic composition, or period effects—that is, over-time changes evident among citizens regardless of their generation, age, or demographics. The analysis will show, for example, that the southern realignment was first fueled by period effects, that those had largely petered out when the effects of generational replacement really kicked in, and that the net effects of shifts in the population's age and demographic composition were nil.

The approach I use is an Age-Period-Cohort (APC) model applied to data from the face-to-face component of the American National Election Studies (ANES) from 1964 to 2016. An APC model is designed to show whether and how outcomes vary with age and other demographics, whether groups defined by when they were born (cohorts or generations[3]) are politically distinctive, and the extent to which outcomes are otherwise changing over time (i.e., are period effects), taking all of these under consideration simultaneously. APC models have their adherents, but have also been met with skepticism and even derision (e.g., Glenn 1976; Markus 1985) and can become statistically very complex. The skepticism arises because APC models try to disentangle causes that are thoroughly entangled, and are able to do so only by making statistical assumptions that may not be warranted. Later, I elaborate on the problem of disentangling age, period, and cohort effects and the solution I employ, which has the advantages of simplicity and transparency of assumptions.

The derision comes from the fact that even if the APC model yields believable results about how outcomes vary with age, period, and cohort, that may not be much of an accomplishment. As Markus (1985,

720) put it, "The APC model is primarily an accounting equation rather than an explanatory one." In one sense, the point is apt. While an APC analysis will identify how outcomes vary by age, period, and generation, it is silent as to why such patterns arise. Of course, we often have clear theoretical reasons to expect age, period, and generation effects, as elaborated below.

Still, APC modeling does serve explanatory goals. One reason is that the effects it uncovers should set the agenda for new research hoping to explain them. Related, only by attempting to disentangle age and generation can we even find the patterns that we next need to try to explain. In two of the cases I consider here, age and generation operate at cross-purposes. With age comes a greater likelihood of affiliating with the Republican Party, but without an APC analysis this would be masked by the fact that newer generations have gravitated more toward the Republicans than did their older counterparts. The likelihood of claiming a party identification also grows with age, but the most recent entrants into the electorate are distinctive in their higher rates of party affiliation. Each of these findings would be missing if not accounting for the other.

Finally, an APC analysis is designed to identify how age (and other demographics), period, and generation are influencing individuals in order to improve our understanding and future expectations regarding macro-political change. One case in point concerns the strong Republican showings in the election of 2016, which undercut arguments foretelling Democratic gains on account of demographic and generational change (Judis and Teixeira 2004; Galston 2013). Though journalistic spins about "demographics are destiny" oversimplified the scholarly arguments (Teixeira 2020), a core idea was that the size of the Democratic advantage would grow because the population was becoming more racially diverse and because of generational replacement, since an age gap had arisen showing that younger Americans—Millennials—were more Democratic than their elders. The APC analysis will show that, yes, the Democrats have been advantaged by the growing nonwhite population, but this advantage has been swamped by other changes in the population's composition that have worked against them. And, yes, today's young people are more Democratic than their elders, something not true two or three decades ago, but these patterns reflect the confluence of age, generation, period, and demographics.[4] Neither inside nor outside of the South are Millennials more Democratic once their age, demographics, and time of entry into the electorate are taken into account.

In what follows, I begin by elaborating on the concept of a political generation, why we expect distinct generations to arise, and how the APC approach I use differs from hypothesis-driven research on generational differences. I follow with a brief discussion of aging and why we might expect it to have consequences for party identification and affective polarization. I then elaborate on the APC framework and the approach I take to disentangle age, period, and cohort effects. In the results section that follows, I consider party identification (Democratic vs. Republican), Independent identification, and affective polarization in turn. The discussion and conclusion sections highlight key findings, implications, and limitations.

Political Generations

A generation is a group defined by the intersection of age and history, with its members having been of a certain age (or within a certain age range) during a specified year or range of years. The concept was elaborated by Karl Mannheim in a famous 1928 essay (1952), "The Sociological Problem of Generations," which inspired volumes of interest by social scientists and emerged as key to theory and empirical work in the field of political socialization (see Stoker 2014 and references therein for an overview).

The political socialization account holds that political orientations are most likely to form in late adolescence and early adulthood, the most "impressionable years" of the life cycle. This is when people are first motivated to define themselves politically and when they are most vulnerable to influence from what is going on in their lives and in the polity (Sears and Brown 2013; Stoker and Bass 2011). Because of this, the political views of a given generation will bear a historical imprint, which will continue to distinguish them from other generations as they age. That is not to say that orientations formed during the impressionable years are unchangeable. Indeed, initial tendencies are expected to strengthen with age due to motivated reasoning and behavioral reinforcement, while events and experiences taking place later in life always have the potential to induce change. Nevertheless, the generation's distinctiveness from others is expected to persist.

Some research on political generations is hypothesis driven, based on explicit ideas about when and why distinct generations form. For example, Gibson and Caldeira (1992) argue that African Americans who went through their impressionable years when Earl Warren presided over the U.S. Supreme Court developed more favorable attitudes toward the Court than those who were either younger or older at the time; Firestone and Chen (1995) argue that women who came of age before passage of the 19th Amendment were throughout their lives less likely to vote than were those who came of age later; and Stoker and Jennings (2008) argue that people who entered the electorate before the two parties diverged on social issues were less likely to develop sorted attitudes than were people entering afterwards.

As with these examples, hypothesis-driven research on political generations begins by identifying historical periods that differ in features thought to shape the political orientations of young, impressionable citizens. This then guides the demarcation of generations—in the examples, respectively those going through their impressionable years during vs. before or after the Warren Court era, before vs. after the passage of the 19th Amendment, and before vs. after the opening of a party divide on social issues. The first two examples also focus their generational arguments on specific subgroups—African Americans and women, respectively. This recognizes that young people may differ in the extent to which they are shaped by the historical moment or react to that moment in divergent ways.

Other work on political generations proceeds inductively, without identifying a specific shift in the society or polity that might be prompting the formation of a new political generation, but still recognizing that sociopolitical changes may be leading the newer cohorts to be politically different from their elders. The APC approach taken in this chapter falls into this category. This kind of work often divides American history loosely into different eras, identifying as generation members those who came into adulthood during those eras. Influential research from the Pew Research Organization distinguishes six generations: *Greatest*—born before 1928 and coming into adulthood in the interwar period or during World War II; *Silent*—born between 1928 and 1945 and experiencing their impressionable years in the quiet period before the storm of the 1960s; *Baby Boomer*—born between 1946 and 1964 and coming into adulthood during or soon after the turmoil over civil rights and Vietnam; *Gen X*—born between 1965 and 1980 and experiencing the Reagan and Clinton presidencies as young adults; *Millennial*—born between 1981 and 1996 and entering adulthood at the turn of the century; and *Gen Z*—born in 1997 or later and coming of age during Obama's second term or Trump's reign

(Dimock 2019; Pew Research Center 2015). Typically, analysts seek to compare the generations across a broad array of attitudinal and behavioral measures and do not use an APC model (e.g., Levine 2007; Putnam 1995; Zukin et al. 2006).

The Political Consequences of Aging

The reasons we expect aging to have political consequences fall into two categories, those that are directly linked to the passage of time and those that are tied to the roles and transitions that accompany aging. The latter are sometimes called life-cycle or life-stage effects instead of aging effects. Ideas in the former category include the growth of experience and understanding that comes with repeated exposure to elections and political news, the sheer length of time one has held on to a social identity, and the effects of repeatedly acting in one fashion or another, as in voting over and over for candidates from a given party. These kinds of ideas give rise to the expectation that political knowledge will deepen with age and that political opinions and identities will strengthen, which have been confirmed by any number of political socialization studies. The growing strength of party identification with age, famously demonstrated by Converse (1976) but shown repeatedly in other research, including APC analyses (Knoke and Hout 1974; Twenge et al. 2016), is a pertinent example. Because of this, we would expect to see rates of Independent identification diminishing with age and affective polarization strengthening, with feelings toward the in-party growing more positive and feelings toward the out-party more negative.

The second category of arguments about why aging has political consequences focuses on how experiences, relationships, and preferences shift as one moves into and through the life stages of adulthood, including college, careers, marriage, parenthood, and retirement. These ideas have been elaborated in the literature on political socialization in adulthood (Sapiro 1994; Sigel 1989; Watts 1999). Research on whether aging prompts conservatism or Republican affiliation is usually of this ilk, where the argument is that aging leads to increases in status, wealth, and obligations, prompting shifts in values and interests that make conservatism and the Republican Party more attractive. Existing evidence on the question is mixed (Peterson, Smith, and Hibbing 2020; Twenge et al. 2016).

The Age-Period-Cohort (APC) Framework

The APC framework attributes macro-level trends to three causes: aging effects, period effects, and cohort replacement effects. Most APC analysts add a fourth, as do I: demographic change. In elaborating on these, it will help to have an example in mind; I will refer to over-time changes in voter turnout rates.

The idea that macro-political trends can be attributed to aging effects has a two-part logic: (1) aging brings about a change in the outcome for reasons having to do with the acquisition of experience or life stage transitions, and (2) as time passes, the age composition of the electorate is shifting. Thus, if (since) the likelihood of a citizen voting tends to rise with age and the U.S. population has been growing older in the aggregate in recent decades, the aging effect would result in higher overall voter turnout rate, ceteris paribus.

Period effects are changes wrought by causes that vary over time and that affect all citizens, regardless of their age or generation. Were the United States to make the November election date a holiday, for example, that would be likely to make it easier for all citizens to vote, prompting an increase in voter turnout rates relative to past elections. Period effects can also be specified as subgroup-specific, as in a change of the Minnesota registration law that affects Minnesotans but not others.

The cohort replacement argument follows a two-part logic similar to that for aging: (1) unique cohorts or generations exist, and (2) as time passes, the generational composition of the electorate is shifting. Through natural mortality, older citizens are dying and being replaced by younger ones entering the electorate. The engine of population replacement turns into generational replacement when older and younger citizens represent distinct political generations. Thus, if the older Americans dying out were part of a highly civically engaged Greatest generation and their replacements are Gen Xers or Millennials who show less inclination to vote, the overall voter turnout rate will decline (on this, see Dalton 2008).

Finally, and likewise, over-time shifts in outcomes can be driven by shifts in the demographic composition of the population on dimensions apart from age or generation, for example, in the rate of union membership or educational attainment. If (since) people are more likely to vote if they are union members or highly educated, then voter turnout rates should rise or fall as the rate of union membership or educational attainment rises or falls.

Using the APC Framework with ANES Data, 1964–2016

Any attempt to estimate the effects of age, period, and cohort in repeated cross-sectional data faces one fundamental challenge: once information on any two of these variables is given, the value of the third one is known. In the case of annual data where period is indexed by year, cohort is indexed by year of birth, and age is indexed by years since birth, then Age = Period − Cohort, Period = Cohort + Age, and Cohort = Period − Age. In the ANES data, studies are spaced four years apart, which means cohorts and age groups need to be binned into four-year groupings if they are to be followed over time. Still, the same indeterminacy arises.

To see this more clearly, consider table 2.1, which shows the frequency of ANES cases classified by period (along the columns) and cohort (along the rows), with the intersection of any row and column indicating the age group.[5] New entrants into the electorate (aged 18–21) are highlighted in bold italics.[6] Once you know the cohort (row) and period (column), then age (intersecting cell) is known. At any one point in time, age and cohort are confounded; those differing in age also differ in when they were born. If following any given cohort over time, age and period are confounded. And if following any given age group over time, cohort and period are confounded.

This means that age, period, and cohort effects cannot be simultaneously estimated unless the analyst imposes statistical constraints or assumptions that break this perfect multicollinearity. Many different solutions have been proposed and illustrated. Good overviews can be found in Fosse and Winship's recent (2019) contribution to the *Annual Review of Sociology* and in a special *Electoral Studies* issue on the topic, introduced by Neundorf and Niemi (2014). One solution is to collect individual cohorts into broader generational groupings, which breaks the perfect association between age and cohort/generation at any given point in time. A second is to simultaneously estimate the APC model on two or more subgroups, constraining one of the three effects (age, period, cohort) to be the same across the groups (Dinas and Stoker 2014). I use one or both of these solutions here.[7]

All of my analyses distinguish five generations instead of the four-year birth cohort groupings shown in table 2.1. In a coding that is similar to the Pew breakdowns, I distinguish those born before 1927 as the Greatest generation; those born between 1927 and 1946 as the Silent generation; those born between 1947 and 1962 as Baby Boomers; those

TABLE 2.1. Face-to-Face Sample Frequencies by Cohort, Year, and (Implicitly) Age

ANES Presidential Election Studies, 1964–2016

	1964	1968	1972	1976	1980	1984	1988	1992	1996	2000	2004	2008	2012	2016
1903–06	85	93	110	94	50	48	27	18	0	0	0	0	0	0
1907–10	106	83	150	118	72	83	56	53	27	0	0	0	0	0
1911–14	135	109	165	144	77	89	60	73	37	23	0	0	0	0
1915–18	121	109	155	124	83	102	75	84	37	35	11	0	0	0
1919–22	125	134	162	133	106	129	102	102	64	44	20	35	0	0
1923–26	147	134	201	149	90	95	94	122	86	57	23	35	22	0
1927–30	126	137	181	125	96	112	111	119	78	66	44	68	24	23
1931–34	126	126	184	119	71	106	88	108	87	66	38	58	34	24
1935–38	139	100	167	133	88	109	111	98	78	86	51	74	37	33
1939–42	125	134	190	157	111	131	96	143	96	99	91	107	69	51
1943–46	26	118	273	182	128	162	128	163	94	132	71	128	77	50
1947–50	0	34	267	247	151	229	200	179	125	131	97	139	126	92
1951–54	0	0	204	186	164	239	227	191	152	141	97	171	123	63
1955–58	0	0	0	146	150	202	182	269	163	160	97	192	146	86
1959–62	0	0	0	0	114	209	208	276	183	172	91	189	171	82
1963–66	0	0	0	0	0	142	145	221	150	174	93	161	124	86
1967–70	0	0	0	0	0	0	103	157	107	133	75	161	118	74
1971–74	0	0	0	0	0	0	0	109	94	107	74	175	152	70
1975–78	0	0	0	0	0	0	0	0	54	98	89	174	150	61
1979–82	0	0	0	0	0	0	0	0	0	74	89	158	175	94
1983–86	0	0	0	0	0	0	0	0	0	0	61	133	145	74
1987–90	0	0	0	0	0	0	0	0	0	0	0	119	173	75
1991–94	0	0	0	0	0	0	0	0	0	0	0	0	128	72
1995–98	0	0	0	0	0	0	0	0	0	0	0	0	0	46

Note: Cohorts from 1800s (1875+) not shown. Rows indicate cohorts by date of birth, columns indicate ANES study year, and cells contain unweighted case frequencies. The diagonals show people in the same age group over time; those newly entering the electorate—aged 18–21—in each ANES study are highlighted in bold. Cohorts are collected into generations as described in the text.

born between 1963 and 1982 as Gen X; and those born between 1983 and 1998 as Millennials.[8]

I also employ the second solution when distinguishing subgroups is essential. When studying the balance of party identifiers, I analyze southerners and nonsoutherners separately, and when studying affective polarization, I analyze Democrats and Republicans separately. In each case, I hold the effects of age (but not period or generation) constant across the subgroups. In other words, I assume that any effect of age on party identification is the same among those living within the South and outside of it, and that the effect of age on in-party and out-party evaluations is the same among Democrats and Republicans.[9]

Of course, the U.S. has experienced substantial changes to its demographic make-up over the past half century, which are also capable of shaping macro-political changes. To isolate the effects of age, period, and generation, these too must be taken into account. Each analysis controlled for education (dummy variables for some college and college degree), union membership (dummy variable for union member in household), race/ethnicity (dummy variables for Black and Hispanic or other nonwhite), nativity (dummy variable for whether one or more parents was born outside of the U.S.), gender (dummy variable for female), and marital status (dummy variable for married or living with a partner).[10]

To summarize, the APC model of party identification distinguishes those residing inside the South from those residing outside the South, allowing the effects of period and generation to vary across the regions. A binary variable of party affiliation (1 = Democrat, 0 = Republican, including leaners) is regressed on (a) a dummy variable for region (South), (b) dummy variables for 13 of the 14 years, (c) dummy variables for 4 of the 5 generations, (d) dummy variables for 17 of the 18 age categories, (e) interactions between South and year dummies, (f) interactions between South and generation dummies, and (g) demographic controls as listed above. The APC model of Independent identification (1 = pure or leaning Independent, 0 = Democratic or Republican identifier), which does not distinguish subgroups, includes the year dummies, generation dummies, age dummies, and demographic variables. The analysis of affective polarization examines two dependent variables, feeling thermometer ratings of the in-party and of the out-party, and distinguishes Democratic from Republican identifiers, allowing the effects of period and generation to vary across the groups. The thermometer ratings (scored 0 to 100) are regressed on (a) a dummy for party identification (PID), (b) dummy variables for 13 of the 14 years, (c) dummy variables for 4 of the 5 generations, (d) dummy variables for 17 of the 18 age categories, (e) interactions between party identification and year dummies, (f) interactions between party identification and generation dummies, and (g) the demographic controls. All analyses are weighted.

Appendix table A2.1 shows how the generation, age, and other demographic variables were changing from 1964 to 2016. The Greatest generation dominated in the early years of the time series but had disappeared by 2016. The Baby Boomers held the plurality from 1984 through 2000, before being eclipsed by the Gen Xers. By 2016, almost 60 percent of the electorate came from the youngest two generations. On average, the electorate grew younger from 1968 (47 years old) to 1984 (45), before growing older with an average approaching 48 years by 2016. Education rates were of course climbing across the time frame while union membership was declining. The share of the electorate identified as Hispanic or other nonwhite grew substantially, while the percentage of those with a parent born outside of the U.S. first declined between 1964 and 1980 and then stabilized, though with volatility. The prevalence of married respondents declined substantially between 1964 and 1988 before rebounding in recent years.

Appendix table A2.2 shows how the generations differ by age and demographics. In addition to the expected age differences, members of the younger generations are more likely to be nonwhite, male, not married, not part of a union household, and to have at least some college education. Millennials come in second to the Greatest generation in terms of the percentage with an immigrant parent, and are less likely to have completed a college degree (yet) than Gen Xers.

In what follows, I first present results on party identification and then turn to the findings on Independent identification and affective polarization. Because of their importance as well as their complexity, I give the partisanship results somewhat more attention. For each topic, I begin by introducing the trends evident in the ANES data. I then show the estimated effects of age, which provides context for what comes next: a display of generational differences over time, which holds the effects of age and demographics constant. I finish by comparing the over-time trends to the period effects, that is, the trends evident after removing confounds from the shifting demographic, age, and generational composition of the electorate. The APC regression results used to generate the figures are given in the appendix (tables A2.3–A2.5).

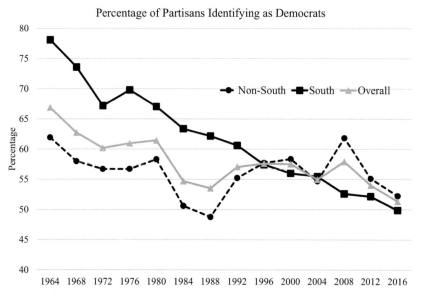

Fig. 2.1a. Trends in Party Balance by Region. (*Note:* Entries show the weighted percentage of partisans [Democrats or Republicans, including leaners] who identified as or leaned Democrat, by region.)
Source: Data comes from the ANES face-to-face studies.

Results: Identifying as a Democrat versus as a Republican

Trends

Figure 2.1a shows how the partisan balance in the electorate shifted from a solid Democratic majority in 1964 to near parity by 2016. The measure here is the percentage of those identifying with a party who identify as a Democrat, including leaners. Pure Independents are, thus, excluded; they number about 10 percent of the electorate, a figure that fluctuates only 1–2 percentage points from election to election and shows no over-time trend. The figure breaks down the results by Census region, distinguishing southern states from others.[11]

What jumps out from the data is the well-known pattern of Southern realignment—the steady decline in Democratic identifiers within the South, which in the ANES data went from nearly 80 percent in 1964 to 50 percent in 2016. The pattern outside the South shows much more election-to-election fluctuation, though a 10-point decline in Democratic identifiers as well, from a percentage in the low 60s in 1964 to a

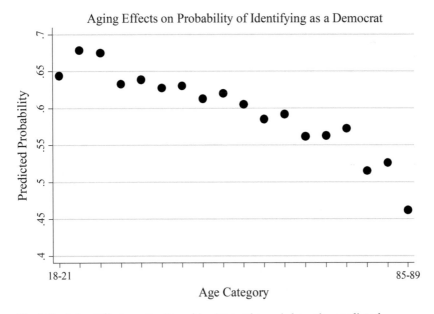

Fig. 2.1b. Aging Effects on Partisanship. (*Note:* Shown is how the predicted probability of identifying as a Democrat varies across age groups, holding all other variables to their means.)
Source: Derived from the Logit results shown in table A2.3.

percentage in the low 50s by 2016. The vast regional variation evident in the 1960s, 1970s, and 1980s had largely disappeared by the 1990s as the Republicans grew slowly and surely in the South and made modest inroads elsewhere. A regional gap popped up again in 2008, this time with Southerners about 10 points more Republican than others.[12] That gap diminished but did not disappear in later years.

Aging

The APC model uncovers a sizeable aging effect on the likelihood of identifying as a Democrat rather than as a Republican, with the probability dropping almost monotonically and by 15 to 20 points across the full age range (fig. 2.1b). With all other variables held constant at their means, the probability of a young person choosing a Democratic identity over a Republican one is about .65. This probability declines steadily to between .45 and .50 among the oldest age groups. This finding is notable in light of the mixed findings from previous research on the aging-brings-conservatism hypothesis, though matches the finding of Twenge et al. (2016), who analyzed non-ANES data, and of Knoke and Hout (1974), who analyzed ANES data from the 1950s through 1972. It is also easily masked, as we will see, because the generation effects work in the opposite direction.

Generational Differences

Figure 2.1c presents the results on generation effects, for Southerners and non-Southerners, respectively. The figure shows generational differences as of each year, holding age and the other demographic variables to their within-region means. To simplify, the over-time trends were smoothed.[13]

One big takeaway is that generation effects are pronounced in the South, which comes as no surprise. The Southern realignment was clearly fueled by the greater draw of the Republican Party to successive generations. Compared to the Greatest generation, the later entrants are more Republican by 9 (Silent), 14 (Boomer), 19 (Gen X), and 20 (Millennial) percentage points, on average. Importantly, Millennials have not extended the pattern; they look no more Republican than the Gen Xers.

Although generational change plays a lesser role outside the South, it too has been contributing to the erosion in Democratic support. There, the Millennials are 16 percent more likely to identify as Republican than the Greatest generation, ceteris paribus, while the Gen Xers are 6 percent more likely. Only the former is statistically significant ($p = .005$) though the later comes close ($p = .104$). The reason why is evident in the figure, where the gap between the Gen Xers and the others diminishes after they entered the electorate in 1984 even if it never quite disappears, while the Millennials remain more distinctive across the four elections in which they appear. Still, the pro-Republican bent for each generation was clearly greatest during the first election in which they were eligible to vote, which were peak times of Republican strength—Reagan's reelection in 1984 (Gen X) and George W. Bush's in 2004 (Millennials).[14] These findings underscore the importance of the contemporary political context to the partisan tendencies of young people entering the electorate.

Period Effects

Generational replacement has helped the Republican Party make gains, especially within the South but also outside of it. So, too, has the

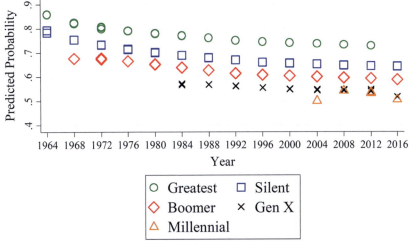

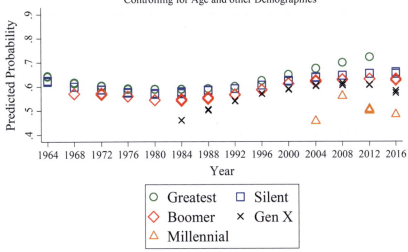

Fig. 2.1c. Generational Differences in Partisanship, by Region. (*Note:* Shown are [smoothed] predicted probabilities of identifying as a Democrat across generation, time, and region. The predicted probabilities hold age and other demographic variables constant at their within-region means.)

Source: Results are derived from the Logit results shown in table A2.3.

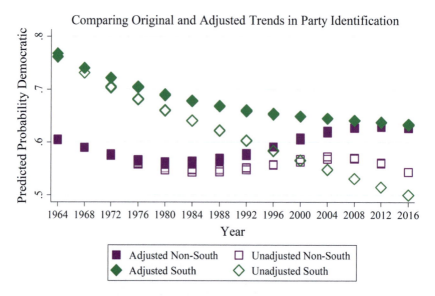

Fig. 2.1d. Trends vs. Period Effects on Partisanship, by Region
Note: Smoothed trends. Adjusted trend holds generation, age, and other demographic variables to the 1964 means, within-region.

greater longevity of population, since people gravitate more toward the Republicans as they age. Other major demographic changes taking place have favored the Republicans as well. The Republicans benefited from the growth in the college educated population, which has more than doubled since 1964, since people with some college education and those with college degrees have identified with the Republicans at higher rates than those with less education (see tables A2.1 and A2.3).[15] The weakening of labor unions has also advantaged the Republicans, since members of union households have been more likely to identify as Democrats than their nonunion counterparts. On the plus side for the Democrats has been the growth in the nonwhite population, a Democratic constituency.

To see the period effects operating on the balance of party identifiers, we need to remove the effects of changes in the population's composition. For each region, figure 2.1d shows a smoothed representation of the original trend alongside a second one that holds population composition constant, specifically setting all compositional variables to their within-region means as of 1964. Thus, for example, the "Adjusted" trend assumes no generational replacement between

1964 and 2016, with the composition instead frozen at 70 percent Greatest and 30 percent Silent in the South, and at 64/36 percent outside the South. It is the adjusted trend that shows the period effects that have been operating on the balance of party identifiers. Differences between the pair of trend lines indicate how much the parties' fortunes were being shaped by generational replacement and demographic change.[16]

As drivers of the Southern realignment, period effects have worked in concert with changes in population composition. Between 1964 and 2016, the percentage of Southerners identifying as Democrat dropped by about 27 points, but this loss is reduced to 13 points by holding population composition constant. Hence, only about 50 percent of the Republican gains in the South can be attributed to generational replacement and other compositional shifts (on this point, see also Erikson, MacKuen, and Stimson 2002; Osborne Sears, and Valentino 2011). Period forces were consistently operating to the advantage of the Republican Party as well, though more strongly in the first few decades than in the post-Reagan years.

Outside the South, the period effects first worked against the Democrats for 20 years before turning around and working in their favor. Had the population's composition not also been changing, the percentage of Democratic identifiers would have declined by about 4–5 percent between 1964 and 1984, before growing by about 6–7 percent across the ensuing years. Yet changes in the population's composition have been working against this bounce-back for the Democrats, leaving them on the whole in a worse position in 2016 than they were in 1964. Generational replacement has been key to this development, but population-level shifts in age, educational attainment, and labor union membership have contributed too. On balance, the pro-Republican compositional shifts well outweighed the major demographic trend going in the Democrats' direction—the changing racial composition of the country.

It is possible to be somewhat more definitive about the relative importance of generational replacement and demographic changes to the shifting balance of party identifiers. The tool is Achen's (1982) "Level Importance" method. I first calculated the mean of each demographic and generation variable at the beginning (1964–68) and end of the series (2012–16) within regions; combining pairs of studies at the beginning and end makes it less likely that peculiarities in any one sample will matter. Multiplying each variable's coefficient by the difference in the two means shows how much it contributed to the shifting outcome across the two time points.[17] This analysis shows compositional shifts costing the Democrats 12 points in the South, of which only one-tenth of a percentage point was due to over-time changes in age and other demographics taken together; the rest was all due to generational replacement. Outside of the South, demographic change has played a more important role but still less than that wrought by generational change. Here the analysis suggests that compositional changes cost the Democrats 8 points, with 3 points attributed to demographic change (including age) and 5 points coming from generational replacement.[18]

Results: Identifying as an Independent

Trends

Figure 2.2a tracks the percentage of American citizens identifying as Independent when asked the first ANES party identification question. On average, two-thirds of these are "leaners" who admit in follow-up questions that they lean toward one or another of the parties. Since there is no over-time growth in the percentage of pure Independents, the trends in figure 2.2a reflect the growth of Independent leaners. The largest jump occurred between 1964 and 1976, when the percentage of Independents went from just over 20 percent to just over 35 percent. Over the next 20 years the percentage identifying as Independent flattened out, only to begin growing again after the mid-1990s—albeit slowly and modestly, increasing another 5 percent by 2016. Nowadays, about 40 percent identify as Independent with about 75 percent of those admitting to a partisan leaning.

Aging

One likely consequence of aging is that the probability of identifying as an Independent declines. The expectations of finding such an association are strong based on theory and past evidence, and the results are as expected. Holding all else constant, the APC model estimates that the probability of calling oneself an Independent drops by more than half when comparing the youngest age group to the oldest, from nearly .55 to about .20 (fig. 2.2b). The decline accelerates to some extent after the early years of adulthood (ages 18–29), plateauing again in old age.

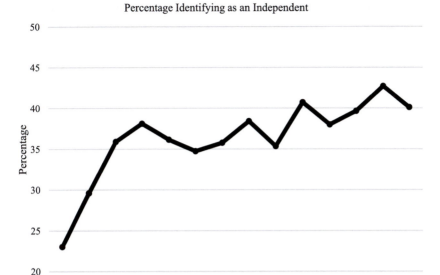

Fig. 2.2a. Trends in Independent Identification. (*Note:* Entries are the weighted percentage of Independent identifiers, including leaners.)
Source: Drawn from face-to-face ANES data.

This is consistent with the portrayal of early adulthood as a key stage of political development, one where many people are figuring where they stand politically.

Generational Differences

What is more novel in these results is the important generational shifts taking place, which work in the opposite direction (fig. 2.2c). Baby Boomers have been slightly less drawn to the Independent label than have members of the Silent and Greatest generations, at least since the 1980s. More clearly, Gen Xers are even less likely to identify as Independent and have consistently been so since entering the electorate in 1984. Millennials have extended the pattern. Compared to the Greatest generation, Gen Xers are 7 points less likely to identify as Independent (.31 vs. .38), on average, while Millennials are 13 points less likely (.25 vs. .38). Thus, even though an Independent identification is more common among the young than the old, the two youngest generations are more partisan than would be expected given their age and other demographic attributes. One likely explanation for this is the fact that Gen

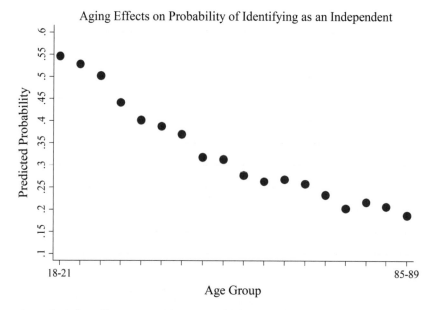

Fig. 2.2b. Aging Effects on Independent Identification. (*Note:* Shown is how the predicted probability of identifying as an Independent varies across age groups, holding all other variables to their means.)
Source: Results are derived from the Logit results shown in table A2.4.

Xers and Millennials entered the electorate in an era of sharper party differences. Another is generational differences in collective memories (Schuman and Scott 1989), notably the fact that the younger generations grew up well after the events spurring antiparty sentiment among their elders, including conflicts over civil rights, the Vietnam War, and Watergate.

Period Effects

Both the aging of the population and generational replacement have worked against an over-time increase in the percentage of Independent identifiers. So, too, has the rise in educational attainment, since the college educated are less likely to claim the identity than are those with a high school education (table A2.4). As a result, the period forces fueling the growth in the percentage of people identifying as Independent are even stronger than those suggested by the simple trend line. This is illustrated in figure 2.2d, which, as before, shows the unadjusted

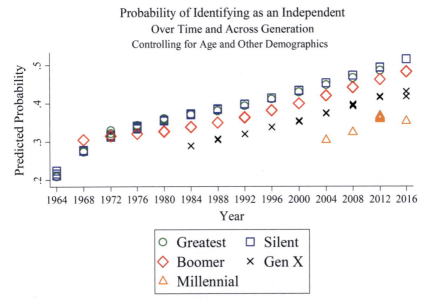

Fig. 2.2c. Generational Differences in Independent Identification. (*Note:* Shown is how the predicted probability of identifying as an Independent varies across generation and time, with age and other demographic variables held constant at their overall sample means.)
Source: Results are derived from the Logit results shown in table A2.4.

(but smoothed) trend as well as the trend under an assumption of no changes in the composition of the population since 1964. Comparing the end points, the over-time growth in percentage of Independents is estimated to have been about 8 points higher had the electorate's composition not also been shifting across this period.

Results: Affective Polarization

Trends

Figure 2.3a displays the trends in affective polarization from 1964 to 2016, with the left panel showing how Democratic and Republican identifiers rated their own party on ANES's 0–100 feeling thermometer and the right panel showing how partisans rated the other party.[19] Previous research has emphasized the steady and steep decline in evaluations of the out-party since their peak point of positivity in the

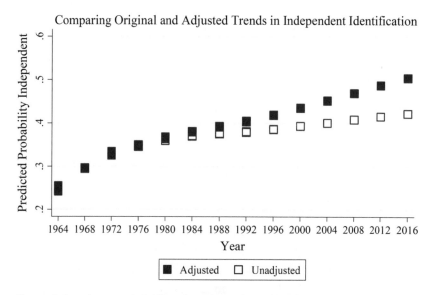

Fig. 2.2d. Trends vs. Period Effects in Independent Identification
Note: Smoothed trends. Adjusted trend holds generation, age, and other demographic variables to the 1964 means.

1970s, trends that are evident in figure 2.3a and very similar for Democratic and Republican identifiers. It is important to remember, though, that out-party ratings had been more negative before that peak. Feelings toward the out-party were neutral in 1964 and rose to being mildly positive by 1972 before beginning their steady descent over the ensuing decades, ending at a rating near 30, about 25 points below the 1972 high.

In-party ratings also show a decline across the period, but one that is milder, varies somewhat across the parties, and manifests more waxing and waning turns. The peak in-party rating for both Democrats and Republicans was in 1964, at about 85 and 80 points, respectively. By 2016, in-party ratings had become 15–20 points more negative, with Democrats maintaining a 5-point edge in in-party esteem. Yet, since the decline between 1964 and 1976 was itself 15 points, the trend across the post-1976 period is best described as flat though fluctuating, which contrasts markedly with the steady decline in out-party ratings.[20]

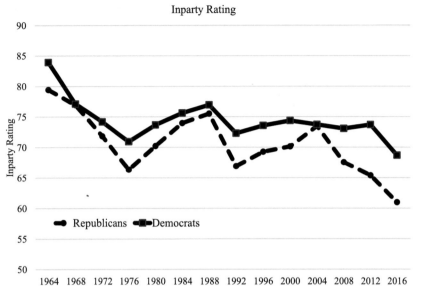

Fig. 2.3a. Trends in In-party and Out-party Ratings, by Party. (*Note:* Entries are weighted means from ANES face-to-face data.)

Aging

Figure 2.3b displays the estimated effects of aging on in-party ratings (*top panel*) and out-party ratings (*bottom panel*). As expected, in-party ratings tend to grow more positive with age, and nearly linearly so, with the oldest partisans expressing feelings that are about 10 points more favorable toward their party than those expressed by the youngest. Unexpectedly, there is no aging effect on out-party ratings. This asymmetry may, however, be possible to square with social identity theory, which holds that strengthening a group attachment prompts more in-group favoritism but not necessarily more out-group antagonism (Tajfel and Turner 2004).

Generational Differences

Figure 2.3c shows results on generational differences, first for in-party ratings (part A) and then for out-party ratings (part B). With minor but interesting exceptions, the overall pattern is of no generation effects. The first exception concerns in-party evaluations from Republicans in the three youngest generations. Compared to their elders, Republican

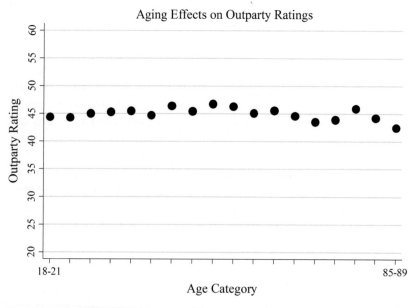

Fig. 2.3b. Aging Effects on In-party and Out-party Ratings. (*Note:* Entries show how predicted in-party and out-party ratings vary across age groups, holding all other variables to their means.)

Source: Results are derived from the OLS results shown in tables A2.5a and A2.5b.

Baby Boomers expressed slightly more negative feelings toward their own party when they first entered the electorate (in 1968), a finding consistent with results from earlier research on generational differences in partisan attitudes (Miller 1992; Norpoth 1987; Stanga and Sheffield 1987; Wattenberg 1981). By contrast, Republican-identifying Gen Xers and Millennials expressed slightly more positive in-party feelings when they first entered the electorate, which was during the second-term elections of Ronald Reagan (1984) and George W. Bush (2004), respectively. These elections followed periods of very high approval for each president, coinciding with each cohort's adolescent and early adult years. Although modest (about 5 points on the 0–100 scale), these differences are consistent with the core idea underlying generation effects, that young people entering the electorate will be especially influenced by the Zeitgeist of the time.

A second exception concerns the out-group ratings of Republican-identifying Millennials, and suggests that their entrance into the electorate is actually mitigating the overall level of out-party hostility. In 2004, 2008, 2012, and 2016, Republican Millennials showed warmer feelings for the Democratic Party than would be expected based on their age or demographic makeup, by about 6 points on average.[21]

Period Effects

We have seen minimal aging and generation effects in figures 2.3b and 2.3c, and demographic differences in these outcomes are, likewise, small (tables A2.5a and A2.5b).[22] Hence, the unadjusted vs. adjusted trends shown in figure 2.3d come as no surprise. There are virtually no differences wrought by adjusting for over-time differences in the composition of the electorate. In other words, the downward trends in partisans' views of their own party and of their opponents cannot be attributed to generational replacement, the aging of the population, or other shifts in its demographic composition. They are pure period effects.

Discussion

Generational replacement has played a big part in the shifting fortunes of the Democratic and Republican Parties since 1964, but the story plays out differently across regions. In the South, period forces favored the Republicans between 1964 and 1980, but their gains were also

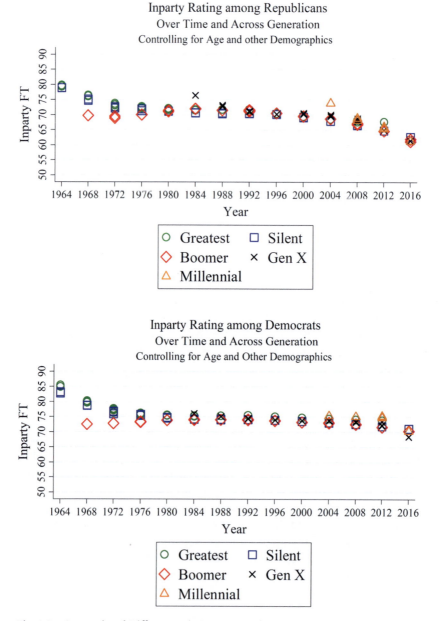

Fig. 2.3c. Generational Differences in In-party and Out-party Ratings, by Party.
(*Note:* Shown in the first and second figures are (smoothed) predicted In-party
Ratings across time and generation among Republicans (*top*) and Democrats
(*bottom*), with age and other demographic variables held constant at their within-
party means. Shown in the third and fourth figures (*opposite page*) are (smoothed)
predicted Out-party Ratings across time and generation among Republicans (*top*)
and Democrats (*bottom*), with age and other demographic variables held constant
at their within-party means.)
Source: Results are derived from the OLS results shown in tables A2.5a and A2.5b.

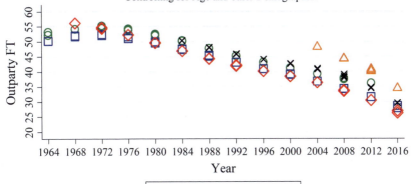

Outparty Rating among Republicans
Over Time and Across Generation
Controlling for Age and other Demographics

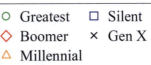

O Greatest	□ Silent
◇ Boomer	× Gen X
△ Millennial	

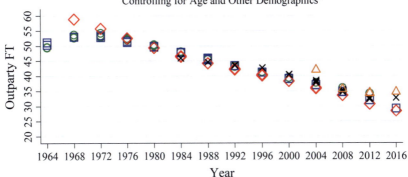

Outparty Rating among Democrats
Over Time and Across Generation
Controlling for Age and Other Demographics

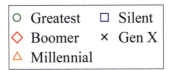

O Greatest	□ Silent
◇ Boomer	× Gen X
△ Millennial	

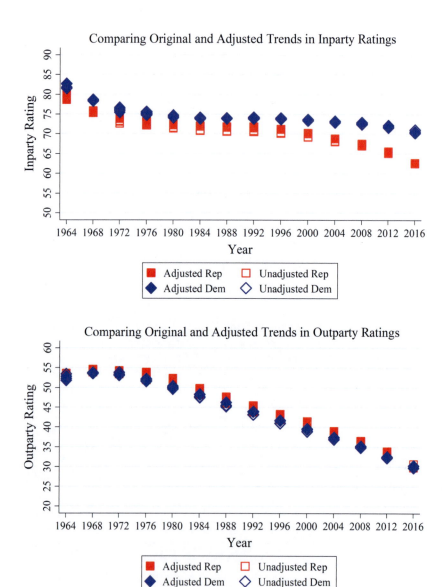

Fig. 2.3d. Trends vs. Period Effects in In-party and Out-party Ratings, by Party

boosted by the dwindling size of the Greatest generation, who in the ANES data went from making up 69 percent of the population in 1964 to 35 percent by 1980. The Republican consolidation after 1980 was powered by a mix of period effects and demographic changes in addition to generational replacement, but the generational dynamic was especially influential. The Millennials, who entered in 2004, look similar to the Gen Xers, who entered in 1984, but both are more Republican than those who came of age earlier, and the younger set grew from making up 0 percent of the Southern population in 1980 to making up 57 percent of the population in 2016. The numbers of those from the older generations dropped accordingly, with the losses largest among the Greatest generation (35% to 0%), followed by the Silent generation (30% to 15%), and then the Baby Boomers (35% to 28%).

Outside of the South, period forces also hurt the Democrats between 1964 and 1980 before they turned around and started working in the Democrats' favor. This reversal is nowhere to be seen in a simple trend chart because it was being countered, not abetted, by ongoing generational replacement and demographic change. The generational differences here are modest compared to those evident in the South, but Gen Xers have been at least slightly more drawn to the Republicans than those from the Greatest, Silent, or Boomer generations and the Millennials have been clearly more so. Their entrance into the electorate and growing size inhibited Democratic gains.

The findings regarding Millennials are particularly important, in that they counter the common journalistic narrative that saw this generation as key to an upswing in the Democratic Party's hold over the electorate. The thought that the Millennials would drive a Democratic resurgence has often been based on simple comparisons of young versus old. But at any one point in time cohort is confounded with age and other demographics. Millennials look more Democratic than their elders because they are younger, more racially diverse, and more likely to be children of immigrants, not because as a generation they are distinctively pro-Democratic.

The question naturally arises as to what these generational dynamics mean for the two political parties going forward. Within the South, the Democrats have faced strong pro-Republican headwinds over the past 50–60 years, which have been weakening. The most Democratic generations have already been greatly diminished in size, and Millennials are no more Republican than their Gen X predecessors. Outside of the South the Democrats' generation problem is both smaller and more recent in origin, since it primarily involves the Millennials. The big question mark, of course, concerns the newcomers, Gen Z, about which the present analysis says nothing at all. One might expect a turn-around in Gen Z based on a favorable Zeitgeist for the Democrats, citing Trump's low approval ratings, Biden's electoral victory, and the prominence of the Black Lives Matter movement, which has over-whelming support among Gen Z (Davis 2020). If they look just like the Millennials, however, the Democrats' headwinds will still be operating, because the newcomers will be replacing the more Democratic members of the Baby Boomer and Silent generations.

The Democrats' edge in partisanship has also been undercut by demographic changes, which on balance have been working in the Republicans' favor, especially outside of the South. America's growing racial and ethnic diversity has been helping the Democrats, but its aging population, weakening labor unions, and rising education levels have been helping the Republicans. How these trends play out in the future will matter to the parties' fortunes. The Census Bureau (Vespa, Armstrong, and Medina 2018) projects that over the next 40 years the population will become older, which should help the Republicans, but also more racially and ethnically diverse and more populated by immigrants, which should help the Democrats. What may be even more important is whether the parties' demographic coalitions are shifting. Results from 2020 suggesting some slippage in Latino support for the Democrats appear overblown (Domínguez-Villegas et al. 2021), but the long-standing pattern of Republican support increasing with education has been reversing in recent years (Pew Research Center 2020).[23] If this trend persists, high and rising educational attainment in the U.S. population will move from a minus to a plus in the Democrats' column.

The APC results regarding Independent identification help make sense of the peculiar fact that across the same time period in which the parties were becoming more clearly differentiated, rates of Independent identification were also growing, if slowly. As we saw, newcomers to the electorate during the era of sharper party differences—the Gen Xers and Millennials—have in fact been more likely to eschew the Independent label and claim a party identification than have those from the generations preceding them. This, however, cannot be seen unless the analyst disentangles the effects of generation and age, since, all else equal, the likelihood of identifying with a party grows with age. Looking ahead, this could mean that the trend toward more Independents will turn around as the proportion of the population coming from the older generations dwindles. Whether this is so will depend on whether the rate of party affiliation in Gen Z matches that of the Millennials, and on whether the period forces enhancing the appeal of the Independent label strengthen, weaken, or stay the course.

These strong period forces can only be seen in an analysis that considers period alongside generation, age, and other demographics. Rates of Independent identification have been kept lower in recent decades by the entrance of Gen X and the Millennials, the aging of the population, and increases in educational attainment. The counterfactual is this: had the composition of the American population not been changing in this fashion, we would have seen the rate of Independent identification grow by 12–13 points instead of just 4–5 points between 1984 and 2016. Yet while the APC analysis has revealed the strength of these period dynamics, it says nothing about what is causing them. This question deserves scholars' attention even if the trend reverses with continued population change, especially since Independent identification is tied up with dissatisfaction with the parties and distrust in government.

The question of what is driving period effects looms even larger regarding affective polarization. Although the APC analysis showed that Millennial Republicans hold slightly less antipathy toward the Democrats than their elders, the changing generational and demographic composition of the population has had no noticeable effect on the substantial trends we have observed—neither the cooling of Democrats' and Republicans' feelings toward their own party, nor the rising hostility they have come to express toward the other.

When an APC model identifies period effects, all we can conclude is that some unspecified variable (or variables)—indexed by and changing over time—is causing similar changes in the outcome across people who differ by generation, age, and demographics. Suspected causes can include macro-level variables and individual-level variables that have been changing among all members of the population.[24] The literature on affective polarization is already burgeoning with ideas and evidence about such suspected causes. These include the proliferation of partisan news outlets, changes in campaigning and advertising, the increased sorting of party with ideology and social group identity, and the greater homogeneity of social networks both online and offline (Iyengar et al. 2019). Despite the limits of observational research for pinning down cause and effect, it would be useful if future work were to use an expanded APC model that included such explanatory variables. Doing so would provide evidence as to whether they are driving the period effects shown here.

Conclusion

The partisan landscape of the United States has transformed over the last half century. In 1964, Democrats outnumbered Republicans 2 to 1, around 20 percent of citizens claimed to be Independents rather than partisans, and both Democrats and Republicans expressed strongly positive feelings toward their own party and at worst neutral feelings toward the other one. By 2016, the percentage of Democrats and Republicans had become evenly matched, the percentage of people calling themselves Independents had doubled, and both groups of partisans had soured toward their own party and—especially—the other party. This chapter has used an APC analysis to gain insight into these developments, parsing how and when they have been influenced by period forces, generational replacement, and the shifting age and demographic composition of the population.

This analysis has provided the clearest evidence to date of the generational dynamics fueling the Southern realignment between 1964 and 2016. Period forces were the prime movers of Republican gains during the 1960s and 1970s, with all segments of the population showing a greater likelihood of affiliating with the party. Over the ensuing decades, however, the realignment gained steam from generational replacement—that is, from the dwindling numbers of the older generations who were still holding to their Democratic identification and the climbing rates of Republican identification among those newly entering the electorate. The realignment slowed down considerably in the mid-2000s as period forces petered out and the Millennials entered, who became the first generation to look no more Republican than their predecessors. On balance, the shifting age and demographic composition of the Southern population favored neither party.

The Democrats' hold on the electorate outside of the South also weakened between 1964 and 2016, though here the losses were on the order of 10 percentage points rather than 30. As in the South, period forces initially drove Republican gains across the 1960s and 1970s, but after the Reagan era they turned around and began working in the Democrats' favor. At the same time, however, generational replacement and shifts in the demographic composition were working in the opposite direction, limiting Democratic gains. Gen Xers and, especially, Millennials have been more likely to identify with the Republican Party than have their age- and demographic-mates from earlier generations, while the net effects of demographic trends favoring the Republicans (the aging of the population, the rise in educational attainment, and the demise of labor unions) have exceeded those favoring the Democrats (the rising racial and ethnic diversity and declining rates of marriage).

Generational replacement has also affected the trend toward Independent identification, which climbed dramatically across the 1960s and 1970s and drifted upward subsequently. The analysis confirmed what earlier research concluded about the initial rise, which is that it was being driven by period forces, leading to increased rates of Independent identification among all segments of the population. What it adds is that, since the 1980s, strong period forces have continued to lead people to eschew an identity as Democrat or Republican and to claim the Independent identity instead. Yet these period effects have been countered by generational replacement, since the most recent entrants into the electorate—Gen Xers and Millennials—have been less likely to identify as an Independent than have those from the generations that preceded them, age and demographics held constant.

If we think of Independent identification as an expression of antiparty sentiment among those who otherwise look like Democrats or Republicans, this pair of findings tells us two things. First, antiparty sentiments are still growing within the electorate, and more so than is indicated by the weak trend toward registration as Independents. Second, it is at the same time lessened among those who entered the electorate during or after the Reagan era. Whether this generational pattern reflects push or pull forces is an open question. Gen Xers and Millennials could be more drawn to a partisan identity because they entered the electorate in an era of clearer party differences, or less drawn to the Independent label because they came of age well after the turmoil of the 1960s and 1970s, which popularized the Independent identity.

Perhaps the most surprising findings regarding generational differences concerns the third development, the rise in affective polarization. One reason is that the slow and steady rise in hostility toward the other party is precisely the trend we would expect to see if generational replacement were a driving force. Moreover, the idea that newer entrants to the electorate would express more out-party hostility than those who entered decades earlier is highly plausible, since they entered in an era notable for the partisan rancor evident in Congress, election campaigns, and mass media communications. Yet the analysis showed that the generational differences are minor and that changes in the composition of the population are irrelevant to understanding the trends. Instead, Americans of all generations, ages, and demographic characteristics have been changing. Whereas in the 1970s the typical partisan held highly positive feelings toward their own party and neutral feelings toward the other, nowadays the pattern is one where in-party feelings are mildly positive and out-party feelings are downright hostile. While surprising, the absence of generational differences may also be comforting. The trend is not doomed to get worse due to the engine of generational replacement; there is more hope that the trend can be stopped or, better, reversed.

The undeniable virtue of an APC analysis is that it links ideas about how individuals develop and change their political orientations to ideas about how the polity writ large changes over time. In so doing it can help us make sense of aggregate trends and, with caution, peek into the future. The individual-level model is skeletal though not atheoretical, positing effects tied to (a) when a person was born and thus came into adulthood, (b) age or life stage, (c) other demographic attributes, and (d) time. As an explanatory model, this leaves much to be desired. It leaves us without an explanation as to why generation, age, or period effects exist, and excludes any number of variables thought to be central to understanding public opinion and political behavior. Even so, the skeletal model is necessary and useful when directed toward understanding macro-political change. It gives us insight into how and when the polity has been changing as time and population replacement marches on.

APPENDIX

(following pages)

TABLE A2.1. Descriptive Statistics on Generation, Age, and Demographic Variables, over Time (%)

	1964	1968	1972	1976	1980	1984	1988	1992	1996	2000	2004	2008	2012	2016
Greatest	65.8	58.8	47.7	44.3	35.4	27.4	22.1	19.1	15.2	9.1	4.1	3.1	0.9	0.0
Silent	34.2	39.1	36.1	31.2	31.4	28.3	27.0	25.7	25.9	24.8	22.5	18.5	11.4	15.0
Boomer	0.0	2.1	16.1	24.5	33.2	38.6	39.4	36.7	35.8	32.6	29.1	28.5	26.7	25.8
Gen X	0.0	0.0	0.0	0.0	0.0	5.8	11.5	18.5	23.2	30.1	32.8	33.5	33.5	31.0
Millennial	0.0	0.0	0.0	0.0	0.0	0.0	0.0	0.0	0.0	3.4	11.5	16.4	27.6	28.2
Average Age	46.0	46.7	44.4	44.8	44.5	44.4	45.0	45.8	44.6	45.5	46.5	46.8	47.2	47.7
Parent(s) not Born US	22.8	21.0	18.4	17.4	16.9	18.0	16.5	17.9	14.8	15.1	17.3	9.9	16.5	18.1
Black	10.2	9.6	9.9	10.3	11.3	11.0	12.8	12.5	11.9	11.8	15.5	11.7	12.0	11.4
Hispanic or Other	0.8	1.3	2.3	2.9	5.1	8.9	11.2	10.9	13.0	14.4	14.0	15.2	17.3	19.6
Female	55.3	56.1	56.8	57.9	56.9	56.2	57.3	53.7	54.4	56.1	51.5	54.9	52.0	52.2
Married	75.9	70.8	66.9	62.5	61.7	58.7	56.5	57.8	59.9	60.4	59.5	51.6	63.4	64.1
Some College	12.7	14.2	16.1	18.4	20.6	24.7	22.5	23.3	26.7	28.1	28.5	28.8	30.1	29.3
College Degree	11.1	13.1	13.1	15.1	16.2	16.7	19.8	23.1	21.7	23.7	25.6	28.0	29.3	32.7
Union Household	24.1	25.1	25.7	23.2	25.7	21.3	19.2	16.3	17.9	15.3	18.9	12.6	16.4	15.0

Note: With the exception of the age variable, entries show the weighted percentage of each group named in the row as of the year named in the column, from the ANES cumulative dataset. The age entry is the weighted average. The generation entries sum to 100% within each year (+/− 1 rounding error).

TABLE A2.2. Descriptive Statistics on Age and Demographics, by Generation

Generation	Average Age	Female	Black	Hispanic or Other	Parents not Born in U.S.	Union HH	Some College	College Degree	Married
Greatest	64.4	58.3	9.6	1.9	27.1	18.7	11.6	10.6	58.5
Silent	47.6	55.1	10.6	4.5	16.1	23.3	19.9	20.6	72.0
Boomer	38.0	54.3	12.0	7.3	10.2	21.9	29.1	25.2	63.8
Gen X	31.5	53.8	13.8	13.3	14.3	14.6	31.0	26.0	53.8
Millennial	23.3	50.3	14.7	16.1	16.5	11.0	35.8	16.8	33.2
Overall	45.6	55.3	11.4	6.5	16.9	19.9	22.8	20.1	61.8

Note: Entries show the age and demographic characteristics overall within the ANES sample I am analyzing (bottom row) and by generation (remaining rows). The age entry is a weighted average. The remaining entries show the weighted percentage of individuals with the characteristic named in the column.

TABLE A2.3. Democrat vs. Republican Party Identification, APC Model Results

Age		Period				Generation		Demographics	
22–25	0.15 (0.101)	1968	-0.16 (0.096)	1968* South	-0.11 (0.196)	Silent	-0.07 (0.074)	Parents not Born in U.S.	0.35*** (0.045)
26–29	0.14 (0.100)	1972	-0.22** (0.089)	1972* South	-0.30 (0.175)	Boomer	-0.14 (0.110)	Black	2.26*** (0.081)
30–33	-0.05 (0.104)	1976	-0.19* (0.095)	1976* South	-0.21 (0.183)	Gen-X	-0.25 (0.153)	Hispanic or Other	0.65*** (0.061)
34–37	-0.02 (0.106)	1980	-0.17 (0.105)	1980* South	-0.30 (0.195)	Millennial	-0.65** (0.232)	Female	0.21*** (0.032)
38–41	-0.07 (0.112)	1984	-0.39*** (0.099)	1984* South	-0.27 (0.184)	Silent* South	-0.35*** (0.093)	Married	-0.34*** (0.035)
42–45	-0.06 (0.119)	1988	-0.47*** (0.107)	1988* South	-0.25 (0.188)	Boomer* South	-0.50*** (0.101)	Some College	-0.35*** (0.040)
46–49	-0.13 (0.127)	1992	-0.12 (0.108)	1992* South	-0.53** (0.182)	Gen-X* South	-0.61*** (1.05)	College Degree	-0.38*** (0.042)
50–53	-0.10 (0.132)	1996	0.00 (0.124)	1996* South	-0.75*** (0.20)	Millennial* South	-0.26 (0.241)	Union HH	0.64*** (0.043)
54–57	-0.17 (0.138)	2000	0.05 (0.130)	2000* South	-0.81*** (0.200)				
54–57	-0.17 (0.138)	2000	0.05 (0.130)	2000* South	-0.81*** (0.200)				
58–61	-0.25 (0.144)	2004	-0.12 (0.143)	2004* South	-0.78*** (0.219)				
62–65	-0.22 (0.150)	2008	0.30* (0.148)	2008* South	-1.03*** (0.202)				

TABLE A2.3—*Continued*

Age			Period			Generation	Demographics
66–69	2012	−0.35* (0.157)	2012	0.05 (0.162)	2012* South	−0.81*** (0.223)	
70–73	2016	−0.34* (0.165)	2016	−0.01 (0.181)	2016* South	−0.87*** (0.238)	
74–77		−0.30 (0.171)					
78–81		−0.53** (0.183)					
82–85		−0.49** (0.203)					
86+		−0.75*** (0.230)					

Note: Entries are coefficients from a logistic regression predicting party identification (Dem = 1, Rep = 0, including leaners; pure Independents excluded), with estimated standard errors in parenthesis below. N = 22,555. The baseline categories are 18–21 for age, 1964 for period, and Greatest for generation. Results for the constant and the South dummy variable, not shown above, are as follows: Constant: b = 0.48, se = 0.14; South dummy: b = .97, se = 0.15. * p < .05, ** p < .01, *** p < .001 two-tailed.

TABLE A2.4. Independent Party Identification, APC Model Results

Age		Period		Generation		Demographics	
22–25	−0.07	1968	0.38***	Silent	0.00	Parents not Born	0.12**
	(0.083)		(0.086)		(0.068)	in U.S.	(0.049)
26–29	−0.18*	1972	0.66***	Boomer	−0.13	Black	−0.63***
	(0.083)		(0.078)		(0.101)		(0.049)
30–33	−0.42***	1976	0.75***	Gen-X	−0.33*	Hispanic or Other	−0.09
	(0.088)		(0.083)		(0.140)		(0.053)
34–37	−0.58***	1980	0.74***	Millennial	−0.60**	Female	−0.28***
	(0.091)		(0.090)		(0.199)		(0.030)
38–41	−0.64***	1984	0.70***			Married	−0.11***
	(0.097)		(0.090)				(0.032)
42–45	−0.72***	1988	0.82***			Some College	−0.10**
	(0.103)		(0.095)				(0.037)
46–49	−0.95***	1992	0.97***			College Degree	−0.32***
	(0.114)		(0.097)				(0.040)
50–53	−0.97***	1996	0.80***			Union HH	0.00
	(0.118)		(0.111)				(0.037)
54–57	−1.14***	2000	1.13***				
	(0.126)		(0.115)				
58–61	−1.21***	2004	1.09***				
	(0.133)		(0.128)				
62–65	−1.19***	2008	1.19***				
	(0.138)		(0.128)				
66–69	−1.24***	2012	1.38***				
	(0.146)		(0.140)				
70–73	−1.37***	2016	1.32***				
	(0.155)		(0.154)				
74–77	−1.55***						
	(0.199)						
78–81	−1.47***						
	(0.175)						
82–85	−1.53***						
	(0.199)						
86+	−1.65***						
	(0.229)						

Note: Entries are coefficients from a logistic regression predicting Independent identification (Independent, pure or leaning, = 1, partisans = 0), with estimated standard errors in parenthesis below. N = 25,629. The baseline categories are 18–21 for age, 1964 for period, and Greatest for generation. Results for the constant, not shown above, are b = −0.17, se = 0.125. Holding all else constant, the probability of identifying as an Independent across the generations is .38 (Greatest), .38 (Silent), .35 (Boomer), .31 (Gen-X) and .25 (Millennial). * $p<.05$, ** $p<.01$, *** $p<.001$ two-tailed.

TABLE A2.5A. In-Party Feeling Thermometer, APC Model Results

Age		Period				Generation		Demographics	
22–25	0.5 (0.82)	1968	−2.1 (1.15)	1968* Democrat	−4.9*** (1.46)	Silent	−1.1 (0.73)	Parents not Born in U.S.	0.1 (0.38)
26–29	0.7 (0.83)	1972	−7.1*** (1.08)	1972* Democrat	−2.4 (1.34)	Boomer	−0.6 (0.99)	Black	8.8*** (0.44)
30–33	0.6 (0.86)	1976	−12.3*** (1.10)	1976* Democrat	−0.6 (1.36)	Gen-X	−0.1 (1.36)	Hispanic or Other	4.0*** (0.54)
34–37	1.4 (0.88)	1980	−8.4*** (1.18)	1980* Democrat	−2.6 (1.45)	Millennial	0.2 (2.10)	Female	2.6*** (0.27)
38–41	3.1*** (0.93)	1984	−4.5*** (1.12)	1984* Democrat	−3.6** (1.37)	Silent* Democrat	−0.2 (0.73)	Married	0.3 (0.29)
42–45	2.7** (0.98)	1988	−3.2** (1.19)	1988* Democrat	−4.5*** (1.43)	Boomer* Democrat	−0.9 (0.79)	Some College	−0.6 (0.33)
46–49	4.4*** (1.07)	1992	−11.4*** (1.20)	1992* Democrat	−0.5 (1.39)	Gen-X* Democrat	−0.9 (1.05)	College Degree	−2.4*** (0.35)
50–53	4.3*** (1.11)	1996	−9.2*** (1.29)	1996* Democrat	−1.1 (1.50)	Millennial* Democrat	0.6 (1.94)	Union HH	0.4 (0.34)
54–57	4.2*** (1.17)	2000	−8.8*** (1.34)	2000* Democrat	−1.1 (1.56)				
58–61	6.4*** (1.20)	2004	−5.6*** (1.48)	2004* Democrat	−5.3** (1.69)				
62–65	6.0*** (1.27)	2008	−11.3*** (1.45)	2008* Democrat	0.2 (1.60)				
66–69	7.4*** (1.32)	2012	−13.4*** (1.59)	2012* Democrat	2.4 (1.73)				

	2016		2016 × Democrat	
70–73	8.6***		−18.2***	2.3
	(1.38)		(1.83)	(2.11)
74–77	7.2***			
	(1.47)			
78–81	8.8***			
	(1.58)			
82–85	7.3***			
	(1.86)			
86+	10.6***			
	(2.03)			

Note: Entries are OLS regression coefficients predicting In-party Ratings (0 = most negative to 100 most positive) among Democratic and Republican identifiers (including leaners), with estimated standard errors in parenthesis below. N = 21,247. The baseline categories are 18–21 for age, 1964 for period, and Greatest for generation. Results for the constant and the Democrat dummy variable, not shown above, are as follows: Constant: b = 74.4, s e= 1.35; Democrat dummy: b = 3.9, se = 1.07. * $p<.05$, ** $p<.01$, *** $p<.001$ two-tailed.

TABLE A2.5B. Out-Party Feeling Thermometer, APC Model Results

Age		Period			Generation		Demographics	
22–25	−0.3 (0.91)	1968	−1.3 (1.42)	1968* Democrat 5.8*** (1.79)	Silent	−2.6** (0.87)	Parents not Born in U.S.	1.0* (0.44)
26–29	0.4 (0.89)	1972	5.2*** (1.31)	1972* Democrat 2.8 (1.65)	Boomer	−3.3** (1.20)	Black	−2.9*** (0.59)
30–33	0.5 (0.96)	1976	1.9 (1.30)	1976* Democrat 1.0 (1.63)	Gen-X	0.8 (1.64)	Hispanic or Other	3.3*** (0.62)
34–37	0.8 (0.98)	1980	1.8 (1.42)	1980* Democrat 1.9 (1.74)	Millennial	6.1** (2.41)	Female	1.4*** (0.32)
38–41	−.1 (1.05)	1984	−3.9** (1.37)	1984* Democrat −0.7 (1.71)	Silent* Democrat	2.6** (0.87)	Married	0.2 (0.35)
42–45	1.6 (1.11)	1988	−5.9*** (1.46)	1988* Democrat 2.1 (1.78)	Boomer* Democrat	2.2** (0.94)	Some College	−1.6*** (0.33)
46–49	0.6 (1.24)	1992	−8.1*** (1.44)	1992* Democrat −0.5 (1.69)	Gen-X* Democrat	0.0 (1.23)	College Degree	−4.8*** (0.40)
50–53	2.1 (1.28)	1996	−11.3*** (1.63)	1996* Democrat 3.6 (1.89)	Millennial* Democrat	−3.3 (2.19)	Union HH	−1.2** (0.40)
54–57	1.5 (1.36)	2000	−11.3*** (1.65)	2000* Democrat 4.3* (1.89)				
58–61	0.3 (1.43)	2004	−11.1*** (1.79)	2004* Democrat 0.7 (2.14)				
62–65	0.8 (1.47)	2008	−15.0*** (1.78)	2008* Democrat −1.8 (1.93)				
66–69	−0.2 (1.57)	2012	−18.5*** (1.95)	2012* Democrat 0.3 (2.08)				

	2016	2016*	
	-24.9***	Democrat	7.2**
	(2.06)		(2.27)
70–73	-1.2		
	(1.68)		
74–77	-0.9		
	(1.77)		
78–81	1.2		
	(1.85)		
82–85	-0.4		
	(2.06)		
86+	-2.1		
	(2.46)		

Note: Entries are OLS regression coefficients predicting Out-party Ratings (0 = most negative to 100 = most positive) among Democratic and Republican identifiers (including leaners), with estimated standard errors in parenthesis below. $N = 21,140$. The baseline categories are 18–21 for age, 1964 for period, and Greatest for generation. Results for the constant and the Democrat dummy variable, not shown above, are as follows: Constant: b = 53.4, se = 1.59; Democrat dummy: b = -3.7, se = 1.36. * $p < .05$, ** $p < .01$, *** $p < .001$ two-tailed.

NOTES

1. Between 1932 and 1964, Democrats took the presidency 7 out of 9 times (the exceptions being Eisenhower's presidencies) and held both the House and the Senate for 15 of the 17 sessions (the exceptions being the 80th in 1947–49 and the 83rd in 1953–55).

2. Exceptions include Osborne, Sears, and Valentino (2011) on the Southern realignment, Ghitza and Gelman (2022) on presidential voting, Twenge et al. (2016) on trends in party identification and ideology, and Erikson, MacKuen, and Stimson (2002) on macropartisanship.

3. See Stoker (2014) on why some distinguish "cohort" from "generation" and on different meanings of "generation."

4. Moreover, the demographic correlates of age have been changing. For example, in the 1980s, older Americans were more likely than younger ones to come from a family of immigrants, whereas today that is true of younger Americans. And while there used to be little to no association between age and race/ethnicity, nowadays the young are much more racially and ethnically diverse than their elders.

5. I start in 1964 to keep the time frame across the analyses constant, since the feeling thermometers used to study affective polarization first become available in 1964. To maintain over-time comparability, I only analyze data from the ANES presidential year studies, since the midterm studies were discontinued after 2002, and use only the face-to-face data even though some of the later studies added internet surveys.

6. Before 1972, when the legal voting age was lowered to 18, the 18–21 group included only 21 year olds. This explains the large jump in the number of new entrants between 1968 ($n = 34$) and 1972 ($n = 204$).

7. Other solutions to the identification problem involve substituting an interval-level period or age variable, or both, for the set of period or age dummies, or both. The APC analysis of immigration attitudes (Dixon, Fullerton, and Nash, chapter 5, this vol.) takes this approach, using a linear time variable and both age and age-squared.

8. Working with multiples of four when defining cohorts leads to generation cutoff points that differ slightly from those employed by Pew. In addition, Pew would call those born in 1997 or 1998 Gen Z, but this group is too small to be distinguished in the ANES data ($n = 18$ in 2016). The age variables collect people into four-year groupings (18–21 and so on) as well, but because of small Ns among the very old, the oldest group included everyone 86 or older.

9. Theoretically, there is no reason to expect the effects of age to vary across the subgroups. Nevertheless, I tested alternative specifications, holding period, generation, and age effects constant across the groups in turn. The results when holding age constant yielded the best fit, though the differences across specifications were small.

10. The principles in selecting demographic variables were that information be available across the entire time frame, that missing data be minimal, and that the variable could not plausibly be viewed as endogenous to whatever is producing generational differences or period effects. Thus, for example, I excluded income

because of missing data limitations and religiosity because of the endogeneity issue.

11. South: AL, AR, DE, DC, FL, GA, KY, LA, MD, MS, NC, OK, SC, TN, TX, VA, and WV.

12. The year 2008 was also something of an outlier in terms of the composition of the weighted ANES sample; see table 2.A1.

13. For each cohort within each generation and region, I first calculated the predicted probability of identifying as a Democrat, holding age and other demographics constant at their within-region means. I then generated smoothed representations of each generation's trend, within regions, using Lowess (with a bandwidth of .8; shorter bandwidth choices made little difference). Multiple instances of the same symbol represent variation in the estimates for a given time point.

14. Green, Palmquist, and Schickler (2004) also report evidence of unusually high rates of affiliation with the Republican Party among Gen Xers entering the electorate during the Reagan years.

15. As I address in the discussion section, a reversal in the association between education and party identification is underway, which has implications for the parties' fortunes going forward.

16. For this analysis and the comparable one for Independent identification (fig. 2.2d), I reestimated the APC model using OLS and used those results to generate the predicted values under the 1964 counterfactual, which were then smoothed and shown in figure 2.1d. The OLS results (shown in Stoker 2020) are substantively very similar to those obtained using Logit. OLS is needed for this counterfactual exercise since its predicted probabilities are additive while those from a Logit analysis are not.

17. This tool relies on the fact that in an OLS regression, the product of each X times its coefficient, summed, yields the overall mean of Y. This analysis, thus, uses OLS coefficients rather than Logit coefficients; see also the next note.

18. Across the two pairs of elections, the percentage of Democrats declined by 24 points in the South and by 6 points outside of the South. Thus, this analysis again has generational replacement accounting for 50% of the over-time decline in support for the Democrats within the South. Outside of the South, it again shows that, had compositional changes not been working against them, the Democrats would have ended up better off by 2016 (+2) rather than worse off (−6) due to the period forces working in their favor since the 1980s.

19. Scores 97 and above, coded "97" in the original data file, were recoded to 100. Between 1964 and 1980 respondents were asked to rate "Democrats" and "Republicans" but afterward they were asked to rate "the Democratic party" and "the Republican party." Iyengar, Sood, and Lelkes (2012) find that this change did not affect in-party ratings but lowered out-party ratings by about 6 points.

20. The difference between in-party and out-party ratings shows a marked curvilinear trend, with in-group favoritism high in 1964, reaching a low in 1972 or 1976, and then climbing again. By the end of the series, Democrats had regained the difference of 35 points evident in 1964, and Republicans had nearly matched that, exceeding their 1964 gap of 25 points. However, these new gaps now combine less positive in-party attitudes (around 65 rather than 85) and more negative out-party attitudes (around 30 rather than 50).

21. This 6-point difference is statistically significant at p = .012 (see table 2.A5b). Republicans from the Silent and Boomer generations expressed slightly more negative feelings toward the Democrats than did those from the Greatest generation, by 3 points in each case. Although small, each difference is statistically significant at p < .01.

22. Holding all else constant, Blacks tend to rate their party more favorably (by about 9 points) and the other party more negatively (by about 3 points), but this does not bear on the trends in affective polarization since the percentage of Black Americans has held steady over time. Race/ethnicity and education also influence party ratings but offset each other, with those of "Hispanic or Other" ethnicity evaluating both parties more favorably and the highly educated rating both more negatively.

23. If I rerun the APC analysis, allowing the effects of the some-college and college degree variables to interact with period in 2012 and 2016, neither of the 2012 interactions are significant but both are in the positive direction, and both of the 2016 interactions are positive, significant and larger than the main effect coefficients. Thus, the tendency for the more educated to be more Republican diminished in 2012 and had reversed by 2016. None of the substantive findings were otherwise changed; the generational results even grew slightly in statistical significance.

24. To explain generational differences, causes of the first type have to have larger effects on younger people (see, e.g., Dinas 2013), while causes of the second type either have to have larger effects on the young or be more prevalent among the young. Of course, causes of the first type are presumably lurking behind causes of the second type.

REFERENCES

Abramowitz, A. I. 2013. "From Strom to Barack: Race, Ideology, and the Transformation of the Southern Party System." *American Review of Politics* 34: 207–26.

Abramowitz, A. I., and K. L. Saunders. 1998. "Ideological Realignment in the US Electorate." *Journal of Politics* 60: 634–52.

Abramowitz, A. I., and S. Webster. 2016. "The Rise of Negative Partisanship and the Nationalization of US Elections in the 21st Century." *Electoral Studies* 41: 12–22.

Abramowitz, A. I., and S. Webster. 2018. "Negative Partisanship: Why Americans Dislike Parties but Behave Like Rabid Partisans." *Political Psychology* 39: 119–35.

Abramson, P. R. 1976. "Generational Change and the Decline of Party Identification in America: 1952–1974." *American Political Science Review* 70: 469–78.

Abramson, P. R. 1979. "Developing Party Identification: A Further Examination of Life-Cycle, Generational, and Period Effects." *American Journal of Political Science* 23: 78–96.

Achen, C. H. 1982. *Interpreting and Using Regression.* Beverly Hills, CA: Sage.

Alwin, D. F. 1998. "The Political Impact of the Baby Boom: Are There Persistent Generational Differences in Political Beliefs and Behavior?" *Generations: Journal of the American Society on Aging* 22: 46–54.

Bafumi, J., and R. Y. Shapiro. 2009. "A New Partisan Voter." *Journal of Politics* 71: 1–24.

Bartels, L. M. 2000. "Partisanship and Voting Behavior, 1952–1996." *American Journal of Political Science* 44: 35–50.

Carmines, E. G., and J. A. Stimson. 1989. *Issue Evolution.* Princeton: Princeton University Press.

Converse, P. E. 1976. *Dynamics of Party Support: Cohort-Analyzing Party Identification.* Beverly Hills, CA: Sage.

Craig, S. C. 1985. "Partisanship, Independence, and No Preference: Another Look at the Measurement of Party Identification." *American Journal of Political Science* 29: 274–90.

Dalton, R. J. 2008. *The Good Citizen: How a Younger Generation Is Reshaping American Politics.* Rev. ed. Washington, DC: CQ Press.

Davis, D. 2020. "The Action Generation: How Gen Z Really Feels about Race, Equality, and Its Role in the Historic George Floyd Protests, Based on a Survey of 39,000 Young Americans." *Business Insider,* June 10. https://www.businessinsider.com/how-gen-z-feels-about-george-floyd-protests-2020-6

Dimock, M. 2019. "Defining Generations: Where Millennials End and Generation Z Begins." Pew Research Center. https://www.pewresearch.org/fact-tank/2019/01/17/where-millennials-end-and-generation-z-begins/

Dinas, E. 2013. "Opening 'Openness to Change' Political Events and the Increased Sensitivity of Young Adults." *Political Research Quarterly* 66: 868–82.

Dinas, E., and L. Stoker. 2014. "Age-Period-Cohort Analysis: A Design Based Approach." *Electoral Studies* 33: 28–40.

Domínguez-Villegas, R., N. Gonzalez, A. Gutierrez, K. Hernández, M. Herndon, A. Oaxaca, M. Rios, M. Roman, T. Rush, and D. Vera. 2021 "Vote Choice of Latino Voters in the 2020 Presidential Election." https://latino.ucla.edu/research/latino-voters-in-2020-election/

Erikson, R. S., M. B. MacKuen, and J. A. Stimson. 2002. *The Macro Polity.* New York: Cambridge University Press.

Fiorina, M. 2017. *Unstable Majorities: Polarization, Party Sorting, and Political Stalemate.* Stanford: Hoover Institution Press.

Firebaugh, G., and K. Chen. 1995. "Vote Turnout of Nineteenth Amendment Women: The Enduring Effect of Disenfranchisement." *American Journal of Sociology* 100: 972–96.

Fosse, E., and C. Winship. 2019. "Analyzing Age-Period-Cohort Data: A Review and Critique." *Annual Review of Sociology* 45: 467–92.

Galston, W. 2013. "The New Politics of Evasion." *Democracy,* no. 30 (Fall).

Ghitza, Y., and A. Gelman. 2022. "The Great Society, Reagan's Revolution, and Generations of Presidential Voting." *American Journal of Political Science* 68: 520–37.

Gibson, J. L., and G. A. Caldeira. 1992. "Blacks and the United States Supreme Court: Models of Diffuse Support." *Journal of Politics* 54: 1120–45.

Glenn, N. D. 1976. "Cohort Analysts' Futile Quest: Statistical Attempts to Separate Age, Period, and Cohort Effects." *American Sociological Review* 41: 900–04.

Green, D. P., B. Palmquist, and E. Schickler. 2004. *Partisan Hearts and Minds.* New Haven: Yale University Press.

Hetherington, M. J. 2001. "Resurgent Mass Partisanship: The Role of Elite Polarization." *American Political Science Review* 95: 619–31.

Judis, J. B., and R. Teixeira. 2004. *The Emerging Democratic Majority.* New York: Simon and Schuster.

Iyengar, S., G. Sood, and Y. Lelkes. 2012. "Affect, Not Ideology: A Social Identity Perspective on Polarization." *Public Opinion Quarterly* 76: 405–31.

Iyengar, S., Y. Lelkes, M. Levendusky, N. Malhotra, and S. J. Westwood. 2019. "The Origins and Consequences of Affective Polarization in the United States." *Annual Review of Political Science* 22: 129–46.

Iyengar, S., and S. J. Westwood. 2015. "Fear and Loathing across Party Lines: New Evidence on Group Polarization." *American Journal of Political Science* 59: 690–707.

Keith, B. E., D. B. Magleby, C. J. Nelson, E. Orr, M. C. Westlye, and R. E. Wolfinger. 1992. *The Myth of the Independent Voter.* Berkeley: University of California Press.

Klar, S., and Y. Krupnikov. 2016. *Independent Politics.* New York: Cambridge University Press.

Knoke, D., and M. Hout. 1974. "Social and Demographic Factors in American Political Party Affiliations, 1952–72." *American Sociological Review* 39: 700–713.

Levendusky, M. 2009. *The Partisan Sort: How Liberals Became Democrats and Conservatives Became Republicans.* Chicago: University of Chicago Press.

Levine, P. 2007. *The Future of Democracy: Developing the Next Generation of American Citizens.* Medford, MA: Tufts University Press.

Mannheim, K. (1928) 1952. "The Sociological Problem of Generations." In *Essays on the Sociology of Knowledge.* London: Routledge and Kegan Paul.

Markus, G. B. 1985. "Dynamic Modeling of Cohort Change: The Case of Political Partisanship." In *Cohort Analysis in Social Research: Beyond the Identification Problem,* edited by William M. Mason and Stephen E. Fienberg, 259–87. New York: Springer.

Mason, L. 2015. "'I Disrespectfully Agree': The Differential Effects of Partisan Sorting on Social and Issue Polarization." *American Journal of Political Science* 59: 128–45.

Mason, L. 2016. "A Cross-Cutting Calm: How Social Sorting Drives Affective Polarization." *Public Opinion Quarterly* 80: 351–77.

Miller, W. E. 1992. "Generational Changes and Party Identification." *Political Behavior* 14: 333–52.

Neundorf, A., and R. G. Niemi. 2014. "Beyond Political Socialization: New Approaches in Age, Period, Cohort Analysis." *Electoral Studies* 33: 1–6.

Norpoth, H. 1987. "Under Way and Here to Stay: Party Realignment in the 1980s?" *Public Opinion Quarterly* 51: 376–91.

Norpoth, H., and J. G. Rusk. 1982. "Partisan Dealignment in the American Electorate: Itemizing the Deductions since 1964." *American Political Science Review* 76: 522–37.

Osborne, D., D. O. Sears, and N. A. Valentino. 2011. "The End of the Solidly Democratic South: The Impressionable-Years Hypothesis." *Political Psychology* 32: 81–108.

Peterson, J. C., K. B. Smith, and J. R. Hibbing. 2020. "Do People Really Become More Conservative as They Age?" *Journal of Politics* 82: 600–611.

Petrocik, J. R. 2009. "Measuring Party Support: Leaners Are Not Independents." *Electoral Studies* 28: 562–72.

Pew Research Center. 2010. "Distrust, Discontent, Anger and Partisan Rancor." April 18. https://www.pewresearch.org/politics/2010/04/18/distrust-discontent -anger-and-partisan-rancor/

Pew Research Center. 2015. "The Whys and Hows of Generations Research." September 3. https://www.pewresearch.org/politics/2015/09/03/the-whys-and-hows -of-generations-research/

Pew Research Center. 2019. "Political Independents: Who They Are, What They Think." March 14. https://www.pewresearch.org/politics/2019/03/14/political-in dependents-who-they-are-what-they-think/

Pew Research Center. 2020. "In Changing U.S. Electorate, Race and Education Remain Stark Dividing Lines." June 2. https://www.pewresearch.org/politics/20 20/06/02/in-changing-u-s-electorate-race-and-education-remain-stark-dividing -lines/

Sapiro V. 1994. "Political Socialization during Adulthood: Clarifying the Political Time of Our Lives." *Research in Micropolitics* 4: 197–223.

Schuman, H., and J. Scott. 1989. "Generations and Collective Memories." *American Sociological Review* 54: 359–81.

Sears, D. O., and C. Brown. 2013. "Childhood and Adult Political Development." In *The Oxford Handbook of Political Psychology*, edited by Leonie Huddy, David O. Sears, and Jack S. Levy. Oxford: Oxford University Press.

Sigel, R. S., ed. 1989. *Political Learning in Adulthood: A Sourcebook of Theory and Research*. Chicago: University of Chicago Press.

Stanga, J. E., and J. F. Sheffield. 1987. "The Myth of Zero Partisanship: Attitudes toward American Political Parties, 1964–84." *American Journal of Political Science* 31: 829–55.

Stoker, L. 2014. "Reflections on the Study of Generations in Politics." *The Forum* 12: 377–96. Berlin: De Gruyter.

Stoker, L. 2020. "Generational Change in Affective Polarization and Partisanship: An Age-Period-Cohort Accounting." Paper presented at the 2020 Annual Conference of the American Political Science Association, San Francisco.

Stoker, L., and J. Bass. 2011. "Political Socialization: Ongoing Questions and New Directions." In *The Oxford Handbook of American Public Opinion and the Media*, edited by Robert Y. Shapiro, Lawrence R. Jacobs, and George C. Edwards III. Oxford: Oxford University Press.

Stoker, L., and M. K. Jennings. 2008. "Of Time and the Development of Partisan Polarization." *American Journal of Political Science* 52: 619–35.

Tajfel, H., and C. J. Turner. 2004. "The Social Identity Theory of Intergroup Behavior." In *Political Psychology*, edited by John T. Jost and Jim Sidanius, 39–68. New York: Psychology Press.

Teixeira, R. 2020. "Demography Is Not Destiny." *Persuasion*, July 16. https://www.per suasion.community/p/demography-is-not-destiny

Twenge, J. M., N. Honeycutt, R. Prislin, and R. A. Sherman. 2016. "More Polarized but More Independent: Political Party Identification and Ideological Self-Categorization among US Adults, College Students, and Late Adolescents, 1970–2015." *Personality and Social Psychology Bulletin* 42: 1364–83.

Vespa, J., D. M. Armstrong, and L. Medina. 2018. *Demographic Turning Points for the United States: Population Projections for 2020 to 2060.* (Updated February 2020). Washington, DC: U.S. Department of Commerce, Economics and Statistics Administration, U.S. Census Bureau.

Wattenberg, M. P. 1981. "The Decline of Political Partisanship in the United States: Negativity or Neutrality?" *American Political Science Review* 75: 941–50.

Watts, M. W. 1999. "Are There Typical Age Curves in Political Behavior? The 'Age Invariance' Hypothesis and Political Socialization." *Political Psychology* 20: 477–500.

Zukin, C., S. Keeter, M. Andolina, K. Jenkins, and M. X. Delli Carpini. 2006. *A New Engagement? Political Participation, Civic Life, and the Changing American Citizen.* New York: Oxford University Press.

3 | Collective Memory and the Pandemic Emergence of Generation Z

Scott L. McLean

In chapter 2 of this volume, Laura Stoker finds that, at least since the 1980s, the process of younger generations replacing older generations has been a prime cause of U.S. party alignment. Generational change, she finds, also accounts for increased levels of "affective polarization," that is, the hostility and fear that supporters of both major political parties feel against the other party. Stoker describes how since the 1970s, each new cohort entering the electorate express slightly more "out-party hostility" than the previous cohort of newcomers decades earlier. Important as these findings are, Stoker also believes that out-party hostility need not get worse with each fresh influx of new young voters. She imagines the possibility of a future class of young voters who may enter young adulthood in a less hotly partisan era. Nevertheless, the question arises: What are the factors that drive partisanship (or independence) of newly maturing young Americans in the first place? To put it slightly differently: Why do the most recent generational cohorts entering the electorate today—Generation Z—appear to have have a higher propensity to vote and identify with a political party than their elders did when they were young? To begin to answer these questions, we need to think in more theoretical terms about the meaning of demographic statistics and public opinion research.

In this chapter I aim to go beyond Stoker's analysis, by using the case of Generation Z to re-think Karl Mannheim's (1928) theory of "political generations." Generation Z (or Gen Z) is the most currently popular term to describe the age cohort born after 1997 and which is now beginning to make up a larger and more politically significant proportion of the U.S. electorate. Generation Z had a record-high voter turnout percentage in 2018 and 2020 national elections (Frey 2021). No previous age cohort has ever voted in higher percentages than Gen Z did in 2020 (CIRCLE 2021). While all age groups had higher turnout in 2020, 18- to 24-year-olds in 2020 reached over 50 percent turnout, the highest youth turnout for that age bracket recorded so far in the 21st century and leaned heavily Democratic (Frey 2021). We can speculate that if not for the extra youth vote in closely fought swing states like Arizona and Georgia, Joe Biden might not have won the election.

How might we explain such a high level of youth voter turnout? Every new age cohort enters young maturity experiencing certain dramatic historical events and even large-scale psychological trauma during their "impressionable years," between late adolescence to early adulthood. These shared experiences leave an imprint that distinguishes each generations outlook and general orientation toward politics. But not every age cohort is a "political generation" having predominant and distinct political orientations and allegiances. There can be little doubt that the norm-shattering presidency of Donald Trump, COVID-19, and the partisan hostilities of the period between 2012 and 2019 were driving forces in Gen Z's high level of engagement in 2020. But did these events leave a "lasting impression" that will drive them to long-term political awareness and engagement? I will present some preliminary evidence from 2016 to 2020 that support the theory that recent world and U.S. political events were experienced as a kind of "collective trauma" by Generation Z. Americans who were in their late teens and early twenties between 2016 and 2020 have experienced dramatic disruptions in culture and politics: accelerating penetration of social media into every facet of work and relationships; the COVID-19 pandemic; the rise of the Black Lives Matter movement; significant percentages of youth involvement in 2020 social and racial protests (Frey 2021); the growing frequency of school shootings and active shooter drills; the overturning of *Roe v. Wade*; the presidency of Donald Trump and its culmination with a violent riot inside the U.S. Capitol. At the same time, youth since 2019 have expressed significant increases in the percentages experiencing anxiety, depression, drug use, and suicide. These are all signs that may contribute to the future development of distinct and even oppositional "generational" consciousness in the post-1997 age cohort of adults who will be engaging in the 2024 and 2026 elections.

Other chapters in this volume have mentioned the work of Karl

Mannheim (1928) and his theory of how rapid disruption in politics and society experienced by an age cohort in the "impressionable years" of late adolescence can imprint the age cohort when they make "fresh contact" with older generations with different outlooks. Sometimes the result is the emergence of a "political generation" (Mannheim 1928; Braungart and Braungart 1986; Braungart 2013). Just as personal trauma can have enduring effects on an individual's memories, national trauma can leave enduring effects on collective memories (Neal 2005). As Laura Stoker in chapter 2 pointed out, events can can also affect age cohorts unevenly, with differing effects over time. Conditions of trauma can grow out of an injury or wound on social life as it was previously known. Something terrible or abnormal has disrupted society and politics, leaving people angry or anxious at the unpredictability of life. For instance, the Great Depression and the 1941 attack on Pearl Harbor played a role in forging the Greatest generation and perhaps accounts for their higher rates of community trust and civic engagement (Putnam 2000). Historical events do not necessarily affect all age groups in exactly the same way. The Kennedy assassination, the Vietnam War, and the 9/11 attacks were shocking to all Americans, but younger generations at those times, lacking few prior experiences for context, probably felt these events more acutely, and they resulted in different patterns of political behavior going forward. Where the World War II generation on the whole showed more trust in political institutions and were avid "joiners," the generations coming of age in the late 1960s exhibited a more cynical and untrusting orientation to institutions and devoted less time to civic pursuits (Putnam 2000). So it goes with Gen Z. The role of Gen Z in the 2020 election, and the particular experiences of high school and college students since the election of Donald Trump and since the pandemic, are signs of a potentially different political orientation and view of politics from their elders, the Millennials.

Gen Z is interesting because it has already demonstrated how it is likely to change the structure of the electorate and the major political parties. In the 2020 election, Gen Z composed about 10 percent of the electorate with 51 percent turnout (U.S. Census 2021). This is the highest voter turnout for youth ages 18 to 24 ever recorded. Even though the turnout rate among 18–24 year olds in 2020 was lower than older age cohorts, youth turnout increased 8 percent over 2016. No other age cohort matched this spike in turnout (Frey 2021). The NBC 2020 election exit poll found that while white voters between ages 18 to 24 favored Trump (53%), minority youth favored Biden by huge margins, resulting in 65 percent of young voters supporting Biden overall—a greater margin than any other age cohort. Even though exit polls have limited accuracy, they do include early voters, and the data supports the claim that Gen Z had record-setting turnout and wide margin of support for Biden and other Democrats in swing states such as Georgia, Arizona, and Pennsylvania. These margins were critical in helping Biden secure an electoral college victory (Hess 2020).

Although it is tempting to attribute high voter turnout among Gen Z to increased opportunities for early voting and mail-in balloting in 2020, the level of youth voter motivation to cast votes against Donald Trump was extraordinarily high in the 2016 and 2018 elections, where youth turnout was also very high. The strategic importance of Gen Z in turning the tide in the next couple of election cycles is clear. Will the 2020 pattern become a trend in future elections, especially if Trump is not on the ballot?

What Is a Generation? And, Is Gen Z Really a Generation?

In this section, I develop a definition of "generation" that goes beyond marking off age cohorts in the population. We can identify, however imperfectly, some key factors that may be pulling Gen Z toward a more consciously politicized view of itself. My argument is that political scientists should build beyond their analyses of age cohorts and focus on ways to account for the role of nationally traumatic and triumphal events in shaping the political concerns and collective memories of emerging generations.

When comparing age cohorts, it is one thing to describe similarities of general outlook, or dominant patterns of political behavior such as protest activity or voting. But it is another thing to marshal evidence that an age cohort is conscious of itself as a distinct political generation, possessing a distinct mindset and distinct political interests opposed to those other generations. This is not as simple as marking off broad age cohorts and declaring that the cohorts think like a "generation." As Mannheim explained, every generation has contending "segments" that pull generations in opposing directions. For example, in the 1960s some young people loudly protested the war in Vietnam, while other youth supported the war, and still others opposed the war but served in the military when drafted, and so on. The meaning, or the "lessons" of the Vietnam conflict, is contestable even among people who came of age during that time. The meaning can be affected by partisan identity, ideology, and subsequent major events. Consider leaders such as Bill Clinton, Al Gore, George W. Bush, Donald Trump, and Joe Biden (though Biden was born in 1942, just before the first wave of the Baby Boom generation). Each of the segments are in a kind of cultural struggle to define whose version of politics and collective memory will stand as definitive.

Not every age cohort is automatically a generation, and generational orientations emerge from politics, which is partly why Mannheim was careful to use the term "political generations" (Mannheim 1928). Individual memories of life during these eventful periods ripple outward with the potential to become collective generational memories. Collective memory of emotional moments is largely subjective and contingent on the generation that experienced them. Political scientists should not treat these generational launching events as a black box; World War II, the Vietnam War, 9/11, and the COVID-19 pandemic do not all have exactly the same political ripple effect on young adults. Moreover, age cohorts can have different ways of incorporating generational memories with their identities such as gender, race, class, and party identification. Comparison of age cohorts is necessary in any study of generational politics. Nonetheless, rather than reflexively presuming that age cohorts are identical to generations, or that whatever events occur in a cohort's political "coming of age" are always generation-defining, political scientists should delve deeper into the events themselves, and attempt to trace how the experiences translate into political behavior across time. Though the focus here is conceptual and theoretical, I will ornament the argument with some early evidence about Gen Z's transition from age cohort to emerging political generation.

Having an interesting label like "Gen Z" or "Millennial" does not by itself make an age cohort into a generation. Nevertheless, we have not seen a period of history where the political responses of young adults have been so distinct from their elders since the 1960s. Does that mean Gen Z is on its way to being a politically distinct generation? Perhaps the tumultuous events surrounding 2020 will shape today's young adults into a generation, but it is not assured that they will remain politically distinct and active in 10 or 20 years when COVID-19, Donald Trump, and Joe Biden have faded into collective memory and mythology.

The early signs of a distinct "Generation Z" consciousness and political orientation became apparent at the end of the Obama administration when scholars wondered if the Millennial generation would retain their enthusiasm for Obama's initial run for president in 2008. Around 2012, popular writers were noticing how this post-1997 age cohort differed from most Millennials. These "Post-Millennials," as they were called at the time, were majority nonwhite and were more glued to smartphones and social media (Horowitz 2012; Dimock 2019). It seems their subculture changes at lightspeed, as if every three weeks when the coolest Millennials decipher a baffling Gen Z meme, this "old meme" is replaced with even more strangely juxtaposed symbols. A major research effort by the Pew Research Center (Parker and Igielnik 2020) profiled these "Post-Millennials." They showed more support than older Millennials for government action to respond to social problems like climate change and gun violence. They are on track to be the most-educated age cohort. They are more accustomed to alternative and neutral gender pronouns (Dimock 2019; Parker and Igielnik 2020). Writers trying to tap into youth culture proposed many names for this group: iGeneration, Generation Snowflake, Boomerangs, the Caring Generation, Digital Natives, Mosaic Generation, Homelanders, and the Zoomers. Eventually, the name "Generation Z" became the most widely used term (Dimock 2019).

The Pew Research Center found significant differences between Gen Z (then called "post-millennials") and the slightly older Millennial generation (defined as those born between 1981 and 1996). Demographically, Gen Z has a higher percentage of nonwhite people (48%) than the Millennials (39%) (Parker and Igielnik 2020). They were more likely to have lived with a college-educated parent; more likely to be enrolled in college than their predecessors at the same age; relatedly more likely to delay their entry into the workforce than their predecessors at the same age; and more likely to be born of immigrant parents and less likely to be foreign-born than their predecessors (Parker and Igielnik 2020).

No generation can extend forever, and an age cohort needs to cut off at some point—scholars may decide the Generation Z cohort should cut off around 2010 or 2012—but there is no obvious point at which one cohort (or generation) should begin or end, and there is no reason a generation should be based on a cohort of 10, 15, or 20 years. There can be demarcations based simply on analytical necessity, and this is the case with the "Millennial generation," defined by the Pew Research Center as those born approximately between 1981 and 1996 (Dimock 2019). In 2017, Pew reported that "trailing Millennials" (as they were called then) born after 1996 "have begun to exhibit notably different characteristics, values, and attitudes, although they are not yet necessarily the norm" (Dimock 2019). The oldest Millennials were pushing 40 for the 2020 presidential election and it was difficult to think of Millennials as "young voters" by the time the 2022 congressional elections arrived.

What are the key differences in perspectives between the Millennials and the Gen Z "Post-Millennials?" Part of the difference has to do with collective memories. Young adults born after 1996 are the first age cohort to lack a direct memory of the 9/11 attacks. They can only view old videos and read about that horrific event in their history books or in "old" movies. Their impressionable childhood years fall outside of the unifying crisis period immediately after 9/11, during the unpopular phase of the Iraq War, and the memorable election of Barack Obama, America's first African American president. According to the Pew Study, 64 percent of Millennials favor government doing more to solve problems, which is higher than Gen X and all the other older cohorts. But the younger Gen Z, at 70 percent support, is even more strongly supportive of government than the Millennials (Parker and Igielnik 2020). Taken together, Pew found that Millennials and Gen Z are the most culturally diverse age cohorts in America, and, not surprisingly, the most "liberal" segment in terms of positions on major political issues (Parker and Igielnik 2020).

Gen Z are digital natives like Millennials, but they are "digital innate" as well, hardly out of the cradle before they were introduced to digital media. Generation Z has an even more natural facility than Millennials with digital communications technology, and also more dependence on social media for news and social connection. Millennials were gradually introduced to multiple changing digital platforms, first as children with PlayStations, then as teens using iPods and Macintoshes, and buying iPhones after college. Generation Z, by contrast, never knew anything but one smartphone platform for their games, socializing, TV shows, casino-style gambling, and music—and, occasionally, speaking on the telephone. For Gen Z, 95 percent have a smart phone, and those in their late teens spend roughly 50 hours a week engaging with social media (Anderson and Jiang 2018; Bond 2020). Political information and news for Gen Z is as fragmented as their games and social media use. And yet Gen Z is showing potential for more faith in government to solve problems, and demanding that government do more on gun control, environmental protection, and health care reform than Millennials.

Pandemic Politics and Gen Z

The COVID-19 pandemic is a singular global event that left a deep impression on the opinions of Generation Z in the United States. As shocking and painful as World War II, the Vietnam War, and 9/11 were, the pandemic has a distinct pattern of impact on youth, compared to older Americans. It is unclear what the meaning of the pandemic will eventually be, and how it might affect the political behavior of Gen Z or how it might amplify or merge with the issues of migration, police brutality, wildfires, hurricanes, the Black Lives Matter protests, or the flailing government response to the coronavirus pandemic in the collective remembering of Gen Z. For example, Jennifer Panning used the name "Trump Anxiety Disorder" to describe the psychosocial stress caused by the current political climate, which affected 62 percent of Americans in 2019 and hit youth in college even harder (Keller 2019). Still, at this time we do not know whether eventually, Gen Z may also lay blame on President Joe Biden for the lingering pandemic.

Time will tell whether the Generation Z pandemic experience qualifies as a trigger period that may lead to a young adult imprint, but as I show below, there are clear indications that the combination of President Trump's challenges to institutional norms with the pandemic made a deep impression on large portions of the Gen Z cohort. For instance, older Americans were far more likely to perish from pandemic-related disease than those aged 18 to 25 years old, but the psychological toll in 2020 was much higher for Gen Z. While all age groups experienced emotional stress during the lockdown, higher proportions of adolescents suffered anxiety and post-traumatic stress (Guessoum et al. 2020). There was already a youth mental health crisis prior to 2019 (Ray 2019). Stress and anxiety were already at a 12-year high in 2018 among 15- to 29-year-olds. The pandemic exacerbated it, especially for those with preexisting mental health problems. According to a Pew survey in March 2020, half of the voting-age members of Gen Z reported that they or someone in their family had lost a job or taken a pay cut because of the pandemic (Parker and Igielnik 2020). This was significantly higher than among Millennials (40%) or Gen X (36%) or Boomers (25%). Added to these economic stresses on Gen Z is political instability. They reported levels of stress and worry nearly as high as those aged 30 to 49 (Ray 2019). The Nation's Report Card (2022) found that reading and math proficiency significantly declined for 4th graders and 8th graders, compared to prepandemic levels in 2019. The

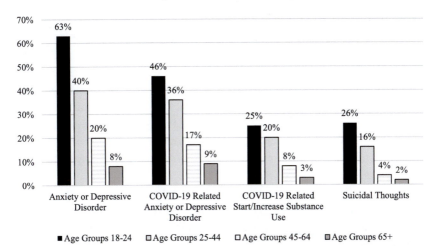

Fig. 3.1. COVID-19 Related Mental Health Problems in June 2020, by Age Group
Source: Czeisler et al. 2020 (https://www.cdc.gov/mmwr/volumes/69/wr/mm6932a1.htm)

COVID-19 pandemic pushed high percentages of Gen Z from general anxiety into even more serious levels of mental illness. The initial lockdown disrupted school-based mental health services, as the initial acute stress response of fear and anxiety set in. Over time during the pandemic, it becomes a chronic stress reaction characterized by denial and minimization of the COVID-19 risk. Emergency department mental health visits increased by 31 percent over 2019 levels, from April through October 2021, according to the Centers for Disease Control (Leeb et al. 2020). After that, frustration and anger emerge, along with increases in the willingness to believe conspiracy theories (Rodriguez 2021). As figure 3.1 shows, depression and anxiety spiked to 63 percent among Americans age 18 to 24 during the first six months of the pandemic compared to 20 percent for people 45 to 64. Over a quarter of 18–24 year olds struggled with thoughts of suicide, compared to just 4 percent among 45–64 year olds (Czeisler et al. 2020)

There are many similarities between Gen Z and Millennials in their political attitudes and behavior. However, a growing amount of evidence suggests that Gen Z is culturally and politically distinct in their issue concerns, level of activism, and party identification. The emerging political consciousness of Gen Z is surely affected also by the wave of protests in response to shocking videos of police brutality. In a CIR-CLE survey in June 2020, 27 percent of 18–24 year-old Gen Z members reported participating in a protest, a remarkable increase from 2016

(5%) and 2018 (16%) for this age group (CIRCLE 2020). In 2018, 73 percent of Gen Z ages 18 to 24 said they believed young people have the power to change things in the U.S. and by summer 2020, that percentage for the same age group rose to 81 percent (CIRCLE 2020). These patterns seem to be holding, and clearly distinguish Gen Z today from Millennials when they were the same age. The Harvard Youth Poll of spring 2021 found that 24 percent of Millennials in 2009 (when they were 18 to 29 years old) considered themselves politically active. Looking at Gen Z, 36 percent considered themselves politically active in 2021 (Harvard Institute of Politics 2021).

Do all these experiences of adults born after 1996 add up to a "new political generation" on the rise? Is Gen Z becoming more than an age cohort, and something more like a distinct cultural unit with its own political tendencies in the future?

Pulse-Rate versus Imprint Approaches to Generations in Political Science

Projecting future political activities from current trends is risky business for political scientists. Over more than a decade, in a series of popular books and articles, William Strauss and Neil Howe (1991, 2000) have developed a popular grand theory of all of American history as a series of recurring generational cycles, and charted them from the late 16th century until the present day. According to them, every 20 to 25 years a new generation with an archetypical persona appears, and automatically establishes a new economic and political climate and new institutions. Eventually, in roughly 80 year cycles, successive generations question and corrode the aging institutions, resulting in a new moment of crisis and then the establishment of a new cultural order, and a new cycle (Howe and Strauss 2000).

Political scientists are rightly skeptical of grand theories like those of Strauss and Howe. As David Schultz (chap. 1, this vol.) remarks, generational analysis is ubiquitous in pop culture and in consumer research, but is in a very underdeveloped state in political science. Visions of inevitable historical cycles, driven automatically by the emergence of each new dominant generation, tend to downplay the impact of unforeseen events and new technologies on mass politics. It also presumes that all events experienced by emerging youth cohorts automatically create a new generational outlook. Yet the evidence for this automaticity is scant. Major events happen almost daily; not all major events have the same identity-producing effect on youth, and they do not appear at regular 20-year intervals. Political scientists still need to develop a better grasp of which major events will make a deep impression on a youth cohort, and which events do not.

At least since Plato's account of generational change in *The Republic*, theorists have tried to define how parents transmit, or fail to transmit, the political regime's norms and values to their offspring. The chain of generations receive an inheritance not only of DNA, but of language, religion, and a way of life that is adapted and passed on to the next generation. In modern political science, thanks to pioneering works such as *Generations and Politics* (1981) by Kent Jennings and Richard Niemi, the emphasis is on how parental upbringing and family environment ripple through an individual's identity and behavior through the life cycle, and how political culture, norms, modes of discourse, and identities are passed on to offspring from generation to generation (Sapiro 1994).

Jennings and Niemi mean "generation" almost literally, and they refer to the ways children are socialized politically by their families, peers, elders and institutions. Jennings and Niemi thought of political identity as an emergent awareness that politics is an important part of their lives that young people experience as they enter young adulthood. Political identity is distinguished from general social identity, because it is less stable and is constantly being formed and re-formed over time with each unfolding period of political history that a person lives through (Erikson 1968). It includes what values they should stand for in their social and political lives, knowledge of how to engage in action within the public sphere, and who their public allies and opponents are (Gentry 2018, 21). Political identity includes things such as party identification (or lack of it), civic belonging, willingness to join community organizations, willingness to protest, and so on.

Moving from the level of individual psychology toward the idea of mass "political generations" in political science requires also seeing large-scale patterns of voting and other forms of civic or political engagement exhibited within national age cohorts. While family and schools are powerful agents of socialization, dramatic or traumatic political events experienced collectively in early adulthood can shock opinion in a whole age cohort. Even brief but dramatic events can affect party identification among age cohorts for long periods of time.

Bartels and Jackman (2014) found that events can affect how an individual first begins to participate as a more mature adult, which in turn affects each subsequent engagement in politics as they move through life (Bartels and Jackman 2014). An awareness that, at an impressionable age, I experienced major events in a way similar to others born around the same time cannot completely override my other identities such as race or gender or nationality. Nevertheless, even personal identities related to gender, class, or race are given a distinct generational flavoring by when they emerge from acting as a generation living through a time of major social change and experiencing those times in a way differently from other age cohorts. Moreover, it might lead me to associate and act differently in civil society and politics than people from other generations.

Generational analysis takes on a different cast when the level of analysis is not individual families, but age cohorts. Where political scientists find greater difficulty is in how to move from the concept of "age cohort" to the much more amorphous concept of "generation."

As other chapters in this book have discussed, Mannheim's theory of "political generations" is a foundation of age-cohort analysis in political science. Less appreciated is Mannheim's skepticism about theories (such as Strauss and Howe's) that define generations in neatly automatic pulses in 20–25-year intervals. Mannheim went on to say that such theories try to establish "a direct correlation between waves of decisive year classes of birth—set at intervals of 30 years, and conceived in a purely naturalistic, quantifying spirit—on one hand, and waves of cultural changes on the other . . . [Yet] whether a new *generation style* emerges every year, every thirty, every hundred years, or whether it emerges rhythmically at all, depends entirely on the trigger action of the social and cultural process" (Mannheim [1928] 2011, 385; emphasis in original). Hans Jaeger's (1985) history of generation theories describes Mannheim's theory as an "imprint" theory of generations, and contrasts it with the "pulse-rate" model that Strauss and Howe use. Imprint theories generally view generations as episodic, as somewhat dependent on contingency or even combinations of chance events. Imprint theories of generation depend on political socialization theories about the "impressionable age," of coming into adulthood responsibilities around age 15 to 25 (Sapiro 2004; Marczewska-Rytko 2020). Major events have different effects on different segments of an age cohort—what Mannheim called "generation units" competing to define the general character of the generation. The generation units might represent a variety of positions within the generation, such as gender, race, religion, ethnicity, even region.

The imprint theory of generations suggests that political scientists would be well served if they resisted the tendency to mark off 20-year age cohorts as "generations." Rather than seeing each age cohort as a generation and then seeking out, post hoc, events presumed to "define a generation" automatically, the analysis should start with major traumatic events, and define the age cohorts more in relation to events. From there, the theory of political generations can drive our questioning about the age cohort, rather than the other way around.

What are the possible candidates for these major imprinting events? Political scientists have had only mixed success in using generational collective memory to predict future political behavior (Jacobson 2012, 2016; Schuman and Corning 2014). That is because the political impact varies for each cohort, and triggers different cultural processes of collective memory and political identity formation. In a preliminary study, the Pew Research Center applied this cohort analysis to determine which historical events each cohort remembered as impactful to them (Deane, Duggan, and Morin 2016). I have summarized the Pew findings in table 3.1. It is important to note that the Pew results report the most widely remembered events, but do not report which of the events had the most impact on groups within each age cohort. Generation Z members were not included in the analysis, but it does provide a roughly quantitative view of what people in various age cohorts mention as memorable historical events occurring in their childhood and youth.

Only a few times in U.S. history do we see simultaneously unsettling events, cultural innovations, demographic bulges, and institutional breakdowns. Braungart (2013) goes on to argue that the 1960s generation of Baby Boomers should be considered a political generation in large part because of the significant role young people played in the civil rights, free speech, antiwar, and other protest and countercultural movements. This is not to say that every individual in the young adult cohorts of the 1960s participated in these movements, only that a large generation-unit was able to challenge institutions controlled by older generations.

Trigger events can appear in many guises, and not only from demographic shifts or trends in public opinion. Hart-Brinson (2018) catalogued multiple types of triggers that can link across many aspects of cohort experience. Linked mechanisms of demographic change, macro-historical change in the broad social environment,

TABLE 3.1. Generation Cohorts and Major Remembered Events

Generation	Birth year start	Birth year end	Pew Survey: Top three most frequently named major historical moments occurring in childhood/ early adulthood	Standout events, mentioned by cohort
Generation Z (or Gen Z)	1997	2012	n/a	n/a
Millennial	1981	1996	• 9/11 attacks (86%) • Obama Election (49%)	Legalized Gay Marriage (19%)
Generation X	1965	1980	• 9/11 attacks (79%) • Obama Election (40%) • Berlin Wall Falls/End of Cold War (21%)	Tech Revolution (20%)
Baby Boomer	1946	1964	• JFK Assassination (45%) • Vietnam War (41%) • Moon Landing (35 %)	Tech Revolution (26%)
Silent Generation	1928	1945	• World War II (44%) • JFK Assassination (41%) • Vietnam War (37%)	Korean War (18%)

Source: Data from Pew Research Center (Parker, Graff, and Igielnik 2020; Deane, Duggan, and Morin 2016).

modes of communication and interaction, and change in world-views can set the stage for a triggering historical period (Hart-Brinson 2018). Moral panic and weakened trust in institutions can follow in the wake of a political scandal like Watergate or a violent crime wave. Alternatively, perhaps artistic innovations such as rock music or hip hop can spark new fashions or new literary genres. An external tragic attack like the attack on the World Trade Center and the Pentagon on 9/11 might have an altogether different sort of effect. Perhaps broader cultural trends such as the decline of religiosity among youth, or the normalization of alternative lifestyles and unorthodox gender identities can shift group identities. Going further back in time, researchers have probed how new definitions of civic membership might alter a generation's relationship with the state, as occurred after U.S. women's enfranchisement, the Great Depression and the New Deal, the rise of Nazism, or alterations in immigrant rights in the 1960s.

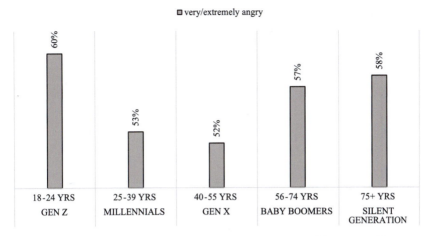

Fig. 3.2. 2020 Anger at "How Things Are Going in the Country," by Generation
Source: 2020 National Election Study (http://sda.berkeley.edu/archive.htm)

The Trump Effect and Generation Z

It is one thing to show how the dramatic events of the pandemic period affected young adult Gen Z youth deeply. It is another thing to see how these emotions are manifested in political attitudes and voting. A major way it was expressed is anger. A significantly greater share of Gen Z who were of voting age in 2020 expressed anger at "how things are going in the country" than Millennials (fig. 3.2).

In this section, I suggest that for a very large proportion of young Gen Z adults, the focus of their negative feelings was on President Donald Trump. One type of identity that is established in these impressionable years is party identification (Dan Wood and Jordan 2018). One of the political characteristics of the older Millennials voting in their first elections in 2008 was their favorable feelings and political support for Barack Obama (Gentry 2018). Yet as Dalton (2016) demonstrated, support for Obama did not translate into strong identification with the Democratic Party (Dalton 2016). Millennials have a strong tendency to think of voting as a "choice" rather than a "duty." They show commitment to social change but they have negative attitudes about achieving it through electoral politics and political parties. Instead, they are significantly more likely than their elders to express loyalty to the political norm of "engaged citizenship" and are more likely than older generations to prefer action

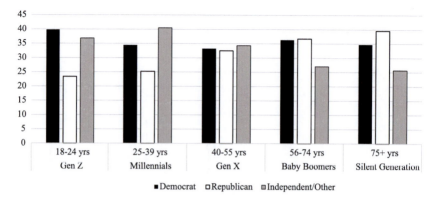

Fig. 3.3. 2020 Party Identification, by Generation
Source: 2020 National Election Study (http://sda.berkeley.edu/archive.htm)

one issue at a time, at the grassroots level of activism and community engagement (Dalton 2016; Gentry 2018). Gen Z parallels the Millennials in their suspicion of parties and voting. Biden is not the charismatic figure for Gen Z that Obama was for Millennials, which makes it significant that they voted in high numbers for Joe Biden and most likely gave the Democrat a winning margin in the closest swing states. We can interpret the Gen Z vote for Biden as anti-Trump sentiment, but what is vital for seeing how Gen Z is beginning to differentiate itself is the unexpectedly higher proportions of Gen Z identifying themselves as Democrats, rather than as independents. Figure 3.3 shows that compared to Milliennials, slightly higher proportions of Gen Z identify as Democrats at least in the first election of their adult life.

No other generational cohort has this large a portion identifying with a party. Even considering only males, Gen Z is the only generation with a greater portion identifying as Democrats than Republicans, 36 percent to 25 percent. Both Gen Z and Millennial voters in the 2018 election were significantly more likely to identify as Democrats than older generations. The trend continued into 2020. Just prior to the 2020 elections, the Harvard Youth Poll (2020) showed that Gen Z (18- to 24-year olds) Democratic identification had reached 40 percent, compared to 24 percent identifying as Republican (Harvard Institute of Politics 2020). Gen Z women, Hispanics, and African Americans identified with Democrats at even higher rates. Among Gen Z women, the proportion of Democratic identifiers is greater than any other generation: 45 percent Democratic, 33 percent independent, and 22 percent Republican (American National Election Study 2021).

Tracing exactly how the events of 2020, presidential approval, and partisan identity are tied together is beyond the scope of this chapter. Having developed a case for merging the quantitative aspects of the pulse rate theory and the qualitative dimension of the imprint theory, we might begin to speculate on Gen Z's distinct political responses in the 2020 election. The mechanisms of how party identification is formed in young adulthood are not fully understood, but one major factor is the role of presidential performance during a cohort's impressionable years. Youthful voting patterns can become more ingrained and habitual as people age (Jacobson 2012; Gentry 2018). There is sturdy evidence that attitudes and identities are more unstable during early adulthood and stabilize soon after. An interesting example of this is Yair Ghitza and Andrew Gelman's work with Jonathan Auerbach (Ghitza, Gelman, and Auerbach 2014; Auerbach, Ghitza, and Gelman 2020), which found that the job approval rating of the president in office when a person is 18 is about three times more powerful in influencing their future presidential party votes than events experienced after a person reaches age 40 (Auerbach, Ghitza, and Gelman 2020; Ghitza, Gelman, and Auerbach 2014). People tend to keep supporting the party of a popular president in power during their youth, and vote against the party of an unpopular president.

Few if any presidents have been as alienating to young adult cohorts as Donald Trump. There have been presidents who have been unpopular or considered unsuited for the job of commander-in-chief by significant segments of the public (Hibbing, Hayes, and Deol 2017). Few presidents have been such an object of anger that they become a rallying point for large segments of generations. Harry Truman, George W. Bush, and Jimmy Carter each were deeply unpopular in office, and yet their unpopularity did not strongly manifest in widespread hatred for them personally, and they became more popular as ex-presidents. Jacobson (2012, 2016) showed that when a young adult age cohort is polarized along party lines in presidential job approval, the long-term effect on voting and party identification is weak. But when a president's performance inspires low polarization in a young cohort (i.e., either the majority has a positive or a negative approval), then the effect on party preferences later in life is more profound (Jacobson 2016; Gentry 2018). Jacobson also notes that Gen Xers who reached age 20 during the more generally popular Reagan presidency tended to remain Republican. The presidencies of G. W. Bush and Obama were polarizing. But they were not polarizing to Millennials, with large majorities disapproving of Bush, and large majorities approving of Obama (Hibbing, Hayes, and Deol 2017).

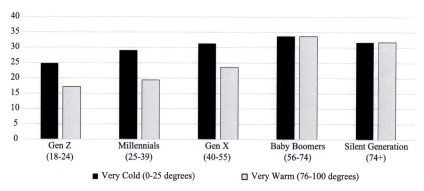

Fig. 3.4. Joe Biden High and Low Feeling Thermometer, by Generation
Source: 2020 National Election Study (http://sda.berkeley.edu/archive.htm)

Adding a quantifiable element to this analysis of Trump as a Gen Z "enemy" symbol, we can review the 2020 American National Election Study "feeling thermometer," which reveals more about Trump's relative unpopularity with voting-age members of Gen Z (fig. 3.5 and fig. 3.6). The feeling thermometer asks respondents to express "warmth" or "coldness" toward a candidate on a "thermometer" continuum between 0 and 100. Low "temperature" indicates unfavorable attitudes toward an object or person, and high "temperature" indicates favorable views. If we focus only on those who gave the lowest temperature (0–25 degrees) or the highest temperatures (76 to 100), we find Millennials gave Trump the highest percentage of low temperature (81 percent rated Trump at 0–25 degrees, and only 20 percent rated him warmly between 76 and 100 degrees), compared to Baby Boomers (69 percent low temperature, 31 percent high temperature). In 2020, sufficient Gen Z voters were in the sample. The Gen Z support for Biden is more complicated than a simple anti-Trump feeling. As figure 3.4 shows, Gen Z was the group with smallest proportion feeling "cold" toward Biden, but also the group with the smallest proportion who felt "warm" toward him. Figure 3.5 and figure 3.6 shows Gen Z voters were more "cold" toward Trump than any other cohort.

Gender is also a factor. Gen Z men were significantly colder toward Trump (54%) than any other cohort of males. Even more generational gaps appeared between women Gen Zers and other generations of women when it comes to Trump. For Gen Z women, 62 percent felt cold toward Trump compared to 55 percent of Millennial women (fig. 3.5). Women across all ages usually viewed Trump more negatively than

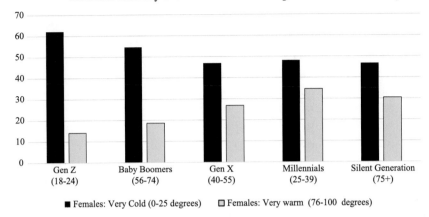

Fig. 3.5. 2020 Women's High/Low Feeling Thermometer for Trump, by Generation
Source: 2020 National Election Study (http://sda.berkeley.edu/archive.htm)

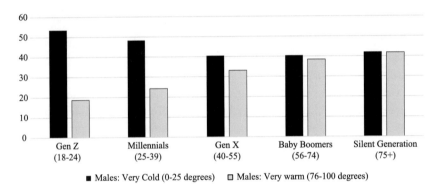

Fig. 3.6. 2020 Men's High/Low Feeling Thermometer for Trump, by Generation
Source: 2020 National Election Study (http://sda.berkeley.edu/archive.htm)

men in the same age cohort. But the gap was smallest between Gen Z women and men.

Are there reasons we can theorize that the "Trump effect" interacted with 2020 events and factors such as gender to generate higher Democratic identification among Generation Z? Past research does show that presidents who are deeply unpopular with key public segments can be catalysts for building political community, at least negatively by becoming "enemy" symbols. For example, both Richard Nixon and Bill Clinton were linked to eras of cultural division and conflict from their ascent into power and office (Fine and Eisenberg 2002). To be clear, Nixon and Clinton were not hated by a majority of Americans and were quite popular with key voter blocs. But for key clusters of detractors, Nixon and Clinton were not merely opposed or disliked. They were villains, and people organized themselves for the purpose of destroying their political careers (Fine and Eisenberg 2002).

For key segments of Republican identifiers, Clinton was a not simply a president blamed for bad policies but a villain and a dark force beneath a number of conspiracy theories. Nixon was seen by the young left in the 1960s and 1970s (and in pop culture) as a kind of paranoid criminal. Nixon's anticommunist activities in the McCarthy era (named for Senator Joe McCarthy) and his prosecution of the Vietnam conflict earned him the hatred of the left in the 1960s. Clinton's role in 1960s anti-Vietnam protests (highlighted by George H. W. Bush in 1992 and Robert Dole in 1996) and the scandal of his inappropriate sexual affair in the Oval Office made him a symbol of post-1960s cultural change for younger Republicans in the 1990s.

Both Nixon and Clinton, like Trump, were symbols of unresolved cultural conflicts stretching throughout their public careers. Donald Trump has a comparable trajectory of being very disliked by a key section of Generation Z. For them, Trump may end up as a powerful partisan generational symbol for many years beyond his time in office. How will Gen Z's memories of Trump and the pandemic affect their future engagement with the political system? When Trump's mythology takes shape for Generation Z, will he be a defeated villain, or a constant reinforcement of their party identity? Finally, after Trump's decision to run for president in 2024, and his indictments, what trajectory might Gen Z's political orientation take?

Conclusion: Gen Z and the 2022 Congressional Elections

One year after a mob violently attacked the U.S. Capitol on January 6, 2021 to disrupt the electoral vote count, 61 percent of Generation Z members saw it as an attack on democracy that should never be forgotten, compared to 46 percent of Millennials age 30 to 44 (see fig. 3.7). Older age cohorts were shocked by January 6 riots, but to them it became less urgent and less worth remembering after a year. They were far more likely than Gen Zers to say that too much is being made of January 6 and that it is time to move on. It would seem that this sustained view of January 6 is related to party identification among Gen Z members, as they prepared to vote in the upcoming congressional elections of 2022. As figure 3.8 suggests, going into the 2022 elections,

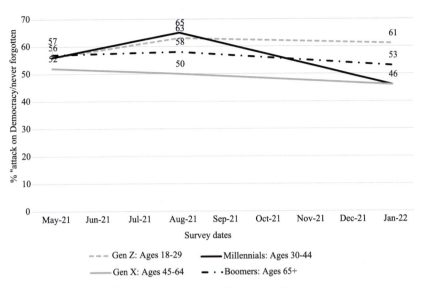

Fig. 3.7. January 6 as "Attack on Democracy," by Generation
Source: Quinnipiac University Polls, May 2021–January 2022 ("The Storming of the U.S. Capitol on January 6, 2021 was an attack on democracy that should never be forgotten").

Gen Z's level of party identification in favor of the Democrats is about as high as it was in the record youth turnout 2018 Democratic Party election year. Pre-2022 election polling found that youth enthusiasm to vote matched that of 2018 (Harvard Institute of Politics 2022). Initial evidence shows that Gen Z's relatively high levels of electoral participation has continued into the 2022 elections. Nationwide, youth 18 to 29 years old turned out at a rate of 28 percent and leaned strongly toward Democratic candidates. It was the second highest midterm election youth turnout in history. Only 2018 reached a higher mark, at 30 percent turnout (CIRCLE 2022). In the end, youth helped Democratic candidates in gubernatorial and congressional elections squeeze through to victory in tight states such as Pennsylvania, Georgia, and Arizona.

Will this level of Gen Z engagement endure? If they continue to have high rates of participation in the next decade, will they follow the pattern of the Millennials, who strongly supported Obama and Democrats in 2008, only to become relatively more supportive of Republicans? For example, the first Millennials to reach voting age were those that voted in the 2008 presidential election. Millennials strongly supported the Obama campaign, and 59 percent of them identified as Democrats, compared to 35 percent as Republicans (Quinnipiac University Poll

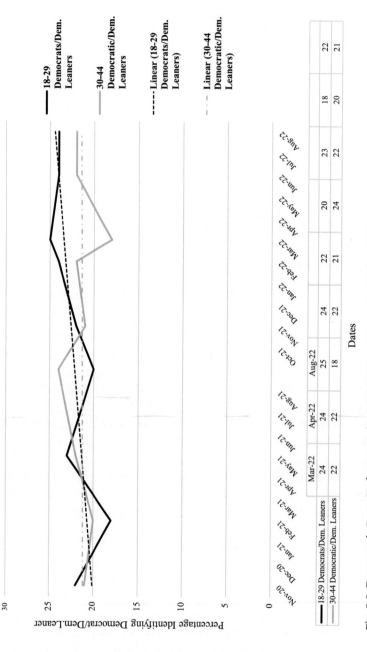

Fig. 3.8. Democratic Party ID for Age Cohort (18–29 Year-Olds vs. 30–44 Year-Olds)
Source: Quinnipiac University Polls, September 2021–August 2022 (Includes Registered/Unregistered and Independent Leaners)

2008). Eight years later, at the time of the 2016 election, only 40 percent identified as Democrats, and 28 percent identified as Republican (Quinnipiac University Poll 2016). As the elections of 2022 approach, around 45 percent of Millennial voters are still Democrats, but now roughly one-third identify as Republicans (Quinnipiac University Poll 2022). This may be a case of more Millennials identifying as Republicans as they age, which political science literature suggests occurs with all age cohorts gradually over time. However, as I have argued in this chapter, Generation Z's coming-of-age differed from that of Millennials. Will the intensity of Gen Z's memories of the 2017 to 2021 period keep them leaning strongly toward identifying as Democrats in the next decade or so? We will have to wait for more post-2022 election data to find more indications of whether Gen Z will again make the difference for Democrats in the 2024 elections.

Throughout this chapter, I have argued that the trying times between 2016 and 2022 were experienced by all age cohorts, but Gen Z experienced them as a community with a distinct demographic makeup and communication style, during their impressionable years, in a way that seems to have politically energized them. But demography is not destiny in politics. Each generation enters public life under contingent historical circumstances that youthful leaders and older allies interpret and make meaningful. These formative events can differ in the mechanisms by which they affect age cohorts and the influence they have on identities over the longer term. Some trigger events, such as technological innovations, can create a relatively gradual shift in generational perspectives. Each generation confronts new circumstances as they age, but they always improvise their responses using frameworks imprinted from the formative years of early adulthood. For previous generations of youth, the Great Depression and the 1960s student rebellion were extraordinarily disrupting and polarizing periods that left a profound mark on the young adults who lived through those times and led to distinct generational perspectives and actions in the public realm. Those were major periods of social change, but in many ways the pandemic and the Trump years had a more direct and intensely emotional impact on youth who are just beginning to reach an age of greater awareness of the political world.

Generation Z engagement in the 2020 election was an all-time high for a young cohort, and one major reason for this is the deep impression the distressing events of 2016 to 2021 made on young adults. The government's poor pandemic response, along with the stress and trauma affecting 18–24 year olds, represented the fragility of Gen Z's illusions of ease and opportunity (Deckman et al. 2020). Added to that, the disruptions of schooling, isolation from friends and family, the spike in unemployment, monthly active shooter lockdown drills, and the eruption of Black Lives Matter protests amounted to a widespread sense of cultural trauma (Hart-Brinson 2018). The Supreme Court's decision in June 2022 to strike down the *Roe v. Wade* precedent and cast abortion rights into uncertainty proved to energize Generation Z in numbers high enough in key states to prevent a major Republican take-over of Congress.

It helps, too, that national elections are defined by rough parity between Democratic and Republican partisans and by tight swing state races where parties and grassroots organizations can mobilize enough young voters to sway the outcome. Some advocacy groups and partisan leaders will continue to appeal to Gen Z anxieties and rage to produce more votes. In 2018 and 2020, youthful emotion prevailed, and Gen Z turned out in high numbers. But the evidence is that the emotions were mainly of anger or fear, with the Democrats reaping greater benefit. Will it play out the same way in the 2024 election? In an ideal world, enlightened citizens participate over the course of their lives because of an enduring sense of civic responsibility. Perhaps someday, that old language of citizenship will motivate most of Gen Z, though no doubt its chorus will be refashioned for a smartphone world. In the long run, American democracy needs both the passion of young people and the acceptance of their responsibility for what the republic is allowed to become. Historical circumstance may have given Generation Z political momentum. The question is how to keep that momentum going. That will take thinking, communicating, and strategy. For the members of Gen Z to emerge in the long run as a new civic generation, they will need to become a community shaped by collective generational memories, mature civic habits, and maybe eventually, a new form of democratic faith.

REFERENCES

Anderson, M., and J. Jiang. 2018. "Teens, Social Media and Technology 2018." Pew Research Center, May 31. https://www.pewresearch.org/internet/2018/05/31/teens-social-media-technology-2018/

American National Election Studies. 2021. ANES 2020 Time Series Study Full Release. July 19, 2021 version. www.electionstudies.org; Berkeley, CA:

Computer-assisted Survey Methods Program (http://sda.berkeley.edu), University of California/ISA, distributors.

Auerbach, Jonathan, Yair Ghitza, and Andrew Gelman. 2020. *A Generational Voting Model for Forecasting the 2020 American Presidential Election.* Unpublished paper. http://www.stat.columbia.edu/~gelman/research/unpublished/2020prediction.pdf

Bartels, L. M., and S. Jackman. 2014. "A Generational Model of Political Learning." *Electoral Studies* 33: 7–18.

Beck, P. A. 1993. "A Socialization Theory of Party Realignment." In *Classics in Voting Behavior*, edited by Richard C. Niemi and Herbert F. Weisberg, 331–45. Washington, DC: Congressional Quarterly.

Bond, C. 2020. "There's a Big Difference between Millennials and Generation Z." *Huffington Post*, August 7. https://www.huffpost.com/entry/millennials-gen-z-di fferences_1_5f2b87f6c5b6e96a22adc439

Braungart, R. G. 2013. "Political Generations." In *Wiley-Blackwell Encyclopedia of Social and Political Movements*, edited by David A. Snow, Donatella Della Porta, and Bert Klandermans, 949–51. Malden, MA: Wiley-Blackwell.

Braungart, R. G., and M. M. Braungart. 1986. "Life-Course and Generational Politics." *Annual Review of Sociology* 12 (1): 205–31.

Bui, Quoctrung, and Claire Cain Miller. 2018. "The Age That Women Have Babies: How a Gap Divides America." *New York Times*, August 4. https://www.nytimes .com/interactive/2018/08/04/upshot/up-birth-age-gap.html

Chang, C. 2001. "The Impacts of Emotion Elicited by Print Political Advertising on Candidate Evaluation." *Media Psychology* 3 (2): 91–118.

CIRCLE. 2012. *CIRCLE 2012 Youth Poll: 52% Support for Obama, 35% for Romney.* https://circle.tufts.edu/latest-research/circle-2012-youth-poll-52-support-obama -35-romney

CIRCLE. 2018. *Are Political Parties and Campaigns Reaching Young People in Civic Deserts?* https://circle.tufts.edu/latest-research/are-political-parties-and-campaigns -reaching-young-people-civic-deserts

CIRCLE. 2020. *Poll: Young People Believe They Can Lead Change in Unprecedented Election Cycle.* https://circle.tufts.edu/latest-research/poll-young-people-believe-th ey-can-lead-change-unprecedented-election-cycle

CIRCLE. 2021. *2020 Election Center.* https://circle.tufts.edu/2020-election-center

CIRCLE. 2022. *2022 Election Center.* https://circle.tufts.edu/index.php/2022-election -center

CNN. 2012. *CNN 2012 Exit Polls.* https://www.cnn.com/election/2012/results/race/pr esident/

CNN. 2016. *CNN 2016 Exit Polls.* https://www.cnn.com/election/2016/results/exit -polls

CNN. 2018. *CNN 2018 Exit Polls.* https://www.cnn.com/election/2018/exit-polls

Czeisler, M. É, R. I. Lane, E. Petrosky, J. F. Wiley, A. Christensen, R. Njai, et al. 2020. "Mental Health, Substance Use, and Suicidal Ideation during the COVID-19 Pandemic—United States, June 24–30, 2020." *MMWR: Morbidity and Mortality Weekly Report* 69 (32): 1049–57. https://doi.org/10.15585/mmwr.mm6932a1

Dalton. 2016. *The Good Citizen: How a Younger Generation Is Reshaping American Politics.* Washington, DC: CQ Press.

Dan Wood, B., and S. Jordan. 2018. "Presidents and Polarization of the American Electorate." *Presidential Studies Quarterly* 48 (2): 248–70.

Deane, C., M. Duggan, and R. Morin. 2016. *Americans Name the 10 Most Significant Historic Events of Their Lifetimes*. Pew Research Center, December 15. https://www.pewresearch.org/politics/2016/12/15/americans-name-the-10-most-signifi cant-historic-events-of-their-lifetimes/

Deckman, M., J. McDonald, S. Rouse, and M. Kromer. 2020. "Gen Z, Gender, and COVID-19." *Politics & Gender* (July): 1–9. https://doi.org/10.1017/S1743923X2000 0434

Denton, R. E. J., and ProQuest Ebooks, eds. 2017. *The 2016 US Presidential Campaign: Political Communication and Practice*. New York: Palgrave Macmillan.

DeSante, C. D. 2017. "They Chose to Go to the Moon: How Birth Cohorts Shape Opinions on Funding for Space Exploration." *Social Science Quarterly* 98 (4): 1175–88.

Dimock, M. 2019. *Defining Generations: Where Millennials End and Gen Z Begins*. January 17. https://www.pewresearch.org/fact-tank/2019/01/17/where-millennials -end-and-generation-z-begins/

Dinas, E. 2014. "Does Choice Bring Loyalty? Electoral Participation and the Development of Party Identification." *American Journal of Political Science* 58 (2): 449–65.

Erikson, E. H. 1968. *Identity, Youth, and Crisis*. New York: W.W. Norton.

Fine, G. A., and E. Eisenberg. 2002. "Tricky Dick and Slick Willy: Despised Presidents and Generational Imprinting." *American Behavioral Scientist* 46 (4): 553–65.

Fisher, P. 2020a. "Generational Cycles in American Politics, 1952–2016." *Society* 57 (1): 22–29.

Fisher, P. 2020b. "Generational Replacement and the Impending Transformation of the American Electorate." *Politics & Policy* 48 (1): 38–68.

Frey, W. H. 2021. "Turnout in 2020 Election Spiked among Both Democratic and Republican Voting Groups, New Census Data Shows." *Brookings Institution Reports*, May 5. https://www.brookings.edu/research/turnout-in-2020-spiked -among-both-democratic-and-republican-voting-groups-new-census-data-sh ows/

Gentry, B. 2018. *Why Youth Vote: Identity, Inspirational Leaders and Independence*. Cham, Switzerland: Springer International.

Ghitza, Y., A. Gelman, and J. Auberbach. 2014. "The Great Society, Reagan's Revolution, and Generations of Presidential Voting." Unpublished manuscript, Columbia University. http://www.stat.columbia.edu/~gelman/research/unpublished/co hort_voting_20191017.pdf

Guessoum, S. B., J. Lachal, R. Radjack, E. Carretier, S. Minassian, L. Benoit, and M. Moro. 2020. "Adolescent Psychiatric Disorders During the COVID-19 Pandemic and Lockdown." *Psychiatry Research* 291: 113624–44.

Hart-Brinson, P. 2018. *The Mechanisms of Generational Change: Triggers and Processes*. https://search.datacite.org/works/10.17605/osf.io/d5ytz

Harvard Institute of Politics. 2020. *Spring 2020 Harvard Youth Poll*. Cambridge, MA.

Harvard Institute of Politics. 2021. *Spring 2021 Harvard Youth Poll*. Cambridge, MA. https://iop.harvard.edu/youth-poll/41st-edition-spring-2021

Harvard Institute of Politics. 2022. *Fall 2022 Harvard Youth Poll*. Cambridge, MA. https://iop.harvard.edu/youth-poll/44th-edition-fall-2022

Hess, A. J. 2020. "The 2020 Election Shows Gen Z's Power for Years to Come." *CBNC. com*, November 18. https://www.cnbc.com/2020/11/18/the-2020-election-shows -gen-zs-voting-power-for-years-to-come.html

Hibbing, M. V., M. Hayes, and R. Deol. 2017. "Nostalgia Isn't What It Used to Be: Partisan Polarization in Views on the Past." *Social Science Quarterly* 98 (1): 230– 43.

Hirschberger, G. 2018. "Collective Trauma and the Social Construction of Meaning." *Frontiers in Psychology* 9: 1441.

Horowitz, B. 2012. "After Gen X, Millennials, What Should Next Generation Be?" *ABC News*, May 3. https://abcnews.go.com/Business/gen-millennials-generation /story?id=16275187

Howe, N., and W. Strauss. 2000. *Millennials Rising: The Next Great Generation*. New York: Vintage Books.

Jacobson, G. C. 2012. "The President's Effect on Partisan Attitudes." *Presidential Studies Quarterly* 42 (4): 683–718.

Jacobson, G. C. 2016. "The Obama Legacy and the Future of Partisan Conflict." *Annals of the American Academy of Political and Social Science* 667 (1): 72–91.

Jaeger, H. 1985. "Generations in History: Reflections on a Controversial Concept." *History and Theory* 24 (3): 273–92.

Jamieson, A., H. B. Shin, and J. Day. 2002. *Voting and Registration in the Election of November 2000*. Washington, DC: U.S. Census.

Jennings, M. K., and R. G. Niemi. 1981. *Generations and Politics*. Princeton: Princeton University Press.

Jennings, M. K., L. Stoker, and J. Bowers. 2009. "Politics across Generations: Family Transmission Reexamined." *Journal of Politics* 71 (3): 782–99.

Keeter, S. 2009. "The Aging of the Boomers and the Rise of the Millennials." In *Red, Blue, and Purple America*, edited by Ruy Teixiera. Washington, DC: Brookings Institution Press.

Keller, J. 2019. "Research Suggests Trump's Election Has Been Detrimental to Many Americans' Mental Health." *Pacific Standard*, January 15. https://psmag.com/ne ws/research-suggests-trumps-election-has-been-detrimental-to-many-america ns-mental-health

Khalid, A., and J. Rose. 2016. "Millennials Just Didn't Love Hillary Clinton the Way They Loved Barack Obama." *NPR.org*, November 14. https://www.npr.org/2016 /11/14/501727488/millennials-just-didnt-love-hillary-clinton-the-way-they-lov ed-barack-obama

Leeb, R.T., R. H. Bitsko, L. Radhakrishnan, P. Martinez, R. Njai, and K. M. Holland. 2020. "Mental Health–Related Emergency Department Visits among Children Aged <18 Years during the COVID-19 Pandemic—United States, January 1–October 17, 2020. *MMWR: Morbidity and Mortality Weekly Report* 69: 1675–80.

Mannheim, K. (1928) 2011. "The Sociological Problem of Generations." In *From Karl Mannheim*, edited by Kurt Wolff, 351–98. New Brunswick, NJ: Transaction.

Marczewska-Rytko, M. 2020. "Political Socialization." In *The SAGE Handbook of Political Science*, vol. 3, edited by D. Berg-Schlosser, B. Badie, and L. Morlino, 641–55. London: Sage.

Mueller, J. T., and L. E. Mullenbach. 2018. "Looking for a White Male Effect in Generation Z: Race, Gender, and Political Effects on Environmental Concern and Ambivalence." *Society & Natural Resources* 31 (8): 925–41.

Nash, L. L. 1978. "Concepts of Existence: Greek Origins of Generational Thought." *Daedalus* 107 (4): 1–21.

National Center for Health Statistics. 2020. *Mental Health Household Pulse Survey.* https://www.cdc.gov/nchs/covid19/pulse/mental-health.htm

Nation's Report Card. 2022. "Mathematics and Reading Scores of Fourth- and Eighth-Graders Declined in Most States during Pandemic, Nation's Report Card Shows." https://www.nationsreportcard.gov/

Neal, A. G. 2005. *National Trauma and Collective Memory: Extraordinary Events in the American Experience.* 2nd ed. Armonk, NY: M.E. Sharpe.

Parker, K., and R. Igielnik. 2020. *On the Cusp of Adulthood and Facing an Uncertain Future: What We Know about Gen Z So Far.* Pew Research Center, May 14. https://www.pewresearch.org/social-trends/2020/05/14/on-the-cusp-of-adulthood-and-facing-an-uncertain-future-what-we-know-about-gen-z-so-far-2/

Pew Research Center. 2018. *An Examination of the 2016 Electorate, Based on Validated Voters.* https://www.pewresearch.org/politics/2018/08/09/an-examination-of-the-2016-electorate-based-on-validated-voters/

Prior, M. 2010. "You've Either Got It or You Don't? The Stability of Political Interest over the Life Cycle." *Journal of Politics* 72 (3): 747–66.

Putnam, R. 2000. *Bowling Alone.* New York: Simon & Schuster.

Quinnipiac University Poll. 2008. National Survey of 2,210 registered voters, November 6–10, with sampling error of +/–2.1%. https://poll.qu.edu/Poll-Release-Legacy?releaseid=1228

Quinnipiac University Poll. 2016. National Survey of 1,007 likely voters, October 17–18, with sampling error of +/–3.1%. https://poll.qu.edu/Poll-Release-Legacy?releaseid=2390

Quinnipiac University Poll. 2022. National Survey of 2,203 registered voters, October 22–26, with sampling error of +/–2.2%. https://poll.qu.edu/images/polling/us/us11022022_demos_udat46.pdf

Ray, J. 2019. *Americans' Stress, Worry and Anger Intensified in 2018.* Gallup Poll, April 25. https://news.gallup.com/poll/249098/americans-stress-worry-anger-intensified-2018.aspx

Rodriguez, T. 2021. "Impact of the Covid-19 Pandemic on Adolescent MentalHealth." *Psychiatry Advisor*, April 30. https://www.psychiatryadvisor.com/home/topics/child-adolescent-psychiatry/adolescent-mental-health-issues-are-further-exacerbated-by-the-covid-19-pandemic/

Ryder, N. B. 1965. "The Cohort as a Concept in the Study of Social Change." *American Sociological Review* 30 (6): 843–61. http://www.econis.eu/PPNSET?PPN=484011146

Saad, L. 2020. *Trump Stuck at 42% Job Approval.* Gallup Poll, September 16. https://news.gallup.com/poll/320303/trump-stuck-42-job-approval.aspx

Samuels, A. 2021. *Why Some Socially Liberal Gen-Z Voters Aren't Leaving the GOP.* August 23. https://fivethirtyeight.com/features/why-some-socially-liberal-gen-z-voters-arent-leaving-the-gop/

Sapiro, Virginia. 1994. "Political Socialization during Adulthood: Clarifying the Political Times of Our Lives." *Research in Micropolitics* 4: 197–223.

Schuman, H., and A. Corning. 2012. "Generational Memory and the Critical Period: Evidence for National and World Events." *Public Opinion Quarterly* 76 (1): 1–31.

Schuman, H., and A. Corning. 2014. "Collective Memory and Autobiographical Memory: Similar but Not the Same. *Memory Studies* 7 (2): 146–60.

Seemiller, C., and M. Grace. 2020. *Generation Z: Voices on Voting: Getting Gen Z to the Polls.* GenZHub. https://static1.squarespace.com/static/54d6c4a6e4b0249186225 602/t/5e4af5f3fd3ee771bdbabf2a/1581970936308/GenZ_Voices+On+Voting.pdf

Stewart, A. J., D. G. Winter, D. Henderson-King, and E. Henderson-King. 2015. "How Politics Become Personal: Sociohistorical Events and Their Meanings in People's Lives." *Journal of Social Issues* 71 (2): 294–308.

Stoker, L. 2014. "Reflections on the Study of Generations in Politics." *Forum* 12 (3): 377–96.

Strauss, W., and N. Howe. 1991. *Generations.* New York: Quill, Morrow.

Taylor, P. 2018. *Millennials Are Allergic to Politics. but They Could Change Anything: Millennials Are Our Most Liberal Generation—but They Still Aren't Politically Motivated.* Washington, DC: WP Company.

Twenge, J. M., N. Honeycutt, R. Prislin, and R.A. Sherman. 2016. "More Polarized but More Independent: Political Party Identification and Ideological Self-Categorization among U.S. Adults, College Students, and Late Adolescents, 1970–2015." *Personality and Social Psychology Bulletin* 42 (10): 1364–83.

U.S. Census. 2017. *Voting and Registration in the Election of November 2016.* Washington, DC: U.S. Census. https://www.census.gov/data/tables/time-series/demo/vot ing-and-registration/p20-580.html

U.S. Census. 2019. *Voting and Registration in the Election of November 2018.* Washington, DC: U.S. Census. https://www.census.gov/data/tables/time-series/demo/vot ing-and-registration/p20-583.html

U.S. Census. 2021. *Voting and Registration in the Election of November 2020.* Washington, DC: U.S. Census. https://www.census.gov/data/tables/time-series/demo/vot ing-and-registration/p20-585.html

Valent, P. 2012. "Trauma, Definitions of." In *Encyclopedia of Trauma,* edited by C. R. Figley, 676–79. Thousand Oaks, CA: Sage.

Part II
Attitudes and Opinions

4 | Generational Divides, Changing Times, or Aging?

Examining Immigration Opinion in the U.S., 2004–2018

Jeffrey C. Dixon, Andrew S. Fullerton, and Victoria E. Nash

The constantly evolving immigration policy is a hot button issue in contemporary U.S. politics and media. Public opinion toward immigration is related to a variety of factors, such as self- or economic interests, labor market competition, "symbolic" or cultural factors, (perceived) group threat, and political conditions (e.g., Espenshade and Calhoun 1993; Quillian 1995; Espenshade and Hempstead 1996; Hopkins 2010; Malhorta, Margalit, and Mo 2013; for reviews, see, e.g., Fussell 2014; Hainmueller and Hopkins 2014; Berg 2015). Yet there is less research focusing on potential generational or cohort divides in public opinion toward immigration policy in the U.S. This is an important oversight because extant studies paint a picture of "Millennials"—those born between circa 1980 and the mid-1990s or later (Dimock 2019)—as having more liberal attitudes than their counterparts on a number of social issues in the U.S. (e.g., Pew Research Center 2011; Rouse and Ross 2018), including immigration (Ross and Rouse 2015).

Still, ostensible generational/cohort divides in immigration policy attitudes may be little more than a sign of changing times—also referred to as periods—or the progression of aging. Some research in the U.S. focuses only on generational divides for a single cross-section (e.g.,

The authors thank the Greisch Family for supporting Victoria Nash's 2019 Summer Research Fellowship in Sociology at the College of the Holy Cross.

Ross and Rouse 2015). Other research using repeated cross-sectional data does not focus on age, period, and cohort effects of U.S. immigration policy attitudes, but includes at most two of these variables, whether as controls (e.g., Amaral, Mitchell, and Marquez-Velarde 2019) or with one (year) as a focal point (Yang and Mena 2019). Some prior research may not have attempted to parcel out the linear effects of cohorts from age and time because of the "identification problem" (Firebaugh 1997): that is, age is equal to the period in which the data is collected minus birth year, or cohort. Yet, age-period-cohort (APC) research offers several potential strategies to address this problem (see Fosse and Winship 2019 for a review; Stoker, chap. 2, this vol., explains age-period-cohort using US partisanship).

It is furthermore possible that Millennials' more liberal attitudes toward immigration are a product of other factors, such as this cohort being more racially/ethnically diverse (e.g., Rouse and Ross 2018). This makes it important to statistically control for these factors. Indeed, studies on immigration policy in Europe and Canada within APC frameworks have accounted for factors beyond age, period, and cohort (e.g., Coenders and Scheepers 1998, 2008; Gorodzeisky and Semyonov 2018; Wilkes and Corrigall-Brown 2011; McLaren and Paterson 2020).

Building on research on immigration attitudes, generational divides, and their synthesis, as well as two of the authors' prior study (Fullerton and Dixon 2010), we investigate immigration policy attitudes in the U.S., employing multinomial logistic regression models on 2004–18 (biannual) General Social Survey (GSS) data. Our study departs from extant studies on immigration policy opinion in the U.S., including research using GSS data during a similar time period (Amaral et al. 2019; Yang and Mena 2019), by substantively focusing on age, period, and cohort effects as well as methodologically examining how such effects may be "asymmetrical" (Lieberson 1985)—that is, associations with immigration policy support are not necessarily the same as the associations with opposition (relative to a neutral viewpoint).

Background

In this section, we review literatures on immigration attitudes, generational/cohort divides, and such divides in immigration policy attitudes, respectively. Given space constraints, our review is necessarily selective, focusing largely—but not exclusively—on studies of the U.S.

Immigration Attitudes

Theories of racial/ethnic prejudice have been evoked to explain immigration attitudes (Fussell 2014). For example, theories of self/economic interests suggest anti-immigrant attitudes are a product of labor market competition, individuals' economic evaluations and perceptions of tax burdens, and socioeconomic vulnerability (e.g., Espenshade and Calhoun 1993; Espenshade and Hempstead 1996; Malhorta et al. 2013; Scheve and Slaughter 2001; Wilson 2001). Theories of symbolic politics/racism represent another perspective, positing that intolerance is rooted in pre-adulthood socialization, as dominant group members are exposed to media and other symbolic messages suggesting that minority groups violate "such traditional American values as individualism and self-reliance, the work ethic, obedience, and discipline" (Kinder and Sears 1981, 416). Symbolic/cultural factors, like negative attitudes toward minority groups, are indeed related to anti-immigration attitudes—and are often more powerful explanations than self/economic interests (e.g., Citrin et al. 1997; Burns and Gimpel 2000; Chandler and Tsai 2001; Malhorta et al. 2013; see Hainmueller and Hopkins 2014; Berg 2015).

This literature also highlights how propinquity may exacerbate, or militate against, antipathy. On the one hand, group threat theory holds that the presence of a minority group poses economic, political, and other threats to the dominant group (Blalock 1967). For example, drawing partly on group threat theory, Quillian (1995) finds that European countries with higher proportions of non-European Economic Community immigrants have higher levels of anti-immigrant prejudice. On the other hand, interpersonal contact with minorities—depending on various conditions—may lead to greater tolerance (Allport [1954] 1979). For instance, McLaren (2003) finds that Europeans who report having minority friends have more favorable attitudes toward immigration. Some earlier studies of U.S. immigration opinion have also focused on contact with *minorities*, rather than immigrants per se; in fact, Ha (2010, 31) suggests that whites may view Hispanics and Asians as proxies for immigrants in the U.S.

Recent scholarship highlights political, social-psychological, and other dimensions of immigration opinion. To move past group threat theory and further specify the "conditions" of symbolic politics theory, Hopkins (2010, 43, 40) proposes the "politicized places hypothesis," which suggests anti-immigrant hostility is a product of "sudden demographic changes" coupled with the politicization of immigration issues. Some research also examines the ways in which immigration opinion is shaped by the immigrant group—or its perceived characteristics, or both—in question (Hainmueller and Hopkins 2015; Flores and Schachter 2018).

Despite the importance of this literature, it is empirically difficult to establish major theories' causal directions (Fussell 2014; Berg 2015), as some research relies on one attitude predicting another in a single cross-sectional survey or a few cross-sectional surveys (see, e.g., Wilson 2001, 495; Malhorta et al. 2013, 395 for discussions). To address these and other causal issues, reviews of the literature recommend using longitudinal, panel, or experimental data, or a combination (Ceobnau and Escandell 2010; Fussell 2014; Hainmueller and Hopkins 2014), as some studies have done (e.g., Hopkins 2010; Hainmueller and Hopkins 2015; Schachter 2016). Though the present study cannot make any definitive claims to causality, we focus on often overlooked generation-related factors, which are assumed to precede policy attitudes and attitudes toward out-groups based on symbolic politics/racism theory (see Sears and Funk 1999) in a repeated cross-sectional context.

Generational/Cohort Divides

Generational or cohort divides have long been a source of theoretical interest (e.g., Mannheim [1927] 1952; Ryder 1965). Suggesting that generations span about 30 years, Mannheim ([1927] 1952) argues that generations are structural locations in society akin to class positions: like individuals in class positions, individuals in a generation may share experiences but may nevertheless express varying degrees of consciousness and social bonds with one another (288–92). He further distinguishes generation location from "*generation as an actuality*," with the latter as one "where a concrete bond is created between members of a generation by their being exposed to the social and intellectual symptoms of a process of dynamic de-stabilization" (Mannheim ([1927] 1952, 303). Ryder (1965) focuses on the concept of a cohort, defining it as "an aggregate of individuals (within some population definition) who experienced the same event within the same time interval" (845) and arguing it is a "structural category with the same kind of analytic utility as a variable like social class" (847).

Prior research has examined generational/cohort and other divides in attitudes toward government spending (e.g., MacManus 1996; Street and Cossman 2006), trust (e.g., Clark and Eisenstein 2013), and tolerance (e.g., Stouffer 1955; Firebaugh and Davis 1988; Quillian 1996; Schwadel and Garneau 2014), among other topics (see Fosse and Winship 2019 for a review). Some of this research points to differences between the "Greatest generation," which was born around 1930, and its counterparts (e.g., Clark and Eisenstein 2013; Street and Cossman 2006; Fullerton and Dixon 2010). Particularly relevant to the present research are studies focusing on tolerance of out-groups: whereas some of these studies find that tolerance is most pronounced among younger cohorts over time (Firebaugh and Davis 1988), which is partly due to their educational levels (Quillian 1996), other research finds that (political) tolerance is most pronounced among the Baby Boom generation (Schwadel and Garneau 2014). Research using GSS panel data between 2004 and 2016 suggests that early socialization helps to explain racial, civil liberties, and other attitudes, albeit with variation (Kiley and Vaisey 2020, 490).

Contemporary scholarship has especially focused on the "Millennial generation" (e.g., Medenica 2018; Ross and Rouse 2015; Rouse and Ross 2018). Building on extant theory, Rouse and Ross (2018, 4) argue that Millennials share a "core persona," furthermore stating that it is "as real and relevant as race and gender in understanding group differences." These researchers empirically define the Millennial generation as those born from the early 1980s to the late 1990s, noting that this cohort is distinct from its earlier-born predecessors in its diversity, digital interconnectedness, and high levels of education and student loan debt (Rouse and Ross 2018, 28–29, 48). Among the "formative events and trends" Millennials have experienced, according to Rouse and Ross (2018, 28–29), are the terrorist attacks on the U.S. on September 11th, 2001, "governance failures" such as those in the wake of Hurricane Katrina (2005), and the 2007–8 economic crisis. Along with this generation's diversity, these experiences have helped to promote shared "values of equality, fairness, respect for diversity and tolerance for differences" as well as "cosmopolitan and collectivist worldviews" (Rouse and Ross 2018, 30). The empirical analyses of Rouse and Ross (2018) have indeed uncovered generational divides in attitudes between Millennials and non-Millennials. We now turn to whether these generational divides extend to immigration policy attitudes.

Generational/Cohort Divides in Immigration Policy Attitudes

There is little research focusing on generational divides in U.S. immigration policy attitudes. Some research on immigration policy attitudes includes cohorts mainly as control variables. For example, Espenshade and Hempstead (1996, table A1) find that the 18–24 and 45–54-year-old age groups expressed greater tolerance of immigration than their 25–44-year-old counterparts, but these differences were not significant after controlling for economic, cultural, and other factors (table A8). Using generalized ordered logit models on 2004–16 GSS data linked to county-level data, Amaral et al. (2019) similarly incorporate cohorts as controls, finding that the 18–24-year-old age group generally expresses more pro-immigration policy attitudes than their older counterparts. The statistically significant difference between this group and 25–44-year olds holds in the face of controls of racial resentment and other factors (Amaral et al. 2019, tables A1 and A2), but is less consistently significant in other models between 2008 and 2016 (table A4).

Other research focuses more squarely on the immigration policy divide between Millennials and non-Millennials. Using survey data from 2015/16, Rouse and Ross (2018, 134–35) find that, on average, Millennials express greater tolerance toward immigrants than non-Millennials. Non-Millennials also seem to support stricter federal immigration policy than Millennials on average (Rouse and Ross 2018). On neither set of issues, however, do Rouse and Ross (2018) examine whether these differences are attributable to other factors or disaggregate non-Millennial cohorts; instead, they focus on accounting for variation in immigration attitudes *among* Millennials (272–73). Using logit analyses on 2008 American National Election Study (ANES) data, Ross and Rouse (2015, table 2) find a main effect of the Millennial generation on immigrant intolerance and an interaction effect between the Millennial generation and a measure of economic self-interest. They interpret these and other findings as supportive of their main hypothesis about the greater tolerance of Millennials (Ross and Rouse 2015, 1376).

Still other research focuses on broader generational divides in immigration attitudes, using different strategies to address the previously noted identification problem in APC research: these strategies include specifying theoretical mechanisms associated with cohorts or periods (see Fosse and Winship 2019 for a review of this and other strategies), using hierarchical age-period-cohort (HAPC) models with random effects (Yang and Land 2006, 2008), or "transforming at least one of the age, period, or cohort variables so that its relationship to others is nonlinear," or both (Yang and Land 2006, 83). For example, Coenders and Scheepers (1998) derive hypotheses from ethnic conflict theory and proxy cohort with such factors as immigration and unemployment levels, finding positive effects of these variables from people's "formative years" on support of "ethnic discrimination" in the Netherlands between 1979 and 1993, net of period and age effects (Coenders and Scheepers 1998). Employing a similar analytic strategy on (West) German data between 1980 and 2000, Coenders and Scheepers (2008) find a positive effect of unemployment levels during people's formative years on their "resistance to the social integration" of foreigners and guest workers, net of period and age effects. Wilkes and Corrigall-Brown (2011) show that unemployment levels help account for the random variation across cohorts and periods in a cross-classified multilevel analysis of Canadians' immigration attitudes between 1987 and 2008. Research in Europe using HAPC models on repeated cross-sectional surveys reveals that unemployment during labor market entry accounts for the random variation in anti-immigrant sentiment across cohorts (Gorodzeisky and Semyonov 2018). Another multilevel study in Europe finds an interaction among cohort, education, and a country-level measure of far-right voting on immigration attitudes, with the researchers noting that "the combined effect of cohort and education diminishes for younger cohorts socialised in the context of a strong far-right anti-immigrant presence" (McLaren and Paterson 2020, 665).

Theoretical Framework

Building on the aforementioned literatures, our theoretical framework recognizes the importance of generations or cohorts (Mannheim, [1927] 1952; Ryder 1965). In particular, Millennials and non-Millennials should differ in their immigration policy attitudes. As prior research has shown, Millennials generally express more pro-immigration attitudes than their (older) counterparts, ceteris paribus (e.g., Ross and Rouse 2015). As such, we hypothesize:

H1: *Millennial cohorts will be less likely to oppose immigration policy than other cohorts, all else equal.*

However, the hypothesized cohort divides might be due to aging or the temporal context, or both. Symbolic politics/racism theory emphasizes the importance of age: policy attitudes are partly a function of pre-adulthood socialization, which may be stable over the life course (e.g., Sears and Funk 1999), and there is support for this view for particular attitudes (Kiley and Vaisey 2020). Mannheim and others also recognize the importance of time periods. Mannheim ([1927 1952) alludes to a cycle between generations and institutions: as institutions change so do people; as people change, so do institutions. Some repeated cross-section research finds that support for U.S. immigration policy has increased in recent times (Amaral et al. 2019), but other research using panel data from several countries suggests that there is some stability in immigration attitudes over time (Kustov et al. 2019). Rouse and Ross (2018) point to the 2007–8 economic crisis as formative for Millennials, but economic conditions may be formative more generally if the research on Europe and Canada above is any indication.

Furthermore, Millennials are distinct from their earlier predecessors in several ways (e.g., Rouse and Ross 2018). These distinctions and other factors may confound the relationship between cohort and immigration policy attitudes. One such difference is Millennials' diversity (Rouse and Ross 2018): factors like foreign-born status, race, and ethnicity (e.g., Bobo and Kluegel 1993; Ha 2010) may shape attitudes toward immigration policy. Another difference is the Millennial generation's experience of higher education (e.g., Kustov, Laaker, and Reller 2019; Reny, Collingwood, and Valenzuela 2019).

Finally, the effects of cohort, age, time period, and other factors may differ depending on whether the attitudinal outcome is conceptualized as "opposition" or "support" relative to a neutral viewpoint (see Fullerton and Dixon 2010). This is rooted in research arguing that attitudes are not necessarily symmetrical (Cacioppo, Gardner, and Berntson 1997; Jordan 1965), and independent variables may have asymmetrical associations with dependent variables (Lieberson 1985, chap. 4). For instance, Fullerton and Dixon (2009) find that education is significantly associated with less opposition to "welfare" spending, but it is not significantly associated with a lack of support. The preceding has implications for the immigration policy attitude we examine here, which is measured as a five-category ordinal variable, with answers ranging from immigration should be "reduced a lot" to "increased a lot" (relative to "remain the same"). Although Millennials may be less *opposed* (e.g., "reduced a lot") to immigration policy than their counterparts (**H1**), they may not necessarily be more *supportive* (e.g., "increased a lot"). Similarly, some factors that may work against *oppositional* immigration policy attitudes, such as education, may not be associated with increased *support* of immigration policy.

Data

To test expectations derived from the aforementioned theoretical framework, we use data from the General Social Survey (GSS) (Smith et al. 2019) collected between 2004 and 2018 (biannually). The GSS is a widely used survey of people aged 18 and older "living in noninstitutionalized arrangements within the United States" based on full probability, multistage sampling, and beginning in 2006, it included Spanish speakers in addition to English speakers according to the codebook (Smith et al. 2019, viii). We limit our sample and analysis to 2004 to 2018 due to the availability of the dependent variable. The number of respondents asked this question is 12,081, about 2.5 percent of which had missing data on the dependent variable, giving us a potential sample size of 11,773. After dropping missing cases on the independent variables, our final sample size is 10,155.

Dependent Variable

The dependent variable in the present study is based on the following question: "Do you think the number of immigrants to America nowadays should be . . ." (GSS Variable: LETIN1A). The response options are "increased a lot," "increased a little," "remain the same as it is," "reduced a little," and "reduced a lot" (Smith et al. 2019). Prior research has used this question (e.g., Aramal et al., 2019) or a similar one, whether from the American National Election Study (e.g., Ross and Rouse 2015) or another survey data set (e.g., Espenshade and Hempstead 1996).

Major Independent Variables

Prior research has empirically defined the Millennial generation as those born between 1980 and 1998 (Rouse and Ross 2018, table 2.1, 36). Other research, especially in the APC context, uses five-year intervals for cohorts (e.g., Coenders and Scheepers 2008; Fullerton and Dixon 2010; Wilkes and Corrigall-Brown 2011; Gorodzeisky and Semyonov

2018); still other research uses 10-year intervals (e.g., McLaren and Paterson 2020). Following the more common strategy in APC research, we code birth year into five-year birth cohorts in this study (except the oldest and youngest cohorts due to group size). As a result, we focus on three approximate Millennial cohorts (1980–84, 1985–89, and 1990–2000), recognizing that the latter birth year grouping by necessity includes a (very small) group of what some may call "Generation Z" (Dimock 2019). We assess the impact of this group of cohort variables in order to test differences between Millennials and older cohorts.

Our other major independent variables are *age* (in years), *age squared*, and *year* (of the survey). Our incorporation of the age squared term follows Yang and Land's (2006) strategy of addressing the identification problem noted earlier. Furthermore, Fosse and Winship (2019, 470–71) argue that "although the linear effects of an APC model are not identifiable, several other quantities are. First and most importantly, the nonlinear effects, that is, the deviations from the linear effects, are fully identifiable." We also considered the possibility of a nonlinear period effect (year + year-sq.), but we found that a single, continuous term best captured the pattern in the data.

Controls

Our analysis controls for many of the variables that Rouse and Ross (2018, 35–38, especially table 2.1) argue constitute the "Millennial persona" and that are rooted in other theories and research. From the perspective of theories of (group) interests (e.g., Bobo and Kluegel 1993), *foreign-born* (= 1, 0 = otherwise) individuals may be most likely to support immigration policy and least likely to oppose it; so, too, may *nonwhites* (= 1, 0 = otherwise; based on the first race mentioned [GSS Variable: RACECEN1]) and *Latinx* (= 1, 0 = otherwise) [Ha 2010]. We also include *education* (in years of schooling), and although we expect education to mitigate opposition to immigration policy, we are unclear whether it will be associated with support. To account for economic considerations, we include (family) *income* in constant dollars (logged). We also include *conservative ideology* (1 = extremely liberal, 7 = extremely conservative) and *Republican Party ID* (0 = strong Democrat and 6 = strong Republican, with "some other party" coded as independents = 3).

In addition to the aforementioned variables, we include other controls regularly included in existing research, such as *female* (= 1; male = 0), *married* (=1; otherwise = 0), *size of place* of residence (a series of binary variables ranging in size from open country to large cities). Regarding the latter, we expect opposition to immigration policy to be more pronounced in rural areas and less pronounced in cities. Finally, we also control for census *region* (a series of nine binary variables). We present descriptive statistics for the independent variables in table 4.1.

TABLE 4.1. Descriptive Statistics for Independent Variables in Models of Immigration Attitudes

	Mean/Pct	SD	Range
Age	47.76	17.18	18 to 89
Age-sq	2,576.14	1,757.53	324 to 7,921
Year	2,011.47	4.52	2004 to 2018
Cohort (ref. = 1915–1934)			
1935–39	4.06		0 to 1
1940–44	5.46		0 to 1
1945–49	7.24		0 to 1
1950–54	7.89		0 to 1
1955–59	9.93		0 to 1
1960–64	10.09		0 to 1
1965–69	9.17		0 to 1
1970–74	9.35		0 to 1
1975–79	9.02		0 to 1
1980–84 (Millennial 1)	9.55		0 to 1
1985–89 (Millennial 2)	7.16		0 to 1
1990–2000 (Millennial 3)	5.33		0 to 1
Female	54.28		0 to 1
Nonwhite	24.09		0 to 1
Latinx	12.15		0 to 1
Foreign Born	11.70		0 to 1
Married	45.18		0 to 1
Education	13.71	2.95	0 to 20
Log Income	9.95	1.11	5.42 to 11.95
Conservative Ideology	4.08	1.44	1 to 7
Republican Party ID	2.70	1.97	0 to 6
Region (ref. = New England)			
Middle Atlantic	11.13		0 to 1
East North Central	17.27		0 to 1
West North Central	6.42		0 to 1
South Atlantic	20.75		0 to 1
East South Central	6.06		0 to 1
West South Central	11.02		0 to 1

Table 4.1—*Continued*

	Mean/Pct	SD	Range
Mountain	8.29		0 to 1
Pacific	14.39		0 to 1
Size of Place (ref. = City, > 250,000)			
City, 50,000–250,000	16.61		0 to 1
Suburb, large city	20.75		0 to 1
Suburb, medium city	10.13		0 to 1
Unincorporated large city	8.84		0 to 1
Unincorporated medium city	8.45		0 to 1
City, 10,000–49,999	4.40		0 to 1
Town >2,500	3.99		0 to 1
Smaller Areas	1.01		0 to 1
Open Country	9.25		0 to 1

Method

Our analysis proceeds in several stages. We begin with bivariate analyses of immigration policy attitudes, noting how they vary across cohorts. Next, we examine age, period, and cohort differences in immigration attitudes with and without controls for other individual-level factors that have been found to shape public opinion. We do not, however, make use of hierarchical age-period-cohort models with random effects as some prior research discussed above has. Fosse and Winship (2019, 478) argue that hierarchical age-period-cohort models, which tend to include age and its square at level 1 and cohort and period variables at level 2, often yield cohort effects with "a zero overall slope." Rather, for this analysis, we make use of a categorical model described below within a fixed-effects framework.

The dependent variable in this study is ordinal, but for the multivariable analyses, ordinal logistic regression (i.e., cumulative logit with proportional odds) is not appropriate. This is because the parallel regression assumption—that is, the assumption that the effects of independent variables are the same across cutpoints of the dependent variable—is violated according to the Brant test. The coefficients for several of the cohort variables, in particular, vary across the cutpoint equations, which makes this traditional ordered model problematic.

For the regression analyses, we thus decided to use multinomial logit, which is equivalent to a lesser-known but useful ordered regression technique: nonparallel adjacent category logit (Fullerton 2009; Fullerton and Xu 2016). Whether one focuses on the baseline comparisons (multinomial logit) or the adjacent comparisons, it is the same model and the key advantage is that it relaxes the proportional odds assumption. In other words, the coefficients are free to vary across equations. In the context of public opinion research, this means that we do not have to assume that support for a policy or group is the mirror image of opposition. The model allows for asymmetries in the data, which is what we found in this study. We chose to focus on the adjacent comparisons in the presentation of results (see table 4.3) given the cohort patterns we observed. The most important gaps between Millennial and older cohorts in models with age, period, and cohort variables are located at the "opposition" end of the ordinal scale; we do not observe a similar cohort difference at the other end ("support"). In our discussion of the results below, we refer to the category of those who say that immigration should be "reduced a lot" as "strong opposition," those who say "reduced a little" as "weak opposition," those who say "increased a little" as "weak support," and those who say "increased a lot" as "strong support."

Results

We present the descriptive differences in immigration attitudes between cohorts based on a cross tabulation with the dependent variable in table 4.2. Across cohorts (from oldest to youngest), the percentage that are strong supporters of immigration ("increased a lot") has slightly increased. The three Millennial cohorts (1980–84, 1985–89, and 1990–2000) have the three highest percentages in the strong support ("increased a lot") and weak support ("increased a little") categories. Millennials have the three lowest percentages in the strong opposition ("reduced a lot") category and are among the lowest in the weak opposition ("reduced a little") category. On balance, the descriptive results support the view that respondents from Millennial cohorts are more liberal in their attitudes toward immigration than older cohorts. However, it will be important to disentangle potential cohort differences from aging and period effects. Therefore, we turn next to the results from multinomial logit models of immigration attitudes.

We present odds ratios from multinomial logit models of immigration attitudes in table 4.3. In Model 1, we only include age, age-squared,

TABLE 4.2. Cohort Differences in Immigration Attitudes in the U.S., 2004–2018

	"The number of immigrants to America nowadays should be":				
Cohort	Increased a lot (%)	Increased a little (%)	Remain the same (%)	Reduced a little (%)	Reduced a lot (%)
1915–34	3.07	10.75	32.76	22.01	31.40
1935–39	2.18	10.19	35.92	21.84	29.85
1940–44	3.25	11.37	32.67	24.19	28.52
1945–49	3.27	13.47	32.52	23.67	27.07
1950–54	4.87	8.86	34.08	24.59	27.59
1955–59	2.68	7.54	37.50	25.10	27.18
1960–64	4.20	9.07	37.66	24.49	24.59
1965–69	5.05	8.38	38.45	24.17	23.95
1970–74	5.16	9.80	38.57	24.55	21.92
1975–79	6.00	8.41	45.09	21.94	18.56
1980–84a	6.70	12.06	42.27	21.13	17.84
1985–89a	6.74	14.86	39.61	23.93	14.86
1990–2000a	7.58	15.16	45.84	20.15	11.28
Total	4.77	10.46	38.21	23.39	23.18

Note: N = 10,155.
a Millennial cohorts.

year, and cohort. The age, period, and cohort differences in immigration attitudes are limited to the "opposition" end of the ordinal scale. Older respondents have higher odds of strong opposition compared to weak opposition, although the relationship is nonlinear. Additionally, the odds of strong opposition (compared to weak opposition) have decreased over time: a standard deviation (4.5 year) change in time is associated with a decrease in the odds by a factor of 0.72, controlling for age and cohort. This yearly trend corresponds to prior research finding more pro-immigration views in more recent years of the GSS (Amaral et al. 2019; Yang and Mena 2019).

For cohort, the reference group is the oldest group (born prior to 1935). If Millennials are more liberal on immigration, then we would expect the odds ratios to be less than 1 for the comparison of strong opposition to weak opposition. Compared to the oldest cohort, the Millennial cohorts actually have greater odds of strong (vs. weak) opposition to immigration. The odds are greater by factors of between 9.14 and 12.92. In a model with only cohort variables (not shown here), those same odds ratios range from 0.39 to 0.59. These results indicate that Millennial cohorts are more supportive of immigration, but it

TABLE 4.3. Odds Ratios from Multinomial Logistic Regression

Models of Immigration Attitudes in the U.S., 2004–2018
(1 = Increased a lot, 2 = Increased a little, 3 = Remain same, 4 = Reduced a little,
5 = Reduced a lot)

	Model 1				Model 2			
	2 vs. 1	3 vs. 2	4 vs. 3	5 vs. 4.	2 vs. 1	3 vs. 2	4 vs. 3	5 vs. 4
Age	0.39	1.62	0.64	4.30**	0.22	2.15	0.72	4.45**
	(−1.12)	(0.93)	(−1.11)	(3.07)	(−1.76)	(1.43)	(−0.79)	(3.10)
Age-sq.	2.45	0.53	1.23	0.58	3.73	0.41*	1.04	0.56
	(1.33)	(−1.60)	(0.66)	(−1.58)	(1.91)	(−2.15)	(0.12)	(−1.66)
Year	0.99	0.88	0.96	0.72***	1.02	0.88	0.97	0.72***
	(−0.08)	(−1.37)	(−0.55)	(−4.25)	(0.11)	(−1.44)	(−0.38)	(−4.22)
Cohort								
1915–34								
1935–39	1.61	0.97	0.86	1.37	1.80	0.97	0.87	1.36
	(0.88)	(−0.11)	(−0.68)	(1.34)	(1.07)	(−0.10)	(−0.63)	(1.28)
1940–44	1.34	0.69	0.99	1.44	1.37	0.68	0.98	1.47
	(0.48)	(−1.03)	(−0.02)	(1.28)	(0.50)	(−1.08)	(−0.09)	(1.33)
1945–49	1.70	0.53	0.93	1.76	1.52	0.55	0.91	1.86
	(0.71)	(−1.46)	(−0.22)	(1.60)	(0.56)	(−1.36)	(−0.29)	(1.74)
1950–54	0.78	0.78	0.87	2.18	0.71	0.84	0.88	2.37*
	(−0.28)	(−0.47)	(−0.35)	(1.85)	(−0.38)	(−0.34)	(−0.32)	(2.03)
1955–59	1.24	0.95	0.76	2.71*	1.21	0.99	0.76	2.99*
	(0.21)	(−0.08)	(−0.60)	(2.03)	(0.18)	(−0.01)	(−0.59)	(2.20)
1960–64	0.95	0.75	0.69	3.24*	0.89	0.78	0.69	3.58*
	(−0.04)	(−0.41)	(−0.72)	(2.09)	(−0.10)	(−0.36)	(−0.71)	(2.24)
1965–69	0.71	0.80	0.61	4.21*	0.62	0.85	0.64	4.79*
	(−0.27)	(−0.29)	(−0.84)	(2.26)	(−0.36)	(−0.21)	(−0.75)	(2.44)
1970–74	0.77	0.68	0.57	5.10*	0.66	0.74	0.61	5.89*
	(−0.18)	(−0.45)	(−0.86)	(2.29)	(−0.29)	(−0.34)	(−0.74)	(2.47)
1975–79	0.52	0.93	0.40	6.64*	0.42	1.05	0.42	7.68*
	(−0.41)	(−0.07)	(−1.27)	(2.40)	(−0.54)	(0.05)	(−1.18)	(2.55)
1980–84a	0.61	0.63	0.38	9.14*	0.47	0.74	0.40	10.35**
	(−0.29)	(−0.45)	(−1.23)	(2.55)	(−0.44)	(−0.28)	(−1.14)	(2.67)
1985–89a	0.69	0.51	0.43	9.34*	0.52	0.59	0.45	10.52*
	(−0.20)	(−0.61)	(−0.98)	(2.36)	(−0.35)	(−0.46)	(−0.91)	(2.46)
1990–2000a	0.56	0.64	0.30	12.92*	0.40	0.71	0.30	14.20*
	(−0.29)	(−0.37)	(−1.27)	(2.44)	(−0.45)	(−0.27)	(−1.26)	(2.49)
−2LL	28553.86				26981.94			
AIC	28681.86				27317.94			
BIC	29144.31				28531.87			
Pseudo R2	0.02				0.07			
Control Variables	No				Yes			

Note: N = 10,155. *p < .05, **p < .01, ***p < .001.
a Millennial cohorts.

TABLE 4.4. Average Discrete Change Coefficients for Millennial Cohorts

(1 = Increased a lot, 2 = Increased a little, 3 = Remain same, 4 = Reduced a little, 5 = Reduced a lot)

Millennial Cohorts	1	2	3	4	5
1980–1984	0.04	−0.01	−0.12	−0.19***	0.28*
	(0.40)	(−0.10)	(−1.06)	(−3.75)	(1.99)
1985–1989	0.04	0.00	−0.16	−0.18***	0.29
	(0.37)	(0.03)	(−1.30)	(−3.57)	(1.88)
1990–2000	0.06	−0.01	−0.14	−0.20***	0.29
	(0.39)	(−0.08)	(−0.96)	(−4.68)	(1.62)

Note: $N = 10,155$. *$p < .05$, **$p < .01$, ***$p < .001$. The results are based on Model 2 from table 4.3.

appears to be due to the fact that they are younger on average or experiencing key life events during a more liberal time period, or both.

The addition of control variables—that is, all of the variables listed in the "Controls" subsection earlier (e.g., foreign-born status, race, ethnicity, education, and so forth)—in Model 2 does not change this picture (results for control variables are available upon request). The odds ratios for the Millennial cohorts remain statistically significant. Odds ratios are not comparable across models due to model differences in residual variance (Karlson et al. 2012), but the odds ratios are actually larger in Model 2.

One measure that is comparable across models is the average discrete change, which is a global measure capturing the average difference in predicted probabilities associated with a change in X. We present the average discrete change results for the Millennial cohort variables in table 4.4. The results are virtually identical for the Millennial cohort variables with or without the controls added to the model. The results in table 4.4 are based on the full model with controls in table 4.3 (Model 2). On average, the Millennial cohorts have a predicted probability of strong opposition to immigration that is 0.28 to 0.29 higher than the oldest cohort, although the coefficient is only significant for the first Millennial cohort (1980 to 1984). The Millennial cohorts also have significantly lower predicted probabilities of weak opposition than the oldest cohort, and these coefficients range from −0.18 to −0.20. Controlling for life cycle and period differences (and the influences of control variables), Millennials display less liberal attitudes toward immigration, and the differences are both statistically and substantively significant. Although no APC model is full proof, the results from this study suggest that we need to rethink the idea that these attitudes among Millennials represent a cohort effect.

Discussion/Conclusion

Immigration policy attitudes and seeming generational divides in public opinion are the focus of a good deal of prior research. Despite the theoretical and political import of each of these topics, these topics have more commonly been examined in isolation from one another. Synthesizing extant theory and research, including the relatively few studies explicitly examining age, period, and cohort effects of immigration policy attitudes in a repeated cross-sectional context particularly outside the U.S., our study analyzed public opinion toward immigration in the U.S. between 2004 and 2018. Our focus was on understanding the extent to which Millennials are more supportive of immigration policy than other cohorts, particularly after accounting for the effects of age and time. Our findings offer important nuance to multiple literatures and suggest possibilities for further research.

Consistent with claims that Millennials are more liberal than other cohorts (Ross and Rouse 2015; Rouse and Ross 2018), descriptive evidence from the GSS between 2004 and 2018 revealed that support for a more inclusive immigration policy—and opposition to a more restrictive immigration policy—was particularly pronounced among Millennial cohorts. Yet, contrary to our expectation, multivariable analyses including age and time reveal few differences between Millennial and other cohorts in their attitudes toward immigration policy. A difference we found was one of degree—that of, strong versus weak opposition—and it was *not* Millennial cohorts who were on the more inclusive end of this spectrum in comparison to older cohorts. The sum total of our results provides less support for cohort effects than for age or period effects, or both. Compared to some research on generational differences with a focus on Millennials (Ross and Rouse 2015; Rouse and Ross 2018), this interpretation more closely resonates with some studies on immigration attitudes and other topics that point to life cycle and other processes as explanations (Kiley and Vaisey 2020; Kustov et al. 2019).

Nevertheless, there are limitations to our study and interpretations. To begin, our study speaks to immigration policy in general, but not toward particular groups of immigrants, which may differ (Hainmueller and Hopkins 2015; Hellwig and Sinno 2017; Flores and Schachter 2018). Moreover, while extant theory and research suggest several explanations for immigration policy attitudes, including group threat and interpersonal contact, our focus on APC processes and data limitations precluded incorporating some of these explanations into our theoretical framework. In addition, extant theory and research suggest different conceptual definitions and measures of cohorts, including the length of their intervals (e.g., Dimock 2019; Mannheim [1927] 1952; McLaren and Paterson 2020; Rouse and Ross 2018). Although we generally used the five-year intervals often employed in prior APC research, at least a small part of our data included what some view as a new generation, Z (Dimock 2019), about which we researchers will know more as additional data is collected in the future. Finally, the use of age-period-cohort models continues to be debated (Fosse and Winship 2019). Based on current and previous research (Fullerton and Dixon 2009, 2010), these debates should be extended to consider asymmetries in people's attitudes, such as whether their opposition to immigration is relatively weak or strong.

In conclusion, the answer to the question posed in the title of this chapter appears to have less to do with generational divides than with time periods or aging, or both. The results from this study provide an early indication that Millennial cohorts may be more liberal on immigration because they grew up in a more liberal time and are still relatively young. Only time will tell if this initial support for immigration diminishes as they age and changes with the times or persists throughout their lives as a true "cohort effect."

REFERENCES

Allport, G. (1954) 1979. *The Nature of Prejudice*. Reading, MA: Addison-Wesley.
Amaral, E. F. L., P. Mitchell, and G. Marquez-Velarde. 2019. "Factors Associated with Attitudes toward U.S. Immigration, 2004–2016." *Open Science Framework*, February 22. http://doi.org/10.31219/osf.io/nkry6
Berg, J. A. 2015. "Explaining Attitudes toward Immigrants and Immigration Policy: A Review of the Theoretical Literature." *Sociology Compass* 9 (1): 23–34.
Blalock, H. M., Jr. 1967. *Toward a Theory of Minority-Group Relations*. New York: Capricorn Books.

Bobo, L., and J. R. Kluegel. 1993. "Opposition to Race-Targeting: Self-Interest, Stratification Ideology, or Racial Attitudes?" *American Sociological Review* 58 (4): 443–64.

Burns, P., and J. G. Gimpel. 2000. "Economic Insecurity, Prejudicial Stereotypes, and Public Opinion on Immigration Policy." *Political Science Quarterly* 115 (2): 201–25.

Cacioppo, J. T., W. L. Gardner, and G. G. Berntson. 1997. "Beyond Bipolar Conceptualizations and Measures: The Case of Attitudes and Evaluative Space." *Personality and Social Psychology Review* 1 (1): 3–25.

Ceobnau, A. M., and X. Escandell. 2010. "Comparative Analyses of Public Attitudes toward Immigrants and Immigration Using Multinational Survey Data: A Review of Theories and Research." *Annual Review of Sociology* 36: 309–28.

Chandler, C. A., and Y-m. Tsai. 2001. "Social Factors Influencing Immigration Attitudes: An Analysis of Data from the General Social Survey." *Social Science Journal* 38: 177–88.

Citrin, J., D. P. Green, C. Muste, and C. Wong. 1997. "Public Opinion toward Immigration Reform: The Role of Economic Motivations." *Journal of Politics* 59 (3): 858–81.

Clark, A. K., and M. A. Eisenstein. 2013. "Interpersonal Trust: An Age-Period-Cohort Analysis Revisited." *Social Science Research* 42: 361–75.

Coenders, M., and P. Scheepers. 1998. "Support for Ethnic Discrimination in the Netherlands 1979–1993: Effects of Period, Cohort, and Individual Characteristics." *European Sociological Review* 14 (4): 405–22.

Coenders, M., and P. Scheepers. 2008. "Changes in Resistance to the Social Integration of Foreigners in Germany 1980–2000: Individual and Contextual Determinants." *Journal of Ethnic and Migration Studies* 34 (1): 1–26.

Dimock, M. 2019. "Defining Generations: Where Millennials End and Generation Z Begins." Pew Research Center, January 17. http://www.pewresearch.org/fact-tank/2019/01/17/where-millennials-end-and-generation-z-begins/

Espenshade, T. J., and C. A. Calhoun. 1993. "An Analysis of Public Opinion toward Undocumented Immigration." *Population Research and Policy Review* 12 (3): 189–224.

Espenshade, T. J., and K. Hempstead. 1996. "Contemporary American Attitudes toward U.S. Immigration." *International Migration Review* 30 (2): 535–70.

Firebaugh, G. 1997. *Analyzing Repeated Surveys.* Thousand Oaks, CA: Sage.

Firebaugh, G., and K. E. Davis. 1988. "Trends in Antiblack Prejudice, 1972–1984: Region and Cohort Effects." *American Journal of Sociology* 94 (2): 251–72.

Flores, R. D., and A. Schachter. 2018. "Who Are the 'Illegals'? The Social Construction of Illegality in the United States." *American Sociological Review* 83 (5): 839–68.

Fosse, E., and C. Winship. 2019. "Analyzing Age-Period-Cohort Data: A Review and Critique." *Annual Review of Sociology* 45: 467–92.

Fullerton, A. S. 2009. "A Conceptual Framework for Ordered Logistic Regression Models." *Sociological Methods & Research* 38: 306–47.

Fullerton, A. S., and J. C. Dixon. 2009. "Racialization, Asymmetry, and the Context of Welfare Attitudes in the American States." *Journal of Political and Military Sociology* 37 (1): 95–120.

Fullerton, A. S., and J. C. Dixon. 2010. "Generational Conflict or Methodological Artifact? Reconsidering the Relationship between Age and Policy Attitudes in the U.S., 1984–2008." *Public Opinion Quarterly* 74 (4): 643–73.

Fullerton, A. S., and J. Xu. 2016. *Ordered Regression Models: Parallel, Partial, and Non-Parallel Alternatives*. Boca Raton, FL: Chapman & Hall/CRC Press.

Fussell, E. 2014. "Warmth of the Welcome: Attitudes toward Immigrants and Immigration Policy in the United States." *Annual Review of Sociology* 40: 479–98.

Gorodzeisky, A., and M. Semyonov. 2018. "Competitive Threat and Temporal Change in Anti-Immigrant Sentiment: Insights from a Hierarchical Age-Period-Cohort Model." *Social Science Research* 73: 31–44.

Ha, S. E. 2010. "The Consequences of Multiracial Contexts on Public Attitudes toward Immigration." *Political Research Quarterly* 63 (1): 29–42.

Hainmueller, J., and D. J. Hopkins. 2014. "Public Attitudes toward Immigration." *Annual Review of Political Science* 17: 225–49.

Hainmueller, J., and D. J. Hopkins. 2015. "The Hidden American Immigration Consensus: A Conjoint Analysis of Attitudes toward Immigrants." *American Journal of Political Science* 59 (3): 529–48.

Hellwig, T., and A. Sinno. 2017. "Different Groups, Different Threats: Public Attitudes toward Immigrants." *Journal of Ethnic and Migration Studies* 43 (3): 339–58.

Hopkins, D. J. 2010. "Politicized Places: Explaining Where and When Immigrants Provoke Local Opposition." *American Political Science Review* 104 (1): 40–60.

Jordan, N. 1965. "The 'Asymmetry' of 'Liking' and 'Disliking': A Phenomenon Meriting Further Reflection and Research." *Public Opinion Quarterly* 29 (2): 315–22.

Karlson, K. B., A. Holm, and R. Breen. 2012. "Comparing Regression Coefficients between Same-Sample Nested Models Using Logit and Probit: A New Method." *Sociological Methodology* 42: 286–313.

Kiley, K., and S. Vaisey. 2020. "Measuring Stability and Change in Personal Culture Using Panel Data." *American Sociological Review* 85 (3): 477–506.

Kinder, D. R., and D. O. Sears. 1981. "Prejudice and Politics: Symbolic Racism versus Racial Threats to the Good Life." *Journal of Personality and Social Psychology* 40 (3): 414–31.

Kustov, A., D. Laaker, and C. Reller. 2019. "The Stability of Immigration Attitudes: Evidence and Implications." SSRN, May 1. http://dx.doi.org/10.2139/ssrn.332 2121

Lieberson, S. 1985. *Making It Count: The Improvement of Social Research and Theory*. Berkeley: University of California Press.

MacManus, S. A. 1996. *Young v. Old: Generational Combat in the 21st Century*. Boulder: Westview.

Malhorta, N., Y. Margalit, and C. H. Mo. 2013. "Economic Explanations for Opposition to Immigration Opinion: Distinguishing between Prevalence and Conditional Impact." *American Journal of Political Science* 57 (2): 391–410.

Mannheim, K. (1927) 1952. "The Problem of Generations." In *Karl Mannheim: Essays*, edited by Paul Kecskemeti, 276–322. London: Routledge.

McLaren, L. M. 2003. "Anti-Immigrant Prejudice in Europe: Contact, Threat Perception, and Preferences for the Exclusion of Immigrants." *Social Forces* 81 (3): 909–36.

McLaren, L. M., and I. Paterson. 2020. "Generational Change and Attitudes toward Immigration." *Journal of Ethnic and Migration Studies* 46 (3): 665–82.

Medenica, V. E. 2018. "Millennials and Race in the 2016 Election." *Journal of Race, Ethnicity, and Politics* 3: 55–76.

Pew Research Center. 2011. *The Generation Gap and the 2012 Election*. November 3. http://www.pewresearch.org/wp-content/uploads/sites/4/legacy-pdf/11-3-11-Ge nerations-Release.pdf

Pew Research Center. 2015. "The Whys and Hows of Generations Research." September 30. http://www.people-press.org/2015/09/03/the-whys-and-hows-of-gen erations-research/

Quillian, L. 1995. "Prejudice as a Response to Perceived Group Threat: Population Composition and Anti-Immigrant and Racial Prejudice in Europe." *American Sociological Review* 60 (4): 586–611.

Quillian, L. 1996. "Group Threat and Regional Change in Attitudes toward African Americans." *American Journal of Sociology* 102 (3): 816–60.

Reny, T. T., L. Collingwood, and A. A. Valenzuela. 2019. "Vote Switching in the 2016 Election: How Racial and Immigration Attitudes, Not Economics, Explain Shifts in White Voting." *Public Opinion Quarterly* 83 (1): 91–113.

Ross, A. D., and S. M. Rouse. 2015. "Economic Uncertainty, Job Threat, and the Resiliency of the Millennial Generation's Attitudes toward Immigration." *Social Science Quarterly* 96 (5): 1363–79.

Rouse, S. M., and A. D. Ross. 2018. *The Politics of Millennials: Political Beliefs and Policy Preferences of America's Most Diverse Generation*. Ann Arbor: University of Michigan Press.

Ryder, N. B. 1965. "The Cohort as a Concept in the Study of Social Change." *American Sociological Review* 30 (6): 843–61.

Schachter, A. 2016. "From 'Different' to 'Similar': An Experimental Approach to Understanding Assimilation." *American Sociological Review* 81 (5): 981–1013.

Scheve, K. F., and M. T. Slaughter. 2001. "Labor Market Competition and Individual Preferences over Immigration Policy." *Review of Economics and Statistics* 83 (1): 133–45.

Schwadel, P., and C. R. H. Garneau. 2014. "An Age-Period-Cohort Analysis of Political Tolerance in the United States." *Sociological Quarterly* 55 (2): 421–52.

Sears, D. O., and C. L. Funk. 1999. "Evidence of the Long-Term Persistence of Adults' Political Predispositions." *Journal of Politics* 61 (1): 1–28.

Smith, T. W., M. Davern, J. Freese, and S. L. Morgan. 2019. General Social Surveys, 1972–2018 [machine readable data file]. Chicago: NORC at the University of Chicago [producer and distributor]. Data obtained through the GSS Data Explorer (gssdataexplorer.norc.org).

Stouffer, S. 1955. *Communism, Conformity, and Civil Liberties*. New York: Doubleday.

Street, D., and J. S. Cossman. 2006. "Greatest Generation or Greedy Geezers? Social Spending Preferences and the Elderly." *Social Problems* 53: 75–96.

Wilkes, R., and C. Corrigall-Brown. 2011. "Explaining Time Trends in Public Opinion: Attitudes toward Immigration and Immigrants." *International Journal of Comparative Sociology* 52 (1–2): 79–99.

Wilson, T. 2001. "Americans' Views on Immigration Policy: Testing the Role of Threatened Group Interests." *Sociological Perspectives* 44 (4): 485–501.

Yang, Y., and K. C. Land. 2006. "A Mixed Models Approach to the Age-Period-Cohort Analysis of Repeated Cross-Section Surveys, with an Application to Data on Trends in Verbal Test Scores." *Sociological Methodology* 36: 75–97.

Yang, Y., and K. C. Land. 2008. "Age-Period-Cohort Analysis of Repeated Cross-Section Surveys: Fixed or Random Effects?" *Sociological Methods & Research* 36: 297–326.

Yang, P., and M. Mena. 2019. "Recent Trends in American Attitudes toward the Level of Immigration." *Ethnic Studies Review* 42 (1): 25–36.

5 | Generational Attitudes toward Drug Policies in the United States

Leah Hutton Blumenfeld

The legalization of marijuana for recreational purposes is a relatively new area of policy, and "the changing legal landscape has coincided with a dramatic increase in public support for legalization" (Geiger and Gramlich 2019). Numerous explanations for this shift in attitudes exist. As more and more states in the union liberalize their drug laws, many have argued that this represents, or is a direct result of, generational differences in attitudes toward marijuana use. Much of the literature on generations focuses on drug use by generation, suggesting that a more relaxed attitude toward drug use has emerged from Gen X onward, while the older generations remain in favor of prohibition. One model of generational learning suggests a linear process whereby each subsequent generation receives instruction from the previous and carries on the same values. These values may be revised or liberalized, but the relationship is unidirectional. Another model suggests rebellion against the previous generation and adoption of different and often more radical values, a defiance of what is taught, and an assertion of a different identity. The subject of marijuana seems to defy both of these models.

Have attitudes shifted overall, or do changes in the laws reflect that a new generation has taken charge of them? This chapter will attempt to show that change is not necessarily a result of generational replacement alone but can also be explained by changing attitudes within and across generations. While the context of one's socialization toward drug use creates views that endure, new contexts and cross-generational interactions can also produce new views and thus new and different

139

policy. I do not seek to redefine generations or cohorts here, and I draw upon existing delineations of age groups. This chapter explores the idea of co-generational learning and change, and will assert that context remains essential; the historical and informational setting matters. Further, I will suggest that age cohorts might influence one another's values in a bidirectional pattern. While each age group may process new information from their own point of view, the content and larger framing of that information can influence attitudes cross-generationally. The old learn from new information; they may even take from the young's interpretation of that information as much as the young learn from the old's wisdom.

Background: Drug Use, Drug Laws, and Socialization in the United States

To understand generational attitudes toward legalization we must consider some of the context and history of prohibition. "Drugs are both physical substances with pharmacological effects and cultural icons with values and behaviors linked to them by the society in which they are found" (Gaines and Kraska 1997, 5). This is true of the United States and its relationship to marijuana and other drugs. The advent of organic chemistry made possible the isolation of morphine from poppies and cocaine from coca leaves in the mid-19th century, which in turn fostered a growing public concern with mood-altering substances and the formation of temperance movements, which eventually expanded to include marijuana. This context informed the lives and politics of the parents of some of the oldest living Americans today; their same concerns and attitudes have helped shape the line of generations thereafter. A different context has also developed over time as new information emerged and different experiences challenged the prevailing wisdom, especially influencing the socialization of middle-aged and younger adults today.

The greatest effort to bring public control over opium and cocaine came in 1914 with the passage of the Harrison Act (Gaines and Kraska 1997; Inciardi 2008; Musto 1997). It "ushered in a half-century of increasingly punitive anti-drug laws" (Boyum and Reuter 2005, 5). It was the first example of the way that drug use and addiction became equated with criminal behavior, an attitude perpetuated by various antinarcotics groups in the early 20th century. Their campaigns, and the hysteria as exemplified in the film *Reefer Madness*, treated drug use as not only a crime but portrayed it as a threat to civilization itself (Schaller 1970; Speaker 2001). The Marihuana Tax Act came just two decades later in 1937, with the same extreme characterization of marijuana and its users as criminal deviants (Schaller 1970; Speaker 2001).

"In the early 1930s, in the wake of reports linking marijuana use with crime (mostly among Mexicans and blacks in the south and southwest), there was renewed agitation for regulation" (Speaker 2001, 594). Marijuana was linked to corrupting elements, especially as defined by race, ethnicity, and poverty, and as such it was a danger to decent white society. Harry Anslinger, Federal Bureau of Narcotics chief in the 1950s, connected drugs to the Mafia, stoking fears and continuing scare tactics. In the 1960s, marijuana was "rediscovered by a broad cross section of the population who . . . found its use both pleasurable and benign" (Schaller 1970, 61). While many hippie Boomers began a relationship with the drug that was more relaxed, prohibition remained the norm. In this same era President Lyndon Johnson proclaimed a war on crime, and by extension, a war on drugs.

President Nixon began the War on Drugs by targeting heroin in the 1970s, but the larger drug war really began to build momentum during the Reagan administration. Inciardi (2008) and Musto (1997) both cite public opinion surveys that indicate a trend among the general public from 1977 through 1987 toward support for increased efforts at drug and crime control. In 1988, the Reagan administration began its zero-tolerance policy and extended the drug war to users, an attitude that did not reflect sympathy. Addiction was still synonymous with crime, as previously established by the Harrison Act, and marijuana was lumped together with all other illicit drugs, despite its pharmacological differences.

Accounts of marijuana induced crimes waves from the early 20th century are difficult to substantiate, and Schaller (1970) notes that newspapers of the 1930s rarely reported any stories about marijuana. The passage of the Marihuana Tax Act was primarily a symbolic gesture, sending a strong message to the public that marijuana was a scourge with the potential to destroy the very fabric of society (Galliher and Walker 1977). A similar rhetoric has characterized leaders' public declarations against the drug's use, including Reagan in the late 1960s and more recently Attorney General Jeff Sessions (Schaller 1970; Vuolo, Kadowaki, and Kelly 2017). The difference is how the resonance of these statements has decreased gradually over time and for each subsequent generation.

The war on drugs also began at roughly the same time that casual use of drugs had begun to increase. Not coincidentally, NORML, the oldest and largest marijuana legalization organization in the country, was founded the same year that the Controlled Substances Act passed—1970. NORML's mission is "to move public opinion sufficiently to legalize the responsible use of marijuana by adults" (2021). They successfully lobbied to decriminalize minor marijuana offenses in some states and to decrease criminal penalties in all states during their first decade. In 1996, California became the first state to legalize marijuana for medical use, and as of August 2023, 38 states and the District of Columbia have followed suit and also legalized recreational marijuana in some form (ProCon.org 2023).

"Despite almost a century of federal, criminal prohibition, an estimated one in seven U.S. adults acknowledge being current marijuana consumers. NORML (2021) opines that our nation's public policies should reflect this reality, not deny it." As we will see below, public opinion is moving toward agreement. Today, we know more about how marijuana works; more have tried it, know someone who has tried it, or use it regularly without ill effect; and an increasing proportion of adults now live in a state where recreational marijuana is legal despite federal prohibition (Miller 2013; Vuolo, Kadowaki, and Kelly 2017). The shift toward the normalization of marijuana use has occurred within a relatively short period of time but that is not necessarily because of a single age group. The larger context has been altered by media, science, and the experience of citizens of all ages. Those with the longest memories may recall the hysteria and fear of the past most vividly; more are beginning to see the drug in a different light and recognize the inequitable and impractical results of the most restrictive prohibitions.

Socialization, Generations, and Drugs: Drug Abuse Awareness Campaigns

Most adults today have seen that marijuana and its use have not brought about the end of the world or the complete destruction of civilized life. The hype and hysteria of the early 20th century softened in the subsequent decades, though scare tactics did not disappear. Some adults today remember that era or stories from those who experienced the sensationalism. These memories of things learned via firsthand experience rather than taught as history distinguish one age group from another. Certain experiences of adolescence and early adulthood often have effects on the formation of outlooks and opinion (Schuman and Scott 1989). These memories include exposure to sensational movies, media, and testimony by experts—or to drug awareness campaigns and educational programs in schools.

Drug abuse awareness campaigns are best classified as demand reduction strategies—those designed to prevent drug abuse by discouraging use before it starts. The film *Reefer Madness* (1936) can be considered one of the earliest examples of a drug abuse awareness campaign through popular media. It depicts the evils of marijuana consumption and was an effort to prevent drug use through scare tactics and moralizing. This was the primary approach experienced by the Silent and Greatest generations in their youth. Drug prevention messages to Boomers also came in the form of scare tactics, but in the 1960s and 1970s, as the Boomers came of age, efforts shifted toward education (Robison 2002a). The idea was that if individuals had more information about the negative aspects of drug use, they would be less likely to even try them. It was also in 1973 that the Special Action Office for Drug Abuse Prevention (today the Office on National Drug Control Policy) stopped production of all federally funded drug prevention materials and issued new rules to end the use of scare tactics and the stereotyping of drug users in future materials, bringing forth a more integrated approach and diminishing racial profiling.

Despite the advent of crack and its connections to gangs—and by extension people of color—in the 1980s, "as the war on drugs escalated and hard drugs moved into the suburbs, a new form of anti-drug education was born" (Robison 2002b, 2). Drug abuse outreach and prevention further replaced the scare tactics. During the Reagan era, the "Just Say No" campaign began, based on the notion that drug use is the result of peer pressure. This slogan-turned-education program aimed at helping teens use reason to resist and say no when offered drugs by friends or "pushers." The Drug Abuse Resistance Education (DARE) program, founded in 1983, followed a similar approach to help kids develop skills to resist involvement in drugs and drug activities, including gangs and violence. DARE continues to be implemented in schools across the U.S. and in more than 50 countries around the world (https://dare.org/where-is-d-a-r-e/).

Awareness campaigns using public service announcements on television also emerged during this era. The Partnership for a Drug-Free America, founded in 1986 and now called the Partnership to End Addic-

diff methods gov't attempted to deter people from drug use throughout history

tion, is probably the best known and most specifically drug focused of the PSA-producing awareness campaigns (Buchanan and Wallack 1998; drugfree.org). According to the organization's website, a small group of professional advertisers thought that advertising could be used to "unsell" drugs as effectively as it is used to market other products. Videos produced by the partnership and its affiliates, including the iconic egg in the frying pan "this is your brain on drugs" PSA, appeared on television for over 30 years. In 2005, the Partnership began the "Above the Influence" campaign, which sought to move beyond the "Just Say No" message and reach teens by demonstrating how drug use might prevent them from pursuing other interests (Buchanan and Wallack 1998; abovetheinfluence.com). The message was that marijuana damages one's ability to think and destroys ambition, rather than turning one into a violent criminal. The imagery of these campaigns is less sensational than the hysteria of *Reefer Madness*, demonstrating a shift in the content—and context—of socialization for Gen X and Millennials. While still antidrug in general, it was more relaxed in relation to marijuana. *More relaxed approach — Shift*

"Just say no" ↓ "above the influence"

These organizations have now moved away from television spots toward digital and social media strategies. The shift away from television to social media and the internet in general extends their reach to younger Millennials and to Gen Z. Not only has the technology shifted, but the content of these campaigns has changed focus. Early campaigns were motivated by marijuana, then cocaine use and underage drinking in the 1980s and 1990s. Today, while underage drinking still remains a major concern, prescription drug use and abuse have become the priority. The reach of social media and the internet dilutes the influence of these organizations as they are just a few of the seemingly infinite sources of information online.

Social media & internet focus

Shift in focus overall

The hysteria of *Reefer Madness* in the early 20th century resonates even less in the 21st century and among teens and young adults who have grown up around an expanded range of legal and illegal prescription and recreational drug use. Decades of educational strategies, appeals to reason, and appeals to all kids with less emphasis on "othering" drug users correlate with the development of different evaluations of marijuana and the policy surrounding it. Rather than being scared away from the drug, a new evaluative and rational approach to its use and regulation has emerged. The impetus has come primarily from the initial targets of these campaigns—Gen X and now Millennial citizens and voters—but as some of the literature

which drugs are targeted

Shift from criminalizing it to regulating its use

on generations suggests, the learning and effects do not necessarily remain solely within these groups.

Generations and Age Group Learning:
How It Informs Drug Policy Preference

Changes in the values and attitudes of a society are said to occur due to social turnover when "the proponents of a certain position may die off more rapidly than they are replaced by young adults with similar points of view" (Klecka 1971, 360). Thus each new generation has the ability to create change. We might think each generation has its own established views and values, but the "progress and stability of attitudes *within* generations over time"—or lack thereof—is something worth considering (Klecka 1971, 360, emphasis added). Do policy preferences shift only through generational replacement, or can you teach an old dog new tricks?

Generations tend to be delineated as they are because "during the first 30 years of life people are still learning" (Mannheim 1952, 278). Even so, we cannot forget that "*all alike are embedded in the general stream of history*" (Mannheim 1952, 279, emphasis added). Every generation is taught by the previous one, based on their existing values and knowledge of past events, though all experience some events concurrently. "The phenomenon of generations is that not merely is the succession of one after another important, but also that their *coexistence* is of more than mere chronological significance" and "the prevailing intellectual, social, and political circumstances are experienced by contemporary individuals" (282). Time "is always experienced by several generations at various stages of development" and so there can be a cross-generational influence of ideas in that context (283). There is both an influence of social context on generations simultaneously and from the ideas of one to another; the case of marijuana seems to suggest that transmission is not just from older to younger alone but also from younger to older.

"Socialization is a continuous process throughout life, shared by every group of which a person may become a member" (Ryder 1965, 852). One is shaped by his or her historical context and formative experiences but not necessarily by these alone. Individuals are continually influenced by interactions with the social context and the people of all ages within it. Learning continues at various stages of life, and opinions and attitudes can change with learning. No generation is completely unaware of others' past experiences or modes of thought. Each successive generation may perceive previous experience and thought as something to be challenged or learned from. Every individual makes "fresh contact" with an accumulated heritage (Mannheim 1952, 293). While this process is often conceived of as unidirectional, we can consider that the new ideas and perspectives that result from this fresh contact can be shared with all. Therefore, the young can be the teachers, too.

"Successive cohorts are differentiated by the changing content of formal education, by peer-group socialization, and by idiosyncratic historical experience" (Ryder 1965, 843). This education, socialization, and experience includes the whole spectrum of attitudes and laws toward drug use at any given time, and in the case of the 20th century, formal drug awareness media campaigns. Each generation reacts to these attempts to influence them within their own time and context. Each generation can also react to and be affected by attempts to influence the next generation, absorbing that same information and the new ways in which it is presented.

Indeed, "to some extent all cohorts respond to any given period-specific stimulus. Rarely are changes so localized in either age or time that their burden falls exclusively on the shoulders of one cohort" (Ryder 1965, 847). Policy preferences may be shifted by a cohort's fresh perspective and sheer numbers, but given how many age groups coexist in any period, fresh perspectives can cross over and be shared by members of all of them. Alwin and Krosnick (1991) found that "people maintain attitudinal flexibility well beyond the earliest socialization" and that social changes "are mere reflections of individual-level changes, instead of being due to unique differences between new and old cohorts" (171). In other words, change across and *within* age groups produces shifts. They also found "only weak support for the hypothesis that young adulthood is the period of greatest mutability of social attitudes over the life span" (180). Generational attitudes toward drug use and policies must be considered in the larger context of norms and values that guide acceptable behavior, and therefore regulations on that behavior. Consider the relaxed attitude that some hippie Boomers carried over to subsequent Gen X and Millennial generations, which may now also carry back to others within the Boomer cohort. While these values may endure for some, change is possible throughout one's lifetime. Next, we will look at the data on where attitudes now stand that demonstrates increased support for legal marijuana is not solely the result of generational replacement and that shifting perceptions of the drug have indeed occurred within and across age groups.

Attitudes and Drug Policy by the Numbers: National Surveys

Gallup first asked about making marijuana use legal in 1969, when just 12% of Americans favored the proposal. Nearly a decade later, a 1977 survey found support had increased to 28%, but it held at about that level through 1995, finally surpassing 30% in Gallup's next measurement, in 2000. Since then, the percentage of Americans advocating legal marijuana usage has more than doubled, with support increasing significantly among all major subgroups.

—"In U.S., Medical Aid Top Reason Why Legal Marijuana Favored," Gallup Poll, June 13, 2019

Surveys have shown that support for legalization passed the 50 percent mark in 2013, and rose to 60 percent in 2016 (Pew Research 2014; Swift 2016). By 2019, the proportion of those in favor of legalization reached two-thirds, with only one major age group where a majority remained opposed (Daniller 2019).

Those age 65 and over were split more or less evenly; of those born before 1945, just 40 percent supported legalization (Jones 2019a). But even this is noteworthy: since 2000 support among the oldest Americans has increased the most, more than doubling by some measures to reach that 40 percent mark (McCarthy 2018). At the time of writing, majorities of all age subgroups favor legalization, the lowest proportion among those over age 65 at 55 percent; the record high level of support for legalization overall held for a second year in a row at 68 percent (Brenan 2020; Gallup 2021; see fig. 5.1). The narrow time frame of these results indicates that many older adults have shifted their own views rather than greater support being a result of generational replacement in the aggregate.

Who typically supports legal marijuana? The conventional logic would suggest those who use it, those who hold liberal ideas, and the young. The three descriptors seemingly go hand in hand, yet the data do not fully support this conclusion. "Views of marijuana legalization differ by generation and political party, though support has increased

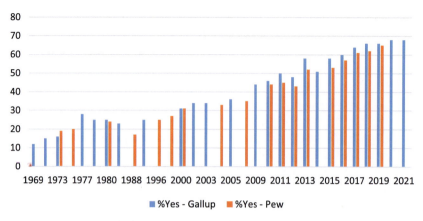

Fig. 5.1. Support for Legal Marijuana Over Time
Source: Analysis by author of Gallup and Pew Research Center Polls.

across demographic groups over time" (Geiger and Gramlich 2019). Even though just over half of people in the U.S. claim to have ever used marijuana, two-thirds favor legalization (Geiger and Gramlich 2019). Available data shows support is highest among Millennials (72%) while roughly two-thirds of Boomers and Gen X are in favor. A gap remains between these three generations and the Silents, but even their portion has grown recently (Pew 2023, see fig. 5.2).

"Across every generational divide, Democrats show higher support than Republicans on this issue" (Gao 2015, 3). Yet partisanship is less of a factor in support for legalization among Gen Xers or Millennials; in 2015, the gap between Republicans and Democrats for both groups was 14 percent, compared to 28 percent and 27 percent for the Boomers and Silents, respectively (Gao 2015). It is also noteworthy that this survey showed a majority in favor among both parties in the Millennial group. Generationally we are moving away from the partisan divide on this issue and it is becoming less of a predictive factor. It is not as simple as those who are younger and more liberal support legalization and those older and more conservative do not; the younger conservatives may be leading the older in a new direction on this issue.

Has support for legalization increased via generational replacement because Millennials are a large age cohort and young people use marijuana in greater numbers? A 2019 poll showed that only 12 percent of adults in the U.S. smoke marijuana. Of these, yes, the largest propor-

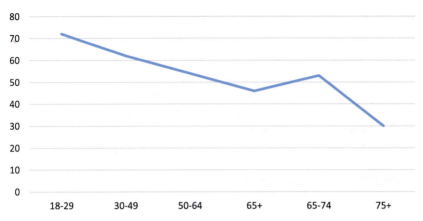

Fig. 5.2. Support for Legal Marijuana by Age Group (2022)
Source: Author's analysis of Pew Research Center data, November 2022 (https://www.pewresearch.org/short-reads/2022/11/22/americans-overwhelmingly-say-marijuana-should-be-legal-for-medical-or-recreational-use).

tions are among those aged 18 to 29, at 22 percent, and liberals are significantly more likely than conservatives at 24 percent compared to 4 percent (Hrynowski 2020). This may not be surprising, but what is genuinely significant about these findings, beyond the expected divide by age or ideology, is that the proportion of users lags far behind the proportion of those who support legalization. Again, two-thirds of adults are in favor of legalization and it has majority support across age groups and political affiliation.

Let us not forget that support has more than doubled in just the last two decades, from 30 percent in 2000 to 68 percent in 2020 and 2021 (Brenan 2020; Gallup 2021). In the even shorter time frame since Washington and Colorado became the first states to legalize recreational marijuana, support rose 20 points. The biggest gaps are seen within party identification and political ideology, but even those who identify as conservative or Republican come in at 49 percent and 48 percent in favor, respectively (Brenan 2020). While liberals and independents favor legalization in greater proportion, there is not complete polarization. Gallup also found that 70 percent of adults now consider smoking marijuana to be morally acceptable (Brenan 2020). In my estimation, this is a huge shift from just a century ago.

Beyond differences between demographic groups, why do people support or oppose legalization? Surveys indicate that supporters and opponents of legalization are split in their reasoning. Majorities of those in favor cite medical benefits or an increased ability for law enforcement to focus on other crime (Pew Research 2015; Geiger and Gramlich 2019). Those who remain opposed tend to cite potential increases in impaired driving or users moving on to stronger drugs. The oldest are most likely to express concern that legalization will lead to more underage people trying marijuana, though younger people also share this concern (Pew Research 2014). Many are worried about personal health and safety; while some stress the medical benefits, others argue marijuana use hurts society in general.

The top two most important reasons cited for supporting legalization are it would help people who need it for medical reasons, and it would free up law enforcement to focus on other types of crime (Jones 2019b). Jones (2019b) finds there are no meaningful differences in reasoning for or against legal marijuana among the various subgroups surveyed. None of these arguments is obviously tied to either age or generation. In spite of some lingering concerns among the opposition, it is clear a change has emerged and support will probably continue to rise. This has resulted from a combination of shifts in the larger social context and attitudes toward drugs, a process of learning within new contexts, and possibly the influence of the younger generation's ideas upon the older.

As mentioned in the introduction, one model of generational learning suggests a linear process whereby each subsequent generation receives instruction from the previous and carries on the same values. These values may be revised or liberalized but the relationship is unidirectional. A second model suggests rebellion against the previous generation and adoption of different and often more radical values. The data above shows the linear direction of changes in attitude suggested by the first model, while it clearly defies the second model, which would indicate a wave-like pattern of reversals in attitudes. As I also noted before, neither model fits perfectly here. Yes, attitudes have liberalized with each subsequent generation, but given the increasing support within generations, the larger context of learning is the better explanation. Within that context are intergenerational interactions that may be a further influencing factor. Perhaps marijuana is an issue that itself is creating intergenerational ties. This is an important area for future research and not something I have yet seen addressed. It is a question that poses various methodological challenges. How might one go about measuring cross-generational learning? Surveys and interviews, certainly, though it is debatable how forthcoming some respondents would be in giving credit to other age groups. The antagonism between Boomers and Millennials, for instance, is well documented in the social media meme-universe. This element of the research goes beyond the scope of my original vision for this project but is worth contemplation. It is an especially valuable question as we look to the next generation that is beginning to assert itself on the national stage.

What Does This Tell Us and What about Gen Z?

According to Laura Stoker (chap. 2, this volume) shifts in the political landscape may be explained by generational replacement, or by larger sociopolitical forces or changes in the sociodemographic composition of the electorate. While her work focuses on questions of polarization and partisanship, the analysis is relevant to our discussion here. She finds that neither generational differences nor individual sociodemographic characteristics are the driving factor; instead, the status of the parties at a given time is most correlated with shifts in identity and evaluation. In much the same way, we can see that attitudes toward drugs seem to shift with the status of that drug in historical context. As the attitudes captured in the data above indicate, the once-evil marijuana enjoys a relatively tamer status today. Thus, support or opposition to legal marijuana is affected by one's generation in combination with the context of socialization. As the context has shifted from the hysteria and fear of the original prohibition era, so have attitudes.

marijuana is viewed very differently today

While policy preference can be described as a function of age-based interests, Fullerton and Dixon (2010) also raise the question about the "assumption of symmetrical effects" in opposition to or support for particular policies among the age groups (649). From this we can understand that strong support for something among voters of one generation does not necessarily mean equally strong opposition from another generation. It is feasible then that the recent trend toward more Silent and especially Boomer support for legal marijuana may be a result of relaxed opposition that may not have been that strong in the first place. Most surveys on these issues rarely capture intensity, and so these attitudes may have been open to influence from a variety of

gen is often not defining factor

sources all along. As noted previously, the hippie Boomers and marijuana are inextricably linked in the popular culture.

Meanwhile, the youngest generations are potentially closer to current issues as a result of their fresh contact, bringing forward new approaches. Opposition among the older generations based on old or limited data is challenged by the accumulated research on both the effects of the drug itself and the downsides of prohibition. "This tension appears incapable of solution except for one compensating factor: not only does that teacher educate his pupil, but the pupil educates his teacher too. Generations are in state of constant interaction" (Mannheim (1923) 1952, 301). The oldest generation can unlearn previously held views. And it is not just the oldest and the youngest—the intermediary generations play a role as well. "Each fresh cohort is a possible intermediary in the transformation process, a vehicle for introducing new postures" (Ryder 1965, 844). This is often seen as the new cohort bringing about change that is broadly accepted within that generation, which then gains majority strength as the previous generations, and their postures, die off. Less often do we think about the younger generation's postures as being adopted by the older, though in the case of legal marijuana, this may be a part of what has happened.

Differences in opinion can be explained as a function of age or point in one's life cycle, or as a function of age cohort and the context of shared experiences, socialization, and values. In the former, the notion is that younger people tend to hold more liberal values and get more conservative as they age. Therefore, we should expect older people today to prefer prohibition to legalization. The latter suggests that each generation or cohort becomes progressively more liberal compared to the one before it, thus shifting policy over time. Neither fully explains the trend toward greater approval of legal marijuana across all age groups as seen in the surveys of the past few decades. The larger context has influenced all, while the young may be leading the change toward more liberalized policy. To demonstrate that definitively would require a more in-depth analysis of who introduced legalization measures in each of the states and the demographics of who voted for them, especially in the cases of ballot initiatives. As more and more states consider the issue, more data will become available for analysis and include the next generation. Gen Z has not yet been formally included in the national opinion surveys cited above; I predict that this age group will continue the trend and push changes in the law further in conjunction with racial justice.

Gen Z is only beginning to form its own consciousness and distinct outlook on the world. We can argue that the shared historical experience for Gen Z that is the crystallizing agent or touchstone historical moment for this group's generational consciousness was the election of Donald Trump or the advent of the Black Lives Matter movement since the mid-2010s. Their ascent into adulthood and engagement with public life at the juncture of social transition definitely provides a moment of fresh contact with our accumulated heritage surrounding multiple issues of law and order, and an opportunity for reappraisal. Legal marijuana is intricately linked to questions of racial justice even though medical use has been the top factor for most adults who support legalization. This is an area where Gen Z can distinguish itself. Not only did young voters increase turnout overall in 2020, but they were more likely than other age groups to cite issues like racism as most important and a factor for their mobilization (CIRCLE 2020). Further, they have grown up with some form of legalization already in place, making legal marijuana more normal than novel.

Generational Attitudes and Drug Policy: The Role of Race

The significance of race for generational shifts in attitudes toward marijuana is that it is a constant undercurrent. In the early 1900s, the connection was outright racism in the association of race to drug use and criminality in general. This was also the era of segregation and Jim Crow. Racism reinforced drug prohibition in general and negative attitudes toward marijuana in particular. The mid-20th century was the era of the civil rights movement and desegregation. While race relations certainly remained fraught, some shift in attitudes toward marijuana was already emerging among the young Boomers of the antiwar movement, among others. Integration may also have meant a softening of that harsh stereotype, the criminal, drug-using person of color.

By the late 1900s, particularly in the 1980s and 1990s, race remained salient but the focus moved away from marijuana even as negative stereotypes continued for people of color in the realm of crack. By this time as well, levels of incarceration had increased significantly since the passage of the Controlled Substances Act; the racial disparity in arrests and convictions became obvious and a new talking point for advocates of decriminalization and legalization emerged (Beckett and Herbert 2008; Levine et al. 2012). It is also worth noting the increase in mixed-race marriages and families during the second half of the 20th century, and a larger emphasis in public institutions and public consciousness toward diversity and multiculturalism. Both trends have continued into the 2000s. The awareness of racial bias in drug arrests and enforcement is rising at the same moment that technology is advancing to distribute that information broadly and rapidly to each new age group. From Gen X through Gen Z, from cable television to the internet to the smartphone, a convergence of factors seems to breed a new stance on marijuana that is beginning to reach across all age groups.

"Marijuana has been a key driver of mass incarceration in this country and hundreds of thousands of people, the majority of whom are Black or Latinx, have their lives impacted by a marijuana arrest each year" (Resing 2019). Early state-level marijuana reform campaigns discussed issues like race but did not always address them directly in the laws as implemented (Morris et al. 2021). Many of these were still supported by voters for the reasons identified by national surveys—access to medical use and additional financial benefits, both in taxes and allocation of resources to law enforcement. As legal marijuana schemes were implemented in the states, the inequality of access to the benefits of the new market began to appear, and attention to the importance of addressing the ongoing effects of discrepancies in enforcement has increased (Morris et al. 2021; Resing 2019).

The recent wave of legalization efforts demonstrates the effectiveness of reformers in framing marijuana policy as a civil rights and racial justice issue (Morris et al. 2021). This observation is noteworthy given that the top reasons indicated in surveys for support of legalization do not explicitly name civil rights or justice. This strategy may have developed—deliberately or otherwise—to connect specific policy proposals to larger issues. It is particularly salient in the context of Gen Z, which has been described as most likely to see the intersectionality of social and political issues (Hess 2020). They are the most likely to approach issues as interconnected and see how the economy, climate change, criminal justice, and even marijuana laws are interwoven. They are also the most diverse generation so far, even more than Millennials, and thus represent a growing voting power and influence across demographics. Many young voters agree that "racial justice is among their top concerns" (Hess 2020).

Racial justice and equity are not explicitly listed among the reasons voters give for supporting legalization in any of the surveys cited here. That is not to say there is no connection; medical benefits and diversion of police resources to more pressing issues are the most popular, but the subject of criminal justice and racial disparities has also been a part of the conversation (see ACLU 2013; Beckett and Herbert 2008; Levine et al. 2012, among others). Legal marijuana is no longer the partisan issue it once was (NPR 2021). Legal and decriminalized marijuana is found in red, blue, and purple states alike. As more states have proposed and passed legalization, they in turn have shifted attention from the marketplace and revenue toward legal reforms as part of the overall process. Morris et al. (2021) note the centrality of social justice in the most recent wave of successful legalization, which in part coincides with events of 2020 that drove large portions of the youngest voters to the polls. It is hard to argue this is not related to the rise in support for the values and teaching of diversity, equity, and inclusion in the past four decades or so that have served as part of the socialization process for Gen X, Millennials, and now Gen Z alike. Of course, the same ideas exist for Boomers in their context and lives; indeed, it is hard to imagine these initiatives taking center stage without their involvement as well. The latest drive to create reforms in tandem with legalization can be seen as an effort initiated in part by the younger generations but clearly one that is also supported more and more by the older ones.

Conclusion

As Robin Boyle-Laisure (chap. 8, this volume) suggests, technology has played a role in the conveyance of ideas and activism among the younger generations. The acclimation to and acceptance of technology, indeed the very way that Gen Z in particular and even Millennials have grown up with smartphones, apps, and social media, has allowed new and different messages about drugs, the laws, and their effects to be shared rapidly among this segment of the population. In turn, the two younger generations have been the driving force in using these same technologies and platforms to communicate with peers, colleagues, and family across generations, thereby further disseminating these ideas and influencing shifts in attitudes. The "ease of access to learning" is demonstrably greater today than it was four generations ago (Boyle-Laisure). I would argue this ease of learning is by no means confined to the younger, supposedly more tech-savvy segment of the population. In fact, 68 percent of Boomers own a smartphone and 59 percent use social media; only 40 percent of Silents have a smartphone and a mere 28 percent of them use social media (Vogels 2019). By some measures, Boomers and Millennials spend an equal portion of their time on social media (Roberts 2019). This provides an opportunity for bidirectional influence of ideas, especially for Boomers who remain in the workforce and thus are in closer contact with Millennials compared to the Silent generation.

Long before this technology came to exist Mannheim (1952) noted how "the older generation becomes increasingly receptive to influences from the younger" and "may even achieve greater adaptability in certain spheres" (302). The younger population, as Boyle-Laisure (chap. 8, this vol.) notes, are perhaps more cognitive of the long-term consequences of the world's collective actions or inaction and are also especially attuned to the necessity of diversity, inclusion, and equity. Their awareness of racial disparity in drug enforcement and the limited resources of police and criminal justice systems may in part explain their stronger support for reforming marijuana laws and refocusing attention on other matters.

Generational differences in attitudes toward drugs are influenced by the messaging in the media and by policymakers of each era. In the early to mid-twentieth century this was primarily a heightened sense of fear and hysteria surrounding the dangers of an evil drug, one that could provoke insanity and violence in its users. The tactic of trying to scare people away from the drug continued into the 1960s and 1970s, even as more tried the drug and found it innocuous. The rhetoric of danger was not abandoned in the last decades of the century but the emphasis turned more toward education and prevention, even as federal and state governments waged a war on drugs.

In addition, the larger context of the society and information about drugs and the effects of policy both matter and influence opinion. The counterculture types allegedly most prone to drug use, such as jazz musicians and later the hippies, did not self-destruct. In fact, many became successful and celebrated, contributing to society. By the turn of the century, the drug war had resulted in huge financial outlays but no corresponding elimination of drugs or drug use. Instead of a drug-free society, drugs had become more readily available, stronger, and cheaper than ever before (Inciardi 2008). Celebrities and popular cul-

Celebs & pop culture "promote" drug use in a sense

ture depicted marijuana use more and more, lifting a taboo and signaling a general liberalization of thought on the subject. Marijuana seemed mild in comparison to heroin, ecstasy, meth, and every other new frontier on the drug map. The U.S. remained rigid in its criminal approach to drugs while other places around the world successfully implemented harm reduction and decriminalization strategies. Voices and voters in places around the U.S. began to wonder if we might choose this path instead.

"mild"

While the Silents remain opposed and their numbers are decreasing, many Boomers have joined the ranks of Gen X and Millennials to back the legalization trend. While it doesn't go as far as legalization, the announcement from the White House in October 2022 that federal pardons for simple possession were forthcoming signals a significant shift in policy from a leader who once fully backed the war on drugs and places it in the frame of racial justice (Daniels and Fertig 2022; Dickson 2019; Wise 2022). Meanwhile, Gen Z is poised to add additional clout; they are diverse, they "are more accepting of some of the ways in which American society is changing," and they are gaining influence in the conversation surrounding social and criminal justice reform, including drug laws and policy (Parker, Graf, and Igielnik 2019). How exactly this plays out remains to be seen, particularly as Gen Z as a cohort has only recently reached voting age and their views are still forming. But their power is already making itself apparent; in the November 2020 election, turnout increased among all age groups but in largest proportion among those 18–34. According to the Census Bureau, for citizens ages 18–34, 57 percent voted in 2020, up from 49 percent in 2016. While turnout was up for all age groups, this was by far the largest increase (Fabina 2021). Hess (2020) notes that 53 percent to 55 percent of voters aged 18 to 29 voted, perhaps the highest ever recorded for that age group. This supports the assertion that Gen Z and Millennials are both "voting generations" that not only have the numbers but are already wielding influence over policy and election outcomes today. As more of Gen Z enters the field, they have the potential to shift the political landscape in ways that may not have seemed possible just a few years ago. So those Boomers and Gen Xers who have long supported legalization, or have come around to it in recent years, may well see it become reality at the national level in their lifetimes. As a member of Gen X myself, I could not have imagined typing that sentence and believing it before now.

Boomers back legalization

power of Gen Z

major influence in U.S.

REFERENCES

Above the Influence. 2021. https://abovetheinfluence.com/

ACLU (American Civil Liberties Union). 2013. *The War on Marijuana in Black and White*. ACLU, June. https://www.aclu.org/sites/default/files/field_document/111 4413-mj-report-rfs-rel1.pdf

Alwin, D. F., and J. A. Krosnick. 1991. "Aging, Cohorts, and the Stability of Sociopolitical Orientations over the Life Span." *American Journal of Sociology* 97 (1): 169–95.

Beckett, K., and S. Herbert. 2008. *The Consequences and Costs of Marijuana Prohibition*, Report commissioned by the ACLU of Washington. https://www.aclu-wa.org /docs/consequences-and-costs-marijuana-prohibition

Biggs, S. 2007. "Thinking about Generations: Conceptual Positions and Policy Implications." *Journal of Social Issues* 63 (4): 695–711.

Boyum, D., and P. Reuter. 2005. *An Analytic Assessment of U.S. Drug Policy*. Washington, DC: AEI Press.

Brenan, M. 2020. *Support for Legal Marijuana Inches up to New High of 68%*. Gallup, November 9. https://news.gallup.com/poll/323582/support-legal-marijuana-inc hes-new-high.aspx

Buchanan, D. R., and L. Wallack. 1998. "This Is the Partnership for a Drug-Free America: Any Questions?" *Journal of Drug Issues* 28 (2): 329.

CIRCLE (Center for Information & Research on Civic Learning and Engagement). 2020. *Election Week 2020: Young People Increase Turnout, Lead Biden to Victory*. Tufts University, November 25. https://circle.tufts.edu/latest-research/election -week-2020#the-top-issues-that-drove-youth-to-the-polls

Daniels, B., and N. Fertig. 2022. "Biden Pardons Marijuana Offenses, Calls for Review of Federal Law." *Politico*, October 6. https://www.politico.com/news/20 22/10/06/biden-to-pardon-marijuana-offenses-call-for-review-of-federal-law-00 060796

Daniller, A. 2019. *Two-Thirds of Americans Support Marijuana Legalization*. Pew Research Center, November 14. https://www.pewresearch.org/fact-tank/2019 /11/14/americans-support-marijuana-legalization/

D.A.R.E. (Drug Abuse Resistance Education). 2021. https://dare.org/

Dickson, E. 2019. "Why Weed Advocates Aren't Happy about Joe Biden's Candidacy." *Rolling Stone*, April 25. https://www.rollingstone.com/culture/culture-features /joe-biden-weed-war-drugs-candidate-2020-827319/

Fabina, J. 2021. *Despite Pandemic Challenges, 2020 Election Had Largest Increase in Voting between Presidential Elections on Record*. U.S. Census Bureau, April 29. https:// www.census.gov/library/stories/2021/04/record-high-turnout-in-2020-general -election.html

Fullerton, A. S., and J. C. Dixon. 2010. "Generational Conflict or Methodological Artifact? Reconsidering the Relationship between Age and Policy Attitudes in the U.S., 1984–2008." *Public Opinion Quarterly* 74 (4) (Winter): 643–73.

Gaines, L. K., and P. B. Kraska, eds. 1997. *Drugs, Crime, and Justice: Contemporary Perspectives*. Prospect Heights, IL: Waveland Press.

Galliher, J. F., and A. Walker. 1977. "The Puzzle of the Social Origins of the Marihuana Tax Act of 1937." *Social Problems* 24 (3): 367–76.

Gallup. 2021. *Support for Legal Marijuana Holds at Record High of 68%.* November 4. https://news.gallup.com/poll/356939/support-legal-marijuana-holds-record-high.aspx

Gao, G. 2015. *63% of Republican Millennials Favor Marijuana Legalization.* Pew Research Center, February 27. https://www.pewresearch.org/fact-tank/2015/02/27/63-of-republican-millennials-favor-marijuana-legalization/

Geiger, A. W., and J. Gramlich. 2019. *6 Facts about Marijuana.* Pew Research Center, November 22. https://www.pewresearch.org/fact-tank/2019/11/22/facts-about-marijuana/

Hess, A. J. 2020. "The 2020 Election Shows Gen Z's Voting Power for Years to Come." *CNBC,* November 18. https://www.cnbc.com/2020/11/18/the-2020-election-shows-gen-zs-voting-power-for-years-to-come.html

Hrynowski, Z. 2020. *What Percentage of Americans Smoke Marijuana?* Gallup, January 31. https://news.gallup.com/poll/284135/percentage-americans-smoke-marijuana.aspx

Inciardi, J. A. 2008. *The War on Drugs IV: The Continuing Saga of the Mysteries and Miseries of Intoxication, Addiction, Crime, and Public Policy.* 4th ed. Boston: Pearson/Allyn and Bacon.

Johnson, K. 2014. "Cannabis Legal, Localities Begin to Just Say No." *New York Times,* January 26.

Jones, J. M. 2019a. *In U.S., Medical Aid Top Reason Why Legal Marijuana Favored.* Gallup, June 12. https://news.gallup.com/poll/258149/medical-aid-top-reason-why-legal-marijuana-favored.aspx

Jones, J. M. 2019b. *U.S. Support for Legal Marijuana Steady in Past Year.* Gallup, October 23. https://news.gallup.com/poll/267698/support-legal-marijuana-steady-past-year.aspx

Klecka, W. R. 1971. "Applying Generations to the Study of Political Behavior: A Cohort Analysis." *Public Opinion Quarterly* 35 (3): 358–75.

Kleiman, M. A. R., J. P. Caulkins, and A. Hawken. 2011. *Drugs and Drug Policy: What Everyone Needs to Know.* New York: Oxford University Press.

Kraska, P. B. 1997. "The Military as Drug Police: Exercising the Ideology of War." In *Drugs, Crime, and Justice: Contemporary Perspectives,* edited by L. K. Gaines and P. B. Kraska, 297–320. Prospect Heights, IL: Waveland Press.

Levine, H. G., J. B. Gettman, and L. Siegel. 2012. *240,000 Marijuana Arrests: Costs, Consequences, and Racial Disparities of Possession Arrests in Washington, 1985–2010.* October. New York: Marijuana Arrest Project.

Love, J. 2004. *Political Behavior and Values across the Generations: A Summary of Selected Findings.* AARP, July. https://assets.aarp.org/rgcenter/general/politics_values.pdf

Mabry, D. J. 1994. "The U.S. Military and the War on Drugs." In *Drug Trafficking in the Americas,* edited by B. M. Bagley and W. O. Walker, 43–60. New Brunswick, NJ: Transaction.

Mannheim, K. 1952. "The Problem of Generations." In *Essays on the Sociology of Knowledge,* edited and translated by Paul Keeskemeti. London: Routledge.

McCarthy, J. 2018. *Two in Three Americans Now Support Legalizing Marijuana.* Gallup, October 22. https://news.gallup.com/poll/243908/two-three-americans-support-legalizing-marijuana.aspx

McWilliams, J. C. 1991. "From the Editor: Drug Use in American History." *OAH Magazine of History* 6 (Fall): 2–5.

Miller, R. J. 2013. "The Cannabis Conundrum." *Proceedings of the National Academy of Sciences of the United States of America* 110 (43): 17165.

Morris, S., J. Hudak, and C. Stenglein. 2021. *State Cannabis Reform Is Putting Social Justice Front and Center*. Brookings Institution, April 16. https://www.brookings.edu/blog/fixgov/2021/04/16/state-cannabis-reform-is-putting-social-justice-front-and-center/

Musto, D. F. 1997. "Opium, Cocaine, and Marijuana in American History." In *Drugs, Crime, and Justice: Contemporary Perspectives*, edited by L. K. Gaines and P. B. Kraska, 21–33. Prospect Heights, IL: Waveland Press.

NORML (National Organization for the Reform of Marijuana Laws). 2021. https://norml.org/about-norml/

NPR (National Public Radio). 2021. *America's Next Generation of Legal Marijuana: New State Laws Focus on Racial Equity*. "Consider This" from NPR, February 26. https://www.npr.org/2021/02/22/970242944/americas-next-generation-of-legal-marijuana-new-state-laws-focus-on-racial-equit

Parker, K., N. Graf, and R. Igielnik. 2019. *Generation Z Looks a Lot Like Millennials on Key Social and Political Issues*. Pew Research Center, January 17. https://www.pewsocialtrends.org/2019/01/17/generation-z-looks-a-lot-like-millennials-on-key-social-and-political-issues/

Parker, K., and R. Igielnik. 2020. *On the Cusp of Adulthood and Facing Uncertain Future: What We Know about Gen Z*. Pew Research Center, May 14. https://www.pewsocialtrends.org/essay/on-the-cusp-of-adulthood-and-facing-an-uncertain-future-what-we-know-about-gen-z-so-far/

Partnership™ for Drug-Free Kids. 2021. www.drugfree.org

Pew Research Center. 2014. *America's New Drug Policy Landscape*. April 2. https://www.pewresearch.org/politics/2014/04/02/americas-new-drug-policy-landscape/

Pew Research Center. 2015. *In Debate over Legalizing Marijuana, Disagreement over Drug's Dangers*. April 14. https://www.pewresearch.org/politics/2015/04/14/in-debate-over-legalizing-marijuana-disagreement-over-drugs-dangers/

Pew Research Center. 2018. *The Generation Gap in American Politics*. March 1. https://www.pewresearch.org/politics/2018/03/01/the-generation-gap-in-american-politics/

Pew Research Center. 2023. *Seven Facts about Americans and Marijuana: Americans 75 and Older Are the Least Likely to Say Marijuana Should Be Legal for Recreational Use*. April 13. https://www.pewresearch.org/short-reads/2023/04/13/facts-about-marijuana/sr_23-04-03_marijuanafacts_4/

ProCon.org. 2023. *Legal Medical Marijuana States and DC*. August 17. https://medicalmarijuana.procon.org/legal-medical-marijuana-states-and-dc/

Resing, C. 2019. *Marijuana Legalization Is a Racial Justice Issue*. ACLU, April 20. https://www.aclu.org/blog/criminal-law-reform/drug-law-reform/marijuana-legalization-racial-justice-issue

Roberts, N. F. 2019. "Forget Generational Stereotypes, Baby Boomers Are Just as Addicted to Smart Phones as Millennials." *Forbes*, May 6. https://www.forbes.com/sites/nicolefisher/2019/05/06/forget-generational-stereotypes-baby-boomers-are-just-as-addicted-to-smart-phones/?sh=7b46de4f4f89

Robison, J. 2002a. *Decades of Drug Use: Data from the '60s and '70s.* Gallup, July 2. https://news.gallup.com/poll/6331/decades-drug-use-data-from-60s-70s.aspx

Robison, J. 2002b. *Decades of Drug Use: Data from the '80s and '90s.* Gallup, July 9. https://news.gallup.com/poll/6352/decades-drug-use-80s-90s.aspx

Ryder, N. B. 1965. "The Cohort as a Concept in the Study of Social Change." *American Sociological Review* 30 (6): 843–61.

Schaller, M. 1970. "The Federal Prohibition of Marihuana." *Journal of Social History* 4 (1): 61–74.

Schuman, H., and J. Scott. 1989. "Generations and Collective Memories." *American Sociological Review* 54 (3): 359–81.

Speaker, S. L. 2001. "'The Struggle of Mankind against Its Deadliest Foe': Themes of Counter-Subversion in Anti-Narcotic Campaigns, 1920–1940." *Journal of Social History* 34 (3): 591–610.

Swift, A. 2016. *Support for Legal Marijuana Use up to 60% in the U.S.* Gallup, October 19. https://news.gallup.com/poll/196550/support-legal-marijuana.aspx

Vogels, E. A. 2019. *Millennials Stand Out for Their Technology Use, but Older Generations Also Embrace Digital Life.* Pew Research Center, September 9. https://www.pewresearch.org/fact-tank/2019/09/09/us-generations-technology-use/

Vuolo, M., J. Kadowaki, and B. C. Kelly. 2017. "Marijuana's Moral Entrepreneurs, Then and Now." *Contexts* 16 (4): 20–25.

Wise, A. 2022. *Biden's Pot Pardon Will Help Reverse War on Drugs Harm to Black People, Advocates Say.* NPR, October 10. https://www.npr.org/2022/10/10/1127708285/marijuana-pardon-biden-black-people-war-on-drugs-harm

6 | Gender and the Generations

You Haven't Come a Long Way Yet, Baby

Whitney Ross Manzo and David B. McLennan

The 2020 election was consequential in many ways. It produced the highest voter turnout in the nation's history, including record turnout for the country's youngest voters (18–24), commonly referred to as Generation Z voters (Hess 2020). Analysts argue that young voters—Gen Z and Millennials—were key to Joe Biden's victory in November. Brett Cohen, executive director of Generations Progress, stated that "Generation Z and millennials are voting generations" (Hess 2020).

Although exit poll data suggests that a strong majority of younger voters voted for the Democratic ticket (NBC 2020), closer examination of the results indicates a more complicated story. Almost 90 percent of Black Gen Z voters supported the Biden-Harris ticket, but a majority of white voters from the same group supported the Trump-Pence ticket. A majority of Latino young voters (69%) supported the Democratic ticket, but almost 30 percent supported Trump's reelection.

Not only are there racial and ethnic differences among young voters in terms of their partisan preferences, but young voters differ in terms of their views of women as political leaders. Recent polling (YouGov 2021) points to a large gender gap among young voters in terms of their approval of the job Kamala Harris is doing as vice president. A majority of women under 30 approve of Harris's early performance, while a majority of men do not. That is not the case for Joe Biden's approval rating, in which both men and women under 30 approved of his job as president.

These differences within the youngest generation of voters, especially about Harris, suggest that sexism may continue to be a reason for one of the most enduring problems in American electoral politics—gender disparity among elected officials. Even after the 2020 elections, women held just over 26 percent of the seats in Congress. In some states, including North Carolina, the number of women candidates and elected officials actually declined from the previous midterm (McLennan 2018).

In recent years, researchers have suggested that the younger generations are fundamentally different than older generations because of their socialization (Bartels and Jackman 2014; Jacobson 2016), with the Pew Research Center proclaiming that most young voters today have a decidedly liberal ideology. Our research on the perception of women political leaders, such as Kamala Harris or Hillary Clinton, raises questions about these claims that the younger generation of voters is really less sexist than previous generations. Specifically, our research demonstrates that younger men have attitudes about women political leaders that mirror those of much older generations of men, and that the idea that gender parity may be on the immediate political horizon may be too optimistic.

Review of Literature

The generational differences we discuss about the view of women as leaders relates to a wide range of scholarship. First, we examine the scholarship examining how political attitudes toward women as political leaders has changed over the past five decades. Then, we summarize the research on political socialization, as it relates to generational differences. Finally, we look at current survey research on Americans' views on challenges women face in achieving gender equality. Our research challenges some of the assumptions in the existing literature by suggesting that we need a more nuanced approach to examining generations' political attitudes and the different ways that members of each generational cohort are socialized.

The issue of sexism within segments of the electorate and its impact of gender parity has a long and uneven history in the research literature. Early research suggested that sexist attitudes were socialized into voters, but there was a belief among researchers that sexist attitudes about women as political leaders have dissipated. However, more recent research has focused on the resurgence of sexism—a more virulent form of sexism in the electorate that manifests itself in overt forms (e.g., hostile sexism) and covert forms (e.g., discussions of whether women candidates are "electable"). Recent research suggests that younger voters are more progressive than their older counterparts, yet our research finds that some younger voters exhibit the same attitudes about women in politics as older generations. This raises the question, at least about gender issues, whether socialization about gender and politics has made any headway.

Early research on sexism within the electorate and its impact on the perceptions of women as political leaders focused on attitudes being passed from one generation to the next through political socialization. The seminal work by Roberta Sigel (1965) argues that political values are passed down from generation to generation almost seamlessly. Her work would support an early thesis to explain the lack of women in politics that there is simply too much discrimination against women by voters and, more importantly, electoral gatekeepers like party officials (Rule 1981; Welch 1978). Studies such as these were popular for a time, but as overt discrimination appeared to decline and more women sought and won elected office, the idea of people being socialized into having sexist attitudes declined (Boxer 1994; Dolan 2004). Since 2016, however, the idea of overt gender discrimination in voting behavior is now accepted and recent research even indicates that some Democratic voters use terms like "electability" as a code word for discriminating against women candidates running for president (Luks and Schaffner 2019). This raises the question about the role of political socialization again, and scholars such as Zoe Oxley and her colleagues (2020) have returned to the idea that children's socialization continues to be important in affecting the political attitudes of voters.

From the 1960s, it has been common to postulate that girls are taught from a young age to be politically passive and cede participation to boys (Campbell et al. 1964; Jaros 1973). As the argument goes, early teachings in traditional gender expectations influence women to believe that politics is a man's game. These expectations get reinforced throughout a woman's life, as she is taught the characteristics often associated with politics and leadership—confidence, assertiveness, self-promotion—are unseemly in women (Thomas 2005; Fox and Lawless 2011). This leads women to doubt their viability as candidates, even if they achieve high levels of education and success in the workplace (Fox and Lawless 2004).

Of course, if women are being socialized about politics and leadership, so are men. They too receive the message that good leaders are male, which may lead to male voters perceiving female candidates as less able and less legitimate (Carli 1990; Ridgeway 2001). Indeed, several studies have demonstrated that both men and women hold two kinds of stereotypes associated with gender and politics: belief stereotypes, which are stereotypes associated with policy position and ideology, and trait stereotypes, which are inferences of personal characteristics derived from gender (Fox and Oxley 2003). In terms of belief stereotypes, women are routinely assumed to be more liberal than men, and, in fact, females tend to do better in Democratic primaries than females in Republican primaries (Koch 2000; Pearson and Lawless 2008). Belief stereotypes also affect policy issues, in which men are perceived to be better at "tough" issues like national security and crime, while women are perceived to be more accomplished at handling "touchy-feely" issues like education and health care. For trait stereotypes, women are assumed to be more compassionate and willing to compromise, which can work for or against them depending on the electoral context (Burrell 1994; Fox 1997). Overall, however, "masculine" traits are often perceived as more important and useful for political office than "female" traits (Rosenwasser and Dean 1989; Huddy and Terkildsen 1993). This is especially true among older generations (Welch 1977).

The question of how voters perceive females as candidates for political office is still relevant, since women are still being elected at lower rates than men. This is especially confusing given research that has shown that exposure to women in elected office leads to more positive views of women as leaders and can break down previously held gender stereotypes (Beaman et al. 2009). How do voters today feel about females as leaders and political candidates? What do regular Americans believe is the source of the problem (if they believe there is one)? Do different demographics believe differently? Specifically, do younger voters perceive women leaders differently than the perceptions of their older counterparts?

Central to our work here and that of many other researchers is the idea of generations. Although historians, sociologists, and political scientists have grappled with the existence of distinct categories and characteristics of political generations, Bartels and Jackman's (2014) age-period-cohort model of examining voters' attitudes is the most useful to our understanding of how people view women political leaders (see also chap. 2 and chap. 4, this volume). They argue that the views of people with identifiable birth cohorts are distinct, specifically as they respond to political events. The youngest voters in 2020, for example, experienced Hillary Clinton primarily as a presidential candidate running against Donald Trump, whereas older voters would have different exposures to Hillary Clinton as a First Lady, a U.S. senator, or a U.S. secretary of state, in addition to her role as a presidential candidate.

The idea that the younger generations of voters see the political world differently has both anecdotal and research evidence to support it. The civic engagement of young people around issues like gun laws and climate change shows a commitment to public activism unseen in the United States since the 1960s. Jacobson (2016) argues that the Obama presidency, as well as experiences from the 2008 recession and its aftermath, had a "generational imprinting" effect on younger Americans that could affect their political behavior for decades. Bartels and Jackman (2014) argue that the political socialization of contemporary young people fundamentally differs from that of previous generations. Pew (2015) also discusses how younger voters are fundamentally more liberal than their predecessors.

The question remains: Do younger voters, even with more liberal attitudes and being socialized differently than previous generations, see the gender disparity in political leadership differently? The Pew Research Center attempted to answer these questions with major studies from 2008 to 2018. What they found was a paradox: while Americans believe women outperform men on five out of six corporate leadership traits (and tie with men on two other political leadership traits), they are evenly divided about whether men or women make better leaders (Horowitz, Igielnik, and Parker 2018).

In their most recent survey, Pew (Horowitz, Igielnik, and Parker 2018) noted generational differences, particularly among women, in terms of the challenges that women faced in achieving leadership positions in business and politics. In their results, about two-thirds (68%) of women under 50 think that discrimination is a major barrier to women's leadership, as compared to half (50%) of women over 50. Younger women are also twice as likely as younger men to see discrimination as a major barrier to women achieving leadership positions. There are virtually no differences in the perceptions of discrimination as a barrier between younger and older men, however.

We build on this research and test the theory of gendered and generational socialization using our own Meredith Poll data to determine whether younger generations do, in fact, have different views than their older counterparts on women in elected office. Ideally, their views about women as political leaders would be less traditional than their older counterparts, thus leading to voting for more women for elected office. However, as our results demonstrate, there is a further bifurcation in the electorate along gender lines with younger women supporting the idea of women political leaders as being equal to or better than male leaders, but young men reflecting the more traditional views of their elders.

Data and Methods

Combining the literature on attitudes toward women in office with what we know about generational views, we expect to see significant differences *between* younger and older generations and gender differences *within* generations regarding various dimensions related to women in political office.

We will seek to answer our research questions using data from the Meredith Poll, an academic survey research program that is administered as part of Meredith College's commitment to civic engagement. The poll uses mixed methods, with part of the survey given to an online panel procured through Dynata and part of the survey given over the phone by Meredith College students. Our respondents are a representative sample of North Carolina voters. We feel North Carolina serves as a good representative for American voters since North Carolina is a true "purple" state—rated by Larry Sabato as one of only two true tossups in the 2020 election—and our other demographics align fairly closely to national demographics.

The following results section is divided into three parts: perceptions of women as political leaders, perceptions regarding barriers to women's participation in politics, and perceptions of mechanisms to improve women's participation. Each of these parts is important to understanding how respondents feel about women in office, as well as whether they believe the problems that face women candidates are individual or systemic. The final part tests just how committed a respondent is to fix the issue of women's representation; after all, it is easy to say that men and women are equally good political leaders generally. Changing electoral rules to help women, as many other advanced democracies have done, signals a much deeper commitment to equality.

A complete list of exactly which poll each question came from, when it was administered, and the poll's margin of error can be found in the appendix. Because we do not survey the same respondents over time, we cannot trace causality; thus, this chapter is an exploration of generational and gender attitudes, rather than proposing any causal relationships. The main demographic variables of interest are gender, generation, and partisanship of the respondent. We have followed the Pew Research Center's guidelines regarding definitions and names of generations. Gen Z includes those aged 18–22, Millennials include those aged 23–38, Generation X includes those aged 39–54, the Boomers are aged 55–73, and the Silent generation includes those 74 and older (these being each group's ages in 2019). In the most recent two polls, we oversampled Gen Z voters in order to develop a more complete picture of the range of this generation's views.

Results

Perceptions of Women as Political Leaders

Because we administer the Meredith Poll from a women's college, we are obviously very concerned with asking questions related to women and politics. First, we have asked whether respondents thought men or women make better political leaders on several iterations of the poll. Every time, a strong majority of respondents said that men and women make "equally good" political leaders. However, dividing these results by gender reveals slight differences; for example, in fall 2016, women were three times as likely as men to say that women make better political leaders (10% vs. 3%). In the same poll, though, more women (15.4%) than men (11.5%) also thought that men make better political leaders. This is different than what we found in fall 2018, when twice as many men as women said that men make better political leaders (20% vs. 10.6%). On the opposite side, 14.1 percent of women said women make better political leaders while only 8.1 percent of men said the same.

In both fall 2016 and fall 2018, between 68 percent and 90 percent of each generation said that men and women make equally good political leaders, but dividing the results by gender and generation at the same time reveals more interesting results. As figures 6.1 and 6.2 show, in general as both men and women get older, they are more likely to say that men make better political leaders. However, Silent generation women were just as likely as younger women to prefer a female leader in fall 2016. Another significant outlier is men from Gen Z in the fall

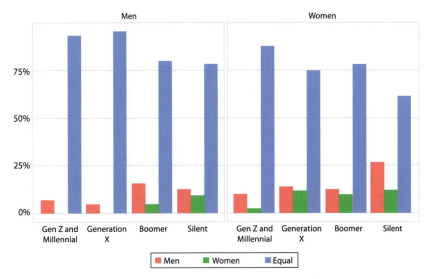

Fig. 6.1. Better Political Leader by Gender and Generation (Fall 2016)
Source: Derived with data collected from authors' conducted Meredith poll.

2018 poll, who were actually the single largest group across both polls to report preferring male political leaders. The group most likely to say that women make better political leaders was Boomer women in fall 2018. Overall, despite the majorities of each generation saying men and women are equally good political leaders in both fall 2016 and fall 2018, we see a distinct growth in the number preferring men over women political leaders in fall 2018. This result corresponds to the growing polarization of many facets of politics from 2016 to 2018.

Because the popular perception is that Gen Z is very progressive, our fall 2018 result regarding Gen Z men was very surprising to us. Accordingly, we fielded a Gen Z-only poll in summer 2020 to try to dig deeper. As figure 6.3 demonstrates, we again found that Gen Z men are surprisingly likely to report preferring male political leaders: fully one-fourth of them gave this answer, compared to 7 percent of Gen Z women. On the other hand, 35 percent of Gen Z women reported preferring female political leaders, by far the highest number we have seen for this answer. Including partisanship makes the source of the polarization clear: Republican Gen Z men. Their polar opposite—Democratic Gen Z women—are the group most likely to prefer women political leaders, but Republican Gen Z women and unaffiliated Gen Z women are not too far behind them.

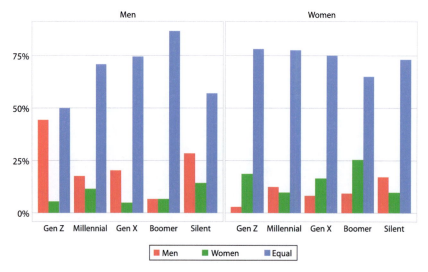

Fig. 6.2. Better Political Leader by Gender and Generation (Fall 2018)
Source: Derived with data collected from authors' conducted Meredith poll.

Our fall 2016 survey asked respondents to determine whether men or women political leaders would be better at representing the interests of people like them, depicted in figure 6.4. While we did find that solid majorities of each generation thought men and women were equally good at representing people like them, the Silent generation was most likely to prefer men at 21.4 percent. However, when gender is added to the equation, our answer becomes more complicated: we find that the group most likely to say men are better at representing them is the women of the Silent generation (21.3%), followed very closely by the men in the combined Gen Z/Millennial generation (21.2%). Women across the generations believe more in descriptive representation than their male counterparts, and women of the Gen Z/Millennial generations believe this the strongest.

Perceptions of Barriers to Women's Participation in Politics

All of the previous questions were about men and women already in political office. However, we are also interested in determining whether respondents believe, as we do, that it is a problem that women are so underrepresented in political office, and what some reasons for this underrepresentation might be. First, we asked what

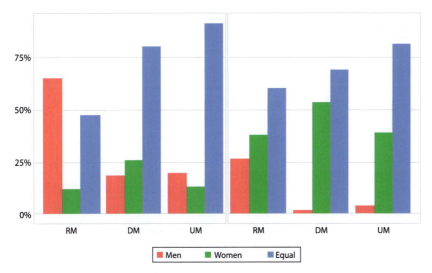

Fig. 6.3. Gen Z Better Political Leader by Gender and Partisanship
Source: Derived with data collected from authors' conducted Meredith poll.

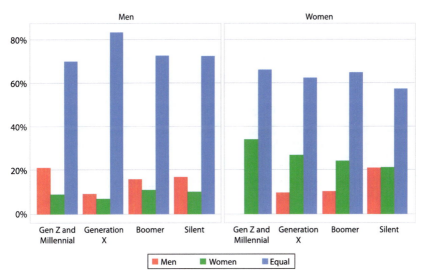

Fig. 6.4. Whether Men or Women Political Leaders Are Better at "Representing People Like Me"
Source: Derived with data collected from authors' conducted Meredith poll.

respondents believed were impediments to women being elected, and these results may be found in table 6.1. Overall, a majority of respondents said that discrimination, women being held back by men in party leadership, and that Americans aren't ready to elect a woman were all reasons why there aren't more women in elected office. Americans being unready was the most given reason, with 80 percent of respondents saying this was either a major or minor reason why there are fewer women in elected office, and this result held across all generations for the most part. However, there were some interesting differences among the generations regarding other reasons. For example, members of Gen Z were much more likely than the other generations to say that women aren't tough enough for politics. Upon closer examination, it is Gen Z men who are driving this result; 66 percent of Gen Z men say women aren't tough enough for politics, while 75 percent of Gen Z women say this isn't a reason at all for fewer women in office. The Silent generation, on the other side of the age spectrum, was the next group to say women aren't tough enough, but there are no significant gender differences within that generation. We find a similar pattern on the responses as to whether "fewer women have experience" is a reason there aren't more women in office. The two generations that agreed the most with this statement were Gen Z, at 56 percent, and the Silent generation, at 55.3 percent. However, again, Gen Z men (78%) are much more likely to say it than Gen Z women (48%), while there are no significant gender differences among the Silent respondents. Regarding barriers to women's full participation in politics, then, it appears that Gen Z men are more similar to members of the Silent generation, and Gen Z women are closer to members of the Millennial, Gen X, and Boomer generations.

We estimated that older Americans would be more likely to say family responsibilities are a major or minor barrier, while younger Americans would name discrimination as a major or minor barrier. Indeed, a full 71 percent of the Silent generation said family responsibilities were an issue for women, compared to only 48 percent of Gen Z. (The middle generations all hovered around 51–55 percent regarding family responsibilities.) Also, 88 percent of Gen Z said discrimination was a major or minor barrier, while only 62 percent of the Silent generation said the same. In fact, as one moves down a generation in age, that group is more likely to feel discrimination against women is a problem for getting women into elected office than the previous generation.

TABLE 6.1. Perceptions by Generation of Why There Aren't More Women in Office

	Major/Minor Reason	Not a Reason
Americans Aren't Ready		
Gen Z	82	18
Millennial	79.5	20.5
Gen X	79.3	20.7
Boomer	87.9	12.2
Silent	72.2	27.8
Women Are Discriminated Against		
Gen Z	88	12
Millennial	76.4	23.6
Gen X	75.5	24.6
Boomer	69	31
Silent	62.3	37.7
Women's Responsibilities to Family		
Gen Z	47.9	52.1
Millennial	51.2	48.9
Gen X	52.5	47.5
Boomer	55.4	44.6
Silent	71	29.1
Women aren't Tough Enough		
Gen Z	40	60
Millennial	28.8	71.2
Gen X	29.8	70.2
Boomer	32.5	67.6
Silent	33.3	66.7
Fewer Women Have Experience		
Gen Z	56	44
Millennial	45.6	54.3
Gen X	45.7	54.3
Boomer	47.2	52.8
Silent	55.3	44.6
Men in Party Politics Hold Women Back		
Gen Z	75.8	24.5
Millennial	72.7	27.3
Gen X	74.1	25.9
Boomer	80.3	19.7
Silent	77.6	22.5

Perceptions of Mechanisms to Help Women Participate

In the fall of 2018, we asked specifically about the importance of having women in office. When we asked the question in a straightforward manner—"Do you believe having women in public office is important?"—a large majority of both genders and all generations said yes, with the only variation coming from partisanship (Republicans were slightly less likely to agree). However, when it came to laws that would guarantee women's presence in public office, like gender quotas for elected office or gender balance laws for appointed office, respondents were a lot less unanimous. Nearly 60 percent of men said that the U.S. should not have a gender quota at either the legislature or party level, and 46 percent of women agreed with them. This leaves us with a complicated result: while women were indeed more likely to favor gender quotas than men, most women still favored no gender quotas. Those women who favored a gender quota liked it at the party level (31.3%) rather than as a rule for the elected legislature (22.7%). When we add the generation variable, we see that while within each generation most men did not favor some sort of gender quota, the strength of the relationship weakens as the men get younger. Indeed, Gen Z men are three times as likely to favor a legislative gender quota as men from the Silent generation. Among women, Boomers and women from the Silent generation favored no gender quotas, while Gen Z women were the only group in our sample who favored any kind of gender quota (at the legislature) over doing nothing.

Regarding gender balance laws for appointed office, we first explained to respondents what they were and said that Iowa had a requirement law, some states have a recommendation law, and that most states have no law regarding gender balance in appointed office. Then, we asked respondents what they thought: Should states require gender balance in appointed office? (We gave them the ability to answer that they liked recommendation rather than requirement.) When examining responses by gender only, we see that nearly half of all men (47%) believe there should be no gender balance laws. Women were much more divided—28.3 percent favored a gender balance requirement, 25.6 percent favored a gender balance recommendation, and 37 percent preferred no gender balance law. As might be expected with this rather obscure topic, 7 percent of men and 9 percent of women didn't know what they thought about the issue. When examining by both gender and generation, again the only group of our sample that

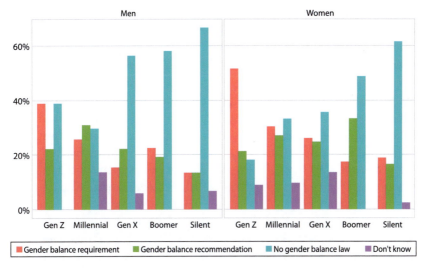

Fig. 6.5. Gender Balance Laws by Gender and Generation
Source: Derived with data collected from authors' conducted Meredith poll.

favored a gender balance law were Gen Z women; over half of them said states should require gender balance for appointed offices. Surprisingly, Gen Z men were right behind them; they favored a gender balance requirement at a higher rate than every other generation of women. As we had estimated, as both men and women grew older, they were less and less likely to say there should be any kind of gender balance law. These results may be seen in figure 6.5.

Discussion

Overall, we found that there are differences between generations and within generations regarding women as political leaders. We were correct that older generations would view male political leaders more favorably, but we did not anticipate finding that Gen Z men shared this view. We also found expected generational differences regarding barriers to women participating in politics, with older generations believing that individual-level factors like family responsibilities are a bigger barrier and younger generations believing that systemic factors like discrimination are a bigger barrier. However, we were surprised to find that all generations were united in the belief that "Americans aren't ready" to elect a woman. There were also unexpected differences within generations, with Gen Z men saying that women "aren't tough enough" for politics and that "fewer women have experience" while Gen Z women are more likely to reject these notions.

These results regarding the gender polarization of Gen Z seem not to bode too well for the future, but Gen Z men complicated matters by agreeing with their female counterparts that gender quotas and gender balance laws are a good way to get more women into office. Indeed, we found the starkest generational divides on these questions. Interestingly, this suggests that Gen Z men simultaneously view systemic-level equality as important and individual women leaders with a suspicious eye. If this is the case, their political socialization may explain the situation; as people who came of age under the United States' first Black president, laws that improve equality may seem natural. However, Gen Z also began to vote under President Trump, whose defeat of Hillary Clinton and emphasis on hypermasculinity may have conditioned Gen Z men regarding women political leaders. Therefore, the theory that we may see more women in elected office as younger voters take over the electorate seems to be unfounded, but it may be possible to see more activity on general equality issues. This is an important finding, as it suggests that groups interested in more representation of women in politics might do better to advocate for laws and policies that benefit women rather than putting the emphasis on electing them to office.

One characteristic that is often considered important regarding the socialization of political attitudes is race/ethnicity. However, we did not include a discussion of this demographic in this chapter because, quite frankly, we found much smaller differences between racial/ethnic groups than between generations and genders for most of our questions. Finally, our results are limited by the fact that, while the Meredith Poll has asked about women as political leaders many times, our other questions are usually one-offs. It would be better if we had more iterations of data for all our questions. We do have data on intention to vote for specific female candidates, however (for example, we have Trump vs. Clinton in 2016 and Elizabeth Warren and Harris vs. a field of Democratic men from earlier this year), so our next step is to examine these questions for generational differences. We suspect, following Pew Research Center analysis from the 2016 election, that older Americans might say they are willing to vote for a generic woman leader, but when it comes time to vote for a specific, real-life woman, they are in fact unwilling.

APPENDIX

All of the respondents of the Meredith Poll are self-reported registered voters in the state of North Carolina. Each poll is weighted to resemble the population of the state of North Carolina. The fall 2016 and fall 2018 polls had respondents from all generations; the summer 2020 poll only had Gen Z respondents.

Fall 2016: Administered September 18–22, 2016

N = 487; Margin of error: +/– 4.43 percentage points

> Q.2 Which of the following comes closest to your opinion of men and women as political leaders?
> | | |
> |---|---|
> | Men generally make better political leaders | 1 |
> | Women generally make better political leaders | 2 |
> | In general, men and women make equally good political leaders | 3 |
> | Don't know/refused | 4 |
>
> Q.8 In general, do you think men or women in political office are better at representing the interests of people like you?
> | | |
> |---|---|
> | Men | 1 |
> | Women | 2 |
> | No difference | 3 |
> | Don't know/refused | 4 |

Fall 2018: Administered October 21–25, 2018

N = 725; Margin of error: +/– 4 percentage points

> Q.5 Which of the following comes closest to your opinion of men and women as political leaders?
> | | |
> |---|---|
> | Men generally make better political leaders | 1 |
> | Women generally make better political leaders | 2 |
> | In general, men and women make equally good political leaders | 3 |
> | Don't know | 4 |
> | No answer/Refused | 5 |
>
> Q.6 Do you believe having women in public office is important?
> | | |
> |---|---|
> | Yes | 1 |

No	2
Don't know	3
No answer/Refused	4

As you may know, our country has 12 women governors out of 50 and 23 US Senators out of 100. There are many reasons why there are fewer women than men in high political office. I am going to read you a list of some of them. For each one, please tell me whether you think it is a major reason, a minor reason, or not a reason why there are fewer women in political office. [The potential responses are listed under Q7, and were the same for the remaining questions in this section.]

Q.7 Many Americans aren't ready to elect women to higher offices.

Major reason	1
Minor reason	2
No reason	3
Don't know	4
No answer/Refused	5

Q.8 Generally speaking, women don't make as good leaders as men.

Q.9 Women are discriminated against in all areas of life and politics is no exception.

Q.10 Women's responsibilities to family don't leave time for politics.

Q.11 Generally speaking, women aren't tough enough for politics.

Q.12 Fewer women have the experience required for higher office.

Q.13 Women who are active in party politics get held back by men.

Q.14 About half the countries in the world have gender quotas, which are designed to ensure that their legislatures are gender balanced. Some countries require that a certain number of elected officials are women, while other countries only require that parties nominate an equal number of men and women. Which comes closest to your view?

The US government should require a certain number of elected women	1
The parties should be required to nominate a certain number of men and women	2
There should be no gender balance requirements	3
Don't know	4
No answer/Refused	5

Q.16 Do you think states should require or recommend gender balance for appointed offices?

Yes, there should be a gender balance requirement	1
Yes, there should be a gender balance recommendation	2
No, they should not have a gender law for appointed office	3
Don't know	4
No answer/Refused	5

Summer 2020: Administered June 30–July 1, 2020

N = 251; Margin of error: +/– 5 percentage points

Q.5 Which of the following comes closest to your opinion of men and women as political leaders?

Men generally make better political leaders	1
Women generally make better political leaders	2
In general, men and women make equally good political leaders	3
Don't know	4

REFERENCES

Bartels, Larry M., and Simon Jackman. 2014. "A Generational Model of Political Learning." *Electoral Studies* 33 (1): 7–18.

Beaman, Lori, Raghabendra Chattapadhyay, Esther Duflo, Rohini Pande, and Petia Topalova. 2009. "Powerful Women: Does Exposure Reduce Bias?" *Quarterly Journal of Economics* 124: 1497–1540.

Boxer, Barbara. 1994. *Politics and the New Revolution of Women in America*. Washington, DC: National Press Books.

Burrell, Barbara C. 1994. *A Woman's Place Is in the House: Campaigning for Congress in the Feminist Era*. Ann Arbor: University of Michigan Press.

Campbell, Angus, Philip E. Converse, Warren E. Miller, and Donald E. Stokes. 1964. *The American Voter*. New York: John Wiley.

Carli, Linda L. 1990. "Gender, Language, and Influence." *Journal of Personality and Social Psychology* 59: 941–51.

"Current Numbers of Women Officeholders." Center for American Women and Politics, Rutgers University.

Dolan, Kathleen. 2004. *Voting for Women: How the Public Evaluates Women Candidates*. Boulder: Westview Press.

Fox, Richard L. 1997. *Gender Dynamics in Congressional Elections*. Thousand Oaks, CA: Sage.

Fox, Richard L., and Jennifer L. Lawless. 2004. "Entering the Arena? Gender and the Decision to Run for Office." *American Journal of Political Science* 48 (2): 264–80.

Fox, Richard L., and Jennifer L. Lawless. 2011. "Gendered Perceptions and Political Candidacies: Central Barrier to Women's Equality in Electoral Politics." *American Journal of Political Science* 55 (1): 59–73.

Fox, Richard L., and Zoe M. Oxley. 2003. "Gender Stereotyping in State Executive Elections: Candidate Selection and Success." *Journal of Politics* 65: 833–50.

Hess, Abigail. 2020. "The 2020 Election Shows Gen Z's Voting Power for Years to Come." *CNBC*, November 18. https://www.cnbc.com/2020/11/18/the-2020-electi on-shows-gen-zs-voting-power-for-years-to-come.html

Horowitz, Juliana M., Ruth Igielnik, and Kim Parker. 2018. "Women and Leadership 2018." Pew Research Center, September 20. https://www.pewsocialtrends.org/20 18/09/20/women-and-leadership-2018/

Huddy, Leonie, and Nayda Terkildsen. 1993. "Gender Stereotypes and the Perception of Male and Female Candidates." *American Journal of Political Science* 37 (1): 119–47.

Jacobson, Gary C. 2016. "The Obama Legacy and the Future of Partisan Conflict: Demographic Change and Generational Imprinting." *ANNALS of the American Academy of Political and Social Sciences* 667: 72–92.

Jaros, Dean. 1973. *Socialization to Politics*. New York: Praeger.

Koch, Jeffrey W. 2000. "Do Citizens Apply Gender Stereotypes to Infer Candidates' Ideological Orientations?" *Journal of Politics* 62 (2): 414–29.

Luks, Sam, and Brian Shaffner. 2019. "New Polling Shows How Much Sexism Is Hurting the Democratic Women Running for President." *Washington Post*, July 11. https://www.washingtonpost.com/politics/2019/07/11/women-candidates -must-overcome-sexist-attitudes-even-democratic-primary/

McLennan, David. 2018. "The Status of Women in North Carolina Politics." Meredith College. https://www.meredith.edu/college-research/the-status-of-women -in-n-c-politics/

NBC News. 2020. "Exit Polls 2020." November 3. https://www.nbcnews.com/politics /2020-elections/exit-polls

Oxley, Z. M., M. R. Holman, J. S. Greelee, A L. Bos, and J. Celeste Lay. 2020. "Children's Views of the American Presidency." *Public Opinion Quarterly* 84 (1): 141– 57.

Pearson, Kathryn, and Jennifer L. Lawless. 2008. "The Primary Reason for Women's Underrepresentation? Reevaluating the Conventional Wisdom." *Journal of Politics* 70 (1): 67–82.

Pew Research Center. 2015. "A Different Look at Generations and Partisanship." April 30. http://www.people-press.org/2015/04/30/a-different-look-at-generatio ns-and-partisanship/

Ridgeway, Cecilia L. 2001. "Gender, Status, and Leadership." *Journal of Social Issues* 57: 637–55.

Rosenwasser, Shirley M., and Norma G. Dean. 1989. "Gender Role and Political Office: Effects of Perceived Masculinity/Femininity of Candidate and Political Office." *Psychology of Women Quarterly* 13 (1): 77–85.

Rule, Wilma. 1981. "Why Women Don't Run: The Critical Contextual Factors in Women's Legislative Recruitment." *Western Political Quarterly* 34 (March): 60–77.

Sigel, Roberta. 1965. "Assumptions about the Learning of Political Values." *Annals of the American Academy of Political and Social Science* 361: 1–9. http://www.jstor.org/stable/1035982

Thomas, Sue. 2005. "Introduction: Women and Elective Office: Past, Present, and Future." In *Women and Elective Office*, 2nd ed., edited by S. Thomas and C. Wilcox. New York: Oxford University Press.

Welch, Susan. 1977. "Women as Political Animals? A Test of Some Explanations for Male-Female Political Participation Differences." *American Journal of Political Science* 21 (4): 711–30.

Welch, Susan. 1978. "Recruitment of Women to Public Office." *Western Political Quarterly* 31 (2): 372–80.

YouGov/Economist. 2021. January 16–19 Poll. https://docs.cdn.yougov.com/4k61xul7y7/econTabReport.pdf

7 | What American Heroism Teaches Us about Generations and Politics

Bruce Peabody

This book explores how generational differences explain distinct political behavior, opinions, and shifting trajectories of party loyalty and other group identifications. This chapter begins with a somewhat different question: Can we use specific rhetorical tropes to overcome (or activate) political differences across generations? In particular, do appeals to heroism and specific heroic figures close gaps in generational attitudes, or do they, instead, teach us about the stubbornness or specific nature of these differences? Here, I explore these issues through survey research regarding public attitudes about historic and contemporary public figures, and the traits different generational groups associate with heroism.

Political references to heroism often have a generational focus. For example, on July 4, 2020, former president Donald Trump traveled to Mount Rushmore, South Dakota to "pay tribute to the exceptional lives and extraordinary legacies of" the four presidents carved into the famous Black Hills monument (Trump 2020). Trump hailed not only George Washington, Thomas Jefferson, Abraham Lincoln, and Theodore Roosevelt, but all the "great heroes" of America, promising that these icons would never be "rip[ped] . . . from our monuments, or from our hearts." While the remarks were a contemporaneous reaction to the removal and defacement of statues and memorials taking place as part of ongoing protests against police violence, the president also gestured to a broader and more overarching project. He sought to link the nation's founders and their political ideals to both a string of (his self-selected) heroic figures and a perceived generational struggle, especially for the hearts and minds of the young. As he warned, "Our children are taught in school to hate their own country, and to believe that the men and women who built it were not heroes, but . . . villains." Instead, the president insisted the country must "raise the next generation of American patriots" by teaching them "they live in a land of legends," iconic figures whose common ideals and virtues both knit different cohorts of Americans together and remind them of their distinctive political culture, including their status as "the most adventurous and confident people ever to walk the face of the Earth."

Invoking heroes to talk about (and erase) generational difference, and to inculcate civic values across them, is neither new nor consigned to one party. In 2014, while touring MacDill Air Force Base, President Barack Obama hailed the "9/11 Generation of heroes" who responded to the September 11 attacks, killed Osama bin Laden, disrupted al Qaeda, and helped Afghani citizens in "reclaiming their communities" (Nakamura 2014). More than three decades earlier, in his first inaugural address, President Ronald Reagan traced an arc of heroism stretching from the military veterans of the American Revolution to the fallen soldiers of "Guadalcanal, Tarawa, Pork Chop Hill, the Chosin Reservoir, and in a hundred rice paddies and jungles of a place called Vietnam" (Reagan 1981). Beyond these notable presidential speeches, countless other elected officials (not to mention pundits and commentators) have appealed to the so-called Greatest generation to teach younger generations about their supposed historical debts and civic responsibilities (Welle et al. 2012, 233; Mettler 2005).

Understanding the Links between Generations and Heroes

What explains this regular intertwining of political discourse about heroism and (purported) generational cohesion? Perhaps most obviously, for American government officials, especially those presiding over a diverse and divided electorate, calling on identifiable heroes is an appealing strategy for bringing together potentially contentious groups and interests. Hero talk, when it resonates, might serve as a unifying gravitational force among a pluralist people. Identifying heroic figures can help to shape an "imagined political community" (Anderson [1983] 2006, 6) of ideals and cultural reference points. As Amber Roessner puts it, "Cultures are regenerated through their stories of great men [and women]. . . . The individual and society are mutually constituted through the practice of hero-worship" (2014, 8). To the extent generational fault lines reflect real or imagined schisms with respect to salient cultural touchstones, policy priorities, party affiliations, and overall attitudes toward governance, turning to heroes is likely to be alluring to leaders. "Heroes may serve as an emblem of unity in a society" and an "important cultural marker of a nation's purported union around key values, symbols, and icons" (Peabody and Jenkins 2017, 210).

But the relationship between heroism and generational difference is also likely to be freighted and conflictual, an observation that helps explain why elected officials regularly expend energy trying to reconcile the two. As numerous chapters in this volume have discussed, generational theory presumes that groups of people possess common political and social attitudes shaped by "their exposure to the same prevailing events" (Klecka 1971, 358). Since these signature events often represent crises or national challenges (such as World War II, the civil rights movement, or 9/11) they are likely to include pivotal leaders and actors (such as Franklin Roosevelt, Martin Luther King Jr., or the veterans of the Afghan and Iraq Wars) who help the public confront, remember, and interpret these historical struggles. But this observation implies that each generation is likely to have a distinctive, powerful, and potentially divisive relationship (vis-à-vis other generational groups) with the heroes of their age. The challenge of those seeking to use heroes to build generational cohesion, therefore, is to find the right figures or narrative structures to overcome experiential and referential divisions between age cohorts.

At least two other factors complicate analysis of the relationship between heroism and generations in the 21st century. First, public trust in government (and institutions more generally) has tumbled since the 1960s. Russell Dalton (2004) captures a scholarly consensus in concluding that the "mass of evidence . . . demonstrates that the American public has become increasingly skeptical and distrustful of the politicians who lead them" over the past half century (27). Such an outcome suggests a powerful and sustained period effect, and that generational attitudes about overtly political heroes (and perhaps institutional or establishment figures more generally) will vary across groups with higher and lower levels of political trust. Second, as Laura Stoker and others have noted, today's analyses of generations must take into account the rise, since the 1980s, of partisan polarization within the electorate including the more recent intensification of this dynamic via negative or affective polarization (Abramowitz and Webster 2018; Hetherington and Weiler 2009; Iyengar and Westwood 2015; Iyengar et al. 2019; see also Stoker, chap. 2, this vol.). These twin developments have pointed implications for an investigation of the relationship between heroes and generations. Specifically, one might wonder whether the shearing forces of political mistrust and partisan polarization make the turn to heroism a largely hopeless or even incoherent strategy for communicating with and binding together disparate generational groups.

This backdrop sets the stage for the puzzles driving this chapter, which I explore by presenting and interpreting data collected from an August 2020 survey asking respondents about their views regarding the hero status of particular figures (such as Trump, George Floyd, Abraham Lincoln, and Christopher Columbus) alongside their evaluations of attributes and behaviors that might be regarded as heroic.[1] In the sections that follow, I briefly explain how I define both heroism and generational difference, before advancing a number of hypotheses regarding the kinds of relationships we might anticipate between generational attitudes, specific heroic figures, and distinct heroic traits in light of the research presented in this book and related scholarship. I then test my hypotheses (in an admittedly preliminary way) against the survey data, discussing the methodology and results of my study and then speculating on the wider importance of this chapter (and its focus on heroism) for understanding the role of generations in American politics in our partisan and distrustful age.

Definitions and Concepts

Exploring the relationship between political heroes and generational attitudes requires a rudimentary understanding of what heroism is at a minimum so one can plausibly identify candidates for evaluation by survey respondents. In other words, without even a crude working theory of heroism, it becomes difficult to know who or what to ask the public about.

There is considerable diversity and imprecision in how both scholars and the public refer to heroes. That said, drawing on prior research, we might identify two general hero types especially pertinent to this chapter. First, one can delineate *great heroes* characterized by their pursuit of a cause larger than themselves, demonstration of some extraordinary and rare talent or attributes, and assumption of significant personal risk (Peabody and Jenkins 2017, 21–22). A figure like Harriet Tubman, whose commitment to abolitionism required enormous bravery and fortitude in the face of danger, fits this conception. In prior scholarship, I found that "ordinary" Americans (with their views captured through surveys, focus groups, and other sources) often supported the association of heroism with these demanding and rather robust standards.

We might also identify a second group of *headline heroes*, individuals who do not embody all (or even any) of the core aspects of "great heroes," but who are nevertheless identified as heroic figures by political, media, or other elite opinion leaders. These figures may be embraced by the public as heroes because of this priming or because of some widespread association with a favored cause, value, or event. In his 2007 State of the Union address, President George W. Bush saluted several of these figures, including the "heroic" Julie Aigner-Clark, who grew the Baby Einstein Company "to more than $20 million in sales" in "just five years" (Peabody and Jenkins 2017, 65–66). Whatever talents and even good intentions Aigner-Clark may have demonstrated in expanding her business, these achievements did not obviously rise to a level of greatness heroism.

The survey research at the heart of this chapter sounded public judgments regarding a range of figures who might plausibly serve as great or headline heroes, or conceivably both. Thus, I asked questions about both enduring American icons (such as Washington and the "Greatest generation" of World War II veterans) and what would likely be more ephemeral figures, at least in the public's consciousness (George Floyd and health care workers).

With respect to how I conceive of generational groups, my approach is fairly traditional and consistent with the chapters in the rest of this book. Thus, I adhere to Stoker's characterization of a generation as "a group defined by the intersection of age and history, with its members having been of a certain age (or within a certain age range) during a specified year or range of years (chap. 2, this volume)." I follow the Pew Research Center's division of these groups into six cohorts, each of which is supposedly associated (to varying degrees) with a distinct "worldview, which in turn affects its members' more specific opinions and behaviors" (Zukin et al. 2006, 11). This political perspective forms during a person's early adulthood through shared experiences of socialization and learning, including pivotal and traumatic events (Hart-Brinson 2018), unique political contexts, and longer-term trends that "lead new generations to reach adulthood in social, cultural, economic, and political circumstances significantly different from prior ones" (Zukin et al. 2006, 11).

Clearly, this process does not produce uniformity in a cohort's consciousness or sense of being distinct, but I follow other scholars in positing that at least a portion of each generational group will develop a particular political identity, namely, a resulting sense that politics is "an important part of their lives" (Gentry 2018, 21). After all, each generation has a somewhat different stake in policy choices and governmental priorities, and different expectations regarding governance and elected officials. Overall, a given generation is expected to carry their distinctive orientations across voting and other political behaviors in ways that continue to delineate them from other generational groups. As Stoker summarizes, "The core idea underlying generation effects, [is] that young people entering the electorate will be especially influenced by the Zeitgeist of the time." Those comprising generational groups can still learn and adapt as they encounter new events and as the nation's political dynamics change, but generational theory presumes that age cohorts revert, at critical moments, to ideas, assumptions, and heuristics decisively imprinted on their youth. As Scott McLean puts it (chap. 3, this volume), "Each generation confronts new circumstances as they age, but they always improvise their responses using frameworks imprinted from the formative years of early adulthood."

Within this theoretical paradigm, I focus my investigation on the five generational cohorts most available at the time of my survey research: Gen Z, Millennials, Xers, Baby Boomers, and Silents. Given the available data, I defined Millennials and Generation Zs as those who were between the ages of 18 to 34 when the survey was conducted, with Generation Xers between the ages of 35 and 54, and Boomers/Silents as those aged 55 and older. These distinctions do not comport precisely with commonly used birth year cutoffs, but my research was limited by the overall sample size. In light of this limitation, I did my best to approximate the various age cohorts currently in the United States. In the same spirit, I combined the two youngest groups (Millennials and Zs) due to the limited number of respondents, especially among Gen Z.

Hypotheses about Generations and Heroism

Within this framework, and in light of the generational research show-cased in this book, what hypotheses might we advance regarding how generational groups are likely to regard heroes and heroism? This question can be further subdivided along three dimensions: (1) *status* (do heroes exist and what role(s) do they distinctively play?); (2) *identity* (what specific individuals or groups of individuals qualify as heroes and meet these standards?); and (3) *attributes* (what specific traits and virtues do we associate with heroic figures and their behavior)?

With regard to status and function, one might hypothesize that those generations (chiefly Boomers and the portion of the Silent generation captured by my survey) will be generally more inclined to identify and recognize political heroes, especially those working within or alongside traditional institutions. The generations represented by these older Americans are more likely to possess institutional and social trust (Hetherington 1998, 792) and to have lived through an age of less media scrutiny and negativism (Sabato [1991] 2000). This is not to claim that these individuals are always trusting of, say, government and the media today. Indeed, as noted in earlier chapters of this book, Boomers in particular are likely to have come of age in an era when they had more negative feelings toward their own party than did members of the other generations (see Stoker, chap. 2, this vol.), making them more likely to look to independent or non-establishment political heroes beyond the traditional corridors of power. Still, these older groups are generally more likely (than Millennials and Gen Zs) to recall figures that came to national prominence in what was arguably a more forgiving political and communications environment (Peabody and Jenkins 2017, 169–70).[2]

With respect to the specific identity of heroes, generally speaking, each generational cohort is more likely to associate heroes with the pivotal crises or events that shaped their political socialization; thus, we can imagine that the Greatest generation would be inclined to consider the figures of Rosie the Riveter or Joe Louis as heroic, while Millennials, many of whom entered the electorate in a political environment inflected with the fear of 9/11, might look to members of Seal Team 6 who were involved in the covert operations that led to the killing of terrorist leader Osama bin Laden.

More generally, we can anticipate the tightening grip of partisanship as a force shaping attitudes about heroes, especially for Millennials and Gen Zs who entered adulthood when ideological polarization was in steady ascendance (McCarty, Poole, and Rosenthal 2006). This influence is likely to be strongest with respect to these younger generations' assessment of alleged heroes associated with party politics and issues, especially where these contemporaneous "headline heroes" have been dubbed as heroic by influential partisan and opinion leaders. In short, one might expect, in particular, that the representatives of Millennials and Gen Z will be more inclined than other groups to see prominent party representatives as heroic and much less likely to see out-group leaders in the same glittering light.[3]

With respect to specific heroic traits and roles, I hypothesize that three characteristics in particular should be generationally salient: challenging the status quo, leading efforts to bring about social and political change, and reflecting American values and beliefs. Given the greater demographic diversity of Millennials and Gen Z, and their correspondingly more liberal attitudes on cultural issues and weaker attachment to some traditional social institutions (like heterosexual marriage and organized religion), the younger generational groups should be generally more likely to associate heroism with challenging the status quo and bringing about social and political change. In contrast, Generation Xers and Silents will be more skeptical about heroes as change agents, and more sympathetic to viewing heroes as those who reflect American values and beliefs (Pew 2015; Rouse and Ross 2018). Anticipating Boomer attitudes is somewhat complicated given that their material success may make them more inclined to support the political and social status quo (Williams 2022), but given their unique history (coming of age in an era of citizen-initiated protest and social change) I expect them to be more inclined to see heroes as transformative rather than conservative.

Survey and Results

To test these hypotheses and explore the linkages between generational attitudes and the call of heroism, I conducted a telephone survey of New Jersey adults.[4] While a more complete explanation of the underlying methodology is available in the appendix, in general the survey sought to probe respondents' views regarding a range of historic (e.g., Christopher Columbus, the veterans of World War II), overtly partisan (e.g., Joe Biden and Donald Trump), "headline" (e.g., George Floyd), and arguably "great" heroes (e.g., Lincoln and Martin Luther King Jr.).

TABLE 7.1. Hero Identification

I'm going to read you some names and groups of people. Can you tell me if YOU think this person is a hero, or not?

	All	Age			Party ID			Gender		Race/ethnicity	
		18–34	35–54	55+	D	I	R	Male	Female	White	Non-white
Health care workers	92%	89%	91%	95%	96%	87%	92%	90%	95%	93%	91%
World War II veterans	92%	86%	91%	96%	93%	84%	96%	93%	91%	95%	87%
Iraq/Afghanistan veterans	90%	84%	92%	92%	89%	86%	95%	89%	91%	93%	86%
Martin Luther King	89%	89%	90%	88%	95%	84%	85%	88%	90%	87%	91%
Abraham Lincoln	80%	68%	79%	88%	78%	73%	88%	84%	76%	86%	71%
George Washington	76%	61%	74%	89%	73%	66%	89%	82%	71%	85%	64%
Jesus Christ	73%	71%	70%	78%	70%	68%	83%	71%	76%	72%	76%
Christopher Columbus	43%	26%	44%	54%	30%	34%	69%	46%	41%	54%	29%
George Floyd	31%	41%	28%	27%	41%	29%	17%	27%	33%	24%	40%
Joe Biden	27%	21%	20%	39%	46%	19%	9%	24%	30%	24%	32%
Donald Trump	23%	16%	22%	29%	2%	15%	57%	26%	21%	32%	10%
N	809	211	272	320	347	185	271	385	424	540	802

Note: Bold denotes significance ≤.05.

Other questions in the survey investigated people's views regarding what specific traits or accomplishments they associated with heroism.

As seen in table 7.1, across my sample, the different generational cohorts do not have difficulty identifying a range of heroes. Thus, on the ontological question of whether heroes exist, my survey respondents across the generations seem to have answered the question in the affirmative, identifying a range of heroic groups (World War II veterans and health care workers) and individuals (Martin Luther King Jr.). This is a somewhat surprising result in light of my expectation that younger generations, growing up in an age of greater political mistrust, would be less inclined to identify heroes.

Once one turns to asking respondents what essential role they believe heroes play in society, generational differences become more apparent, as seen in table 7.2. As hypothesized, Boomers/Silents are the most likely to say that heroes are important for reflecting American values and beliefs, with percentages that are more than double that for Millennials/Gen Z (14% versus 29%). Conversely, young adults and Xers are more likely than Boomers/Silents to recognize the importance of heroes for inspiration. Almost half of Millennials/Gen Zs and Xers say this is why heroes are important for society, as compared with a third (33%) of Boomers/Silents. These attitudinal differences occur independent of partisanship, as both Democratic and Republican Millennials/Zs and Xers believe in the importance of heroic inspiration in numbers that are significantly greater than among Democratic and Republican Boomers/Silents. Focusing on inspiration may well capture some institutional skepticism of younger respondents, insofar as it suggests that heroes effect change indirectly and not by virtue of their privilege or place.

With respect to the question of *what* figures are heroes, there was broad agreement about some names, but also notable differences that reinforce some of my hypotheses regarding generational difference. The figures who garnered the greatest cross-generational support as heroes were arguably nonpartisan (including military veterans, health care workers, and Jesus[5]) and political figures with limited direct association with contemporary party politics (Martin Luther King Jr.).

In contrast, across nine of the 11 potential heroic figures posed on the survey, there were notable generational differences reflecting support for both explicitly political and more apolitical heroes. As table 7.1 demonstrates, there is a trend of greater hero identification among older respondents for George Washington, Abraham Lincoln, veterans (of both World War II and the recent conflicts in Iraq and Afghanistan),

TABLE 7.2. Heroic Roles in Society

In your opinion, which of the following reasons best describes how, if at all, heroes are important in society? Do they . . . [insert option] OR are they unimportant in society?

	All	Age			Party ID			Gender		Race/ethnicity	
		18–34	35–54	55+	D	I	R	Male	Female	White	Non-white
Inspire others to do something they wouldn't otherwise do	**41%**	**46%**	**45%**	**33%**	**42%**	**44%**	**37%**	**43%**	**39%**	**39%**	**43%**
Lead efforts to bring about social and political change	25%	33%	23%	20%	34%	24%	14%	21%	28%	21%	30%
Reflect American values and beliefs	**21%**	**14%**	**18%**	**29%**	**15%**	**15%**	**34%**	**24%**	**19%**	**26%**	**16%**
Heroes are not important in society	3%	1%	4%	2%	1%	4%	3%	4%	2%	3%	2%
Combination (vol)	5	1%	5%	8%	6%	5%	4%	3%	7%	5%	5%
N	809	211	272	320	347	185	271	385	424	540	802

Note: Bold denotes significance ≤.05.

Joe Biden, and Donald Trump, to name a few. Although the percentage differences between Millennials/Zs and Boomers/Silents is relatively small for some figures, it is sizable for others. For example, fewer than two-thirds (61%) of Millennials/Zs regard George Washington as a hero, while three-quarters (74%) of Xers and 89 percent of Boomers/Silents feel that he is a hero.[6] Christopher Columbus, George Floyd, and Joe Biden were three other figures that seemed to prompt the greatest generational splits. Given the contemporary prominence of the protests over Floyd's murder and the Black Lives Matter movement generally, it is reasonable to posit that some of these evaluations were charged by racial politics and might not be replicated in subsequent studies. Stated differently, period effects are surely evident in the data collected from my survey.[7] Unless one sees Biden as a polarizing racial figure, his generational evaluation is likely different from, say, Floyd's, and may simply reflect representational and life cycle issues: greater comfort (and discomfort) with the candidate based on his age (Biden was 78 at the time the survey was distributed).

Table 7.1 shows that, not surprisingly, the major party representatives elicited significant partisan differences when it came to assessing their heroic status. Thus, almost half of Democrats (46%) regarded then presidential candidate Joe Biden as heroic, compared with only 9 percent of Republicans. Incumbent president Donald Trump garnered over half of his own party's respondents endorsing him as a hero (57%), compared with almost no Democrats (2%). Beyond these evaluations of presidential figures, even long-revered public figures now appear to be evaluated through a partisan lens. For example, even though broad majorities of both Democrats and Republicans regarded Lincoln and Washington as heroic, Democrats were less inclined to come to this conclusion. Seventy-three percent of Democrats endorsed Washington's heroic status while significantly more Republicans said the same (89%). The survey also revealed that Christopher Columbus is a partisan figure today, at least among New Jersey adults; less than a third (30%) of Democrats identified Columbus as a hero, while more than two-thirds (69%) of Republicans come to this positive evaluation.

Scrutinizing the relationship between age cohort and partisanship (table 7.3) illuminates the data a bit more. On the one hand, partisan differences remain regardless of generational grouping for certain figures (e.g., Columbus). But older respondents, regardless of party identification, appear more similar than dissimilar for other hero candidates including Lincoln and Washington (with Millennials/Zs

TABLE 7.3. Hero Identification by Major Party Identification and Age

I'm going to read you some names and groups of people. Can you tell me if YOU think this person is a hero, or not?

	All	Democrat			Republican		
		18–34	35–54	55+	18–34	35–54	55+
Health care workers	92%	**98%**	91%	100%	93%	92%	95%
World War II veterans	92%	97%	92%	99%	96%	100%	98%
Iraq/Afghanistan veterans	90%	89%	93%	95%	96%	99%	96%
Martin Luther King	89%	**98%**	95%	98%	94%	90%	86%
Abraham Lincoln	80%	**76%**	83%	94%	93%	92%	92%
George Washington	76%	**69%**	76%	92%	89%	93%	97%
Jesus Christ	73%	**86%**	77%	81%	**86%**	**82%**	95%
Christopher Columbus	43%	**24%**	30%	44%	**61%**	**74%**	80%
George Floyd	31%	**60%**	47%	49%	29%	18%	18%
Joe Biden	27%	**30%**	40%	79%	13%	6%	10%
Donald Trump	23%	**6%**	1%	1%	**54%**	**57%**	67%
N	809	96	105	142	46	100	124

Note: Bold denotes significance ≤.05.

accounting for much of the observed partisan difference in assessing these figures).

Still other survey results seem to confound some of my earlier predictions regarding generational attitudes. Thus, one does not find a distinctively strong relationship between Boomers and "non-establishment" heroes like Martin Luther King, George Floyd, or health care workers. Indeed, contrary to expectations, Democratic Boomers seem *much* more inclined to support the party candidate, Joe Biden, than Millennials and Zs. Again, life cycle effects may simply swamp anticipated party effects, especially for a candidate who would go on to become the oldest person ever inaugurated as president.

Before pivoting to examining heroic traits and what the public believes are the distinctive roles heroes provide society, we might consider a final and finer point on how Americans distinguish and group alleged heroes. Drawing on my respondent data, I factor analyzed the 11 personalities surveyed with a principal component analysis and varimax rotation and found three groupings of hero types with eigenvalues that equal or exceed one. These groupings can be found in table 7.4.

Consistent with my earlier observations, regardless of party or age, New Jersey adults embrace the identified "nonpartisan" heroes in overwhelming numbers. But turning to the other groupings paints a more

TABLE 7.4. Factor Analysis Hero Groups

Nonpartisan Heroes	World War II veterans
	Iraq/Afghanistan veterans
	Health care workers
	Jesus Christ
	Martin Luther King Jr.
Generational Heroes	Christopher Columbus
	George Washington
	Abraham Lincoln
	George Floyd
Partisan Heroes	Donald Trump
	Joe Biden

complex picture. Republicans, regardless of age, were more inclined to extend hero status to iconic figures including Washington, Lincoln, and Columbus—presumably regarding them as falling under the "nonpartisan" hero label. But Millennials and Gen Z respondents were the *least* likely to endorse these individuals as heroes even within the Republican Party. How do we explain this relatively powerful generational effect for this class of figures? Again, a plausible explanation for this result is that distinct generational attitudes regarding race and diversity—primed by contemporary racial politics—found unique expression with this group of "generational heroes." As noted, the immediate context in which the poll was conducted included civil rights protests in full swing across the nation (Floyd had been killed just three months earlier), the broader Black Lives Matter movement, and resulting discussions (and sometimes direct action) concerning public monuments that celebrated Confederate soldiers and generals and other figures marred by their support for slavery and other racist causes. This environment, I posit, was especially likely to activate generational differences regarding racial justice and diversity within both parties (Pew 2019b). Thus, George Floyd was greeted more sympathetically as a heroic figure by Millennials and Gen Z respondents than Boomers and Xers. On the other hand, Columbus's treatment of American Indians, Washington's status as a slaveholder, and even Lincoln's complex legacy of delivering racial freedom fared relatively poorly in the eyes of our younger generations. Among other considerations, the Black Lives Matter movement sparked in 2013 brought into greater focus the personal failings of national leaders like Washington and Lincoln, despite their iconic roles in founding and preserving the nation. The role of the "Great Emancipator" in helping to end slavery did not obviously resonate with younger generations galvanized by racial inequality in wealth, social mobility, and criminal justice.

With respect to the third group identified as heroes in my factor analysis, Biden and Trump were roundly rejected by their partisan out-groups. However, older and younger Democrats evaluated Biden quite differently, which is likely a reflection of youthful reluctance to embrace Biden contrasting with Boomers' and Silents' long-standing life cycle patterns of supporting establishment politicians.

As shown in table 7.5, Millennials/Zs, Xers, and Boomers/Silents are not terribly distinct when it comes to assessing heroic traits, with a few important exceptions. Risking your life to help others rings true as a heroic characteristic for 90 percent or more of Millennials/Zs, Xers, and Boomers/Silents—corroborating earlier research showing that this is an essential ingredient of the "great" heroism admired by the public (Peabody and Jenkins 2017). One finds a similar if somewhat diminished consensus across the generations regarding "standing up for what you believe in." As anticipated, however, one finds substantial generational differences with respect to the importance of, on the one hand, heroes who effect "social and political change," and, on the other, those who reflect and reinforce "American values and beliefs." The surveyed Zs and Millennials were noticeably more supportive of heroic change agents and less inclined to embrace value conservatism than older generational groups. The remaining traits surveyed attracted similar (and lower) levels of support, regardless of age.[8]

Turning to partisanship uncovers more significant differences. Most notably, Democrats were more likely to endorse challenging the status quo, overcoming adversity, and commanding respect and admiration as key elements of heroic behavior.

Discussion

As already indicated, some, but not all, of my initial hypotheses are supported by the survey data. I expected that older respondents would be more likely to identify a range of historic and traditional political heroes (including veterans of World War II and Washington and Lincoln), because of their relatively higher levels of political trust. While this is certainly true for Washington and Lincoln, this generational bias

TABLE 7.5. Heroic Traits

Please tell me if you personally associate the following traits with heroes

	All	Age			Party ID			Gender		Race/ethnicity	
		18–34	35–54	55+	D	I	R	Male	Female	White	Non-white
Risking your life to help others even if not required by your job	92%	**90%**	**92%**	93%	92%	88%	94%	91%	92%	92%	91%
Standing up for what you believe in	84%	84%	84%	82%	87%	82%	80%	80%	87%	83%	85%
Overcoming adversity in your life	77%	77%	76%	77%	80%	77%	73%	73%	80%	75%	79%
Commanding the respect and admiration of others	60%	**60%**	**49%**	**69%**	65%	53%	57%	57%	62%	58%	63%
Not expecting personal recognition	70%	70%	70%	68%	**76%**	**68%**	**63%**	69%	70%	67%	73%
Challenging the status quo	60%	66%	56%	60%	**70%**	55%	**52%**	58%	63%	**56%**	**66%**
N	809	211	272	320	347	185	271	385	424	540	802

Note: Bold denotes significance ≤.05.

is somewhat weaker for military heroes (World War II veterans and the veterans "of the Wars in Iraq and Afghanistan after 9/11"). In general, across the sample, veterans, health care workers, and other nonpartisan figures received high levels of recognition as heroes, perhaps reflecting a widespread sense that these groups of citizens were somewhat insulated from the cloud of mistrust associated with their military commanders and government policymakers. Indeed, respondents across our generational groups identified several apolitical or nonpartisan individuals who garnered support as heroic figures, notably Jesus and Martin Luther King Jr.

I did not anticipate other generationally driven results. For example, as the correlation coefficients indicate (table 7.5), in comparison with their younger cohorts, older voters were more likely to identify both Donald Trump and Joe Biden as heroes, with, obviously, considerable variation by party. This result is somewhat perplexing given that one might expect Boomers (as the children of the iconoclastic 1960s) to favor more independent (nonparty based) heroes, while Gen Xers and Millennials (who came of age in an era of greater party division) would be more supportive of in-group partisan figureheads.

Instead, the generational split regarding Trump and Biden may reflect what Hanna Pitkin has identified as the political sympathies garnered by descriptive representation, that is, how closely a leader actually resembles a constituent or demographic group (Pitkin 1967). In a similar vein, older respondents were somewhat more likely than younger respondents to identify health care workers as heroes. The simplest explanation here may be that our surveyed Boomers and Silents were expressing anxiety and gratitude for medical providers given their greater demographic risks in the face of the COVID-19 pandemic.

Perhaps the best way to interpret the survey results is to concede that the partisan effects one finds in identifying various heroes (and in identifying heroic traits) generally swamp generational effects, with a few exceptions. Thus, in looking at correlations, partisanship exhibits a stronger independent effect than age on the likelihood of identifying heroes for 8 of the 11 figures surveyed. For self-identified Republicans, the figures they are most likely to identify as heroes are (in descending order) Donald Trump, Christopher Columbus, and George Washington. For Democrats, heroes are less identifiable generally, but they include Joe Biden, George Floyd, and Martin Luther King Jr.

The three heroes who induced stronger generational as opposed to

TABLE 7.6. Bivariate Correlations between Heroic Personalities, Attributes, Roles, and Age and Partisanship

	Age	Democrat	Republican
Personalities			
World War II veterans	.137**	.042	.097**
Iraq/Afghanistan veterans	.097**	−.045	.102**
Health care workers	.072*	.090*	−.01
Donald Trump	.152**	−.452**	.578**
Christopher Columbus	.261**	−.267**	.366**
George Washington	.261**	−.097**	.186**
Abraham Lincoln	.158**	−.053	.098**
Jesus Christ	.054	−.078*	.088*
Martin Luther King Jr.	−.003	.149**	−.099**
George Floyd	−.122**	.253**	−.274**
Joe Biden	.127**	.406**	−.353**
Heroic qualities			
Risking your life to help others	.023	.029	.022
Standing up for what you believe in	−.012	.076*	−.084*
Overcoming adversity in your life	−.001	.063	−.083*
Commanding the respect and admiration of others	.084*	.080*	−.03
Not expecting personal recognition	−.063	.105**	−.141**
Heroic roles in society			
Challenging the status quo	−.053	.150**	−.145**
Inspiring others to do something they would not normally do	−.107**	−.01	−.039
Lead efforts to bring about political and social change	−.107**	.173**	−.180**
Reflect American values and beliefs	.125**	−.156**	.237**

* Correlation is significant at the 0.05 level (2-tailed).
** Correlation is significant at the 0.01 level (2-tailed).

partisan effects were World War II veterans, George Washington, and Abraham Lincoln.[9] Presumably, the Silents, Boomers, and Xers who favorably identified these "nonpartisan"[10] figures as heroes discarded partisan frames for interpreting politics and instead tapped into their political self-identity and socialization norms. For younger generations, as argued earlier, the heightened profile of racial justice concerns may have inflected their judgments about whether Washington and even Lincoln were contemporary heroes.

Overall, however, the 2020 survey results confirm that the refractory power of partisanship extends to the identification of heroes.

While, as noted, Silents, Boomers, and Xers evinced distinctive generational support for the veterans of World War II and the American icons Washington and Lincoln (perhaps reflecting decades of acculturation—periods through which these figures were hailed without much controversy), party was generally a stronger and more determinative factor in ascertaining heroes. Consider in this regard that while the identification of Martin Luther King Jr. as a hero was not independently affected by one's membership in a specific generational cohort, Republicans were less likely to identify him as a hero and Democrats more so—reflecting the degree to which today's party polarization is linked to the prominence of divisions over race in the electorate as well as elites (Abramowitz 2011).[11]

Turning to the traits that stamp someone as a hero, I hypothesized that generational attitudes would be expressed through three characteristics in particular: challenging the status quo, leading efforts to bring about social and political change, and reflecting American values and beliefs. While the data in this chapter show that leading social change and reflecting American values reflected generational attitudes in the direction anticipated (with younger respondents more likely to see leading change as heroic and older respondents inclined to think that heroes should reflect U.S. values), challenging the status quo did not exhibit an obviously strong generational effect. As discussed earlier, perhaps Boomers (whose political consciousness formed during a period of dynamic social movements and mobilization outside of government) joined with younger respondents in associating heroism (somewhat abstractly) with challenging the status quo. But at the same time, our oldest surveyed group (which included Boomers and some Silents) was the *least* likely to recognize heroes as important in leading "efforts to bring about social and political change." This tension or juxtaposition *might* be explicable when viewed in the light of the racial justice protests roiling many neighborhoods. Conceivably, the "social change" aspect of heroism may have represented a bridge too far for many of the oldest (and less racially diverse) generational respondents if they associated it with dramatic criminal justice and policing reforms. In contrast, upsetting the status quo may have struck them as more removed from the immediate headlines (and protests) of the day and therefore less threatening. One might also note that given that the survey was conducted in the midst of a stubborn pandemic affecting all generational groups and both parties—and at a time when American satisfaction with the "way things are going" was at a historic low (Jones

2020)—linking heroism to upsetting the status quo may have seemed like a more inviting and inclusive idea than bringing about social and political change.

Perhaps more interesting, the capacity of a person to inspire others to do something they would not otherwise do showed a modest generational effect (with older respondents somewhat *less* likely to see this trait as heroic in comparison with younger respondents), but not an obvious partisan effect (see table 7.6). While somewhat puzzling, one might speculate that for some older generational cohorts this facet of heroism triggered a skeptical judgment about the capacities of the followers of heroes to achieve meaningful change or advance significant projects, perhaps a judgment born of decades of experience. For younger survey respondents, the Floyd and Black Lives Matter protests may have bolstered the opposite conclusion. As with naming particular heroes, identifying heroic traits often reflected partisan effects more powerfully than generational effects. For example, to take up our earlier example, Democrats were more likely than Republicans to believe that heroism could be defined by upsetting the status quo (an aspect of heroism that did not obviously trigger a generational effect).

Conclusion

This chapter makes a preliminary case that heroes help to imprint generational identity and serve as a source of consensus and divergence across the generations. What is the broader importance of these findings for how we think about generations and politics?

First, given the willingness of respondents in each age cohort to identify heroes, and the widespread cross-generational recognition of some figures as heroic (such as health care workers and Martin Luther King Jr.) we can surmise that the idea of the hero still has some resonance. This study has found notable differences in how members of different generational groups assess specific heroic figures (seen, for example, in the cases of Columbus and Floyd). Moreover, declining political trust and the rise of hyperpartisanship have triggered changes in how different groups identify heroes, making it exceedingly difficult, for example, for prominent party leaders to be recognized as heroic by partisan out-groups. In general, national political figures tend to be polarizing rather than unifying in recent decades, a claim supported by noting the rising partisan gap in approval of American presidents (Taylor 2016, 2).[12] Similarly, changes in our consumption of media and the greater homogeneity of in-person and online networks (Iyengar et al. 2019) pose significant challenges to anyone seeking to identify a unifying national heroic figure.

All this said, the preliminary survey data discussed in this chapter tell us that it is premature to conclude that the era of national heroes is decisively over. Again, for leaders trying to find cohesion in our diverse, divided, and "imagined political community," hero talk remains a complex if valuable tool.

As a second broad observation, one might note that a key component of my analysis is the supposition that generational attitudes about heroes can be importantly impacted by fairly specific (albeit intense) political environments. In the data considered here, I speculate that the electric climate formed by racial justice protests and the murder of George Floyd brought out political "frameworks imprinted from the formative years of early adulthood"—in this case, triggering disparate judgments regarding the nature of racial justice and the best tools to achieve this good. This argument invites additional research to evaluate whether this dynamic of racially activated generational beliefs can be replicated under similar conditions, or with different issues and generational triggers.

While this chapter and book is primarily interested in reflecting on the relationship between generations and U.S. politics, grappling with the nature of heroism is also politically significant for several reasons. First, historically, widely revered, public heroes have been used to secure distinctive political ends, including public goods. Hero talk has leveraged participation in national causes ranging from military conflicts like two world wars to participation in civil rights campaigns. Consider how Lyndon Johnson was able to invoke the martyred John F. Kennedy to help advance a legislative revolution in civil rights (Gittinger and Fisher 2004).

A second observation about the arguable importance of heroes concerns how we communicate norms of civic behavior and pass them from one generation to the next. As Cliff Zukin and his coauthors have argued, "Generational replacement is one of the most fundamental issues any polity faces, since over time it literally involves the placing of its future into the hands of an entirely new and untested public. At the heart of this process is the generational transfer of a society's collective norms, values, beliefs, and knowledge" (Zukin et al. 2006, 10–11). Heroic figures (and their accompanying mythos) can transmit "values associated with good character and responsible citizenship" (Sanchez 1998). Notwithstanding George Washington's moral failings concerning slavery (not to mention his shortcomings as a military general), for generations his heroic iconography reinforced the ideals of public honor, limited political service, and classical virtues like temperance and courage (Peabody 2001).

The findings of this chapter cast doubt on whether the familiar icons of the past can continue to transmit the "basic norms" that bolster our democratic institutions and temper the rough edges of partisan competition (Levitsky and Ziblatt 2018).[13] But this conclusion underscores the ongoing value of studying whether groups like Millennials and Gen Zs coalesce around different and even their own set of anointed heroes, and whether they can use these figures to transmit a conception of civic responsibility to future generations. Such an inquiry will help plumb the depths of generational research while simultaneously contributing to the project of diagnosing our democratic well-being.

APPENDIX

The survey referenced in this chapter was conducted by live callers on both landlines and cellular phones from June 18 through June 30, 2020, with a scientifically selected random sample of 809 New Jersey adults, 18 or older. Interviews were in English and included 263 adults reached on a landline phone and 546 adults reached on a cell phone, all acquired through random digit dialing. The data were weighted to be representative of the noninstitutionalized adult population of New Jersey. The weighting balanced sample demographics to target population parameters. The sample is balanced to match parameters for sex, age, education, race/ethnicity, region, and phone use. The sex, age, education, race/ethnicity, and region parameters were derived from 2018 American Community Survey PUMS data. The phone use parameter was derived from estimates provided by the National Health Interview Survey Early Release Program. The simple sampling error for 809 New Jersey adults is +/−3.8 percentage points (including the design effect) at a 95 percent confidence interval. The specific questions included the following:

- I'm going to read you some names and groups of people.

Can you tell me if YOU think this person is a hero, or not?
[ROTATE H1 OPTIONS]
George Washington
Abraham Lincoln
Martin Luther King Jr.
Jesus Christ
Christopher Columbus
George Floyd
Donald Trump
Health care workers
Joe Biden
Veterans of the Second World War
Veterans of the Wars in Iraq and Afghanistan after 9/11

We selected these figures to measure public assessments of three classes of heroes. First, we included arguably great heroes, figures like Washington, Lincoln, and King. Second, we sought to solicit views about headline heroes, individuals the public might not ordinarily regard as heroic but who garnered a second look because of their heightened profile or association with important contemporaneous causes (Floyd, health care workers, Trump, Biden). The expressed attitudes concerning these figures were likely to be more circumstantial, time-bound, and ephemeral. Third, and at times overlapping with these other categories, we tried to probe the public's attitudes about those held up as heroic icons in the past, but whose status seemed to be in flux, perhaps as a result of generational changes. This group included such individuals as Washington, Lincoln, Jesus Christ, Columbus, and the veterans of World War II, Iraq, and Afghanistan.

Other questions in the survey asked about the characteristics and importance of heroism in general, rather than specific individuals:

• Please tell me if you personally associate the following
  traits with heroes:
    Risking your life to help others even if not required by your
        job
    Standing up for what you believe in
    Overcoming adversity in your life
    Commanding the respect and admiration of others
    Not expecting personal recognition
    Challenging the status quo

- In your opinion, which of the following reasons best describes how, if at all, heroes are important in society? Do they . . . [insert option] OR are they unimportant in society?

  Inspire others to do something they wouldn't otherwise do

  Lead efforts to bring about social and political change

  Reflect American values and beliefs

  Heroes are not important in society

  Combination of above (volunteered)

The survey data and resulting findings are limited by a number of factors, common to anyone seeking to use cross-sectional survey data to address public attitudes. First, the survey work is novel in asking about something (heroism) few think to include on telephone surveys, limiting my ability to make comparisons with similar research. At the same time, I was restricted in what I could ask and the number of respondents I could request. The questions appeared on a statewide omnibus survey that was funded by a nonprofit university, Fairleigh Dickinson. Given this chapter's interest in generational comparisons, I would have preferred oversampling Millennials and Zs, and, of course, comparing the results to additional polls conducted nationally and in other states. This was not possible and, to put it simply, I took what I could get. The N size is therefore too small to offer a more robust generational analysis.

Beyond these points, one might note that generational research is always vexed with questions of why—that is, are differences between the provided age groupings the result of life cycle, cohort, or period effects? The reluctance in some of the younger respondents' willingness to believe, for example, that Abraham Lincoln and George Washington were heroes may change as they age. Their maturation may bring greater reverence for these historical icons, despite their flawed characters. It is also plausible that the cynicism, distrust, and the tendency of the mass media and social networks to both elevate and scrutinize heroes has marked today's younger generations in ways that differentiate them from those socialized in more trusting times.

NOTES

1. The author thanks Krista Jenkins, senior officer, Pew Charitable Trusts, for her survey analysis and other invaluable work contributing to this chapter. George

Floyd was a Black man who was murdered by Minneapolis police in 2020, sparking nationwide protests about racial justice.

2. In addition to the points already made, one wonders if younger generations are less inclined generally to see heroes in a categorical or dichotomous mode ("hero" or "not hero") and are instead more likely to evaluate individual actions or the specific effects of specific figures in evaluating heroic deeds or traits.

3. Overall, one might also anticipate that any identified heroes will tend to skew ideologically liberal for the younger generations: while only 15% of Millennials express consistent conservative views (on such matters as the performance and responsibilities of government, and the proper status and treatment of minority groups like the poor, African Americans, immigrants, and gays), Xers (25%), Boomers (33%), and Silents (39%) express more support for these conservative positions (Pew 2015).

4. Given the importance of generational and demographic changes in effecting realignment, especially in the South, it would be valuable, of course, to obtain similar survey data from southern respondents.

5. The widespread view of Jesus as a hero across age groups is somewhat notable given the decline in Christian affiliation among Millennials and Zs (Pew 2019a).

6. Significant positive correlations can be found between age and seven of the 11 heroes queried on the survey (World War II veterans, Afghanistan/Iraq veterans, health care workers, Christopher Columbus, Donald Trump, Abraham Lincoln, Joe Biden). A negative correlation exists between age and identification of George Floyd as a hero. See table 7.6 for correlations between measures of heroism, major party identification, and age.

7. As noted, public opinion concerning heroes is not something that regularly populates databases and I am therefore unable to demonstrate trend lines for our more iconic personalities.

8. The consistency of many of the heroic traits across age groups may speak to a distinctively American vision of the qualities necessary for a healthy civil society, what Alexis de Tocqueville famously called the "habits of the heart." In this interpretation, respondents who identified, say, "Standing up for what you believe in" or "Overcoming adversity in your life" as heroic traits were giving expression to admirable but accessible aspects of the U.S. democratic character.

9. The icons George Washington and Abraham Lincoln showed a generational effect (greater support from older respondents) and a weaker partisan effect.

10. In identifying World War II soldiers, Washington, and Lincoln as nonpartisan, I am arguing that, across my surveyed age groups, respondents are unlikely to link these figures to 21st century party politics. Lincoln is a Republican president, but he is unlikely to be associated with today's Republican Party in the same way as Donald Trump.

11. For historical context, one might note that federal approval of King's birthday as a national holiday took place in 1983 (the law was signed by President Reagan), with Republican leaders Jack Kemp and Newt Gingrich advocating for the measure with floor speeches, and a Republican-controlled Senate supporting the initiative with the support, among others, of South Carolina segregationist Senator Strom Thurmond (National Constitution Center 2020).

12. For example, while an average of 49% of Democrats expressed approval for

President Dwight Eisenhower, only 14% of Republicans reported similar approval for President Barack Obama.

13. After all, younger Americans will likely resist and even reject this transmission of many traditional icons and values; in our study, the 28-point gap between Millennial/Z and Boomer evaluations of Columbus as a hero arguably speaks to this generational tension.

REFERENCES

Abramowitz, A. 2011. *Disappearing Center: Engaged Citizens, Polarization and American Democracy* New Haven: Yale University Press.

Abramowitz, A. 2013. *The Polarized Public: Why American Government Is So Dysfunctional.* New York: Pearson Longman.

Abramowitz, A., and S. Webster. 2018. "Negative Partisanship: Why Americans Dislike Parties but Behave Like Rabid Partisans." *Advances in Political Psychology* 39 (Suppl. 1).

Anderson, B. [1983] 2006. *Imagined Communities: Reflections on the Origin and Spread of Nationalism.* 3rd ed. London: Verso.

Dalton, R. 2004. *Democratic Challenges, Democratic Choices: The Erosion in Political Support in Advanced Industrial Democracies.* Oxford: Oxford University Press.

Gentry, B. 2018. *Why Youth Vote: Identity, Inspirational Leaders and Independence.* New York: Springer.

Gittinger, T., and A. Fisher. 2004. "LBJ Champions the Civil Rights Act of 1964." *Prologue Magazine* 36 (2). https://www.archives.gov/publications/prologue/2004/summer/civil-rights-act

Hart-Brinson, P. 2018. *The Gay Marriage Generation: How the LGBTQ Movement Transformed American Culture.* New York: NYU Press.

Hetherington, M. J. 1998. "The Political Relevance of Political Trust." *American Political Science Review* 92 (4): 791–808.

Hetherington, M. J., and J. D. Weiler. 2009. *Authoritarianism and Polarization in American Politics.* Cambridge: Cambridge University Press.

Iyengar, S., Y. Lelkes, M. Levendusky, N. Malhotra, and S. J. Westwood. 2019. "The Origins and Consequences of Affective Polarization in the United States." *Annual Review of Political Science* 22:129–46.

Iyengar, S., and S. J. Westwood. 2015. "Fear and Loathing across Party Lines: New Evidence on Group Polarization." *American Journal of Political Science* 59 (3) (July): 690–707.

Jones, J. M. 2020. "U.S. Satisfaction at 13%, Lowest in Nine Years." Gallup.com, August 4. https://news.gallup.com/poll/316736/satisfaction-lowest-nine-years.aspx

Klecka, W. R. 1971. "Applying Generations to the Study of Political Behavior: A Cohort Analysis." *Public Opinion Quarterly* 35 (3): 358–75.

Levitsky, S., and D. Ziblatt. 2018. *How Democracies Die.* New York: Crown.

McCarty, N., K. T. Poole, and H. Rosenthal. 2006. *Polarized America: The Dance of Ideology and Unequal Riches.* Cambridge, MA: MIT Press.

Mettler, S. 2005. *Soldiers to Citizens: The G.I. Bill and the Making of the Greatest Generation.* New York: Oxford University Press.

Nakamura, D. 2014. "In Speech to US Troops, Obama Vows to Avoid 'Another Ground War in Iraq.'" *Washington Post*, September 17.

National Constitution Center. 2020. "How the Martin Luther King Jr. Birthday Became a Holiday." January 20. https://constitutioncenter.org/blog/how-martin-luther-king-jr-s-birthday-became-a-holiday-3

Peabody, B. 2001. "George Washington, Presidential Term Limits, and the Problem of Reluctant Political Leadership." *Presidential Studies Quarterly* 31 (3): 439–53.

Peabody, B., and C. Jenkins. 2017. *Where Have All the Heroes Gone? Changing Conceptions of American Valor.* New York: Oxford University Press.

Pew Research Center. 2015. "The Whys and Hows of Generations Research." September 3. https://www.pewresearch.org/politics/2015/09/03/the-whys-and-hows-of-generations-research/

Pew Research Center. 2018. "The Generation Gap in American Politics." March 1. http://www.people-press.org/wp-content/uploads/sites/4/2018/03/03-01-18-Generations-release2.pdf

Pew Research Center. 2019a. "In U.S., Decline of Christianity Continues at Rapid Pace." October 17. https://www.pewforum.org/2019/10/17/in-u-s-decline-of-christianity-continues-at-rapid-pace/

Pew Research Center. 2019b. "Generation Z Looks a Lot Like Millennials on Key Social and Political Issues Among Republicans." January 17. https://www.pewresearch.org/social-trends/2019/01/17/generation-z-looks-a-lot-like-millennials-on-key-social-and-political-issues/

Pitkin, H. 1967. *The Concept of Representation.* Berkeley: University of California Press.

Reagan, R. 1981. "First Inaugural Address." January 20. https://www.presidency.ucsb.edu/documents/inaugural-address-11

Romano, A. 2020. "Why We Can't Stop Fighting about Cancel Culture." *Vox.com*, August 25. https://www.vox.com/culture/2019/12/30/20879720/what-is-cancel-culture-explained-history-debate

Rouse, S., and A. Ross. 2018. *The Politics of Millennials: Political Beliefs and Policy Preferences of America's Most Diverse Generation.* Ann Arbor: University of Michigan Press.

Ryder, N. B. 1965. "The Cohort as a Concept in the Study of Social Change." *American Sociological Review* 30 (6): 843–61.

Sabato, L. J. [1991] 2000. *Feeding Frenzy: How Attack Journalism Has Transformed American Politics.* Baltimore: Lanahan.

Sanchez, T. R. 1998. "Using Stories about Heroes to Teach Values." *ERIC Digest.* http://files.eric.ed.gov/fulltext/ED424190.pdf

Stoker, L. 2014. "Reflections on the Study of Generations in Politics." *The Forum* 12 (3): 377–96.

Taylor, P. 2016. *The Next America: Boomers, Millennials, and the Looming Generational Showdown.* New York: Public Affairs.

Trump, D. 2020. "Remarks at an Independence Day Celebration." July 4.

Welle, J., John Ennis, Katherine Kranz, and Graham Plaster, eds. 2012. *In the Shadow of Greatness: Voices of Leadership, Sacrifice, and Service from American's Longest War: The U.S. Naval Academy Class of 2002.* Annapolis, MD: Naval Institute Press.

Williams, T. 2022. "Millennials Have a Steeper Hill to Climb to Afford the Same Life-style Their Boomer Parents Enjoyed." *Fortune.com*, October 27. https://fortune.com/2022/10/27/millennials-versus-boomers-wealth-gap-doubled/

Wrone, D. R. 1979. "Lincoln: Democracy's Touchstone." *Journal of the Abraham Lincoln Association* 1 (1): 71–83.

Zukin, C., S. Keeter, M. Andolina, K. Jenkins, and M. X. Delli Carpini. 2006. *A New Engagement? Political Participation, Civic Life, and the Changing American Citizen.* New York: Oxford University Press.

Part III

Participation and Political Engagement

8 | "The Times They Are a Changin'"

Generational Comparisons of the Civil Rights Movement with the Current-Day Climate Movement

Robin Boyle-Laisure

Andrew Young, referring to the Black Lives Matter wave of protests: "'A phenomenal moment,' but . . . they cried out for organization and structure." (Barry 2020)

Bob Dylan's famous song lyric, capturing the spirit of the 1960s, is just as apropos today: "The times they are a changin'" (1964). The civil rights movement changed history by securing legislation and court decisions advancing the constitutional rights of black people (Dalton 2008, 7). The movement took flight at a time when the Baby Boomer generation was politically active and seeking social change. As outlined in the introduction to this book, the generations and their birth years are as follows: Silents (1925–45); Baby Boomers (1946–64); Gen X (1965–80); Millennials (1981–95); and Gen Z (1996–2013). Baby Boomers "experienced the height of the civil rights movement from 1954 to 1968, where African Americans and other allies fought to end institutionalized racial discrimination, segregation, and disenfranchisement" (CFI 2021). Although some of the leaders of the civil rights movement were born prior to 1946 (for example, Rosa Parks was born in 1913), nevertheless, the Boomer generation supplied momentum and gravitas for this movement.

Political movements often are fueled by young adults, and the civil rights movement and the climate movement are no different. As observed by Laura Stoker (chap. 2, this volume), young adults, those in late adolescence to early adulthood, are in the most "impressionable years" of their life cycle. During these impressionable years, young adults are more likely to define themselves politically.

The civil rights movement and the climate movement were populated by different generations. In contrast with the Baby Boomers in the former, the Millennials and Generation Z are the galvanizing, media-grabbing activists for the climate movement. These generations have grown up in very different time periods, with the digital age affecting the younger generations. Although the climate movement has been in existence for several decades, it has risen to prominence only recently. Those promoting the goals of the climate movement and who are gaining media attention range in age from teenagers to college students and recent graduates. These activists fall into the categories of the Millennial generation and Generation Z.

The two movements share some common characteristics in how they have employed similar organizing tactics, yet they differ fundamentally on how their members interact with other members and with building coalitions of community support. These differences can be traced to generational distinctions due to acculturation. They differ in their respective approaches to organizing marches and rallying people to their causes. The Gen Zers have been described as activists, independent, and nontraditional (Atkins 2020). Millennials are also independent-minded. More so than their older counterparts in the Gen X and Boomer generations, Millennials are much more likely to describe themselves as political independents (Bloom, Dendy, and Wilson 2019). Their independent nature, as this chapter explains, becomes apparent when studying how a movement with which they associate is relatively less engaged with institutions, other nonprofit groups, and the greater populace.

The impact of the digital age has had a profound effect upon the members of the Millennial and Gen Z generations. They are impacted by the ever-expanding explosion into homes and classrooms of electronic devices (Newell 2015). The younger generations are being trained to rely upon their devices for school assignments, for sports, and for extracurricular sign-ups. They also feel peer pressure to use chat groups, text messages, and social media for staying in touch with their social group. According to a 2012 survey, 95 percent of teenagers use the internet, with 93 percent of them owning their own computer or accessing one at home (Newell 2015). Those in the Gen Z and Millennial generations are "more likely to communicate with other people in their lives via text message than by talking to them on the phone or in person" (Newell 2015, 776). Reliance upon electronic devices, as opposed to verbal and in-person communication, has contributed to a generational distinction in the organizing tactics of the climate movement and the civil rights movement.

The digital age has so entrenched itself in the younger generations that most youth check their devices as often as every 15 minutes. They multitask, using multiple devices at once and for various purposes (Newell 2015). The younger generations' ability to socialize (Newell 2015) and communicate has been affected. The way the younger generations' brains process information, how they communicate, and their day-to-day functioning with school and social tasks are different from that of the Baby Boomer and older generations.

Neuroscientists embrace the theory of neuroplasticity, which is premised upon the theory that the brain is not static as it was once postulated, but that the brain can change like a pliable organ (Newell 2015). The modern-day view of the brain is that it consists of networks of neurons and many pathways that can be forged within one's lifetime. With the inculcation of electronic devices in most aspects of a young person's life (Newell 2015), their brains are wired differently from that of the Boomers.

Polls indicate that concerns about climate change can be detected along generational lines, with those in the Boomer generation being more resistant to the climate movement, whereas those taking up the rallying call are the Millennials and the Gen Zers (Farber 2020). Boomers are less invested and less worried about the long-term effects of climate change because environmental science was not studied in school, but the younger generations were exposed to climate change while in school (Farber 2020). The younger generations were also exposed to climate change issues in the news media and on social media. As reported by a recent Pew Research Center survey, Gen Z and Millennial social media users are more likely than the Baby Boomer generation to engage with climate change content online (Thigpen and Tyson 2021). The younger generations are more concerned about the long-term effects of climate change. A 2016 University of Texas poll found that twice the number of Millennials wanted to reduce the use of coal than those in the Baby Boomer generation. The poll results were similar with Millennials supporting carbon taxes and prioritizing public policy regarding climate change (Farber 2020).

Within a subset of the American registered voters, Pew poll results show that a majority of Republicans as a group deny the existence of climate change (Farber 2020; Funk and Tyson 2020). However, out of the Republicans surveyed, 29 percent of younger Republicans—Millennials and Gen Z—say that human activity contributes to climate change, as opposed to 16 percent of the Baby Boomer or older Republicans (Farber 2020; Funk and Tyson 2020). The Millennials and Gen Zers embrace the political goals of the climate movement more than the Baby Boomers.

The differences in generations become apparent when comparing the organizing tactics of the two social movements. Arguably the civil rights movement has reached pinnacles of success, whereas the climate movement has diminished results thus far, despite both movements having beginnings at approximately the same time. While an extensive network of support propelled the civil rights movement forward, a comparable widespread community network supporting the climate movement has been slow to develop. Absent from the infrastructure of the climate movement are branches of government, corporations, community leaders, and the populace. The gap in community support for the climate movement can be traced to the maturation of the Millennials and Gen Zers in the digital age with technology deeply affecting how they interact with others and with their independent-minded spirit.

The pivotal moments marking the beginning of the civil rights movement was the 1955 killing of Emmett Till and when Rosa Parks, supported by the National Association for the Advancement of Colored People (NAACP) and Women's Political Council, refused to sit in the back of the city bus (Farber 1994). In response to Rosa Parks's actions, a groundswell of support got underway with a boycott of bus ridership and a community organizing task involving printing 50,000 leaflets in the middle of the night and on a moment's notice. Jo Ann Robinson, on behalf of the Council, and with the help of churches and volunteers, distributed these leaflets throughout Montgomery, setting up a carpool system with 40 pickup locations. The boycott was effective in accomplishing its purpose—disrupting the bus system and revenues that would have been generated (Theoharis 2021).

The movement was propelled forward five years later, by the "sit-in" of four male Black college students on "Whites Only" stools at a Woolworth's lunch counter in Greensboro, North Carolina, in defiance of the Jim Crow laws (Farber 1994, 67, 76). These preplanned nonviolent sit-ins and store boycotts sparked mass demonstrations by thousands of Black and white protesters throughout the South (Farber 1994; Barry 2020). The events involved participation by a generation of Boomers rallying for change but were additionally supported by networks that were orchestrating it.

Although there is no clear end to the civil rights movement, arguably the culminating events were the enactment of the Civil Rights Act of 1964 and the Voting Rights Act of 1965 (Dalton 2008). Another culminating moment was on April 4, 1968, when Martin Luther King Jr. was assassinated. Although it was not the end—the work of the civil rights movement continued with groups providing community outreach (Bloom and Martin 2013). While the ultimate goals of the civil rights movement will not be achieved until racial injustice is eliminated and its work is ongoing, threshold legislative and judicial landmarks were accomplished.

The current-day climate movement refers to a collective of individual youthful protesters from the Millennial and Z generations, along with the Big Green groups, which are large nonprofit organizations, all seeking to end climate change. The movement has a multidecade history, but in contrast to the civil rights movement, its progress has been slow, indicated by the continuing rise in carbon emissions (Gardiner 2021). In fact, the amount of carbon in the atmosphere increased even during the pandemic-driven economic shutdown, when it should have decreased (Gardiner 2021). According to the Environmental Protection Agency, climate change is getting worse, not better, when calculating the severity and frequency of wildfires, rising temperatures on land and in the ocean, and flooding (Flavelle 2021).

The climate movement took root as the "environmental movement" in the 1960s and 1970s. Over time, Millennial and Gen Z activists got involved. The movement suffered setbacks in 2009–10 when comprehensive climate change bills were defeated in Congress (Wines 2014). It suffered a further setback when former president Donald Trump was in office (Sengupta 2021). In a rejuvenating moment, international teenage activist Greta Thunberg sailed to the United States and captured headlines (Baker 2019). But the efforts of the movement have always faced opposition by the well-funded and politically connected coal, oil, and gas industries. Big Green groups expend resources to pressure lawmakers just to retain existing environmental protections (Wines 2014), hampering their ability to promote additional ones. Activists from the Millennial and Gen Z generations have taken climate change to the streets by holding marches and sit-ins, as well as lobbying lawmakers, drawing upon lessons from the civil rights movement.

The goals of the climate movement are couched in terms of emission reduction standards, with movement proponents looking toward public pronouncements by businesses and regulations by lawmakers (Eavis and Krauss 2021). The movement has not reached benchmarks of success because lacking are meaningful corporate pronouncements and their demonstrated efforts to meet those goals. Also lacking are stringent administrative regulations setting standards for corporations (Eavis and Krauss 2021).

The climate movement could be viewed as gaining momentum when considering how President Joe Biden placed climate change high on his agenda improving this country's air quality (EDF 2021), and is positioning the United States as a global leader by rejoining the Paris Agreement, a pact among 200 countries to slow down climate change (Sengupta 2021). President Biden's priorities—pushing climate change to the top of his presidential agenda—is unprecedented even for Democratic presidents (*New York Times* 2021). However, the movement has suffered setbacks and slow progress. The movement's organizing tactics provide insight into the generational differences between the Baby Boomers and the younger generations—the Millennials and the Gen Zers.

The first part of this chapter explains the similarities between the civil rights movement and the climate movement. Leaders of each were motivated by the feeling that they had the greatest stake in the outcome. Tactics from the 1960s were reinvigorated in the current-day movement, with nonviolent civil disobedience and demands for legal reform through legislative and judicial branches of government taking center stage.

The second part of this chapter examines a significant distinction between the tactics of the two movements—networks of support—that were apparent in the civil rights movement but are visibly missing from the climate movement. The civil rights movement drew upon strength from many corners of society, and organizations such as the Student Nonviolent Coordinating Committee (SNCC) spent time planning and mobilizing marches. In contrast, the climate movement's Big Green groups, with their focus on legislative environmental protections, is on a parallel track with marches and lobbying efforts organized by youthful individuals. Adding to the schema is the White House agenda and corporate America's public statements of commitment toward emission reduction. However, the younger generations are not building an extensive network of societal support to propel the climate goals into reality, which the Baby Boomers achieved with the civil rights movement. The independent-minded Millennials and Gen Zers are not accomplishing the goals quickly enough due to their reliance upon quick-action technology, rather than deeper human-to-human relationship building.

Sociologist Mario Diani (2004, chap. 15) views networks within movements as "dynamic" in that participants become involved in these political activities through preexisting links and their very participation also forges new bonds. A typical component of a social movement is "a network of informal interactions between a plurality of individuals, groups and/or organizations" (Diani 1992). To make a sustainable environmental impact, the climate movement needs to forge sustainable bonds between its young activists, who are not used to such cooperation, and corporate leaders, Big Green groups, governmental agencies, and lawmakers. The reasons why these bonds have not been formed can be traced back to differences in how the Baby Boomer generation and the younger generations (Millennial and Gen Z) interact, mobilize, and organize a movement.

David Schultz (chap. 1, this volume) asks whether the rise of social media has transformed the way generations are formed. The answer in sum is "yes," social media has transformed the Millennials and Gen Zers because social media is encompassed within the digital age that has shaped these generations. The effect of the powerful influence of technology is evident in the shift in how political movements are being conducted. Social media should not be fully replacing the old-fashioned strategies of communication, and continuing on this path may lead to further disengagement within political movements.

I—The Similarities between the Civil Rights Movement and the Climate Movement

A "movement" is a broad term encompassing many smaller events. There are common characteristics shared by the civil rights movement and the climate movement. First, those who felt that they had the most to lose with respect to the political issue, those feeling a stake in the outcome, emerged as leaders. In both movements, it was the younger generation that felt the weight of these causes. A second identifiable characteristic common between the civil rights movement and the climate movement is that the latter eventually adopted tactics from the civil rights movement by using nonviolent civil disobedience and demands for legal reform through the legislative and judicial branches of government.

A. Youthful Generations Feel a Stake in the Outcome

1. Both the Civil Rights Movement and the Climate Movement Were Composed of Youthful Generations

The civil rights movement had multiple leaders from various reaches of society. The leaders of the movement felt that they had a significant stake in its outcome, many of them from the Baby Boomer generation. There was an outpouring of support from Black college students, particularly those in the South, who had little opportunity for professional advancement in fields of law, medicine, or business (Farber 1994). They were excluded from public facilities, and even from state-run universities in the South, which were reserved for white students only (Farber 1994). This realization likely caused Black college students to feel an investment in the movement. And the numbers support this—approximately 70,000 Black college students in the South participated in the sit-in movement held in public spaces such as lunch counters, despite risking beatings by police and bystanders (Farber 1994). The southern students were aided by northern white and Black freedom fighters who traveled from their college campuses (Farber 1994). The leaders of the civil rights movement, the most visible of which were primarily Black men, and who were supported by college students, pushed to achieve access to institutions, economic opportunity, housing, and the right to vote.

Similarly, young people have taken the climate movement to the streets because they feel they have a stake in the outcome. High school and college-age students (Millennials and Gen Zers) have seen dramatic weather pattern changes cause environmental catastrophes and desperate human immigration patterns. Our young people today fear that they will bear the long-term consequences of the world's collective actions or inactions in climate change.

Gen Zers are the largest segment of all the generations—comprising 74 million people (Atkins 2020). They are currently in their early to mid-20s and are known for wanting to improve the world (Graham 2019). Gen Zers are motivated by political causes and their generation's profile describes them as particularly insistent upon diversity, inclusion, and equity (Graham 2019), in contrast to the more complacent older Millennial generation (Boyle and Ingham 2006; Bohl 2008). Gen Zers in college have helped to raise awareness about climate change, such as by writing articles for their college newspaper (Reith 2019). Both the Gen Zers and the Millennials are on average more likely than the older generations to say that the Earth is getting warmer due to human activity (Parker and Igielnik 2020). Given the large numbers in Gen Z, their commitment to political causes, and their feeling of having a stake in the outcome, they have proliferated the climate movement.

Public statements by youthful activists in the climate movement indicate that the younger generation feels the burden of long-term environmental consequences. In a headlines-grabbing moment, teenage activist Greta Thunberg addressed the United Nations in New York City in 2019 (Baker 2019). She warned them, "'We are in the beginning of mass destruction'" (United Nations Climate Action Summit 2019).

Why is climate change important to college students and teenagers? Dana Fisher, a sociologist, explains why we have seen such widespread protests around the world on the topic of climate change: "'We all know the burden of climate change will fall on these kids' shoulders when they are adults. They are acutely aware as well'" (Sengupta 2019b).

While both the civil rights movement and the climate movement included youth as organizers of marches and meetings, there were differences between the two in the age and gender of the leaders. The civil rights movement was predominantly led by Black male leaders, ranging from college age to older adult. The most prominent leader was Dr. Martin Luther King Jr., who seized the spotlight in his 20s. Only pockets of high school-aged students in the 1960s were engaged and active then (Stern 1969).

In contrast, current social movements' most prominent activists are most noticeably female teenagers. International activist Greta Thunberg attracted international attention, as the most renowned spokesperson for the movement, when in her teen years. The relatively youthful leadership was also seen in other recent movements. March for Our Lives, formed after the Parkland shooting, was led by high school students, including female leaders (Interlandi 2019). And teenagers, often young women, are taking leadership roles with Black Lives Matter protests (Bennett 2020).

Although the Gen Zers seem more impassioned and have more numbers than their older counterparts, the Millennials are also supporting the climate movement. For instance, Millennials expressed their disapproval of President Trump's and congressional Republican's policies on climate change, among other issues, by voting at a higher rate in 2018 than in 2014 (Ross and Rouse, chap. 11, this volume).

In general, young generations often defy social norms and mores. Arguably, younger generations are more likely to take risks for a cause that they feel strongly about, and they are most likely expressing themselves through the ballot box or by way of community organizing. Both movements—civil rights and climate—have been fueled by the actions and words of the youth feeling the weight on their shoulders.

B. Similar Tactics between the Civil Rights Movement and Climate Movement

Leaders of both the civil rights movement and the climate movement have deployed similar organizing tactics to achieve their goals. The civil rights movement served as a successful model for nonviolent protest, a principal component of the leaders' strategy. Some youthful climate control groups have emulated this tactic. Eventually the civil rights movement (Farber 1994), and later the climate movement, sought to make change through the legislatures and the courts.

1. Civil Rights Movement—Use of Civil Disobedience

Leaders of the civil rights movement from organizations such as SNCC instructed participants to use nonviolent civil disobedience, a practice previously used by Mahatma Gandhi (Farber 1994). One tactic was the "sit-in," in which the demonstrators occupied a space for a period to time (Farber 1994, 67, 76), during which they found ways to express their cause, through chanting, sign-carrying, and so forth. It was estimated that protesters in over 150 cities had participated in sit-ins. By late 1965, approximately 120 colleges and universities had held teachins to share information and hold intellectual debates about war and society (Farber 1994).

Young climate control activists have emulated the 1960s tactics of nonviolent marches and sit-ins. Nonviolent marches were a tactic employed in 2017 for the national People's Climate March held in Washington, DC that attracted 200,000 people (Fisher 2019). On a local level, young activists formed part of a larger initiative called the Sunrise Movement, founded in 2017 by college graduates. They have held nonviolent marches and sit-ins for climate change in several cities. Their participants range in age from elementary school to college graduates (First-Arai 2020).

Greta Thunberg was heralded for inspiring six million people in 150 countries to participate in nonviolent marches for the environment (Baker 2019). Thanks to social media, on September 20, 2019, "masses of young people poured in the streets on every continent" to protest climate change In the United States, Thunberg inspired rallies in all 50 states (Sengupta2019b). Thunberg and other youthful leaders relied upon social media in organizing school strikes in several countries to raise awareness about climate change issues. (Sengupta 2019a; Sengupta 2019c). These climate change protests were relatively peaceful, borrowing the tactics of the civil rights movement.

2. Similar Tactics—Applying Pressure for Legislative Reform

The gains of the civil rights movement grew from not only civil disobedience tactics but also from judicial and legislative reform. Landmark Supreme Court precedent was achieved through, in part, the strategic investigatory work of the NAACP. It was the NAACP that strategically sought African American families to serve as plaintiffs for *Brown v. Board of Education* of 1954 (Farber 1994). The basis of their lawsuit was that racially segregated schools perpetuated inferior education. The research behind that argument led the Supreme Court to hold that states must end school segregation. This decision established precedent for future cases.

The civil rights leaders also put pressure on Congress to pass federal legislation. The 1964 Civil Rights Act passed, followed by the passage of the Voting Rights Act of 1965. Also momentous was the 1964 Economic Opportunity Act, with its purpose to wage a war on poverty. This landmark legislation created programs to be administered by the Office of Economic Opportunity, and later the Community Services Administration (Klein, Lazar, and Zeisel 1981). Community Action Agencies were created on the local level to provide programs for children, youth, adults, and senior citizens to improve access to nutrition and health services, jobs, and legal services (Klein, Lazar, and Zeisel 1981). The federal programs created community-based programs that were designed to influence change on a grassroots level.

The campus protest tactics used in the earlier 1960s civil rights and antiwar movements—namely, sit-ins, teach-ins, marches—eventually gave way to working within the system to advocate for legislative reform (Goeken 1999) and corporate divestment. By the 1970s, college students demanded that colleges divest funds from South Africa in support of the antiapartheid movement (Slack 1988; Rierden 1990; Buckley 2012). Other campus groups, such as the Public Interest Research Groups, sought to work within the legislative system to bring about reform (Goeken 1999).

The climate movement has, like the civil rights movement, sought to lobby legislators with the goal of affecting legislation. The Sunrise Movement claims to have 260 hubs across the country, with 20,000 followers (First-Arai 2020). For instance, their pressure in Nashville, along with the influence of Greta Thunberg and Al Gore, convinced congressional representative Jim Cooper to sign the Green New Deal resolution (First-Arai 2020).

The Green New Deal was introduced in 2019 by one of the younger members of Congress, Representative Alexandria Ocasio-Cortez of New York. Initially, it called for the United States to get 100 percent of the country's power from renewable sources, and to eliminate carbon emissions, within 10 years (Flavelle 2020). Since then, climate change legislation on Capitol Hill continues to evolve.

Teen activists have had some success on the state level with climate legislative initiates. For example, a Utah teen, Mishka Banuri, helped to organize the People's Climate March in March 2016 (Larsen 2020). Banui worked with other high school students to meet with the state's largest utility company and pressure lawmakers (Gomez and Ahmed 2018). By May 2018, Governor Gary Herbert signed a resolution for the state legislature to acknowledge climate change (Gomez and Ahmed 2018). In Seattle, teenager Jamie Margolin founded Zero Hour, an advocacy group promoting climate change legislation (Jarvis 2020). She has addressed a joint congressional committee, seated next to Greta Thunberg.

Operating on a parallel track are the Big Green groups, such as the Sierra Club and the Natural Resources Defense Council (Wines 2014). They have been successful at raising money and pressuring legislators and the main federal administrative agency—the Environmental Protection Agency (Wines 2014). When these groups launched a campaign about limiting new coal-burning power plants they drew four million comments that were sent to the EPA (Wines 2014) during the public comment period for regulations.

In both the civil rights movement and climate movement, activists turned to making change through the lawmaking process. All three branches of government helped reach the goals of the civil rights movement—with the assistance of presidents, the judicial landmark decisions affecting voting rights and education, and the creation of grassroots Community Action Agencies (CAAs) through the administrative branch. Similarly, the climate movement has pursued congressional and state initiatives—sparked by young lawmakers and teenagers, as well as by Big Green groups. It too has received, in the 2020 presidential election, support from President Biden. Missing currently are administrative regulations mandating and ensuring corporate compliance with emission reduction goals. Also missing is deep and far-reaching coalition building.

II—Differences between the Two Movements

A. The Race of the Movement's Leadership as an Issue

The differences between the civil rights movement and the climate movement are significant. First is the issue of race. The essence of the civil rights movement was to achieve racial integration and to end discrimination. It was a race-based movement, with its supporters drawing primarily from organizations (the NAACP, for example) representing persons of color. The color of its supporters was not a point of contention for reaching its ultimate goals. In contrast, the climate movement, with its environmental focus, has drawn criticism for its lack of inclusiveness. The climate movement has been criticized for its whiteness (Jones 2020).

Although persons of color are not entirely absent from the climate movement, there has been historical and current-day racial controversies. One of the long-term conservationist organizations, the Sierra Club, recently criticized its founder, John Muir, for his racist beliefs (Jones 2020). In 2020, the Associated Press publicly apologized for making a "terrible mistake" when it cropped an African climate activist, Ugandan Vanessa Nakate, out of a photo, but retained four white girls including Greta Thunberg (Bauder 2020). That incident led to newsroom soul-searching, diversity training, the restoration of Nakate to the photo, and to its republication (Bauder 2020).

As a college student, activist Leah Thomas reflected on the intersectional theory expounded by the legal scholar Kimberlé Williams Crenshaw, which "'posits that oppression affects certain groups on multiple levels, including race, class, gender, religion, and other aspects of their identity'" (Jones 2020). Thomas has reached out on social media to express why environmentalists should embrace the Black Lives Matter movement, and her message went viral. She is currently working with nonprofits engaged in environmental issues to better promote inclusivity of voices (Jones 2020).

Other activists have expressed how the environmental movement needs to be more racially inclusive (Campbell and Rosa-Aquino 2020). A Puerto Rican attorney and environmental justice leader, Elizabeth Yeampierre, advises that the Big Green groups should support '"frontline leadership because we're the ones that are being impacted by climate change. Not the other way around'" (Campbell and Rosa-Aquino 2020). A teenage activist with the Sunrise Movement in Michigan, Savitri Anantharaman, advises that the movement should be '"intentionally creating opportunities for lower capacity volunteers to contribute'" and '"truly investing in leaders of color as organizers and people instead of further marginalizing and tokenizing them'" (Campbell and Rosa-Aquino 2020).

This perceived lack of diversity in the climate movement and its association with a white-dominated cause indicates the lack of a supportive network, which was apparent in the civil rights movement. The absence of a supportive network is the second reason why the climate movement is not realizing its goals.

Climate change has more recently been examined through the lens of its impact on persons of color. "Environmental racism" and the "climate gap" are phrases used to describe the effect of "climate events involve[ing] hurricanes, wildfires, extreme heat or increased exposure to air pollution" (Wesson 2021, 35). Will the impact of climate change upon persons of color motivate more segments of society to support the movement? That will depend upon organizing tactics.

B. The Supportive Network for the Civil Rights Movement, Currently Lacking in the Climate Movement

For the civil rights movement, supportive networks, loosely defined, connected national organizations with local chapters and college campuses, national leaders, church leaders, and the public. For instance, the Montgomery bus boycott gave rise to the Southern Christian Leadership Conference (SCLC), which, in turn, at a conference in 1960, gave birth to SNCC, focused on the younger generation (Farber 1994). Soon, chapters of SNCC sprouted on college campuses, engaging college students in the civil rights movement (Barker 1984). The Baby Boomer generation participated in these efforts. These extensive networks are missing from the climate movement. Instead, the Big Green groups seemingly operate separately from the grassroots mobilization.

The civil rights movement was propelled forward by the preplanning and organizational efforts of groups like the SCLC and SNCC. In addition to the sit-ins, the SCLC, along with other civil rights leaders, organized marches. In 1963, after hundreds of adults were arrested, SCLC organized schoolchildren to march in Birmingham. Thousands continued with marches and sit-ins, until President John F. Kennedy announced that he would introduce federal legislation guaranteeing desegregated public facilities, schools, and voting rights (Farber 1994).

Acting in solidarity, a thousand northern white students piled into buses and headed to the South marking the 1964 Mississippi Freedom Summer in a program sponsored by SNCC (Barker 1984, C3; Farber 1994, 93). The goal was to register Black voters (Farber 1994). Following President Kennedy's assassination, President Lyndon Johnson took office and signed the Civil Rights Act in 1964 and the Voting Rights Act of 1965, after they passed through Congress.

The next year, in 1966, Huey Newton and Bobby Seale launched the militant Black Panther Party. It grew in membership and drew the country's attention to racial injustice issues. The Panthers were organized on multiple levels. They published a newspaper to raise money and publicize the party's mission. They reached into the community. Seale, who had formerly worked with CAAs, began organizing breakfast programs for children, and they eventually provided a range of services—such as health care and senior care (Bloom and Martin 2013).

When faced with adversity, many organizations and individuals came to the Panthers' defense, indicating a broad network of support. The police made several arrests of Panther members starting in 1967 with the arrests of Seale and Eldridge Cleaver. Thousands of college students attended Panther rallies to show support for the movement (Bloom and Martin 2013). When Huey Newton was shot and arrested later in 1967, a coalition of groups was formed to aid in his defense, including the Progressive Labor Party, Students for a Democratic Society, and SNCC (Bloom and Martin 2013).

After the highly publicized police killing of Panther leader Fred Hampton in 1969, there was further evidence of a supportive network when groups rallied (Bloom and Martin 2013). When Panther leader

Bobby Seale was arrested and put on trial as part of the Chicago Seven, who were accused of organizing riots at the 1968 Democratic National Convention in Chicago (Bloom and Martin 2013), the largest antiwar organization in the country, the New Mobilization Committee to End the War in Vietnam, supported Seale's claims of innocence (Bloom and Martin 2013). The trial caused national media attention and an outpouring of support. The heightened interest in these events is indicative in the streaming of a 2020 film on Netflix, *The Trial of the Chicago 7*. The rallying around the trials of Black Panther Party members, despite ideological disagreement with the party, indicated how far-reaching the network of support for the civil rights movement ranged.

Purportedly, SCLC's and SNCC's success was in "bringing de jure racial segregation to its knees" (Bloom and Martin, 2013, 113). But SNCC's student protests and organizing were not isolated events; instead, they were influenced and supported by a greater network of national organizations and leaders: the NAACP, the SCLC, and individuals such as Dr. King. Black women were less visible in leadership roles, but they led the voting rights movement and other civil rights campaigns (Bennett 2020), like the Montgomery Bus Boycott.

In addition to organizations led by Black leaders, support for the civil rights movement also came from white college students in campus chapters of the National Student Association (Franklin 1969). Their members held annual national meetings with 900 attendees in 1965 (Janson 1965), growing to 1,200 delegates in 1967 (Roberts 1967). Students debated the Vietnam War, and they also focused on extending their reach off campus, to organize "people in the ghettos" (Roberts 1967). In 1967, 200,000 students acted as tutors for children of color (Roberts 1967). The National Student Association also received grants to study communities of persons of color (Franklin 1969).

There was a nationwide effort, beyond college campuses, to end racial discrimination and poverty, which are inextricably linked. President Johnson sought to create the "Great Society" (Farber 1994, 104). Over 1,000 CAAs were set up around the nation to help eradicate poverty (Farber 1994; Klein, Lazar, and Zeisel 1981). The CAAs were meant to involve the poor while helping underserved communities, fostering a grassroots structure (Klein, Lazar, and Zeisel 1981). One-third of CAA boards of directors were to consist of representatives of the poor and the rest from the private sector and lawmaking bodies. Head Start was created through this federal legislation, which was designed to provide low-income children with learning skills (Klein, Lazar, and Zeisel 1981).

Thus, the 1960s civil rights movement was supported—by other organizations, community leaders, churches, programs created by our government, all three branches of government—to defend movement leaders and promote racial equality.

C. Generational Differences Observed in Today's Black Lives Matter Movement and Climate Movement

Commentators have helped us to understand the organizing tactics employed by the Millennials and the Gen Zers. Their observations of the Black Lives Matter movement are insightful for understanding the climate movement.

1. Black Lives Matter

A striking difference surfaced with the organizational planning and modes of communication for today's Black Lives Matter movement, as opposed to the 1960s civil rights movement. These differences can be attributed to how our more youthful generations, Millennials and Gen Zers, interact with each other and with the public.

Criticism about the lack of planning and seemingly disorganized structure surfaced during the Black Lives Matter protests following George Floyd's death. The 1960s civil rights movement exerted months of planning and coordination to pull off marches and sit-ins. Andrew Young, at age 88, former mayor of Atlanta and ambassador to the United Nations, and a key SCLC staff member, contrasted the 1960s organizational planning with the 2020 Black Lives Matter protests: the "wave of protests were 'a phenomenal moment,' [but that] they cried out for organization and structure" (Barry 2020, A22). According to Young, the absence of digital technology in the 1960s meant that organizing and planning took time. Young recalls that the events in Birmingham took three or four months to organize (Barry 2020).

An example of a teenage organizer and her facilitation of technology to organize a Black Lives Matter protest comes from the Nashville Black Lives Matter protest. Zee Thomas told the press that despite her lack of experience with protest movements, she received support on social media: "'Social media was like my best friend. . . . I met my other organizers there. They contacted me on Twitter and Instagram'" (Bennett 2020, 4). Similarly, Tiana Day, who led the march in San Francisco, was contacted initially by a co-organizer who put out a comment on

Instagram that a leader was needed. Day described the speed of the results this way, "'I D.M.-ed her. We organized the entire thing in 18 hours, pushing out a single flier'" (Bennett 2020, 4). The result was a march that spread for miles.

A march can be organized in a couple of days, as opposed to months, and no one needs to find the money to make hundreds of copies of fliers, nor do they need to find ways to get the fliers to campuses or to community groups to distribute them. But then missing are the lines of communication around campus and community groups and the hours of face-to-face event-planning meetings. Replacing human contact are smartphones and virtual messages. The recent use of technology to organize a movement can be traced to the acculturation of the Millennials' and Gen Zers' formative stages of development.

2. Millennials and Gen Zers and the Digital Age

The digital age helped to shape the mindset of the Millennials and the Gen Zers. The Millennials, growing up in the digital age (Rouse and Ross 2018), are "the first digital natives" (Ross and Rouse, chap. 11, this volume). "Technology and the internet have shaped the way Millennials think, communicate, and learn" (Allen and Jackson 2017, 5). By the turn of the century, the vast majority of American children were "computer literate" (Bohl 2008, 779–80). Even more than the Millennials, Gen Zers' formative years were most directly affected (Graham 2018, 2019). Impacting Gen Z was the iPhone's release in 2007; Gen Zers were just at the age (young teens) to use this new and addictive mode of communication.

Commentators have observed that the Millennials and Gen Z are "wired" (Ricci and Sautter 2021, 70) and "are more than at ease using technology, including smartphones, apps, and online forums" (Ricci and Sautter 2021, 52). Because of their growing up with technology, in ways that previous generations have not, they "communicate differently" (Ricci and Sautter 2021, 52).

The ease of access to planning events is remarkably different today than it was for the Baby Boomers who helped to organize sit-ins and marches for the civil rights movement. A single video clip or single-sentence post by anyone with a TikTok or Twitter app can attract hundreds of thousands of followers. The Gen Zers can easily express political beliefs, across the spectrum from conservative to progressive, on TikTok (Herman 2020). It was through the use of TikTok that this young generation spread word to buy seats at a Tulsa, Oklahoma rally for President Trump, but not attend (Herman 2020), thus accomplishing the goal of embarrassing the former president.

Even though technology makes communication swifter than in the past, helping to mobilize bodies to a protest march at a moment's notice, paradoxically it has added physical distance to our human interactions culturally (Twenge 2017). The Gen Zers and Millennials spend less time together than the Baby Boomers or Gen Xers—in terms of dating and socializing, and instead the younger generations spend a considerable amount of time more physically isolated, such as in their bedrooms, and on their smartphones and electronic devices (Twenge 2017). As Twenge (2017) explained, "The arrival of the smartphone has radically changed every aspect of [Gen Zer]'s lives, from the nature of their social interactions to their mental health. These changes have affected young people in every corner of the nation and in every type of household."

The availability of technology has become ingrained in the mode of communication among Millennials and Gen Zers, but to the detriment of the movements.

3. Generational Divide within the Climate Movement

The climate movement is divided by generational differences. The Big Green groups operate on a parallel track with the younger activists. They are not seemingly linked to each other, nor to the greater supportive networks such as those seen with the civil rights movement.

An example of the generational divide within the climate movement arose during a recent interview. A sharp difference in opinions surfaced in an interview with Jim Tripp, 80, former general counsel of the Environmental Defense Fund, and Jamie Margolin, 18, teen activist and Zero Hour spokesperson (EDF 2020). Tripp advocated solutions that work within the current legal and corporate systems, such as creating policies to reduce carbon emissions and to increase offshore wind investments. Margolin took a more drastic stance that the answer was not solely more renewable energy but that oil companies need to switch to a different business and end fossil fuel production (EDF 2020).

Margolin's position is representative of Generation Z, who are characteristically more risk averse about climate change than the older generations. Gen Zers are independent and nontraditional (Atkins 2020). They are also concerned about social justice (Atkins 2020). It is predictable, therefore, that Gen Zers would be passionate about climate change and would take a more extreme stance on the goals of the movement.

Although the civil rights movement involved what now seems to be antiquated tools, such as duplicating machines and telephones, it offered activists an opportunity to talk to each other face-to-face during strategy and planning meetings, to design a flier using words and graphics, to weigh tactics and prepare for the press (Theoharis 2021; Atkins 2020). As Andrew Young said, missing from the swift use of smartphones to organize a current day march is "organization and structure" (Barry 2020, A22). This author argues that climate movement organizers could benefit from the Baby Boomer's slower, more deliberate, human to human connection.

4. The Fragility of the Social-Media-Based Occupy Wall Street

The fragility of a social-media-based movement like Occupy Wall Street (OWS) caused it to fade quickly. Led by the Millennials, in 2011–12 (Rouse and Ross 2018), the protests started with people camping out in Zuccotti Park near Manhattan's Wall Street. The protests spread to college campuses and cities around the country (Buckley 2012). The OWS protesters were initially objecting to the connection of big government with Wall Street, in bailing out the big banks after they had crashed the economy and their general support for the wealthiest 1 percent over 99 percent of Americans (Buckley 2012). The issues went beyond this initial call and in some locations were site specific, such as at Tufts, where OWS protests pushed for an Africana studies department at their school (Buckley 2012). The rallying call seemed unfocused, which likely contributed to the movement's short lifespan.

Additionally, OWS lacked national leadership, unlike the civil rights movement, which produced leaders. And it also lacked an infrastructure of networking support with other groups and segments of society. Without an extensive network of support and connectivity among human activists, the climate movement may face a fate similar to that of OWS.

5. Lessons Learned

Both the civil rights movement and the climate movement are fueled by those who felt they had a stake in the outcome. Furthermore, both embraced similar organizing tactics, such as civil disobedience, sit-ins, marches, and electoral and legislative reform. However, the civil rights movement demonstrated that a network of support helped to effect change. Although the Millennials and the Gen Zers are using technology that they matured with, and it can provide swift connectivity, these younger generations are socially isolated and are missing greater networks of support. The young activists are unaccustomed to the effort necessary to build coalitions.

The civil rights movement demonstrated remarkable connectivity among leaders and the populace. Rosa Parks's activism was deeper rooted than the moment she refused to give up her bus seat in Montgomery, Alabama (Theoharis 2021), saying, "'over the years, I have been rebelling against second-class citizenship. It didn't begin when I was arrested'" (Theoharis 2021). Nor did Mrs. Parks's arrest by itself draw the public's attention. Rather, established leaders and networks helped to thrust this event into the history books.

The evolution of social movements sheds light on the motivations of the generations that fuel them and their tactical approaches to propelling the movements toward success. These movements also provide insights into the similarities and differences of generations that populate them.

Conclusion

Although technology can be a useful tool for rallying people, this author finds that the tool actually causes a wedge between potential constituencies. Rather than human to human contact, which was evident in the civil rights movement, nowadays Gen Zers and Millennials are so dependent upon their smartphones for communication that the political ends are hampered.

Generation Z and the Millennials' approach to community organizing and lobbying are fundamentally different from their older generational counterparts. The younger generation's reliance upon smartphones in everyday life (Twenge 2017), and their diminished reliance upon meeting with coalition leaders, live planning of events, connecting the populace and the more seasoned environmentalists, have affected the potential success of the climate movement.

The Millennials' and Gen Zers' reliance upon technology as an organizing tool stems from their acculturation in this digital age. Unlike previous generations, these younger sets grew up with gadgets for entertainment, communication, and education. The use of electronics is so ubiquitous that the brains of the Millennials and the Gen Zers are likely wired differently than of the Baby Boomer generation. It would be nearly impossible not to use the devices for an organizational task.

As former mayor, ambassador, and activist Andrew Young cautioned the Black Lives Matter activists, there is still value in meeting, discussing, planning—employing thoughtful organizational tactics (Barry 2020).

ACKNOWLEDGMENTS

For contributions to this chapter, I gratefully acknowledge Renee Nicole Allen, Christine Nero Coughlin, Andrea J. Laisure, Corey P. Laisure, Paul Skip Laisure, Sandy Patrick, Cheryl Wade, and Alexis A. Zobeideh.

REFERENCES

Allen, R. A., and A. R. Jackson. 2017. "Contemporary Teaching Strategies: Effectively Engaging Millennials across the Curriculum." *U. Det. Mercy L. Rev.* 95, 1–34.

Atkins, T. D. 2020. "#Fortheculture: Generation Z and the Future of Legal Education." 26 *Mich. J. Race & Law* 26, 101–55.

Baker, K. C. 2019. "Fighting for the Planet." *People*, October 21, 72.

Barker, K. 1984. "If You Think My Generation Was Crushed, Wait 'til the Next Fight." *Washington Post*, October 21, C3.

Barry, E. 2020. "They Made History in the 1960s and See It on the March Again." *New York Times*, June 19, A1.

Bauder, D. 2020. "Photo Cropping Mistake Leads to AP Soul-Searching on Race." AP News, January 27. https://apnews.com/article/us-news-sally-buzbee-race-and-et hnicity-greta-thunberg-business-6a853a81f34164ab85713e68a889976d

Bennett, J. 2020. "Teen Girls Fighting for a More Just Future." *New York Times*, June 28, Style, 1.

Bloom, J., and W. E. Martin Jr. 2013. *Black against Empire: The History and Politics of the Black Panther Party*. Oakland: University of California Press.

Bloom, J. S., C. Dendy, and K. Wilson. 2019. "Generation Differences. State Bar of Texas CLE Oil and Gas Disputes Course 9–1 (Chapter 9. Not Your Father's Jury: The Rise of the Millennial)."

Bohl, J. C. 2008. "Generations X and Y in Law School: Practical Strategies for Teaching the 'MTV/Google' Generation." *Loyola University New Orleans Law Review* 54: 775–798.

Boyle, R. A., and J. I. Ingham. 2006. "Generation X in Law School: How These Law Students Are Different from Those Who Teach Them." *Journal of Legal Education* 56 (2): 281–95.

Buckley, C. 2012. "The New Student Activism: The Occupy Movement on Campus Seems to Have Legs. But How Strong Is Their Will?" *New York Times*, January 22, A16.

Campbell, S. R., and P. Rosa-Aquino. 2020. "Five Ways to Make the Climate Movement Less White." *Guardian*, September 21. https://www.theguardian.com/us -news/2020/sep/21/five-ways-to-make-the-climate-movement-less-white

Corporate Finance Institute (CFI) Team. 2021. "Baby Boomers: A Generation of People Born between 1946 and 1964." September 21. https://www.corporatefinance institute.com/resources/knowledge/other/baby-boomers/

Dalton, R. J. 2008. *The Good Citizen: How a Younger Generation Is Reshaping American Politics*. Washington, DC: CQ Press.

Diani, M. 1992. "The Concept of Social Movement." *Sociological Review* 40 (1): 1–25.

Diani, M. 2004. "Networks and Participation." In *The Blackwell Companion to Social Movements*, edited by D. A. Snow, S. A. Soule, and H. Kriesi, 339–59. Malden, MA: Blackwell.

Dylan, B. 1964. "The Times They Are A-Changin." Retrieved from https://www.yout ube.com

Eavis, P., and C. Krauss. 2021. "The Climate Talk vs. the Walk." *New York Times*, February 23, B1.

Environmental Defense Fund. 2020. "In Conversation: Can We Agree?" *EDF Solutions* 51 (2): 17.

Environmental Defense Fund. 2021. "Tackling Climate, Jobs, and Justice." *EDF Solutions* 52 (2): 9.

Farber, D. 1994. *The Age of Great Dreams: America in the 1960s*. New York: Hill and Wang.

Farber, D. 2020. "Climate Perspectives across the Generations." *Natural Resources Journal* 60: 293–303.

First-Arai, L. 2020. "Sunrise in Nashville: Young Activists Are Pushing Lawmakers to Care about Climate Change." *Sierra Magazine* (May/June): 33–37.

Fisher, D. R. 2019. *American Resistance: From the Women's March to the Blue Wave*. New York: Columbia University Press.

Flavelle, C. 2020. "Democrats' Climate Plan to Embrace Racial Justice." *New York Times*, June 30, A21.

Flavelle, C. 2021. "Climate Change Is Getting Worse, E.P.A. Says. Just Look Around." *New York Times*, May 13, A1.

Franklin, B. A. 1969. "U.S. Student Group Maps New Protest Tactics." *New York Times*, February 23.

Funk, C., and A. Tyson 2020. "Millennial and Gen Z Republicans Stand Out from Their Elders on Climate and Energy Issues." Pew Research Center, June 24. https://www.pewresearch.org/fact-tank/2020/06/24/millennial-and-gen-z-repub licans-stand-out-from-their-elders-on-climate-and-energy-issues/

Gardiner, Beth. 2021. "The Deadly Cost of Dirty Air." *National Geographic* 40 (April): 62.

Goeken, C. 1999. "Letter to Editor." *New York Times*, April 4.

Gomez, I., and S. Ahmed. 2018. "How a Group of Teenagers Convinced the Utah Legislature to Recognize Climate Change." *CNN Health*, May 22. https://www .cnn.com/2018/05/22/health/utah-students-climate-change-trnd/index.html

Graham, L. P. 2018. "Generation Z Goes to Law School: Teaching and Reaching Law Students in the Post-Millennial Generation." *U. Ark. Little Rock Law Review* 41: 29–95.

Graham, L. P. 2019. "Welcoming Generation Z to the Legal Workplace." *Wyoming Law* (August): 22–23.

Herman, J. 2020. "TikTok Is Shaping Politics, but How?" *New York Times*, June 28. https://www.nytimes.com/2020/06/28/style/tiktok-teen-politics-gen-z.html?smid=em-share

Interlandi, J. 2019. "Opinion: Amid the Tears, She Took Action." *New York Times*, September 23, A26.

Janson, D. 1965. "Student Congress Emphasizes Political Activism." *New York Times*, September 5.

Jarvis, B. 2020. "A Teenage Climate Activist Grows Up in the Shadow of an Uncertain Future." *New York Times Magazine*, July 26, 28.

Jones, R. 2020. "The Environmental Movement Is Very White: These Leaders Want to Change That." *National Geographic*, July 29. https://www.nationalgeographic.com/history/article/environmental-movement-very-white-these-leaders-want-change-that

Klein, R., K. S. Lazar, and L. Zeisel. 1981. *Studies in Community Action. Vol. I: A Legislative and Administrative History*. Ithaca, NY: Foundation for Human Services Studies.

Larsen, B. 2020. "Civics Lesson: This Teen Activist Has Learned to Combine Legislation with Direct Action." *Sierra Magazine* (May/June): 23.

Newell, L. A. 2015. "Redefining Attention (and Revamping the Legal Profession?) for the Digital Generation." *Nev. L.J.* 15: 754–824.

New York Times. 2021. "The Task Ahead for Biden on Climate." Editorial. *New York Times*, February 7, A6.

Parker, K., and R. Igielnik. 2020. "On the Cusp of Adulthood and Facing an Uncertain Future: What We Know about Gen Z So Far." Pew Research Center, May 14. https://www.pewresearch.org/social-trends/2020/05/14/on-the-cusp-of-adulthood-and-facing-an-uncertain-future-what-we-know-about-gen-z-so-far-2/

Reith, K. 2019. "IC Students Must Combat Climate Crisis." *The Ithacan* (student-run publication of Ithaca College, NY), August 29, 12.

Ricci, S. A. G., and C, M. Sautter. 2021. "Corporate Governance Gaming: The Collective Power of Retail Investors." *Nev. L. J.* 22, 51–97.

Rierden, A. 1990. "Campuses See a New Spirit of Involvement." *New York Times*, April 15, CN1.

Roberts, S. V. 1967. "The Voices of the Campus." *New York Times*, August 20, E9.

Rouse, S. M., and A. D. Ross. 2018. *The Politics of Millennials: Political Beliefs and Policy Preferences of America's Most Diverse Generation*. Ann Arbor: University of Michigan Press.

Sengupta, S. 2019a. "She Didn't Mince Words: 'Listen to the Scientists.'" *New York Times*, September 19, A9.

Sengupta, S. 2019b. "Young People around the World Take It to the Streets." *New York Times*, September 21, A14.

Sengupta, S. 2019c. "Meet 8 Youth Protest Leaders (This is Our Terrifying World)." *New York Times*, September 21, A16.

Sengupta, S. 2021. "Climate Efforts to Alter Role of U.S. in World." *New York Times,* January 28, A19.

Slack, K. 1988. "Vassar Severs Ties with South Africa." *Vassar Miscellany News* 2 (2) (December 1). On file with the author.

Stern, M. 1969. "Teen-agers Protesting Too." *New York Times,* January 9.

Theoharis, J. 2021. "Rosa Parks's Real Story." *New York Times,* February 7, SR8.

Thigpen, C. L., and A. Tyson. 2021. "On Social Media, Gen ZX and Millennial Adults Interact More with Climate Change Content Than Older Generations." Pew Research Center, June 21. https://www.pewresearch.org/fact-tank/2021/06/21/on-social-media-gen-z-and-millennial-adults-interact-more-with-climate-change-content-than-older-generations/

The Trial of the Chicago 7. 2020. Netflix film.

Twenge, J. M. 2017. "Have Smartphones Destroyed a Generation?" *The Atlantic,* September. https://www.theatlantic.com/magazine/archive/2017/09/has-the-smartphone-destroyed-a-generation/534198/

United Nations Climate Action Summit. 2019. September 23. Retrieved from www.YouTube.com

Wesson, V. D. 2021. "Environmental Racism: How Lawyers Can Help Close the Climate Gap." *New York State Bar Assoc. Journal* (January/February), 35.

Wines, M. 2014. "Environmental Groups Focus on Change by Strengthening Their Political Operations." *New York Times,* June 1.

9 | Building Youthful Habits of Voting

Niall Guy Michelsen

This chapter presents a tale of two generations. The senior members of one generation are slowly fading into memory and the other has not yet arrived, politically speaking. Let's begin with a puzzle. The 1960s was a turbulent political era with one of its major characteristics how young people burst onto the political scene with a vigor that both scared and excited older generations. Great numbers of young citizens embraced some form of reform or revolution of the existing status quo. They added their voices loudly and colorfully to topics ranging from how colleges are run, what the role of women in society should be, the rights of African Americans, protection of the environment, and the wars we fight. As a reward for their vigor and perhaps to deter more disruptive political actions, the nation passed the 26th Amendment in 1971, dropping the voting age from 21 to 18. However, the first of the generation to get the vote at 18 led in a direction that no one anticipated— they became the leading edge of a decline in voting turnout. How did this highly energetic generation become lethargic voters? This chapter contends the cause is found in the failure to instill the habit of voting in these young people. Ironically, the chapter also contends that the solution to this problem of low voting rates is found in applying the same medicine that caused the problem. Drop the voting age again, this time to 16.

Setting the Stage, 1971

Sometimes, turbulent political times engender frantic attempts to provide a fix. Political reforms completed in haste may be wise or unwise, but they are likely to have unanticipated consequences. As humans we naturally harken back to earlier times when we find ourselves in an unsettling situation. It is not saying much to say that American politics today is unsettled. When looking for a comparable period, many have been drawn to the years at the end of the 1960s and early 1970s. Then, as now, cities were battlegrounds, racial issues inflamed political debates with outrage and fear. One missing element from that earlier time is the intense disagreements over a foreign war. Then we were in the midst of the Vietnam War and now, by contrast, we are involved with several low intensity military engagements around the world, none of which spark much interest, although U.S. assistance to the war in Ukraine might be one possibility. We do have the COVID-19 pandemic to provide us with reasons for political bickering.

Looking back at the extraordinarily rapid passage of the 26th Amendment, which dropped the minimum voting age to 18, we can evaluate the wisdom of that reform while considering some of the unexpected ramifications. Our concern is not with the debates that gave rise to this amendment except to the degree that its advocates advanced grand, but not irrational, claims. The 26th Amendment can be seen as a product of the war, specifically, the antiwar contingent in Congress. Advocates advanced a couple of powerful arguments. One claimed that drafting young men to fight in Vietnam without allowing them to vote was unjust. In this way society could repay that generation for drafting some of them to fight in Vietnam, by extending the rights of suffrage to them. The second argument was not as prominent but was essential. This maintained that the highly energized generation would energize a badly frayed political system. Thus, where one argument aimed to repay the youth for Vietnam, the other was hoping that the youth would redeem the political system that seemed to be in great trouble.

We are now in a position to evaluate the reform. Certainly, the emergence of dynamic young politicians was noticeable in the wake of this reform. Joe Biden (elected to the U.S. Senate in 1972 at age 31) and Dennis Kucinich (elected mayor of Cleveland in 1977 at age 31) come to mind. But they might have been elected with or without the amendment. We can, however, look at the impact upon voting rates of this new generation of voters, who I will designate as Votes@18. Generations can be viewed in sociological ways with analysts discerning special characteristics that distinguish one generation from another. The characteristics that we select depend on our larger purposes and here our concern is

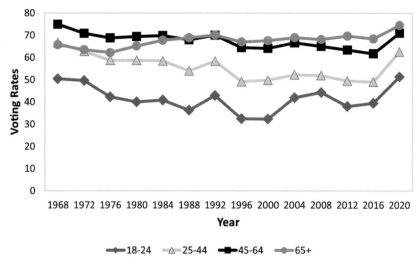

Fig. 9.1. Voting Rates by Age in Presidential Election Years
Source: Updated data from Wattenberg 2016.

specifically with voting and voting turnout rates, so we will draw a line at 1972 with the generation of Votes@18 representing our relevant cohort. These pioneers who were between 18 and 21 years old on Election Day in 1972, and the cohorts who followed them, have the common experience of coming of age to vote at the age of 18. We will suggest later that this is unfortunate and should give way to a new voting age and a new generation of Votes@16. At the time, no one knew that this was going to set up the Votes@18 generation for low voting rates.

Using updated data from Wattenberg (2016) we see the following pattern in presidential election years in figure 9.1. Prior to the passage of this amendment the gap between the youngest and oldest eligible cohorts was relatively minor, but that gap was set to increase as more and more younger voters entered the electorate. Clearly there is an ordering pattern in effect here: the older the cohort, the higher the voting rate. The exception to this is that from 1968 through 1984, the 45–64 cohort voted at higher rates than the 65+ cohort. Thereafter the oldest cohort has become the highest voting cohort. Note that the lowest young voting category is always the youngest (in 1968 this was 21–24).

The line in figure 9.2 indicates how much more likely someone in the first category (65+) is to vote compared to someone in the second

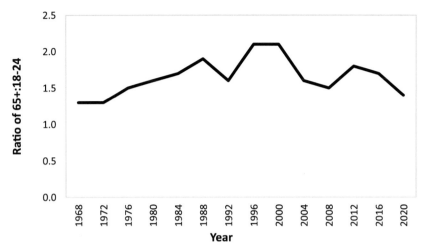

Fig. 9.2. Ratio of 65+ to 18-24 in Presidential Election Years
Source: Updated data from Wattenberg 2016.

category (18–24). So, in 1968 those 65+ were 30 percent more likely to vote than the 21–24 year olds. Over time, this rose as high as more than twice as likely (1996 and 2000) and then dropped fairly steadily. The gaps in 2008 (50%) and 2012 (80%) demonstrate how Barack Obama's first candidacy energized young citizens but his reelection did not have the same magic. The 2020 election results reflect the closing of the gap to its lowest point. Figure 9.3 presents data from the midterm elections and it follows the same pattern as in the first figure. There is more crossing over between the age cohorts. The older cohort's rates are nearly as high as in the presidential elections, whereas the youngest cohort rates are considerably lower.

The story in figure 9.4 is similar to figure 9.2, but the ratio numbers are much more pronounced, indicating that in the midterm elections the gap between the oldest voters and the youngest is much larger. For example, only in the presidential elections years of 1996 and 2000 was the ratio as high as 2.1:1 (meaning that older voters were more than twice as likely to vote as the youngest voters). By contrast, only in 1970 and 2018 were the ratios as low as that during midterm elections. The 2018 midterm election stands out from the others with energized voters and the turnout was of historic proportions. Even so, the ratio of old voters to young voters was 2.1:1. But this is minor in comparison to the preceding midterm in 2014, when the gap was a whopping 3.6:1. Simi-

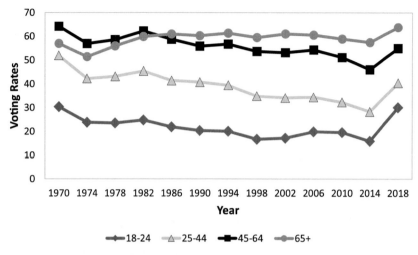

Fig. 9.3. Voting Rates by Age in Midterm Elections
Source: Data compiled from midterm elections.

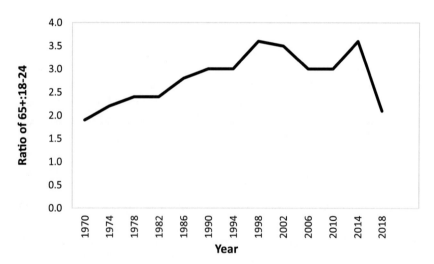

Fig. 9.4. Ratio of 65+ to 18-24 in Midterm Elections
Source: Data compiled from midterm elections.

larly, in 2022, youth vote was high. What is not clear at this point is whether the strong showing of youth is a harbinger of a renewed youthful engagement in electoral politics, or whether it is a product of a peculiar time in political history.

Understanding the Decline

Perhaps this is throwing too much blame on the Votes@18 folks. Certainly, the declining turnout rates between 1968 and 2018 were unintended. This has generated a number of explanations that account for some of the decline. Instead of seeing the 26th Amendment as a crowning achievement followed by disappointing voting turnout, perhaps the timing was inauspicious. For example, dropping the voting age coincided with a series of national events that marked a decline in trust in government, characterized by severe economic troubles and defeat in Vietnam and the resignation of President Richard Nixon. The 26th Amendment was still fresh when Watergate erupted onto the national stage, robbing the American public of its political innocence.

Other potential long-term factors include declines in economic equality and in trust in government. Both of these could push down voting rates and both of these roughly coincide with the period of the Votes@18 generation. The 1972 voting rate for the 18–24 age group was low compared to older age groups, but higher than any election since, and this corresponds to the declining political trust. Figure 9.5 shows trust in government survey results in comparison to the 18–24 voting rates since 1972. There is some similarity in the early periods but, even then, the turnout rates are not tied very closely to changes in trust. And the 21st century period exhibits a wide discrepancy.

One explanation for this pattern focuses on the social and media environments in which young generations are coming of age. Here we see another puzzle of sorts. On one hand, today's youth have exponentially more political news and information in their hands compared to earlier generations. On the other hand, they have not, until very recently, shown much interest in and knowledge of politics. Some analysts contend that the developments in technology have changed much in society, including our inclinations to see voting as an important civic act (Foa and Mounk 2017). Recent generations have come of age during a period where media itself has taken on entirely new forms. Old folks speak wistfully of the time when Walter Cronkite of CBS News could be

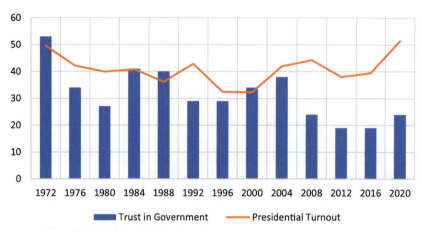

Fig. 9.5. Voting Rates and Trust in Government
Source: Updated data from Wattenberg 2016 and data from Trust in Government Surveys.

the most trusted person in the country, and when he said we could not win the war in Vietnam, public opinion moved strongly against the war. Now, no one has the position of most trusted because no one is trusted by everyone. Evidence also shows that reliance on electronic news sources for political information is associated with lower levels of political knowledge and with the acceptance of political misinformation (Milner 2020).

It is commonplace to recognize that major national events can have an impact on the turnout rates of citizens. It is also widely understood that state and local actions to suppress voting can have an impact on turnout rates including among specific populations. Thus, some events, such as economic recessions and wars, whether popular or unpopular, can push turnout rates up or down. Turnout rates are also responsive to deeper trends. Among the positive trends are the growing percentage of college-educated Americans, the increasing wealth of the overall population, and the aging of the population. These trends should be pushing turnout rates up because old, educated, more affluent people vote at higher rates than others. Instead, until 2018 at least, the trend has been in the other direction. The argument here maintains that dropping the voting age in 1971 initiated a major depressing impact on voting turnout rates for the Votes@18 generations (1972–present).

A different view suggests that perhaps there is nothing wrong with younger generations of citizens and in fact there is not a political participation problem. Rather than being disaffected and apathetic, perhaps young citizens are expressing their political views in ways that are not captured in voting statistics. Netizens is a term that has been used to describe the essence of this perspective (Milner 2010). Survey data shows that there is not a noticeable drop-off in political activities by newer generations when these nonvoting forms of political participation are included. While they might not vote as often, they are more likely to join political boycotts, sign online petitions, and so forth (Dalton 2008).

Another view suggests that the problem of declining participation rates is not with the entire population of younger people, but rather a subset of the generation. Many analysts who engage in this debate are only capturing the changes in behavior of youthful citizens who are in college, or who are college graduates. If we measure changes in nonvoting political engagement, and if this is something that is mostly associated with college-educated people, we miss the big picture, which includes noncollege citizens.

In some ways the collegiate population is of less concern here than the rest of the population—those young people who are not going to attend college. There are a couple of reasons why we should be most concerned with the less educated citizens. The first reason is that there is a positive link between education and voting rates, with more educated citizens voting at higher rates than less educated citizens. Gallego (2015) identified the education gap as central to political inequality in her study of democracies around the world. Dalton (2017) identifies education as the most significant independent variable in predicting who does and does not vote.

The second reason is that colleges, often intentionally, sometimes unintentionally, encourage their students to register and vote (Voter Friendly Campus 2019). The deliberate assistance usually comes with students setting up voter registration tables and the university putting voter registration forms and instructions in the physical mailboxes of residential students (required by federal law in 1965). Increasingly, colleges and universities manage to bring polling booths to campus so that student voters merely must walk to a central location on campus. It is noteworthy that those specialized messages and encouragements are not offered to their former high school classmates who are not

TABLE 9.1. Voting Rates by Education Level

Education	Voting rate as percentage of population rate		Difference
	1972	2008	1972–2008
Less than High School	.79	.62	−.17
High School Graduate	1.03	.86	−.17
Some College	1.18	1.07	−.11
College Graduate	1.33	1.24	−.09

Source: Adapted from Leighley and Nagler 2014, 36. Modified by author.

attending college. What encouragement they do receive is general and goes to people of all ages and situations, including their college-attending cohorts.

A compelling reason for the great interest in less-educated citizens is that it is within those less educated populations that voting has dropped most precipitously. Comparing data from 1972 and 2008 shows the decline in voting across different educational levels (Leighley and Nagler 2014, 36). In table 9.1 if there was zero educational gap in turn-out rates, each of the cells would be scored as 1.0. Numbers less than 1.0 indicate an educational category whose voting rate is less than their percentage of the voting age population. Numbers greater than 1.0 indicate an educational category whose voting rate is higher than their percentage of the voting age population.

Table 9.1 shows that in 1972 only the citizens without a high school degree voted at rates less than their percentage of the population. In 2008 that group had been joined by high school graduates who were now voting at lower rates than their percentage of the population. Meanwhile, the non-high-school graduates declined even further. The positive news is that the percentage of the population with some college education or a college degree grew substantially in the intervening 36 years, as is shown in table 9.2. It shows that the two underperforming voting categories (less than high school, and high school graduates) comprised a much smaller proportion of the overall population in 2008. The two overperforming voting categories (some college, and college graduates) constituted twice as large a proportion of the overall population in 2008 (57.1%) compared to 1972(26.0%).

Leighley and Nagler (2014, 21) show the overall voting rate dropped from 63.6 percent in 1972 to 58.2 percent in 2008. The implications of this are astounding. The overall American electorate is much more

TABLE 9.2. Education Rates as Percentage of Total Population

Education	1972 as percentage of total population	2008 as percentage of total population	Difference
Less than High School	36.6	11.2	−25.4
High School Graduate	37.5	31.7	−5.8
Some College	14.3	29.6	15.3
College Graduate	11.7	27.5	15.8

Source: Adapted from Leighley and Nagler 2014, 36; modified by author.

educated than in the past, but it does not vote at the same levels as previous electorates. The anticipated rise in voting rates due to the increases in the wealth, education, and age of the electorate is being counteracted by the decline of voting among those Americans with the least education. And this is occurring even as those less educated Americans are declining as a percentage of the population. The more educated citizens still vote at high rates. This is a very troubling development. A promising solution as we shall see is Votes@16. Moreover, there are undeniable patterns with who goes to college and who does not. Not everyone is going to college, and those who do tend to be from more privileged backgrounds (Kam and Palmer 2008).

Similarly, the voting decline mirrors the increasing gap between college-educated citizens and non-college-educated citizens. Of course, higher education is tied not only to higher voter rates but also to higher incomes. Something that is not considered here is one of these causing the other—in other words, are less educated people voting less because of greater inequality, or is there greater inequality in part because of the declining voting power of less-educated people (and fewer union voters as well).

We have discussed alternative long-term factors that coincide with the Votes@18 generation that include rising economic inequality, declining trust in government, fragmentation of news sources, rising education levels, and an aging population. Our attention is on the first three that each represent trends that should constantly be pushing voting rates for the youngest voters down. Instead, figure 9.1 showed a strong decline between 1968 and 2000, followed by an upward trend from 2000 to 2020. With that firmly in mind, let us approach the problem from another direction. The unifying element among the members of the Votes@18 generation is that they became eligible to vote at an age where good habits are difficult to establish.

Nurturing Habits

When we address the elements of voting we will see why reducing the voting age to 18 led to lower voting and why reducing the voting age to 16 might lead to higher voting rates. The key is to focus on establishing the habit of voting. An activity becomes habitual after a certain number of occurrences so that it becomes natural and not a matter of weighing costs and benefits. Scholars have established that 3–4 elections in a row where someone votes can establish the habit of voting. The flip side is also true—three or four elections where a citizen is of age to vote but does not vote can create a habit of nonvoting.

Dinas (2012) points out that explanations for any particular choice to vote or not vote can be expressed in cost-benefit terms. However, research shows that over time those calculations are less important and that habit (having voted in election #1 makes a citizen more likely to vote in election #2) becomes more important as an explanatory variable. Habits of voting (or nonvoting) are established like other habits after repeated experiences. Ultimately, habitual behaviors, including voting, become second nature. Some scholars employ terms such as the "footprint" of the first election and "young initiation" as the larger process by which youth are brought into voting (Franklin, Lyons, and Marsh 2004). Eventually, the habit becomes a greater predictor of whether someone will vote in the next election than the race, age, economic status, or educational level of the citizen (Dinas 2012). So, costs of voting are important in determining the first and second voting experiences, but less important as habits build. But nonvoting is also habitual. In fact, it is always easier to not vote than it is to vote. When habits are weak or nonexistent it takes dramatic political circumstances to move a nonvoter to pay the costs of getting registered to vote and to take all the other steps needed.

A habit of voting (or not voting) can be considered as a product of the following elements: the cost of voting; distractions from voting; resources for voting; the habit of voting. Table 3 shows how these factors affect the likelihood of voting.

Ultimately, our goal is to generate voters, and by reducing costs and distractions, or by increasing resources and habits, we can increase the expected likelihood of voting. The converse is also true: increasing costs and distractions, and reducing resources and weaken habits, will decrease the expected likelihood of voting.

Costs are considered the activities a citizen must perform in order

TABLE 9.3. Factors of Voting

Factors	Impacts
Costs	Reduce the likelihood of voting
Distractions	Reduce the likelihood of voting
Resources	Increase the likelihood of voting
Habits	Increase the likelihood of voting

Source: Created by author.

to cast a meaningful ballot. Costs are important because elections are structured by rules and procedures that citizens must respond to if they wish to cast a legitimate ballot. Thus, elections prescribe who can vote, when they can vote, and where they can vote. All those rules and procedures by their very nature impose costs upon the citizen. The process of becoming an eligible voter and casting a vote requires citizens to undertake actions that require them to expend things such as time, energy, and mental contemplation, though typically very little actual money aside from what it might cost to get to a polling booth. The costs of voting are especially important because they have the largest impact on the newest voters, and these tend to also be the youngest voters.

Costs vary across individuals as when one citizen lives within easy walking distance of the polling site and another citizen lives two bus rides away. The first faces low costs in terms of getting to the voting booth while the second faces much higher costs. These costs vary across the United States and across the democratic world. And they vary over time. Governments change the rules and procedures periodically. Costs also vary over time for individuals. Having voted once or more reduces the costs of voting—not all steps, such as getting registered or learning where the polling place is located, need to be replicated at each election.

Distractions are things that could stand in the way of someone going through the steps involved with voting. Distractions are factors of life that can make voting seem less important. Among these are getting married, starting a new career, and moving to a new location. Of these factors, distractions are the most problematic because they are the things that are part of everyday life. Government policies can affect these, as in providing more day-care facilities that would ease the ability of single parents to make it to the polling booth. Nonetheless, most distractions come at the individual or family level.

Against these costs and distractions, individuals bring varying resources to the decision of whether to undertake the steps required to cast a vote. Some very important resources are political knowledge; prior experience in voting; a sense of voting as an obligation; a sense of community; and environmental factors such as peers or family who vote (Foa and Mounk 2017). The sources of these qualities include families, schools, media, government, political actors, religion, and peers. These resources are lowest at the youngest age, which implies that helping the first-time voter is the most important.

In theory, all Americans can increase their resources. For example, nearly everyone has the opportunity to gain adequate political knowledge, internalize the sense of citizen obligations to vote, and generate an interest in politics (McAvoy, Fine, and Ward 2016). In reality, individuals develop these characteristics in different measures. Holbein and Hillygus (2020) focus their attention on the gap between what young citizens want to do (participate actively in politics) and what they actually do. They maintain that young people lack the noncognitive skills to navigate the voting bureaucracy. Holbein and Hillygus (2020) maintain that current civics is so full of cognitive elements that noncognitive elements are left out. Ultimately, they suggest that state public education standards should be expanded to have more than one civics type class mandated. There is much to say in favor of this, but it seems like a distant aspiration.

The first time a citizen becomes eligible to vote is critically important. Since nonvoting tends to lead to future nonvoting, setting the initial voting age at a time when voting is likely to pose the highest costs to the first-time voter only seems to set a pattern for future nonvoting. For most citizens this happens when they reach the minimum age required for voting. Green and Shachar (2000) say, "Lure someone to the voting booth, and you will raise his or her propensity to vote in a future election (562)." When youth face their first election, the costs are high. Plutzer (2002, 42) puts it this way:

As young citizens confront their first election, all the costs of voting are magnified: they have never gone through the process of registration, may not know the location of their polling place, and may not have yet developed an understanding of party difference and key issues. Moreover, their peer group consists almost entirely of other nonvoters: Their friends cannot assure them that voting has been easy, enjoyable, or satisfying.

As a citizen moves from a first-time voter to a regular voter, costs go down, resources go up, distractions may or may not get worse, and habits grow stronger. Costs decrease with voting experiences. Having successfully navigated the voting process once means that the citizen will ordinarily be registered when the next election comes around, and will know how to get to the polling booth. As costs go down, voting gets easier, and with experiencing more elections, habits grow stronger. Reforms that lower costs can therefore make habits easier to form. In turn, habits make the costs less consequential. When habits are ingrained, citizens follow the pattern they have already established. Ultimately, a regular voter becomes oblivious to the costs and feels highly efficacious in the role of voter, handles distractions easily, and thus becomes a bona fide habitual voter.

This is how things are supposed to unfold. Of course, participating in the second election is not certain. The first election could be a bad experience or might even conclude without a vote being cast. These individual choices made to register and vote, or not, are not truly individual choices. They are always taken within a social context and the characteristics of the social context vary considerably over space and time. Thus, individual behavior can be shaped if not determined by government policies and regulations. It is possible for governments to raise or to lower those costs. Raising the costs of voting will negatively affect the new voters more than experienced voters. Conversely, reducing the costs would predictably have a greater positive impact on newer voters than on experienced voters.

Younger voters are more susceptible to factors that disrupt or complicate an election since they have not yet developed the habits involved with all the steps in the voting process. Following Franklin (2004), Gallego (2009) says that "just after leaving school or when attending university young adults are more likely to be in situations that are not conducive to learning to vote": They are otherwise busy, don't have older role models to show them the ropes, and are unattached to locality. The positive effects of staying in school and going to college hide the negative impact of having new adult roles and responsibilities.

It has been argued that setting the voting age at 18 is the wrong time to initiate voters into the electoral process, and that 16 is much more opportune. Mark Franklin argues that 18 is the worst time to start the voting (nonvoting) habit. "Ironically, almost any other age from 15 to 25 would be a better age for individuals to first be confronted . . . the most promising reform that might restore higher turnout would be to lower the voting age still further, perhaps to 15" (Franklin 2004, 213). One way to understand how dropping the voting age from 21 to 18 was a mistake is found by looking at the costs of elections, and the distractions facing the youngest voters.

The current minimum voting age of 18 is in the middle of a period of intense transitions. All are leaving high school, some to go to college, some to join the military, some to follow their dreams to Philadelphia. Some are staying at home and working at a nearby retail center. Some are also falling in love and perhaps having babies and thinking about moving to a new place. Moving and changing one's role in society all interfere with picking up a new positive habit of voting. Worrying about health considerations and financial issues along with myriad other everyday concerns could easily distract a citizen from getting registered to vote and making it to the polling place on the right day. Thus, the distractions will be plentiful, and many are very demanding upon the time and energy of those citizens. Many of these matters immediately go to the top of the pecking order and their obligations to their fellow American citizens gets shunted off to the side.

Switching our attention to the prospective 16-year-old voters, instead of beginning new lives after school, nearly all 16 year olds are in school, most living at their childhood homes (Marshall 2019). In terms of costs, resources, and distractions this is a much better circumstance than what faces 18 year olds who are trying to make their way in the adult world. Since 18 is a time of change (of location very often, of social standing very often), by contrast, 16 is a more tranquil period of youth. The changes that are experienced are largely nonpolitical ones (renegotiating relationship with parents and siblings, becoming an adult in some ways, remaining a child in others).

The most important positive implication of dropping the voting age to 16 is that the high school, through its courses in civics or related subjects, can help the students to pay the costs of voting the first time and build resources. In fact, it seems reasonable to split the focus of those courses on reducing these costs and building resources. The first would explore details of elections and the roles of citizens. The second would involve content covering the essential nature of American democracy, including the nature of elections in a representative democracy.

In the civics classes, simple things that can cause headaches for prospective new voters can be laid out in clear fashion. How does one register to vote? Where does one find the dates for registration and the steps that are necessary? When will the next election be held? Where are the polling booths? How does one get there? When? What offices are up for election? What are the differences between the political parties on the ballot? What are the major issues in the upcoming election? These questions and a host of others can be answered by the schoolteacher. Given the importance of building habits of voting, the potential of dropping the voting age to where the public schools could be directly involved in helping students get registered to vote, and even to assist them in getting to the polling booth as colleges are increasingly doing, might facilitate good voting habits or practices.

One can expect that students, with their first election as a full citizen coming up, will pay more than cursory attention to these matters. Thus, another one of the ancillary expected benefits of the reform is the invigoration of civics and American government high school classes. This expects that 16-year-old students will be more engaged in the course materials when they are connected to an upcoming election this semester or next, rather than when the very distant 18th birthday finally arrives.

Once the first election is successfully completed, we have a full citizen who will be confident that they can negotiate the steps to vote thereafter. These citizens will not need to be encouraged by their college to get registered and vote because they are already registered and have already voted once. While it will take a few elections for the habit to be fully formed, they are on their way. In the process they may provide a positive role model for nonvoting parents (Dahlgaard 2018).

Table 9.4 is an expanded version of the previous table. The new table adds three columns representing three different types of voters. The first is the status quo with the minimum voting age at 18. The second column represents the reformed situation where the first vote is at age 16 (or the earliest one after 16). The third new column represents the reformed situation where the voter is voting the second time at age 18. This table also added a row on the likelihood of voting.

Expanding our previous table and populating it with estimates of how these three types of voters rank shows clearly the importance of dropping the voting age to 16. Beginning with the current status quo first-time voter 18@First Vote, we see the costs are the highest among the three groups, and the distractions are tied for the highest. Meanwhile the resources are the lowest. Hence, the likelihood of voting is not good and the habit of voting is either weak or nonexistent.

If we turn to the second column of voters, the proposed first-time

TABLE 9.4. Factors and New Voters

Factors	18 @ First Vote	16 @ First Vote	18 @ Second Vote
Costs	Highest	*Middle*	*Lowest*
Distractions	Tied Highest	Lower	Tied Highest
Resources	Lowest	*Highest*	*Middle*
Likelihood of Voting	Lowest	Highest	Middle
Habit	Weakest	Middle	Strongest

Source: Created by author.

voter 16@First Vote, we see a different picture. The costs have been reduced via the support provided in the civics courses. Distractions, though building, are not as high as they will be in a couple of years. Resources will be higher because the young citizen will have adult role models who are encouraging them to register and to vote. They should be more interested in learning about politics and the upcoming election. Hence the likelihood of voting is the highest, and the habit of voting will be born, but one election does not a habit make.

Moving to the final first-time voter, 18@Second Vote, we see that the costs are the lowest because this citizen already voted once. Distractions will still exist, but the second-time voter will have more resources and receives the highest ranking on habits since it is the only voter who has already voted. Ultimately this voter is the second likeliest to vote because despite its low costs and strong habit, he or she will not have a teacher who is overseeing the preparation for voting.

Concluding Comments

The irony of the 26th Amendment is strong. It was implemented because society wished to atone for their wartime sacrifices society demanded of that generation. Yet, by giving 18 year olds the vote at an inopportune age, they consigned them to a history of low voting. The irony is compounded since the young generation being rewarded was arguably the most politically engaged young generation in American history. That it was the generation to be responsible for lowering U.S. voting rates for decades is especially sad.

Most proposed and recently implemented electoral reforms focus on expanding the voting electorate by reducing the costs of voting. In 1993 the federal National Voter Registration Act went into effect, requiring states to offer voter registration when someone applies for a new or renewed driver's license. Researchers have discovered that impacts of these reforms will be felt more heavily among younger voters (Gallego 2009). This is because older citizens have mostly developed ingrained habits of voting, or not voting, and they also have more resources. For them a little more convenience in the voting process is not very important. But for first- or second-time voters this might be consequential in determining whether someone bothers to vote or not. Holbein and Hillygus (2020) found that some election reforms just help those who are already habitual voters vote more easily. The ones that help young (and poor and less educated) voters the most are those that make registration easier. Same-day registration, automatic registration, and preregistration options have been shown to have positive impacts on youth voting and therefore reducing the voting age gap. Early voting and no-excuse absentee balloting do not close the voting age gap.

This proposed change fits with other potential changes in the way we handle elections. Among these are some that are politically feasible and others that are less feasible. One that is moderately feasible in the near term is ranked-order voting. This system does not penalize the voter who votes for a third- or fourth-party candidate. Miller and Shanks (1996) point out that young voters are more prone to vote outside the two-party dominant model than are older voters. Some see this as a lack of political maturity, others see it as youth being more creative and imaginative. One of the potentially negative aspects of the voting habit is that the habit often extends to which party a voter prefers. This means the more habitual voter is less receptive to third-party candidates.

Though the goal of reforms is to increase voting rates, the outcome is often the reverse (Burden et al. 2014). For example, citizens in some states can vote by mail, and in many states voting days have been expanded under the name of early voting. The unintended and unwanted impact of these reforms was to make it more difficult for political parties to mobilize voters. A recent law review article focused on these in the context of the United States and highlights a number of concerns that are rarely, if ever, raised by advocates (Silbaugh 2020). The article focused on the impact of dropping the voting age on ancillary legal and social aspects that use the age of majority as a crucial dividing line. For example, some rights accorded to children up to the age of 18 might disappear if it is decided that since 16-year-olds can vote they are effectively adults. By focusing primarily on the United

States case, this analysis fails to consider whether such negative consequences have happened in other locations. This should serve as a cautionary tale about reforms, even if they enjoy wide political support. While no one can be certain of outcomes in these matters, some clues can be drawn from elsewhere if the reform has been tried in other places. Although different political systems can respond differently to identical reforms, if we see similar outcomes in a wide variety of political systems, we can have some confidence.

Fortunately, while the voting age change proposed here might seem radical in some senses, it has been tried in some countries and in several municipalities. Some of those countries are nondemocratic (Cuba and Nicaragua) and some have compulsory voting (Argentina and Brazil—though both of these make voting voluntary for 16–17 year olds). Austria adopted 16-year-old voting for all its elections in 2007. A few American cities have begun reducing their voting age and there are occasionally national politicians making the argument in favor.

A valuable book published in 2019 reported on the status of Votes@16 where it has been implemented around the world (Eichhorn and Bergh 2019). They found some success stories and identified some important factors. For example, the work on the U.S. municipalities with Votes@16 highlighted the complexities of operating school systems that did not directly correspond to the lines that define voting districts. Because the chapters in the book were comparative in nature and reported on developments in several different political systems, the results often did not drill down into some of the second and third order effects of these changes.

While this chapter has provided a thorough explanation of why the Votes@18 generation became the generation that brought down voting rates that dramatically expanded the gap in turnout rates between the 65+ and the 18–24 age groups, it has not said nearly as much about the Votes@16 generation. The obvious reason is that it does not yet exist in the political sense. Nonetheless, we can say a few things about this generation when it does arrive.

Whenever the Votes@16 generation reaches voting age, they will have a deeper knowledge of politics and civics than prior generations. They will be more intrinsically interested in learning about politics because their first voting experience is coming soon. Another vitally important result of this reform is that Votes@16 schools are teaching students who come from a wide range of backgrounds. They will be more racially diverse than previous generations, although they might or might not attend college at the same rate as previous generations. According to projections done by Tufts University's Center for Information & Research on Civic Learning and Engagement (CIRCLE 2020), which researches youth civic engagement, in 2005 approximately 61 percent of the Americans aged 14–24 were white. This dropped to 55 percent in 2015 and is expected to be down to 50 percent in 2025. This decline is offset by a growing percentage of Latino youth rising from 17 percent in 2005 to 28 percent in 2025. As a consequence, these students who will become at least for one election voters are going to be much more representative of the American population than is the college population. In the view of those researchers "today's youth are the most diverse in American history and the most diverse segment of the electorate" (CIRCLE 2020). Overall voting rates will slowly move up as more and more age cohorts follow. And, as those overall rates go up, so will the percentage of nonwhite and noncollege voters. The American electorate will move in the direction of being a reasonable representation of the entire population.

Today's youth have demonstrated in a couple of high-profile examples that they are full of politically engaged energy and can speak very passionately on political issues of the day, and of the future. The eloquence of the Parkland School shooting survivors was heartbreaking but also inspiring. Their voices called out for the middle-aged and elderly lawmakers to take real action to protect schoolchildren, even if it risked their own political futures. The contrast was visible for all to see. We saw a young Greta Thunberg sail across the Atlantic to address the United Nations about climate change. Once again, the confidence and determination of the youth were starkly contrasted with the national and international gridlocks on these important matters. On the electoral stage the strong youth turnout in the 2018 and 2020 elections confirmed that youthful political activism did not perish with the fading of the Baby Boom generation. The two issues highlighted here (mass shooting and climate change) seem likely to be with us for a long time. There will surely be more issues coming that will be handled better if more voices are heard.

REFERENCES

Burden, B. C., D. T. Canon, K. R. Mayer, and D. P. Moynihan. 2014. "Election Laws, Mobilization, and Turnout: The Unanticipated Consequences of Election Reform." *American Journal of Political Science* 58 (1): 95–109.

CIRCLE (Center for Information & Research on Civic Learning and Engagement). 2020. "Youth Voter Turnout by Race/Ethnicity and Gender." July 27. https://circle .tufts.edu/latest-research/2020-youth-voter-turnout-raceethnicity-and-gender

Cultice, W. W. 1992. *Youth's Battle for the Ballot: A History of Voting Age in America.* Westport, CT: Greenwood Press.

Dahlgaard, J. O. 2018. "Trickle Up Political Socialization: The Causal Effect on Turnout of Parenting a Newly Enfranchised Voter." *American Political Science Review* 112 (3): 698–705.

Dalton, R. J. 2008. *The Good Citizen: How a Younger Generation Is Reshaping American Politics.* Washington, DC: CQ Press.

Dalton, R. J. 2017. *The Participation Gap: Social Status and Political Inequality.* Oxford: Oxford University Press.

Dinas, E. 2012. "The Formation of Voting Habits." *Journal of Elections, Public Opinion and Parties* 22 (4): 431–56. https://doi.org/10.1080/17457289.2012.718280

Eichhorn, J., and J. Bergh, eds. 2019. *Lowering the Voting Age to 16: Learning from Real Experiences Worldwide.* New York: Springer Nature.

Foa, R. S., and Y. Mounk. 2017. "The Signs of Deconsolidation." *Journal of Democracy* 28 (1): 5–16. https://www.journalofdemocracy.org/articles/the-signs-of-deconso lidation/

Franklin, M. N. 2004. *Voter Turnout and the Dynamics of Electoral Competition in Established Democracies since 1945.* Cambridge: Cambridge University Press.

Franklin, M. N., P. Lyons, and M. Marsh. 2004. "Generational Basis of Turnout Decline in Established Democracies." *Acta Politica* 39: 115–51.

Gallego, A. 2009. "Where Else Does Turnout Decline Come From? Education, Age, Generation and Period Effects in Three European Countries." *Scandinavian Political Studies* 32 (1): 23–44. https://doi.org/10.1111/j.1467-9477.2008.00212.x

Gallego, A. 2015. *Unequal Political Participation Worldwide.* Cambridge: Cambridge University Press.

Green, D. P., and R. Shachar. 2000. "Habit Formation and Political Behaviour: Evidence of Consuetude in Voter Turnout." *British Journal of Political Science* 30 (4): 561–73. https://doi.org/10.1017/S0007123400000247

Holbein, J. B., and D. S. Hillygus. 2020. *Making Young Voters: Converting Civic Attitudes into Civic Action.* Cambridge: Cambridge University Press.

Kam, C. D., and C. L. Palmer. 2008. "Reconsidering the Effects of Education on Political Participation." *Journal of Politics* 70 (3): 612–31.

Leighley, J. E., and J. Nagler. 2014. *Who Votes Now? Demographics, Issues, Inequality, and Turnout in the United States.* Princeton: Princeton University Press.

Marshall, J. 2019. "The Anti-Democrat Diploma: How High School Education Decreases Support for the Democratic Party." *American Journal of Political Science* 63 (1): 67–83. https://doi.org/10.1111/ajps.12409

McAvoy, P., R. Fine, and A. H. Ward. 2016. *State Standards Scratch the Surface of Learning about Political Parties and Ideology.* No. 81, K-12 Schools and Civic Education. Medford, MA: Tufts University Press. https://circle.tufts.edu/sites/default/files /2020-01/WP81_StateStandardsPoliticalIdeoloy_2016.pdf

Michelsen, N. G. 2020. *Votes at 16: Youth Enfranchisement and the Renewal of American Democracy.* Blue Ridge Summit, PA: Lexington Books.

Miller, W. E, and J. M. Shanks. 1996. *The New American Voter*. Cambridge, MA: Harvard University Press.

Milner, H. 2010. *The Internet Generation: Engaged Citizens or Political Dropouts*. Medford, MA: Tufts University Press.

Milner, H. 2020. "Populism and Political Knowledge: The United States in Comparative Perspective." *Politics and Governance* 8 (1): 226–38.

Pew Research Center. 2019. *Public Trust in Government: 1958–2019*. April 11. https://www.pewresearch.org/politics/2019/04/11/public-trust-in-government-1958-2019/

Plutzer, E. 2002. "Becoming a Habitual Voter: Inertia, Resources, and Growth in Young Adulthood." *American Political Science Review* 96 (1): 41–56. https://doi.org/10.1017/S0003055402004227

Silbaugh, K. 2020. "More Than the Vote: 16-Year-Old Voting and the Risks of Legal Adulthood." *Boston University Law Review* 100 (5): 1689–1726. http://www.bu.edu/bulawreview/files/2020/10/SILBAUGH.pdf

Voter Friendly Campus. 2019. *Voter Friendly Campus*. October. https://www.voterfriendlycampus.org/

Wang, T. 2020. "Union Impact on Voter Participation—and How to Expand It." Harvard Kennedy School Ash Center for Democratic Governance and Innovation, Cambridge, MA.

Wattenberg, M. 2016. *Is Voting for Young People?* 4th ed. New York: Routledge.

10 | Presidential Candidates on Campus and Civic Engagement among College Students

Mobilizing a New Generation

Kenneth W. Moffett and Laurie L. Rice

Generations' worldviews and shared experiences with defining events in their younger years subsequently shape their orientation toward civic and political life (Jennings and Niemi 1981; Putnam 2000; Zukin et al. 2006). For example, growing up during the Great Depression and fighting in World War II gave the Greatest generation foundational experiences that would make them civically active throughout their lives (Mettler 2005). Additionally, those parents that are politically engaged and active are more likely to transmit those values to their children (Jennings, Stoker, and Bowers 2009). Yet this parental socialization does not prevent one generation from having a markedly lower predisposition toward political participation than the one that raised it, as evidenced by the differences in participation between Baby Boomers and Generation X (Zukin et al. 2006).

Younger generations have typically been viewed as less engaged by political scientists and practitioners because of their comparatively low levels of political participation, especially voting, relative to earlier generations (Ansolabehere, Hersh, and Shepsle 2012). In particular, the generations that contain college students between the traditional ages of 18 to 25 years old in 2016, or Millennials and Generation Z, seemed the least likely to politically participate (Holbein and Hillygus 2016, 2020).

While life cycle theories expect the participation rates of younger generations to increase with age (Niemi, Stanley, and Evans 1984), this begets a question: Are life cycle explanations of participation the only hope for increasing political participation among Millennials and Generation Z over time? Or can something occur now to enhance their participation? We argue that campaign visits on college campuses counter substantial barriers to young adults' political participation, including not being asked to participate. After reviewing the literature on campaign visits, we argue that campaign visits to college campuses should increase college students' political participation, both through voting and other forms of engagement. To initially investigate our hypothesis, we analyze data on voter turnout at public universities where candidates visited in 2016. We follow this analysis with more finely grained survey data from a campus that Bernie Sanders visited in 2016 because, to test the impact of a visit, data needs to be sufficiently localized to capture those potentially exposed to it (see, e.g., Rice 2018). Our findings indicate campaign visits on college campuses can significantly increase the voting and civic engagement rates of young adults. We conclude with the implications for the generations just entering political life.

The Impact of Presidential Campaign Visits

Previous research reveals that visits from presidential candidates during the general election lead to increased vote totals for candidates (Shaw 1999). In fact, President Harry Truman's famous whistle-stop campaign in 1948 helped lead to his come from behind victory (Holbrook 2002) and more recent candidates have also benefited from their visits (Herrnson and Morris, 2007). Visits to battleground states help raise voter turnout (Holbrook and McClurg 2005; Hill and McKee 2005) and increase candidates' standings in state-level polls (Hill, Rodriquez, and Wooten 2010). While visits during presidential primaries have attracted less study, they are a regular staple of presidential primary campaigns. Candidates' visits during presidential primaries can increase their vote shares (Rice 2018). In a multicandidate race for the nomination, multiple candidates may visit the same area, shaping one another's vote totals (Rice 2018).

While visits sometimes successfully mobilize voters, not everyone agrees that visits increase votes (Wood 2016). Visits do not always work as intended, as some candidates' visits do not help at the state level (Wendland 2017) or even depress their own vote totals (Johnston,

Hagen, and Jamieson 2004). Moreover, analyses of state-level exit polls suggest that only a few candidates in recent primaries have success-fully mobilized key subgroups of voters (Wendland 2017). Altogether, these disparate findings indicate that these mobilization attempts can work, but success is not guaranteed.

Effects of Campaign Visits to College Campuses

College campuses make attractive venues for campaign stops because they house venues with large seating capacities to hold the crowds a candidate might draw. Often, these facilities host ticketed concerts, plays, and sporting events that make entrances and exits relatively easy to secure. Thus, they serve the needs of both candidates and their secu-rity details. College campuses were the most common venue to host campaign visits in 2016, both for these practical considerations and because they provided a place to reach young voters (Devine 2019).

Yet, by itself, holding a campaign event at an attractive venue that is close to an underreached demographic does not automatically mobi-lize college students. The campaigns must mobilize a population that political scientists and pundits cite as frequently lacking resources, skills (Rosenstone and Hansen 1993; Verba et al. 1995; Brady et al. 1995), the internal motivation to be civically active (Brady et al. 1995; Beaton 2016; Condon and Holleque 2013), or even face a collection of state and local laws that actively discourage political engagement (Campbell 2016). For example, many college students have relatively limited financial means, which requires balancing their studies with working to support themselves such that they graduate with less stu-dent loan debt (Perna 2012).[1] This emphasis on resources, skills, and motivation frequently places the blame for low levels of participation among college students squarely on their shoulders.

Yet political campaigns frequently do not ask students to participate because they have few ties to their current residence and have yet to appear on voter contact lists (Squire, Wolfinger, and Glass 1987).[2] Also, many campaigns do not target young adults with their limited resources since this group is less likely to vote. Thus, even students who commute from their hometowns are less likely to be high on campaign contact lists. Consequently, those who are not asked to participate are much less likely to do so (see, e.g., Rosenstone and Hansen 1993). One reason for young adults' low electoral participation levels may be because under typical circumstances "nobody asks" (Brady et al. 1995; Rosen-stone and Hansen 1993).

However, activity among mobilized college students in recent American political history has helped elect candidates. In the 1970s, their efforts helped elect a new group of anti–Vietnam War candidates into Congress (Murphy 1971). And their enthusiasm helped bring Barack Obama from a long-shot candidate for the Democratic nomination in 2008 to president of the United States (Keeter 2008; Reilly 2016). In both instances, a candidate specifically targeted college students, invited them to participate, and inspired them to make a difference.

First, purposeful appeals to young people like these are one necessary ingredient for boosting young people's political participation. It makes them feel included in the electoral process, something they were legally excluded from until turning 18. When a candidate visits a campus, they bring the excitement of the campaign and a chance to become part of the broader election story directly to students. These visits make students central to the election story and counter feelings of separation and isolation from the political process. Coming to a college campus with young people present and discussing issues that matter to them strongly signals that a candidate thinks they are important political actors and values their participation. Young adults tend to respond favorably to these targeted appeals.

Second, the campaigns must ask college students on campus to participate in additional ways for a visit to successfully mobilize this group. Campaigns frequently ask students to help with the event, and by doing so, they gain access to opportunities for additional political involvement beyond those offered by the visit. Campaign staffers also use these visits to recruit campaign volunteers who perform activities that range from door knocking to securing pledges of support. These invitations and the sense of inclusion facilitated by campaign visits can attract students to the political process. Campaign visits to college campuses directly counter what Rosenstone and Hansen (1993) label the "nobody asks" problem, particularly with respect to mobilizing college students. Thus, we expect that students at college campuses that candidates visited should experience higher levels of political participation.

When Bernie Sanders Comes to Campus

While campaign visits to college campuses can mobilize college students, candidates who focus on issues of importance to this age group are likely to successfully do so. During the 2016 election cycle, Senator Bernie Sanders (D-VT) made issues that are salient to college students central to his campaign by campaigning for single-payer health care, free college tuition at public colleges and universities, action on climate change, and lower student loan rates (Friedman 2019; Prokop 2015). These issues appealed to college students at the time because most paid tuition at public colleges and universities, 9 percent lacked health insurance (Bauer-Wolf 2018), and 69 percent of college graduates left with student loan debt that averaged $29,650 (Institute for College Access and Success 2019). Further, members of this generation believe that climate change should be a preeminent policy priority (Boyle-Laisure, chap. 8, this volume; Ross and Rouse, chap. 11, this volume; Stoker, chap. 2, this volume; Tyson, Kennedy and Funk 2021). Also, Millennials "look more Democratic than their elders because they are younger . . . and more likely to be children of immigrants" (Stoker, chap. 2, this volume).

Additionally, these issues appeal to this generation because they are more racially diverse than their elders, as only 52 percent of Gen Z members self-identify as white (Parker and Igielnik 2020; Stoker, chap. 2, this volume). Members of racial minority groups are more likely to have higher levels of student loan debt and not to have health insurance (Elliott and Lewis 2015; Keisler-Starkey and Bunch 2022). Belanger and Meguid (2008, 477) find that voters "identify the most credible party proponent of a particular issue and cast their ballots for that issue owner." A large proportion of young voters voted for Sanders in 2016 (Blake 2016) and also engaged in other ways in favor of that issue owner, as college student participation can increase when campaigns focus on issues that they find important (Moffett and Rice 2016; Rice and Moffett 2022).

In fall 2016, there were over 11 million college students between the ages of 18 and 25 (U.S. Department of Education 2017). According to the generational dividing lines employed by the Pew Research Center, this age range spanned two generations, with Millennials ending with those born in 1996 and Generation Z beginning with those born in 1997 (Dimock 2019). If generations are shaped by shared experiences with defining events (Mannheim 1952), the two oldest years of Generation Z and the youngest Millennials are likely to have more in common with each other than they do with those at the far end of their own generation (Rice and Moffett 2022; Stoker, chap. 2, this volume). Yet this group differs from previous generations, including in their positions on many social issues (Ross and Rouse, chap. 11, this volume; Rouse and Ross

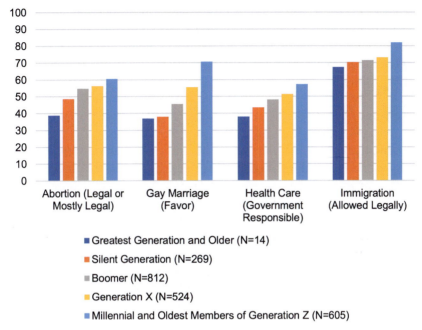

Fig. 10.1. Views on Issues by Generation at the Time of the 2016 Presidential Primaries
Source: Data from Pew Research Center Polls (2016).

2018; Stoker, chap. 2, this volume). Figure 10.1 shows generational differences in opinions on four issues that Pew Research Center asked about at the time of the 2016 presidential primaries.

Figure 10.1 shows that with each generation, views on abortion, gay marriage, immigration, and health care become more progressive, with Millennials and members of Generation Z old enough to vote noteworthy for their embrace of gay marriage and immigration. Thus, while separated from his young supporters by age and generation, Sanders' campaign reached out to a demographic that is similar to him politically. Their more liberal positions on these and other issues made them particularly ripe for mobilization by progressive candidates like Sanders.

Sanders regularly visited college campuses to attract young adults' votes and to engage them in the political process. While other candidates may have successfully fostered civic engagement of college students through their campaign visits in 2016, we expect the biggest increases to be among students on campuses Sanders visited because he shared many of their positions on issues. Thus, Sanders' visits provide a good opportunity to test whether campaign visits mobilize college students to get more involved in politics.

Campaign Visits to College Campuses and College Student Turnout

To initially test our hypotheses, we consider whether voter turnout in the general election was higher at universities visited by Sanders during the primaries compared to campuses lacking visits. This requires the impact of a visit on voting to be enduring and not limited to support for the candidate who visited. To do so, we collected voter turnout data for all public universities that participated in the ALL IN Campus Democracy Challenge and supplied their 2016 National Study of Learning, Voting, and Elections (NSLVE) report. By limiting our analysis to public universities that participated in the ALL IN Challenge, we can explore the impact of campaign visits while considering institution type and a campus commitment to increase their students' levels of civic engagement.

Then, to determine whether a presidential candidate visited these campuses, we gathered data on the town in which each university was located and searched the *National Journal* Travel Tracker (2016) for presidential candidate visits to that location. For each record of a candidate visit to a college town, we conducted a Google search including the name of the candidate and the name of the university and examined the first two pages of search results to see if there was any indication that a candidate visited the university while in town.

Figure 10.2 shows the mean level of general election turnout among campuses without any candidate visits, campuses that had a candidate other than Sanders visit, campuses that Sanders visited, and campuses with multiple candidate visits (including Sanders). The means progressively increase across these categories, but their differences are not statistically significant. This minimally supports our hypothesis, as it suggests that primary visits could have small effects on voter turnout months later in the general election. Yet this analysis is limited because it does not consider several other factors that affect voter turnout.[3] Thus, to better understand the impact of campaign visits on college campuses, we investigate the impact of one specific visit among students on the campus where it occurred.

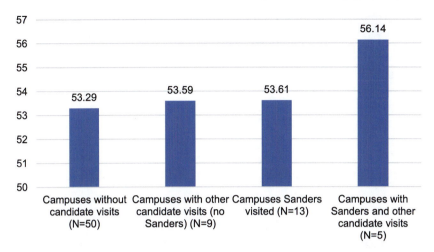

Fig. 10.2. Campaign Visits and Voter Turnout
Source: Election Data

Did Bernie Sanders' Visits Help Mobilize the Youngest Generations?

Bernie Sanders' March 2016 visit to Southern Illinois University at Edwardsville, announced less than 48 hours earlier, packed the university's gymnasium to capacity. Media estimates reported a crowd of 4,700 with another 1,000 waiting outside (Donald 2016). Among these crowds to see Sanders in person were many students, some of whom lined up in the middle of the night. As the crowd waited to enter, Sanders campaign volunteers asked them multiple times to sign up to volunteer for his campaign and to vote for him. Thus, instead of remaining one of many young adults whom "nobody asks" (Rosenstone and Hansen 1993), those who shared their contact information with the campaign became part of lists of people who could be contacted later and asked again to participate.

We examine the effects of three opportunities that came because of the visit: attending the rally, volunteering at it, or livestreaming it. While only two of these require physical presence at the event, we expect that all three will lead to greater participation. In the heavily networked world of Millennials and Generation Z, one can experience and participate in an event without being there through social media apps like Facebook Live and Snapchat Live. If the direct mobilization efforts are the only part of a campaign visit that increases participation, then only those students who volunteered at the rally or attended it should show higher participation levels. However, if the opportunity to be a part of something greater and the sense of inclusion created by a campaign visit where a candidate addresses issues of concern to young people also drives participation, then we should also see increases in participation among those who livestream.

Our data structure allows us to estimate the average effect of the treatment on the treated (ATT) for those who capitalized on the opportunities that a visit to campus by Sanders provided. To investigate whether these opportunities yield higher participation levels, we consider two potential impacts on participation. The first, and more immediate, is on the likelihood that students who volunteered at, attended, or livestreamed the rally voted in the 2016 presidential primaries. This is, after all, the primary goal of campaign mobilization efforts. If campaign visits only drive participation through direct mobilization efforts, their effects might end there. The second effect, both broader and enduring, is whether this led to increased levels of civic engagement through the 2016 general election. If visits counter a sense of exclusion by welcoming students into politics, then their effects likely persist longer than election-specific mobilization efforts. Thus, we expect that the opportunities that students have to engage with the visit yield higher levels of participation among those who capitalized on them. Our measurement of civic engagement, described in more depth in the section that follows, focuses on offline activities and includes commonly asked about forms of participation from both political and civic life. This enables us to test the broader impacts of campaign visits.

Data

We performed web-based surveys of full-time undergraduate students between 18 and 25 years old at Southern Illinois University at Edwardsville, a public university with approximately 14,000 students at the time.[4] In table A1, located in the online appendix, we compared the samples to the overall population from which they were drawn based on race, sex, and age. Based on this comparison, these samples reasonably represent the population from which they are drawn with respect to each of these characteristics. Thus, we have no reason to believe that the results are a function of differences across types of higher education institutions (e.g., other public or private universities).

To encourage students to participate in the survey, we held a drawing to win a free iPad. Because we are specifically interested in testing whether campaign visits on college campuses have broad benefits on young adult participation, we do not limit our analysis to young Democrats or Sanders supporters. Further, since we investigate whether these effects last into the general election, we performed our survey between October 11 and October 25, 2016, and used the complete list of university-assigned student e-mail addresses to comprise our sample.[5] Approximately 933 of the 9,576 students eligible to complete the survey did so. While our response rate for this survey (approximately 9.7%) is less than ideal, it lies within the range that other organizations have provided (Pew Research Center 2016).

There are two dependent variables.[6] The first is whether the student voted in a 2016 primary. The second is an additive index measuring the frequency with which each student participated in a set of 10 *offline* civic activities ($\alpha = .76$).[7]

We utilized three different binary treatment variables. We asked whether each respondent had attended the rally, volunteered at it, or livestreamed it.[8] We anticipate positive signs for the ATT for each of these variables.[9]

Because we use a series of matching analyses, we "match" based on the values of a series of covariates. These measures capture other motivations and predispositions to participate. Since those who participate online are also more likely to be participatory apart from the internet (Cantijoch, Cutts, and Gibson 2016; Moffett and Rice 2016; Vaccari and Valeriani 2016),[10] we utilize an additive index of social media activity ($\alpha = .86$). We also match using an additive index of online political expression ($\alpha = .86$) and on the basis of frequency of blog reading about politics and current events.[11] To control for the effects of general political engagement on offline civic activity, we match on the basis of level of attention to the 2016 presidential campaign, level of interest in politics, and an additive index of peer civic engagement ($\alpha = .68$).[12] We anticipate positive signs for each variable as both campaign attention and interest in politics routinely predict voting and other forms of offline engagement (Verba et al. 1995), as can positive peer pressure through social networks (Lin 1999).

Finally, we match for personal characteristics that may shape offline engagement. First, we considered the strength of each respondent's partisan attachment because this predicts many forms of political activity (Rosenstone and Hansen 1993; Verba et al. 1995). Second, we match on the basis of whether students are political science majors as this major has been associated with greater civic engagement (Conroy, Feezell, and Guerrero 2012). We anticipate positive signs on both coefficients.

Third, we match on the basis of whether students identify as liberal or conservative.[13] We have no theoretical expectations about the sign on either ideology variable but control for them as others have found that identifying as a conservative or liberal shapes some forms of participation (Beck and Jennings 1979; Best and Krueger 2005).[14] Further, we match on the basis of age, race, and sex as these can drive political participation (Collins and Block 2020; Fox and Lawless 2014).

Methods

We utilize matching to perform our empirical tests. Matching allows us to determine whether the treatments of attending the rally, volunteering at it, or livestreaming it affected voting in the 2016 primary or offline civic activity. Through matching based on many respondent characteristics known to make individuals more likely to participate, we can isolate the impact of a visit beyond individuals' other predispositions to participate. Moreover, matching allows us to compute ATTs for each of our treatments, and by doing so, to ascertain some degree of causality using observational data.[15] Conversely, regression models do not generate ATTs, and may yield biased results because model coefficients are conditioned on other values of the other independent variables. More specifically, matching can tell us how much of an effect that volunteering at the rally, livestreaming it, or attending it had on the likelihood that one voted in the 2016 primary and on one's offline civic activity.

Since we satisfy the statistical assumptions that underlie matching, we need to choose a matching technique[16] that optimizes across two competing criteria: highly similar treatment and control groups,[17] and a sufficiently large sample from which to make inferences (Imai, King, and Stuart 2008; King et al. 2017).[18] Thus, we need to reduce imbalance *and* get a large enough sample from which we can make inferences. To do so, we implement an algorithm developed by King et al. (2017) that optimizes both criteria to generate a matching frontier. At each position along the frontier (denoted by the size of the matched sample), this approach "offers a matched subset of the complete data such that no other possible subset of the same size has lower imbalance" (King et al. 2017, 474). The matching frontier is "a set of matched samples that fully characterize the tradeoff between imbalance and sample size"

(King et al. 2017, 473). The Matching Frontier technique improves upon many alternatives because most utilize manual, ad hoc adjustments that researchers make along the way to generate their results (Austin 2008; Caliendo and Kopenig 2008; Stuart 2008). Thus, we use the Matching Frontier technique to perform our analyses.[19] Finally, we use the Mahalanobis discrepancy to match our observations, as this tends to provide accurate matching using all observations in the data set (Faber and Kademon 2003).

Results

Figure 10.3 visualizes the ATT for each treatment variable—rally attendance, volunteering at the rally, and livestreaming it—on our two dependent variables.[20] The left side of each graphic under the relevant treatment visualizes the ATT for voting in the 2016 primaries while the right side visualizes the ATT for civic engagement.[21] The ATT estimates the effect size of each treatment variable on each dependent variable. Put differently, figure 10.3 shows the impact of rally attendance, volunteering at the rally, or livestreaming the rally on individuals' probability of voting or on the amount of offline civic activities in which they engage.

When we analyze the ATT for voting in the 2016 primary election, the ATTs for rally attendance and livestreaming it are positive as we prune observations, even after accounting for model dependence using Athey-Imbens (2015) intervals (designated in gray).[22] While the increase in instability of the estimates for each treatment after one prunes 200 observations shown in the graphics located on the left side of figure 10.3 for each treatment appears initially worrisome, it is difficult to make valid statistical inferences given that there are so few cases from which to do so. Consequently, it is better to draw statistical conclusions based on the entire frontier, not just on a selected set of points along it.

As shown in figure 10.3, those who attended the Sanders rally experience a 20 to 25 percent increase in their probability of voting in the 2016 primaries. However, those who volunteered at the rally or livestreamed it experienced no statistically significant increases in their probability of voting in the 2016 primaries. Although the effect size is positive for volunteering at the rally, it is eliminated at most points along the frontier by an Athey-Imbens (2015) interval that includes zero. In addition, the effects of livestreaming the rally are near zero for most points along the frontier.

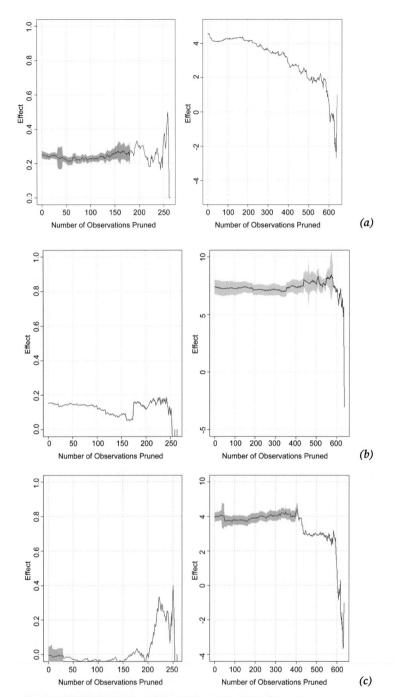

Fig. 10.3. ATT Plots by Number of Pruned Observations: (*a*) rally attendance;
(*b*), volunteering at rally; (*c*), livestreaming rally
Source: Derived with data collected from authors' conducted survey.

When computed for civic engagement, the ATTs for rally attendance, volunteering at the rally, and livestreaming it are positive as we prune observations, even after considering model dependence using Athey-Imbens (2015) intervals. While the decrease in effects for each treatment after one prunes 600 observations shown in the graphics located on the right side of figure 10.3 initially appears concerning, it is because one has difficulty making valid statistical inferences given that there are so few cases from which to do so.

As figure 10.3 depicts, those who attended the Sanders rally or livestreamed it experienced between 2 and 4-point increases in mean offline civic engagement. Substantively, a 2-point increase means having participated in one additional civic activity sometimes or having participated in an activity in which one was already involved at a higher frequency. Moreover, those who volunteered at the rally experience an 8-point increase in mean offline civic engagement.[23] Substantively, this means participating very often in two activities that otherwise would not have occurred.

Change in Covariate Values for Voting in the 2016 Primary and Civic Engagement

Figures 10.4 through 10.6 display the change in the mean of each covariate as we prune observations for the treated observations, relative to the untreated ones, for each dependent variable. These figures illustrate how much of an effect each of the differing matching covariates has on our outcome variable. These figures give additional insights that are not readily available from other matching techniques, as these other techniques frequently estimate ATTs and not much else. The Matching Frontier technique provides effect sizes of the matching covariates on each dependent variable, visualized across the entire matching frontier.

The first illustration in each figure corresponds to voting in the 2016 primaries while the second corresponds to offline civic engagement. Further, figure 10.4 examines rally attendance as a treatment, figure 10.5 examines volunteering at it, and figure 10.6 examines livestreaming it. Each line corresponds to a different covariate on which matching took place.[24] In general, the higher the line on the figure for a covariate, the bigger its effect on the outcome variable. However, these figures cannot tell us whether the effects are statistically significant.

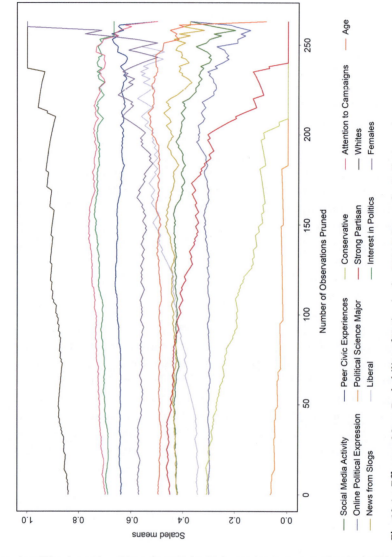

Fig. 10.4a. Effect on Mean Probability of Voting in the 2016 Primary for Rally Attendance by Number of Pruned Observations

Source: Derived with data collected from authors' conducted survey.

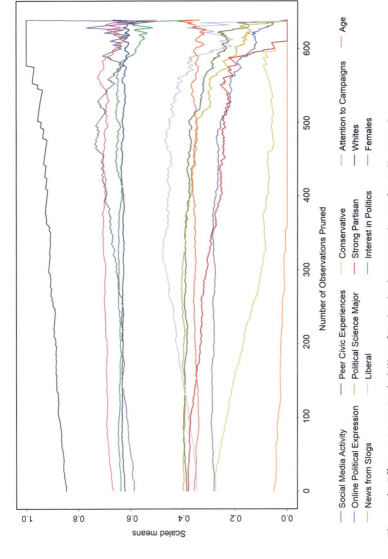

Fig. 10.4b. Effect on Mean Probability of Voting in the 2016 Primary for Rally Attendance by Number of Pruned Observations

Source: Derived with data collected from authors' conducted survey.

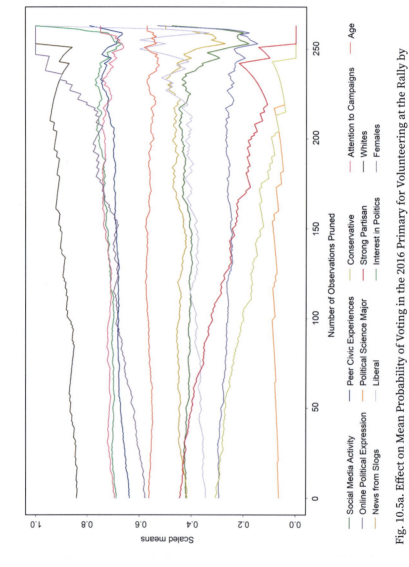

Fig. 10.5a. Effect on Mean Probability of Voting in the 2016 Primary for Volunteering at the Rally by Number of Pruned Observations

Source: Derived with data collected from authors' conducted survey.

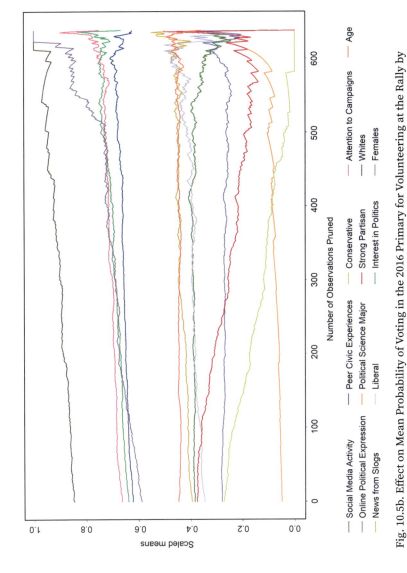

Fig. 10.5b. Effect on Mean Probability of Voting in the 2016 Primary for Volunteering at the Rally by Number of Pruned Observations

Source: Derived with data collected from authors' conducted survey.

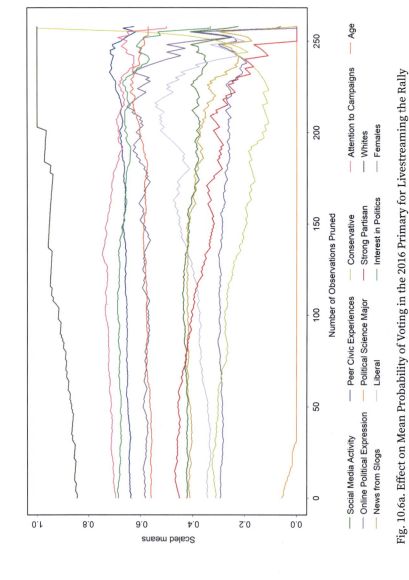

Fig. 10.6a. Effect on Mean Probability of Voting in the 2016 Primary for Livestreaming the Rally by Number of Pruned Observations

Source: Derived with data collected from authors' conducted survey.

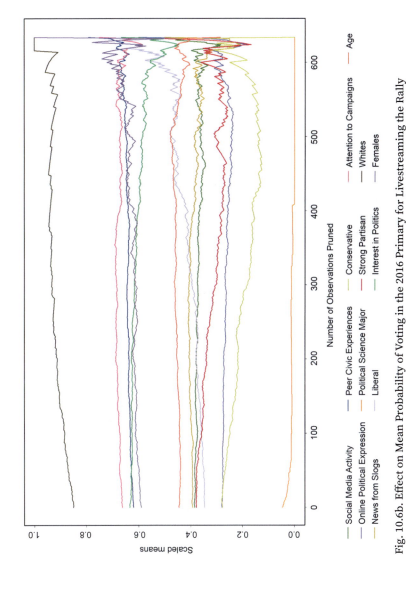

Fig. 10.6b. Effect on Mean Probability of Voting in the 2016 Primary for Livestreaming the Rally by Number of Pruned Observations

Source: Derived with data collected from authors' conducted survey.

Based on the results of logistic regressions for voting in the 2016 primaries, and OLS regressions for offline civic engagement using the matched data from each treatment in table 10.1, several statistically significant trends emerge.[25]

Voting in the 2016 Primary

Attending the rally or livestreaming it increases the likelihood of voting in presidential primaries as well as offline civic activity. Different, but complementary, factors underlie these increases. Those who self-identified as liberal experienced a .2 to .4-point increase in the probability of voting in the 2016 primaries if they either attended, volunteered at, or livestreamed the rally. Thus, the results partly confirm the conventional wisdom that visits by Sanders engaged liberals (Sargent 2016).

Among the treated, students who reported an average interest in politics were more likely to vote in the 2016 primaries, experiencing around a .6 to .8-point increase in the probability of voting in the primaries for having attended the rally, volunteered at it, or livestreamed it. This shows the mobilizing power of a visit, as it occurred on a Friday, with the primary on the following Tuesday. Those with average levels of interest in politics tend to be less motivated to participate, yet their likelihood of voting in the primary increased if they livestreamed, attended, or volunteered at the rally. Yet online civic activity, several political engagement predictors, and most of the demographic predictors associated with motivation are unconnected with additional increases in the likelihood of voting in the 2016 primaries. The lack of statistical significance for age suggests that members of Generation Z and Millennials responded in similar ways to Sanders' visit.

Civic Engagement

When we examine offline civic engagement, differing, but complementary, dynamics emerge. Among the treated with a mean level of peer civic engagement, we observe a .6-point increase in mean civic activity for having attended, volunteered at, or livestreamed the rally. While these students' networks of friends are not predisposed to participate at high rates, these students become more likely to participate because of their rally experience. At least one treatment (livestreaming) that does not require attendance at the rally is connected with increases in mean civic engagement.

Moreover, those already likely to participate become even more inclined to do so because of the opportunities afforded by the rally. The results indicate an approximately .4-point increase in mean civic engagement among those with average levels of politically oriented social media activity if they attended the rally, volunteered at it, or livestreamed it. A similar increase (.4) for those who attended, volunteered at, or livestreamed the rally is seen among those with an average level of acquiring their news from political blogs. And among students with average levels of online political expression, there is between a .2 to .4-point increase in mean offline civic engagement if they attended, livestreamed or volunteered at the rally. These results are largely consistent, regardless of the number of pruned observations.[26]

Interestingly, though, demographic characteristics are less connected with increases in mean offline civic activity. On the one hand, political science majors who attended the campaign rally or volunteered at it engaged in higher levels of mean civic engagement than those who did not. Being a political science major exerts a .1 to .2-point increase in mean civic engagement among rally attenders and volunteers. However, other personal characteristics of respondents have limited effects on mean offline civic activity, regardless of whether they engaged with Sanders' visit to campus. There was no evidence that age or a respondent's level of campaign attention related to changes in civic activity or the likelihood that one voted in the 2016 primaries. Self-identifying as a strong partisan had no statistical connection with voting in the 2016 primaries or with changes in mean offline civic engagement, regardless of whether one engaged with Sanders' visit or bypassed that opportunity. Participation in the rally was not limited to liberals, as 7.54 percent of rally attenders, 7.41 percent of rally volunteers, and 11.86 percent of those who livestreamed it self-identified as politically conservative. Yet being a conservative conferred no unique benefit in civic activity beyond the higher civic activity that exists among those who participated in one or more of the opportunities that Sanders' visit provided.

Finally, we investigated whether our results are model-dependent (Ho et al. 2008) beyond the use of Athey-Imbens (2015) intervals. One limitation of solely relying on Athey and Imbens's (2015) approach is that the functional form of the covariates can be ad hoc, and itself problematic (480). To verify whether this concern affects the analyses, we reran the matching routines for both dependent variables by exclud-

TABLE 10.1. Impact of Sanders Rally Activities Using Matched Data

	Voting			Civic Engagement		
	Model 1	Model 2	Model 3	Model 4	Model 5	Model 6
Treatment Variables						
Rally Attendance	.201*	—	—	1.329**	—	—
	(.079)			(.505)		
Volunteering	—	.077	—	—	3.258**	—
		(.154)			(1.099)	
Livestreaming	—	—	-.084	—	—	1.529*
			(.099)			(.679)
Online Civic Activity						
Social Media Activity	.005	.004	.006	.163***	.168***	.177***
	(.007)	(.007)	(.007)	(.041)	(.042)	(.041)
Online Political Expression	-.006	-.006	-.006	.363***	.377***	.352***
	(.008)	(.009)	(.009)	(.055)	(.056)	(.056)
Frequency of Blog Reading	-.031	-.025	-.024	.435**	.404**	.436**
	(.024)	(.024)	(.024)	(.146)	(.148)	(.146)
Political Engagement						
Interest in Politics	.141**	.147**	.149**	.521	.416	.529
	(.051)	(.052)	(.053)	(.317)	(.320)	(.310)
Campaign Attention	-.001	-.002	-.002	.394	.470*	.342
	(.035)	(.035)	(.036)	(.231)	(.225)	(.223)
Peer Civic Engagement	.013	.014	.012	.370***	.389***	.365***
	(.013)	(.013)	(.013)	(.081)	(.080)	(.079)

Demographic Characteristics

Strong Partisan	.091	.095	.097	.041	.001	.188
	(.063)	(.064)	(.065)	(.408)	(.414)	(.406)
Political Science Major	-.149	-.094	-.093	2.616**	1.990*	2.121
	(.124)	(.132)	(.127)	(.914)	(.860)	(1.229)
Liberal	.155*	.201**	.198**	-.019	.367	.236
	(.075)	(.073)	(.074)	(.444)	(.438)	(.437)
Conservative	.079	.057	.044	.034	.119	-.063
	(.078)	(.079)	(.079)	(.481)	(.485)	(.472)
Whites	-.057	-.047	-.025	-.513	-.432	-.413
	(.080)	(.080)	(.082)	(.502)	(.517)	(.517)
Females	-.058	-.062	-.059	-.294	-.222	-.230
	(.060)	(.060)	(.061)	(.372)	(.379)	(.370)
Age	-.016	-.020	-.019	-.024	-.056	-.114
	(.018)	(.018)	(.019)	(.116)	(.116)	(.113)
Constant	.634	.701	.665	2.485	2.945	4.367
	(.440)	(.442)	(.449)	(2.631)	(2.631)	(2.558)
Observations	265	265	260	600	600	600
R2	.139	.121	.121	.447	.454	.442
Adjusted R2	.091	.071	.071	.434	.441	.429
F Statistic	2.890***	2.452**	2.419**	33.755***	34.777***	33.097***

Source: Student Election Survey Data.

Note: First, the numbers in parenthesis are standard errors. Second, * denotes $p < .05$, ** denotes $p < .01$, and *** denotes $p < .001$, all two-tailed tests. Finally, the coefficients for the voting models are logistic regression coefficients while the coefficients for the civic engagement models are ordinary least squares coefficients.

ing one variable at a time using Athey-Imbens (2015) intervals. This allows us to vary the functional form of covariates and to determine whether this limitation operates meaningfully (Athey and Imbens 2015, 480). These results are similar to those reported here. Thus, the results are neither model-dependent nor an artifact of our model specification.[27]

Conclusion

Bernie Sanders' visit helped mobilize college students. Those who attended the rally were more likely to have voted in the 2016 primaries. Moreover, students who volunteered at the rally, livestreamed it, or attended it became more civically active than those who did not participate in these ways. Thus, the evidence indicates that one of the reasons college students tend to participate at lower levels is that campaigns typically do not ask.

While generations may have different dispositions toward participation in civic and political life (Putnam 2000; Zukin et al. 2006; Dalton 2007), we find that even those with a low predisposition to electoral participation respond favorably to mobilization attempts. Further, there was no significant difference among Millennials and Generation Z in their response to these attempts at mobilization. Thus, our results identify one method for increasing the participation rates of the United States' youngest generations. This suggests that generational studies must go beyond just examining defining events to understand a generation's participatory rates. After all, as young adults Baby Boomers were mobilized first in support of Robert Kennedy and Eugene McCarthy and then to support a slate of antiwar congressional candidates (Murphy 1971). Had candidates similarly sought to mobilize Generation X when they were of similar age, perhaps their trajectory of participation might have changed.

Campaign mobilization matters and attempts to mobilize college students work. However, the results for livestreaming indicate that student participation increases not just through specific attempts at mobilization or by physically being at the rally, but more broadly by invitations to participate in the election. Campaign visits provide students a chance to participate in the political story, and those who capitalize on this opportunity are more likely to continue engaging, even after the election that was the focus of the direct mobilization attempts ends.

This has important implications for the participation rates of generations as they enter American political life. We leave it to others to track the lingering impact of targeted generational mobilization attempts over the course of the life cycle.

Yet the increases in voting in the 2016 primaries and mean offline civic activity that accompany a presidential candidate's visit to campus are not uniformly distributed. Motivation matters, too. Those who self-identified as liberal or had average levels of interest in politics became more likely to vote in the 2016 primaries if they attended the rally, livestreamed it, or volunteered at this event. Further, students who engaged with the visit and had peers who were civically active experienced higher increases than those who declined the opportunities that a visit afforded, ceteris paribus. Those who were engaged on social media or expressed themselves politically online also experienced higher levels of offline civic activity when they engaged with Sanders' visit. This fits within the larger literature on civic activity tying interest in politics and online political activity with voting and other forms of civic engagement (Vitak et al. 2011).

Yet our results comport with Leighley's (1995) call to investigate the importance of mobilization compared to other factors to explain why individuals participate and with Highton and Wolfinger's (2001) conclusion that scholars must look beyond adult-role theory to explain young adults' low turnout rates. Perhaps the reason many fail to participate is because under normal circumstances "nobody asks" (Rosenstone and Hansen 1993; Brady, Verba and Schlozman 1995). Given that we found more substantial and consistent campaign visit effects on civic engagement than we did on voting, both life cycle and generational tendencies against voting are harder to overcome than are orientations toward other civic and political activities (Dalton, 2007). As Niall Michelsen (chap. 9, this volume) argues, these life cycle explanations should not serve as cause to give up on young people voting. Scott McLean's (chap. 3, this volume) look at the emerging political identity of Generation Z suggests that college campuses may become more fruitful places for mobilizing voters as more of its members join the ranks of college students. If these experiences with enhanced civic engagement remain over the long run, Jennings, Stoker, and Bowers (2009) suggest that this increased engagement will carry over to one or more generations.

As with all studies of politics, our study has some limitations. First, we examined the effect of a single presidential candidate's visit at a particular university at a single time point.[28] Yet we have no reason to believe that students at this college campus systematically differ in their participation patterns from those at other universities around the United States,[29] so these results should be generalizable. Second, there is very little data that is localized enough and of sufficient quality to be able to model the causal effects of any campaign visit. Yet this limitation is precisely what allows us to test for causality, and in this way, allows for this meaningful scientific contribution.

These results could be the artifact of a candidate-specific effect because Sanders targeted his appeal to college students (Levenson 2016). Nonetheless, candidates who take issue positions consistent with a young generation's worldview can successfully mobilize that generation through their visits to college campuses. Future research can examine whether advancing similar views is necessary to successfully mobilize these generations. It is possible that the "Bernie Sanders" effect that we discovered on a single college campus in 2016 may also have manifested itself as a "Hillary Clinton" or "Marco Rubio" effect, for example, on campuses those presidential candidates visited. Given that most candidates made fewer campaign stops at college campuses than Sanders did, and that visits are rarely announced far in advance, opportunities to do so are limited. We lack data from other campuses to test whether these effects exist, and are aware of no such data that is publicly available or suitable to perform such an investigation. Yet the causal mechanism we specify likely holds for other candidates provided they visit college campuses and specifically work to involve college students while there. Through appearing where college students are and inviting them to be part of something bigger by participating, young college students are drawn into politics.

In many election cycles, college students are excluded from the election story. Campaign visits are one way of changing that. When campaigns engage students where they are rather than ignore them, students respond. Thus, one of the reasons young adults tend to participate at lower rates may be that candidates do not ask. Those who became a part of the election story in 2016 through engaging with the rally live,[30] whether through volunteering at the event, attending in person, or livestreaming,[31] caught much of the excitement from the visit, became a part of the election saga, responded to invitations to participate, and became involved in other ways. For example, campaigns can contact those who attend or volunteer at rallies for subsequent participation opportunities and may be able to do so for those who livestream as well.[32] Thus, it is possible that partaking in these other participation opportunities can yield higher levels of civic engagement and voting. Unfortunately, we do not have the data on these participation opportunities to investigate those queries.

In 2020, Sanders lacked a monopoly in the Democratic field of presidential candidates on progressive positions and other issues of concern to young adults. Thus, young adults' votes and enthusiasm were split across these candidates, instead of centering on Sanders. In addition, the emerging COVID-19 pandemic curtailed the normal pattern of campaign visits. This limited candidates' ability to use campaign visits to mobilize young people. However, social media offers an alternative mechanism for attracting young voters (Moffett and Rice 2016) that campaigns could employ. As the 2020 general election neared, Donald Trump began holding more large campaign rallies while Joe Biden held lesser numbers of socially distanced campaign events. This skewed campaign visit pattern may offer an additional reason why Ashley Ross and Stella Rouse (chap. 11, this volume) find that Trump's support grew among white Millennials in 2020 over 2016.

While the pandemic temporarily halted visits on college campuses in 2020, attempts by presidential campaigns to mobilize college students are not wasted. Those campaigns that visit college campuses and provide opportunities for students to become involved can successfully mobilize them to become more civically engaged. This effect exists even if the candidate who visits is unsuccessful in his or her pursuit of the presidency. This is good for democracy because citizens need to have meaningful opportunities to participate in the democratic process (Dahl 1989). Democracy functions best when all citizens have a voice (Schlozman, Verba, and Brady 2012), and campaign visits to college campuses help mobilize new generations to engage in ways that makes their voices heard.

ACKNOWLEDGMENTS

We presented an earlier version of portions of this research at the 2017 Meeting of the Midwest Political Science Association, Chicago. We thank Grete Graf, Scott McLean, Jennifer Merolla, Brian Newman, the reviewers, and especially Sally Friedman and David Schultz for comments and Christopher Lucas for providing helpful methodological advice. Any remaining errors or omissions are our responsibility.

NOTES

1. However, a sizable minority of college students do not work while attending college and may have more free time to devote to civic activity (Perna 2012).

2. There are, however, civic-minded groups such as the ALL In Campus Democracy Challenge, Campus Compact, and the Campus Vote Project tackling the problem of low voter turnout rates among college students. The effects of these efforts are outside the scope of this analysis.

3. It is possible that campaigns select universities known to be more participatory as venues for campaign rallies. However, the campuses candidates visited had significantly varied voter turnout rates according to National Study of Learning, Voting, and Elections (NSLVE) reports. This provides some confidence that candidates prioritize other factors such as the electoral rules in the state and the visit patterns of their opponents (Rice 2018) as well as the size and location of the university over its past voting rates in deciding which campuses to visit.

4. The margin of error for this survey is 3.79%. The online appendix is available at http://www.kenmoffett.net/research

5. All decisions have trade-offs. While this timing allows us to study whether a visit by Sanders might have lasting impacts on participation despite his failure to secure the Democratic nomination, it does leave out those who might have volunteered at, attended, or livestreamed the video but graduated or otherwise left the university in the time between the visit and the survey. Ideally, we might have conducted two surveys, with one at the time of the visit. However, the very short time periods in between this visit's announcement and occurrence (as is typical for most campaign visits) would not allow the necessary time to gain Institutional Review Board approval for such a survey.

6. The complete question wording and coding for each variable, along with summary statistics, can be found in the online appendix available at http://www.kenmoffett.net/research

7. Civic engagement substantially varies across young people, and we have found this in repeated surveys that we have taken in 2008, 2012, and 2020 of this population, and also using mTurk surveys of young adults in the United States in 2018 and 2020 (Moffett and Rice 2016; Rice and Moffett 2022). Thus, we have no reason to believe that high levels of variance in one of our dependent variables drives the results of this analysis. If anything, this high level of variance indicates that we have captured high and low participators alike. This enhances the generalizability of these findings because we can discuss more than high participators.

8. It is possible that students chose to answer that they had participated in one or more events related to the rally despite having not done so, as they may have seen participating as socially desirable. However, only 17% of respondents said they attended the rally, 3% volunteered, and 7% livestreamed it. These percentages are in line with (or below) the actual numbers of volunteers and attendees. Thus, we are confident in the reliability of this measure and we can eliminate widespread social desirability bias as a possible explanation for having stated that a student has received one or more of these treatments.

9. Some may be concerned that there is too great of an elapsed time between when Sanders visited the campus (March 2016) and when we fielded the survey (October 2016). This concern can manifest itself in terms of inaccurate or biased

memories about a particular respondent's participation in the rally. If any bias exists, it is nonsystematic because it is unclear about what direction the bias would run since Sanders did not win. Nonsystematic biases do not alter the conclusions that one can draw from social science research (see King, Keohane, and Verba 1994). Further, although we ask students to recall events that occurred months earlier, their self-reports appear in line with overall figures on rally attendance.

10. This suggests an interesting hypothesis beyond the scope of this analysis that is certainly an implication of it: that each of the treatment variables (attending the rally, volunteering at it, and livestreaming it) is also connected to higher levels of online political participation. We encourage interested researchers to test this more formally, as this generation engages online politically at far higher levels than their elders (see e.g., Moffett and Rice 2016; Rouse and Ross 2018).

11. Response choices for each question ranged from "never" to "very often" on a 5-point scale. We anticipate positive signs for all three coefficients.

12. "Don't know" responses were coded as missing for the purposes of index construction. Thus, no peer civic engagement score exists for those who answered "don't know" for at least one of the questions.

13. While our surveys lack a measure of strength of ideological attachment, considering ideology in this manner allows us to investigate the effect of ideological direction on civic activity and voting in the 2016 primary.

14. We do not use other demographic characteristics beyond those mentioned for the matching routines. Questions about other characteristics like residence hall or academic ability were not asked in this survey.

15. One can also use matching as part of a structural equation model to analyze voting and offline civic engagement. To do so, though, one must know the complete directed acyclic graph (DAG) structure to satisfy the assumptions of matching (VanderWeele and Shpitser 2011). In particular, directed acrylic graph structures must include all direct causal effects and all common causes for any pair of variables in the graph. Given the data that we have here, this is impossible to specify. Consequently, matching as part of any structural equation approach is not a good option here.

16. Please see the online appendix (http://www.kenmoffett.net/research) for more details about how we satisfy the matching assumptions in this chapter.

17. If we do not reduce imbalance by a series of rebalancing routines, then we cannot estimate any causal effect of attending the rally, livestreaming it, or volunteering at it on either of our dependent variables.

18. If one matched perfectly based on covariates (as with exact matching), then the inevitable consequence is a sample size so small that one cannot make statistically valid inferences.

19. To implement this technique, we use the MatchingFrontier package in R while matching based on closest unit measured in Mahalanobis distance.

20. Those who volunteered at, attended, or livestreamed the rally were not limited to members of one political party. Thus, we consider the impact of Sanders' visit on voting in any of the presidential primaries.

21. While this technique provides transparency with respect to imbalance reduction across the entire frontier, it does not give a precise level that indicates an unacceptable level of imbalance across the frontier.

22. We used these intervals because they provide a more systematic robustness

check on the results than analyses often report. These intervals rely upon the internal evidence provided by the data. They are estimated by a four-step process. First, these estimates are computed by estimating a series of alternative models that include the base model specified in the matching routines (Athey and Imbens 2015, 476–77). Second, the model is split into varying subsamples based on each value of each control variable (Athey and Imbens 2015, 477). Third, the model is reestimated for each of these subsamples to generate a new ATT, less the control variable whose value is being conditioned. Finally, the low and high values of the reestimated ATTs comprise the Athey-Imbens (2015) interval because all other ATT estimates, given the data, are located within this interval. Once estimated for each point along the frontier, they are plotted with the lower and upper bounds being the outer parameters of the orange region in figures 10.1 and 10.2. However, technical issues with implementing the routines prevented us from estimating Athey-Imbens (2015) intervals for all points along the frontier.

23. This trend happens until we converge toward a more balanced data set, when the effect decreases.

24. We assume that each binary variable is held at one, and all continuous variables are held at their means.

25. Fewer respondents reported having voted in the 2016 primary election than participated in the array of offline civic activities in 2016.

26. The one exception is for the model for those who livestreamed the rally while acquiring news from political blogs. These estimates vary from this discussion.

27. The results are substantially similar to what we report and are available upon request from the authors.

For example, it is possible that interest in politics, strong partisanship, and being a political science major are interrelated such that the individual effects of each variable are muted by including all of them in the same model. To consider this possibility, we removed each of these variables one at a time to investigate whether our results change. The results were substantially like what we report.

28. This campus experienced no other presidential candidate visit during the 2016 election cycle.

29. Moffett and Rice (2016) discuss similarities between students at this university and the population of young adults. More details are also contained in the online appendix (http://www.kenmoffett.net/research).

30. We examined whether those who waited outside of the event but could not get in had higher levels of civic activity or were more likely to vote in the 2016 primary than those who got in. We used the same covariates, a question that asked whether one waited in line outside but could not get inside of the rally location, as our treatment variable and performed the same matching technique. We discovered that those who waited outside, but were unable to get into the rally, experienced an approximately 10–20% increase in the probability of voting in the 2016 primary versus those not in this group. However, waiting outside but being unable to get into the rally had very little causal effect across the frontier to indicate higher levels of civic engagement among this group versus those not in this group. These results are available upon request.

31. It is possible that some of those who livestreamed the rally had waited in line but could not get in; those waiting outside had contact with campaign staffers and volunteers and were also greeted by Sanders.

32. If someone chooses to livestream on a campaign website, they can be directly asked for contact information and provided opportunities to sign up to volunteer. If they choose to watch on another platform, as many students at the university studied here did, the campaign will only be able to find them through purchasing advertising geared toward specific web traffic patterns.

REFERENCES

Ansolabehere, S., E. Hersh, and K. Shepsle. 2012. "Movers, Stayers, and Registration: Why Age Is Correlated with Registration in the U.S." *Quarterly Journal of Political Science* 7 (4): 333–63.

Athey, S., and G. W. Imbens. 2015. "A Measure of Robustness to Misspecification." *American Economic Review Papers and Proceedings* 105 (5): 476–80.

Austin, P. C. 2008. "A Critical Appraisal of Propensity-Score Matching in the Medical Literature between 1996 and 2003." *Journal of the American Statistical Association* 27 (12): 2037–49.

Bauer-Wolf, J. 2018. "After the ACA, Fewer Uninsured Students." *Inside Higher Ed,* March 30. https://www.insidehighered.com/news/2018/03/30/obamacare-has-led-fewer-uninsured-students-study-finds

Beaton, C. 2016. "The Science behind Why Millennials Don't Vote." *Forbes,* November 4. https://www.forbes.com/sites/carolinebeaton/2016/11/04/whymillennials arentvoting/#5f51f02a89c2

Beck, P. A., and M. K. Jennings. 1979. "Political Periods and Political Participation." *American Political Science Review* 73 (3): 737–50.

Belanger, E., and B. M. Meguid. 2008. "Issue Salience, Issue Ownership, and Issue-Based Vote Choice." *Electoral Studies* 27 (3): 477–91.

Bernie Sanders Campaign. "On the Issues: It's Time to Make College Tuition Free." https://berniesanders.com/issues/its-time-to-make-college-tuition-free-and-de bt-free/

Best, S. J., and B. S. Krueger. 2005. "Analyzing the Representation of Internet Political Participation." *Political Behavior* 27 (2): 183–216.

Blake, A. 2016. "More Young People Voted for Bernie Sanders Than Trump and Clinton Combined—by a Lot." *Washington Post,* June 20. https://www.washingtonpo st.com/news/the-fix/wp/2016/06/20/more-young-people-voted-for-bernie-sande rs-than-trump-and-clinton-combined-by-a-lot/?utm_term=.e5115fc11b9b

Brady, H. R., S. Verba, and K. Lehman Schlozman. 1995. "Beyond SES: A Resource Model of Political Participation." *American Political Science Review* 89 (2): 271–94.

Caliendo, M., and S. Kopenig. 2008. "Some Practical Guidance for the Implementation of Propensity Score Matching." *Journal of Economic Surveys* 22 (1): 31–72.

Campbell, E. 2016. "Voting Hurdles Often Keep College Students Away from the Ballot Box." NBC News, August 25. https://www.nbcnews.com/feature/college-ga me-plan/voting-hurdles-often-keep-college-students-away-ballot-box-n637046

Cantijoch, M., D. Cutts, and R. Gibson. 2016. "Moving Slowly up the Ladder of Political Engagement: A 'Spill-Over' Model of Internet Participation." *British Journal of Politics and International Relations* 18 (1): 26–48.

Collins, J., and R. Block Jr. 2020. "Fired Up, Ready to Go: The Impact of Age, Campaign Enthusiasm, and Civic Duty on African American Voting." *Political Behavior* 42: 107–42.

Condon, M., and M. Holleque. 2013. "Entering Politics: General Self-Efficacy and Voting Behavior among Young People." *Political Psychology* 34 (2): 167–81.

Conroy, M., J. T. Feezell, and M. Guerrero. 2012. "Facebook and Political Engagement: A Study of Online Political Group Membership and Offline Political Engagement." *Computers in Human Behavior* 28 (5): 1535–46.

Dahl, R. A. 1989. *Democracy and Its Critics.* New Haven: Yale University Press.

Dalton, R. J. 2007. *The Good Citizen: How a Younger Generation Is Reshaping American Politics.* Washington, DC: CQ Press.

U.S. Department of Education. 2017. Digest of Education Statistics: 2017. Retrieved from https://nces.ed.gov/programs/digest/d17/

Devine, C. J. 2019. "Voter Mobilization 101: Presidential Campaign Visits to Colleges and Universities in the 2016 Election." *PS* 52 (2): 261–66.

Dimock, M. 2019. "Defining Generations: Where Millennials End and Generation Z Begins." January 17. https://www.pewresearch.org/fact-tank/2019/01/17/where-millennials-end-and-generation-z-begins/

Donald, E. 2016. "Bernie Sanders at SIUE: 'We Can Create the Nation We Want to Become.'" *Belleville News Democrat,* March 4.

Elliott, W., and M. K. Lewis. 2015. *The Real College Debt Crisis: How Student Borrowing Threatens Financial Well-Being and Erodes the American Dream.* Santa Barbara, CA: Praeger.

Faber, O., and R. Kademon. 2003. "Assessment of Alternative Approaches to Bioclimatic Modeling with Special Emphasis on the Mahalanobis Distance." *Ecological Modeling* 160 (1–2): 115–30.

Fox, R., and J. Lawless. 2014. "Uncovering the Origins of the Gender Gap in Political Ambition." *American Political Science Review* 108 (3): 499–519.

Friedman, Z. 2019. "Bernie Sanders: I Will Cancel All $1.6 Trillion of Your Student Loan Debt." *Forbes,* June 24. https://www.forbes.com/sites/zackfriedman/2019/06/24/student-loans-bernie-sanders

Herrnson, P. S., and I. L. Morris. 2007. "Presidential Campaigning in the 2002 Congressional Elections." *Legislative Studies Quarterly* 32 (4): 629–48.

Highton, B., and R. E. Wolfinger. 2001. "The First Seven Years of the Political Life Cycle." *American Journal of Political Science* 45 (1): 202–9.

Hill, D., and S. C. McKee. 2005. "The Electoral College, Mobilization, and Turnout in the 2000 Presidential Election." *American Politics Research* 33 (5): 700–725.

Hill, J. S., E. Rodriquez, and A. E. Wooten. 2010. "Stump Speeches and Road Trips: The Impact of State Campaign Appearances in Presidential Elections." *PS: Political Science and Politics* 43 (2): 243–54.

Ho, D., K. Imai, G. King, and E. A. Stuart. 2008. "Matching as Nonparametric Preprocessing for Reducing Model Dependence in Parametric Causal Inference." *Political Analysis* 15 (3): 199–236.

Holbein, J. B., and D. S. Hillygus. 2016. "Making Young Voters: The Impact of Preregistration on Youth Turnout." *American Journal of Political Science* 60 (2): 364–82.

Holbein, J. B., and D. S. Hillygus. 2020. *Making Young Voters: Converting Civic Attitudes into Civic Action.* New York: Cambridge University Press.

Holbrook, T. M. 2002. "Did the Whistle-Stop Campaign Matter?" *PS: Political Science and Politics* 35 (1): 59–66.

Holbrook, T. M., and S. D. McClurg. 2005. "The Mobilization of Core Supporters: Campaigns, Turnout, and Electoral Composition in United States Presidential Elections." *American Journal of Political Science* 49 (4): 689–703.

Imai, K., G. King, and E. Stuart. 2008. "Misunderstandings among Experimentalists and Observationalists about Causal Inference." *Journal of the Royal Statistical Society, Series A* 171 (2): 481–502.

Institute for College Access and Success. 2019. "Quick Facts about Student Debt." https://ticas.org/files/pub_files/qf_about_student_debt.pdf

Jennings, M. K., and R. M. Niemi. 1981. *Generations and Politics.* Princeton: Princeton University Press.

Jennings, M. K., L. Stoker, and J. Bowers. 2009. "Politics across Generations: Family Transmission Reexamined." *Journal of Politics* 71 (3): 782–99.

Johnston, R., M. G. Hagen, and K. H. Jamieson. 2004. *The 2000 Presidential Election and the Foundations of Party Politics.* New York: Cambridge University Press.

Keeter, S. 2008. "Young Voters in the 2008 Presidential Primaries." Pew Research Center, February 11. http://www.pewresearch.org/2008/02/11/young-voters-in-the-2008-presidential-primaries/

Keisler-Starkey, K., and L. N. Bunch. 2022. "Health Insurance Coverage in the United States: 2021." https://www.census.gov/content/dam/Census/library/publications/2022/demo/p60-278.pdf

King, G., R. O. Keohane, and S. Verba. 1994. *Designing Social Inquiry: Scientific Inference in Qualitative Research.* Princeton: Princeton University Press.

King, G., C. Lucas, and R. A. Nielsen. 2017. "The Balance-Sample Size Frontier in Matching Methods for Causal Inference." *American Journal of Political Science* 61 (2): 473–89.

Leighley, J. E. 1995. "Attitudes, Opportunities and Incentives: A Field Essay on Political Participation." *Political Research Quarterly* 48 (1): 181–209.

Levenson, M. 2016. "Bernie Sanders Becomes Unlikely Leader of a Youth Movement." *Boston Globe*, January 19. https://www.bostonglobe.com/metro/2016/01/18/bernie-sanders-unlikely-appeal-college-students/muC3jazXBjXv7myW1wKOtL/story.html

Lin, N. 1999. "Building a Network Theory of Social Capital." *Connections* 22 (1): 28–51.

Mannheim, K. 1952. "The Problem of Generations." In K. Mannheim, *Essays on the Sociology of Knowledge,* 276–320. London: Routledge and Kegan Paul.

Mettler, S. 2005. *Soldiers to Citizens: The G.I. Bill and the Making of the Greatest Generation.* New York: Oxford University Press.

Moffett, K. W., and L. L. Rice. 2016. *Web 2.0 and the Political Mobilization of College Students.* Lanham, MD: Lexington Press.

Murphy, W. T., Jr. 1971. "Student Power in the 1970 Elections: A Preliminary Assessment." *PS: Political Science and Politics* 4 (1): 27–32.

National Journal Travel Tracker 2016. "Visits by Presidential Candidates during the 2016 Election Cycle." https://www.nationaljournal.com/s/29520/2016-presidential-candidate-travel-tracker/

Niemi, R. G., H. W. Stanley, and C. L. Evans. 1984. "Age and Turnout among the Newly Enfranchised: Life Cycle versus Experience Effects." *European Journal of Political Research* 12 (4): 371–86.

Parker, K., and R. Igielnik. 2020. "On the Cusp of Adulthood and Facing an Uncertain Future: What We Know about Gen Z So Far." May 14. https://www.pewresea rch.org/social-trends/2020/05/14/on-the-cusp-of-adulthood-and-facing-an-unce rtain-future-what-we-know-about-gen-z-so-far-2/

Perna, L. W. 2012. *Understanding the Working College Student: New Research and Its Implications for Policy and Practice.* Sterling, VA: Stylus Publishing.

Pew Research Center for the People and the Press. 2016. "Flashpoints in Polling." October 24. http://www.pewresearch.org/2016/08/01/flashpoints-in-polling/

Prokop, A. 2015. "Bernie Sanders 2016: A Primer." *Vox*, October 12. https://www.vox .com/2015/7/28/18093566/bernie-sanders-issues-policies

Putnam, R. D. 2000. *Bowling Alone: The Collapse and Revival of American Community.* New York: Simon and Schuster.

Reilly, K. 2016. "Read Michelle Obama's First Campaign Trail Speech for Hillary Clinton." *Time*, September 17, 17. http://www.time.com/4498086/michelle-oba ma-hillary-clinton-campaign-trail-transcript/

Rice, L. L. 2018. "Campaign Visits, Party Ties, and Challenges to the Party Establishment." In *Parties under Pressure: Strategic Adaptations for a Changing Electorate,* edited by C. Rackaway and L. L. Rice, 143–68. New York: Palgrave Macmillan.

Rice, L. L., and K. W. Moffett. 2022. *The Political Voices of Generation Z.* New York: Routledge.

Rosenstone, S., and J. M. Hansen. 1993. *Mobilization, Participation and Democracy in America.* New York: Macmillan Press.

Rouse, S. M., and D. A. Ross. 2018. *The Politics of Millennials: Political Beliefs and Policy Preferences of America's Most Diverse Generation.* Ann Arbor: University of Michigan Press.

Sargent, G. 2016. "Bernie Sanders Has Already Succeeded in a Huge Way (Even if He Loses)." *Washington Post,* February 11. https://www.washingtonpost.com/blogs /plum-line/wp/2016/02/11/bernie-sanders-has-already-succeeded-in-a-huge -way-even-if-he-loses/?utm_term=.5351adfaa25a

Schlozman, K. L., S. Verba, and H. E. Brady. 2012. *The Unheavenly Chorus: Unequal Political Voice and the Broken Promise of American Democracy.* Princeton: Princeton University Press.

Shaw, D. R. 1999. "The Effect of TV Ads and Candidate Appearances on Statewide Presidential Votes, 1998–1996." *American Political Science Review* 93 (2): 345–61.

Squire, P., R. E. Wolfinger, and D. P. Glass. 1987. "Residential Mobility and Voter Turnout." *American Political Science Review* 81 (1): 45–65.

Stuart, E. A. 2008. "Developing Practical Recommendations for the Use of Propensity Scores: Discussion of 'A Critical Appraisal of Propensity Score Matching in the Medical Literature between 1996 and 2003.'" *Statistics in Medicine* 27 (12): 2062–65.

Tyson, A. B. Kennedy, and C. Funk. 2021. "Gen Z, Millennials Stand Out for Climate Change Activism, Social Media Engagement with Issue." Pew Research Center, May 26. https://www.pewresearch.org/science/2021/05/26/gen-z-millennials-sta nd-out-for-climate-change-activism-social-media-engagement-with-issue/

U.S. Department of Education. 2017. "Digest of Education Statistics: 2017." https://nc es.ed.gov/programs/digest/d17/

Vaccari, C., and A. Valeriani. 2016. "Party Campaigners or Citizen Campaigners? How Social Media Deepen and Broaden Party-Related Engagement." *International Journal of Press/Politics* 21 (3): 294–312.

VanderWeele, T. J., and I. Shpitser. 2011. "A New Criterion for Confounder Selection." *Biometrics* 67 (4): 1406–13.

Verba, S., H. E. Brady, and K. L. Schlozman. 1995. *Voice and Equality: Civic Voluntarism in American Democracy.* Cambridge, MA: Harvard University Press.

Vitak, J., P. Zube, A. Smock, C. T. Carr, N. Ellison, and C. Lampe. 2011. "It's Complicated: Facebook Users' Political Participation in the 2008 Election." *Cyberpsychology, Behavior and Social Networking* 14 (3): 107–14.

Wendland, J. 2017. *Campaigns That Matter: The Importance of Campaign Visits in Presidential Nominating Contests.* Lanham, MD: Lexington Press.

Wood, T. 2016. "What The Heck Are We Doing in Ottumwa, Anyway? Presidential Candidate Visits and Their Political Consequence." *ANNALS of the American Academy of Political and Social Science* 667 (1): 110–25.

Zukin, C., S. Keeter, M. Andolina, K. Jenkins, and M. X. Delli Carpini. 2006. *A New Engagement? Political Participation, Civic Life, and the Changing American Citizen.* New York: Oxford University Press.

Part IV

Impact

11 | Millennial Generation Political Engagement

Democratically Motivated or Disenchanted?
Insights from the 2020 Election

Ashley D. Ross and Stella M. Rouse

In 2016, Millennials were excited by the presidential candidacy of a 74-year-old white Jewish senator who spoke bluntly and seemed to never comb his hair. Given the generational gap, support for Bernie Sanders among Millennials seemed odd. However, he had a platform and message of a more just economy—free college tuition, higher minimum wage, and guaranteed family leave—that deeply appealed to a generation that had disproportionately endured the financial turmoil of the Great Recession. In fact, once Sanders lost the Democratic presidential primary, many Millennials did not switch their support to Hillary Clinton. Of the 46 percent of Millennial voters who cast a ballot in 2016, only 55 percent of those supported Clinton (Center for Information and Research on Civic Learning and Engagement [CIRCLE] 2016). Some voted for Donald Trump or a third-party candidate, and many stayed home, disillusioned by institutional rules that robbed them of their preferred choice, a two-party system that they believe does not work, and lack of interest among party candidates about issues that mattered to their generation (Galston and Hendrickson 2016; Rouse and Ross 2018).

Fast forward to 2018, when Millennials were motivated to express their disapproval of the Trump administration's and congressional Republicans' policies, such as the denial of man-made climate change, attempts to rescind the Affordable Care Act, and hardline immigration initiatives, by turning out to vote at much higher rates than in the previous midterm election (42% in 2018, compared to 22% in 2014) (Cilluffo and Fry 2019). That election also saw the highest midterm turnout rate for young people in the last quarter century (CIRCLE 2018). Millennials were also electorally motivated by the emergence of new, young, and diverse Democratic candidates for Congress, like Alexandria Ocasio Cortez, who ran on similar platforms as Sanders that challenged the politics of status quo. Overall, in 2018, 67 percent of Millennials cast a ballot for Democratic House candidates, compared to just 32 percent who voted for Republican House candidates (CIRCLE 2018).

A lot has occurred since 2016, the last year we surveyed Millennials on a broad scale about their political attitudes and their interest in and engagement with politics (Rouse and Ross 2018). At the time, Millennials were still recovering, at a slower pace than the general population, from the employment and financial struggles they incurred during the Great Recession that began in December 2007 and lasted until June 2009. Those hardships included massive student loan debt, unemployment or underemployment, a smaller share of household wealth (compared to older generations), and the first generation projected to have less earning potential across their lifespan than the previous generation (Kent 2020).

Likely due in part to these hardships, we found in our 2016 survey of American adults some evidence of disenchantment or general disappointment and dissatisfaction with the political system among Millennials, a sense of distrust in institutions, and a belief that the system is rigged against them. However, despite these disappointments, Millennials also reported being politically engaged, particularly in less traditional forms of engagement such as marching, volunteering, canvassing, and supporting referendums. Dalton (2016) calls this a model of "engaged citizenship," and argues that Millennials eschew more traditional forms of political participation, such as voting and giving to a political campaign, in favor of these more direct and individual actions. Furthermore, given this generation's unique set of values (Rouse and Ross 2018), especially their belief that government has an important role to play in addressing problems, Millennials in 2016 believed that government could help improve their lives. Therefore, the Millennial story of being motivated or disenchanted is not black and white. We suspect that as Millennials have aged and as circumstances of the last few years have further impacted their lives and ability to prosper, some attitudes will have changed more than others.

Just as Millennials were working to establish a financial foothold after 2008, another economic recession hit—this one with potentially greater economic implications, plus added health concerns. The COVID-19 pandemic is yet another crisis for the Millennial generation, and it occurred at the point in their lifespan when they are at the height of their earning potential (Sewell 2020). Furthermore, the diversity of the Millennial generation—about 44 percent are people of color (Frey 2018)—increases this cohort's economic vulnerability because minorities have been disproportionately impacted by the pandemic (Collins 2020).

The effects of both the Great Recession and the COVID-19 pandemic may have significant and irreversible consequences for the Millennial generation. Add to this the increasing effects of climate change (Ross and Rouse 2020) and the social unrest about high-profile incidents of police brutality that led many young people to march in the streets for racial justice and reforms (Fisher and Rouse 2022), and it is little surprise that Millennials are feeling the stress of an uncertain future, much more so than older generations (Frazee 2020). Against this backdrop, this chapter examines how the political attitudes and levels of political engagement of the Millennial generation have evolved, from 2016 to 2020, as this generation has aged. The election of 2020 is the first where Millennials make up the largest voting bloc (Fry 2020). In an election seen by many as a test for democratic resolve, the way Millennials engage not only sheds light on how contemporary politics has affected this cohort but also how the youngest fully adult generation will be at the forefront of shaping the future of American democracy.

Background: Millennial Generation Identity and Political Engagement

While generational boundaries are not absolute, Millennials are generally understood to comprise the age cohort born from 1981 to 1996 (Dimock 2019) and, thus, came to age at the turn of the third millennium. As we have established in previous work (Rouse and Ross 2018), the Millennial generation shares a unique identity or generational persona that is relevant for understanding group differences (Campbell et al. 2015). This shared identity broadly frames the political beliefs and attitudes, policy preferences, and priorities of this generation. The Millennial generation identity is rooted in shared experiences—broad cultural shifts resulting from social, economic, and political events that occurred during this group's formative or "impressionable" years. As described by Laura Stoker (chap. 2, this volume), this is when people are first motivated to define themselves politically and most influenced by personal and social events. For Millennials these include the proliferation of technology—*Millennials are the first digital natives*; the rapid pace of globalization—*Millennials have a strong sense of being global citizens*; and the growing ethnic diversity of young people—*Millennials are the most racially and ethnically diverse adult generation*. In addition, Millennials grew up observing political instability surrounding the September 11 terrorist attacks, the government response to Hurricane Katrina, and the gridlock and discord in Congress and the White House. Furthermore, Millennials experienced—and have been severely impacted by—the Great Recession of the early 2000s. These events have shaped Millennial values of tolerance and social justice, but they have also been an undercurrent in this generation's political dissatisfaction and disengagement. On the whole, Millennials tend to eschew traditional institutions, including religion, marriage, and politics. However, they continue to look to government as "the greatest tool at society's disposal to address the collective action problems of today" (Roosevelt Institute 2013, 8).

Millennials share a collectivist worldview that sees government as a platform for solving problems and improving the lives of citizens, both in our nation and around the world (Molyneux and Teixeria 2010; Parker et al. 2019; Rouse et al. 2022). The majority of Millennials believe the government should be more involved in order to make college affordable, help the poor, create jobs, provide a basic standard of living, protect the environment, and address climate change (Rouse and Ross 2018). Given these beliefs and policy priorities, Millennial political ideology is largely liberal, which most Millennials recognize in their self-described political stances (Maniam and Smith, 2017). The question remains, however, how this ideology may have changed as this generation ages. Furthermore, given its diversity, how does the Millennial generation identity interact with other social identities, namely race and ethnicity, to affect political engagement?

The Millennial generation has ushered greater race and ethnic diversity into the broader American public. In 1980, only 22 percent of young adults, aged 18–34 years, belonged to a racial or ethnic minority group. In 2015, 44 percent of young—Millennial—adults were racial and ethnic minorities (Frey 2018). While post-Millennials, known as Generation Z, are even more diverse in their demographic composition, racial and ethnic diversity grew in unprecedented ways with the

Millennial generation. Millennials are, in the words of demographer William Frey, the "bridge between an older, largely white America and a much more diverse post-millennial America" (Frey 2018). Race and ethnic identity, therefore, is a central part of the shared Millennial generation identity and the complex individual social identity of many Millennials. Garcia-Rios et al. (2019) introduce the concept of an "identity portfolio" to understand the complexity of social identities. An identity portfolio holds all the identities or identity categories that an individual subscribes to when making political decisions. Within this portfolio, the extent of attachment to each identity varies, but more salient identities have greater importance and are more easily politicized. The activation of different identities is more likely to occur in the context of an increasingly multicultural society like the U.S., where multiple identities are more common and more salient. However, the effects of these types of identities on attitude formation and political engagement remain underexplored. For example, in another project (Ross and Rouse 2020), we find that the overlapping identities of Millennial and Latino are associated with heightened concern about climate change, and that strong attachment to one identity is sufficient to cause concern when the other identity is weak.

The racial and ethnic diversity of Millennials is particularly important, not only for their shared generation identity and for individual identity portfolios but also for the levels of political engagement of Millennial minorities. Past research has established that the greatest external impediment to political participation and engagement is rooted in socioeconomic status (SES) (Campbell et al. 1960; Verba and Nie 1972; Wolfinger and Rosenstone 1980). Individuals with higher SES—in terms of income, education, occupational status, and social networks—are more politically engaged and active because they have the skills, time, and resources to be involved (Tam Cho, Gimpel, and Wu 2006) and because they typically glean greater benefits from political engagement than those with lower SES (Campbell et al. 1960). SES is part of the reason that minority populations, in particular African Americans and Latinos, have struggled to be politically engaged at rates similar to those of whites (Verba, Schlozman, and Brady 1995). Disparities in income and education persist among African Americans and Latinos, as compared to whites, and have grown larger in the past decade with the Great Recession. Recent analyses of Millennial wealth show major gaps between race and ethnic groups—white Millennials have more than three times the median wealth of Black Millennials

(Cramer et al. 2019). Given that the impacts of the COVID-19 health crisis have disproportionately affected Hispanic and Black communities the hardest (Lopez et al. 2020), SES gaps between Millennial race and ethnic subgroups are likely to only grow in the future and continue to affect political engagement. In this important context, we examine race and ethnic differences among Millennials. We also compare Millennial and older adult racial and ethnic groups in an effort to determine if Millennials as they age are looking more like older adults of their race or ethnic group, or both, or if they appear to share more of a generational identity.

Data: Two Snapshots of Millennial Political Attitudes and Engagement

To explore Millennial political engagement, we employ two data sets that surveyed a nationally representative group of Millennials in the month following the presidential elections of 2016 and 2020. These surveys are cross-sectional and do not involve a repeated panel of respondents. As such, they should be understood as "snapshots" of Millennial political attitudes and behaviors and not used to make causal inferences across time based on panel data trends. We use these surveys to establish broad comparisons in order to examine Millennial ideology, political party affiliation, and presidential vote choice in 2016 and 2020 and investigate differences between Millennials and older adults in levels of political engagement.

The 2016 survey was launched online and included 1,250 respondents recruited by Qualtrics to fill a set of demographic quotas on sex, geographic region, and race and ethnicity. Millennials were purposively oversampled ($n = 576$) to provide a sufficient number of observations to analyze subgroups. The 2020 survey was also launched online using a panel of 1,220 respondents recruited by Qualtrics. The panel filled a set of demographic quotas, including age, sex, race and ethnicity, as well as political party affiliation. The quotas for age were nested within race and ethnic groups so that a representative subgroup of respondents was collected for whites, Blacks, and Latinos, enabling comparisons of a sufficient size. The sample included 407 Millennial respondents.

Due to low response rates, high costs, and poor coverage of probability surveys, nonprobability surveys such as the ones used in this chapter are increasingly used by researchers (Baker et al. 2013). While quota-based sampling aims to match a panel to a set of population parameters and, therefore, enhances the representativeness of the sample, there is a critical disadvantage: no measures of precision (i.e., response rate, margins of error). This likely introduces unknown sampling biases into the survey estimates (Battaglia 2008). A study by Kennedy, et al. (2016) from Pew Research Center concludes that such biases may be reduced through the use of survey weights. Accordingly, we carefully compared sample to population parameters on multiple factors; there were substantial discrepancies for age groups. Therefore, we created a weight for each survey that adjusts the sample to more closely match population age groups. This method is appropriate for managing the limitations of nonprobability survey samples (Baker et al. 2013), but we recognize it does not completely eliminate biases.

Throughout the remainder of this chapter, we rely on weighted tabulations of the survey data to compare Millennials to older adults as well as make comparisons between race and ethnic subgroups—whites, Blacks, and Latinos—among Millennial and older adult groups. Where there are differences in the number of observations reported for these descriptive statistics, it is due to missing observations. For the purposes of analysis, we adopt the conventions of the Pew Research Center in defining generational boundaries. We consider the Millennial generation to be composed of those born between 1981 and 1996 while older adults are those born before 1981. The youngest adult cohort—Generation Z—include individuals born after 1996. We do not incorporate analyses of Generation Z because, as outlined in Scott McLean (chap. 3, this volume), this cohort shares some different characteristics and values than Millennials.

Millennial Generation Identity: Steadfastly Liberal

A central part of the Millennial generation identity is their shared political liberalness. Millennials have demonstrated more liberal values than older adults at the same age (Rouse and Ross 2018). Furthermore, Pew Research data has also shown that Millennials appear to be staying liberal as they age—a departure from the trends of older generations (Pew Research Center 2018). The survey data we have collected across four years does not show significant change among Millennials in their ideology. Certainly, Millennials are not monolithic, and there are some shifts in ideology among Millennial racial and ethnic subgroups.

In 2016, our survey data indicated 39 percent of Millennials considered themselves liberal; in 2020, 40 percent of Millennials said they were liberal. In 2016, 34 percent of Millennials identified as moderate while 27 percent identified as conservative. In 2020, this had shifted to 29 percent moderate and 31 percent conservative. The increase in conservatives may be indicative of life cycle effects; Laura Stoker (chap. 2, this volume) provides evidence to support the "aging-brings-conservatism" hypothesis. Alternatively, this change may reflect the divisiveness of the 2020 election and resultant ideological sorting. We can draw more inferences by looking at race and ethnic subgroups and comparing Millennials with older adults of their group.

As shown in figure 11.1, all racial and ethnic subgroups of Millennials were more liberal than older adults of their group in 2016: white—36 percent of Millennials versus 29 percent of older adults; Blacks—35 percent of Millennials versus 34 percent of older adults; and Latinos—42 percent of Millennials versus 36 percent of older adults. In 2020 there are some changes to these percentages. The percentage of white Millennials who are liberal are about equal to the portion of older adult whites who are liberal (33% and 34%, respectively). At the same time, conservative white Millennials are more aligned with conservative white older adults in 2020: 34 percent of Millennials and 39 percent of older adults are conservative in 2020, compared to 29 percent of Millennials and 41 percent of older adults in 2016. Black and Latino Millennials in 2020 remain more liberal than older adults in their minority group: 43 percent and 42 percent of Millennial Blacks and Latinos, respectively, are liberal, compared to 38 percent and 27 percent of older adult Blacks and Latinos, respectively. However, there are nearly equal portions of conservatives in minority racial and ethnic groups: 25 percent of Millennial Blacks and 22 percent of older adult Blacks say they are conservative, as do 34 percent of Millennial Latinos and 36 percent of older adult Latinos. These trends imply that among Black and Latino subgroups, Millennials are more liberal but equally conservative in comparison to older adults. White Millennials look more similar to older adults in their liberal and conservative sorting.

In addition to remaining liberal as they age, Millennials are steadfastly Democratic in their political party affiliation. In 2016, our survey data indicated that a greater portion of Millennials affiliated with the Democratic Party than older adults: 46 percent of Millennials com-

POLITICAL IDEOLOGY

4-in-10 Millennials
identified as liberal in 2016 and 2020

Millennials, as a whole, have remained liberal as they have aged. However, there are shifts in ideology among race and ethnic subgroups.

Ideology among race & ethnic subgroups

■ liberal ■ moderate ■ conservative

		0%	10%	20%	30%	40%	50%	60%	70%	80%	90%	100%

2016
- White — Millennial
- White — Older adult
- Black — Millennial
- Black — Older adult
- Latino — Millennial
- Latino — Older adult

2020
- White — Millennial
- White — Older adult
- Black — Millennial
- Black — Older adult
- Latino — Millennial
- Latino — Older adult

Fig. 11.1. Political Ideology and Millennials
Source: Derived with data collected from authors' conducted surveys.

pared to 39 percent of older adults. At the same time, fewer Millennials said they were Republican: 22 percent of Millennials compared to 28 percent of older adults. In 2020, 45 percent of Millennials identified as Democrats, 32 percent said they were Republicans, and 23 percent identified as independents. These trends, however, slightly shift when we examine race and ethnic subgroups.

As shown in figure 11.2, in 2016, the majority of Black (71%) and Latino (55%) Millennials affiliated with the Democratic Party, while a slight plurality of white Millennials (39%) identified as independents. Similar political affiliations as their respective young cohort were observed among older white adults—38 percent identifying as independents—and Black adults—72 percent affiliating with the Democratic Party. While a plurality of Latino older adults affiliated with the Democratic Party (46%) in 2016, this was 9 percentage points lower than Latino Millennials. In 2020, there were marked changes in party affiliation among all subgroups. The majority of white Millennials (56%) and a plurality of older white adults (46%) now identify with the Democratic Party, with a slight uptick among both in Republican Party affiliation (30% in 2020, compared to 28% in 2016 among Millennials; 35% in 2020, compared to 33% in 2016 among older adults). Among Blacks and Latinos, there was a decline in Democratic Party affiliation. This was the case for both Black and Latino Millennials (45% and 36%, respectively) and older Black and Latino adults (65% and 31%, respectively). For both Black and Latino Millennials, the decline in Democratic Party affiliation was sizable—26 percentage points, compared to 2016 for Blacks, and 19 percentage points, compared to 2016 for Latinos. At the same time, Republican Party identification among Black Millennials increased from 3 percent in 2016 to 24 percent in 2020, and for Latino Millennials from 19 percent in 2016 to 41 percent in 2020. While figures from a national survey conducted by Pew Research Center in 2020, including an oversample of Black Americans, indicates our survey may be inflating the rate of identification with the Republican Party among Black and Latino Millennials (Pew Research Center, 2020), recent shifts to the right among voters of color could signal more lasting change. In 2018, Donald Trump made gains among both Latinos and African American voters (Nagesh 2020), and the Republican Party made notable gains among young Black voters in 2022 (Parker 2022). While the majority of Blacks and Latinos remain loyal to the Democratic Party, and Millennials largely seem to find it the best fit for their liberal views, it is important to remember that minority Millennial

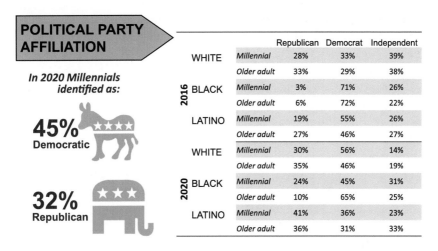

			Republican	Democrat	Independent
	WHITE	Millennial	28%	33%	39%
		Older adult	33%	29%	38%
2016	BLACK	Millennial	3%	71%	26%
		Older adult	6%	72%	22%
	LATINO	Millennial	19%	55%	26%
		Older adult	27%	46%	27%
	WHITE	Millennial	30%	56%	14%
		Older adult	35%	46%	19%
2020	BLACK	Millennial	24%	45%	31%
		Older adult	10%	65%	25%
	LATINO	Millennial	41%	36%	23%
		Older adult	36%	31%	33%

POLITICAL PARTY AFFILIATION

In 2020 Millennials identified as:

45% Democratic

32% Republican

Fig. 11.2. Political Party Affiliation and Millennials
Source: Derived with data collected from authors' conducted surveys.

subgroups are quite diverse. There could be life cycle effects at play, as well as factors particular to the last two electoral contests. More trend data is needed to determine whether these shifts in party affiliation among Millennial subgroups will persist.

Despite some changes in party affiliation between 2016 and 2020, Millennials have and continue to predominantly vote for Democratic candidates. According to our 2016 survey, fewer Millennial respondents, compared to older adults (30% versus 42%), reported voting for Republican candidate Donald Trump, and more Millennials voted for Democratic candidate Hillary Clinton than older adults (59% versus 48%). In 2020, our survey results indicated that 64 percent of Millennials and 66 percent of older adults voted for Democratic candidate Joe Biden while 34 percent of Millennials and 32 percent of older adults voted for incumbent President Trump.

Among Millennials, more whites voted for Trump in 2016 (39%) while a higher percentage of Black and Latino Millennials (87% and 64%, respectively) voted for Clinton. In 2016, Trump support was much higher among white older adults (50%) while Black and Latino older adults predominantly supported Clinton (82% and 51%, respectively). In 2020, race and ethnic subgroup differences looked similar. Among Millennials, 30 percent of whites, 27 percent of Blacks, and 44 percent of Latinos said they voted for Trump while 69 percent of whites, 71 percent of Blacks, and 53 percent of Latinos said they voted for Biden. Among older adults, 42 percent of whites, 10 percent of Blacks, and 42 percent of Latinos said they voted for Trump while 58 percent of whites, 88 percent of Blacks, and 55 percent of Latinos voted for Biden.

These trends demonstrate that the liberalness of the Millennial generation identity has not changed in relation to political ideology, and party affiliation may not necessarily be fully indicative of vote choice. There have been some shifts among white Millennials toward increasing conservatism that make them more closely aligned with older adults of their racial group. However, the majority of Millennials generally remain affiliated with the Democratic Party and supported Joe Biden in the 2020 presidential election.

Millennial Political Engagement: Disenchanted or Democratically Motived?

In 2015, when first gathering data for our book *The Politics of Millennials*, we asked a panel of respondents a simple question: *Do you feel engaged in the political system or politics?*[1] The responses from Millennials and older adults were similar—only 31 percent of both groups felt engaged (see fig. 11.3). We were surprised because prevailing depictions of Millennials made them seem more apathetic, less engaged; some criticize this cohort for their political "slacktivism" (Gendron and Lienesch 2015). So, we dug a little deeper, posing an open-ended question that asked respondents to tell us what would make them more engaged. Emergent theme analysis revealed that about a third of Millennials and older adults are just not interested or don't know what could make them more engaged. Many, however, were looking for better political representation (15% of Millennials and 19% of older adults) and more honesty and accountability from politicians and less politics (12% of Millennials and 16% of older adults). Another 10 percent of Millennials indicated they would like politics to be more relevant to them and still another 10 percent said they wanted better political information, including from the media.

We posed the same questions about feeling engaged in our 2020 postelection survey. Remarkably, political engagement doubled: 69 percent of Millennials and 64 percent of older adults said they felt engaged in the political systems. When asked what it would take to make them feel more engaged, responses indicating disinterest or not

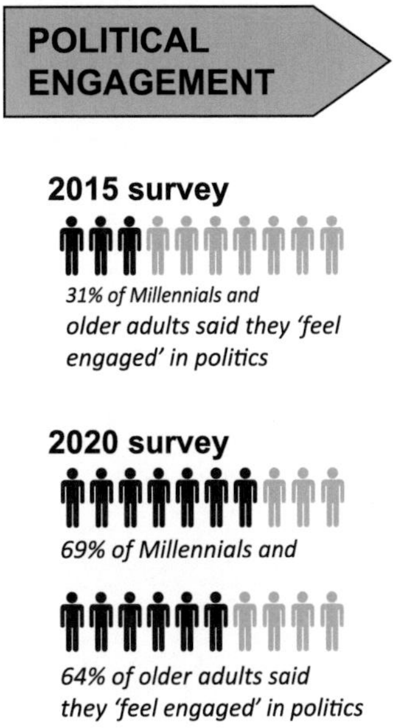

POLITICAL
ENGAGEMENT

2015 survey

👤👤👤👤👤👤👤👤👤👤

31% of Millennials and older adults said they 'feel engaged' in politics

2020 survey

👤👤👤👤👤👤👤👤👤👤

69% of Millennials and

👤👤👤👤👤👤👤👤👤👤

64% of older adults said they 'feel engaged' in politics

| What would it take to make you more engaged in politics? | | | | |
| | 2015 survey | | 2020 survey | |
	Millennial	Older Adult	Millennial	Older Adult
Better political representation	15%	19%	22%	15%
More trust, honesty, and accountability of politicians	12%	16%	30%	41%
Make political participation easier	7%	7%	8%	5%
Greater relevance of politics to me	10%	6%	7%	4%
Better political information, including from the media	10%	6%	7%	6%
Different or improved political institutions	5%	4%	5%	5%
Make politics more interesting	7%	5%	4%	2%
Feel like I make a difference in the political system	5%	3%	4%	6%

Fig. 11.3. Political Engagement and Millennials
Source: Derived with data collected from authors' conducted surveys.

knowing what could improve engagement were nearly halved, and responses from both Millennials and older adults focused on better political representation and more trust, honesty, and accountability of politicians. There were more frequent mentions of better political representation among Millennials (22% versus 15% among older adults), while older adults focused more on trust and accountability of politicians (41% versus 30% among Millennials).

Voter Turnout

Early in their voting life, Millennials made a big impact in the 2008 presidential election of Barack Obama with 50 percent of eligible Millennials turning out to vote (Fry 2018). Millennial turnout was less impressive in 2012 with 46 percent of eligible Millennials saying they voted. Since then, Millennials have improved their turnout, making some of their biggest strides in the 2018 midterm election when they nearly doubled their midterm turnout rate from 22 percent in 2014 to

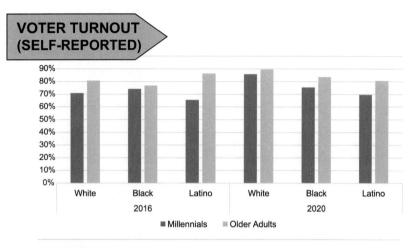

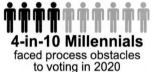

4-in-10 Millennials
faced process obstacles
to voting in 2020

In 2020, 40% of Millennials said they did not vote because they did not have the required documents, were not sure of the process of how to vote, or were not able to mail in their absentee ballot in time.

Fig. 11.4. Voter Turnout and Millennials
Source: Derived with data collected from authors' conducted surveys.

42 percent in 2018 (Cilluffo and Fry 2019). Improvements in Millennial voter participation are also evident in our survey data. According to our 2016 survey, fewer Millennials self-reported as voting in the presidential election than older adults: 68 percent versus 81 percent.[2] Voter turnout among Millennials increased in 2020, according to our data: 76 percent of Millennials surveyed said they voted as did 85 percent of older adults. Overall, Millennials seem to have overcome many of these challenges, which is what we expect to see as generations grow older. Self-reported voter turnout improved for all Millennial racial and ethnic subgroups, as shown in figure 11.4.

What motivates Millennials to vote? Our 2020 survey asked respondents: *In your opinion, which of the following brings about the most political change?* Only 53 percent of Millennials, compared to 64 percent of older adults, selected "voting." We asked this question in a previous survey, and results were similar—56 percent of Millennials and 62 percent of older adults identified voting as bringing about the most political change. This implies that attitudes about the efficacy of voting as a medium of political change have not evolved. What did change was the political environment. The election of 2020 was highly divisive. As a result, more independents chose sides (either Republican or Democrat), and voter turnout set record highs. Our survey results also indicate that political integrity was at stake, and this may have motivated political participation from Millennials and older adults alike. Responses to a survey question asking about the importance of various reasons behind presidential choice reveal that trust was most important in 2020 (74% of Millennials and older adults said this was "very important") while opposition voting was central to motivations in 2016 (76% of Millennials and 80% of older adults said this was "very important"). These results reflect the polarizing nature of the 2020 elections and speak to a contest that was largely a referendum on the Donald Trump presidency.

Equally illuminating of political participation are reasons for not voting. Among those who reported not voting in the 2016 election, a sizeable portion of Millennials and older adults said the reason they did not vote was because they could not support any of the presidential candidates (31% and 40%, respectively). The second most frequently cited reason for not voting among Millennials was lack of efficacy: 18 percent of Millennials said they felt their vote would not matter to the outcome of the election, compared to only 11 percent of older adults feeling the same way. This feeling dropped in 2020 with only 12 percent of Millennials saying they did not feel like their vote would matter.

Millennials who did not vote in the 2020 presidential election more frequently cited not being able to make it to polls (18%); yet, another substantial portion of Millennial nonvoters said they did not have the required documents (17%), were not sure of how to vote (12%), or were not able to mail in their absentee ballot in time (12%). This indicates that in 2020, reasons for not voting among Millennials had less to do with a lack of desire to vote and more to do with voting barriers. Four-in-ten Millennials encountered some type of process obstacle to voting in 2020; similar challenges were faced by 3-in-10 older adults.

Negative personal experiences with the voting process were coupled with prevailing concerns about voter fraud: 47 percent of Millennials and 41 percent older adults said they agreed that there was voter fraud in the 2020 election, and about 19 percent of both groups said they did not recognize Joe Biden as the winner of the 2020 presidential election. These concerns about voter fraud and voting process obstacles are not unique to the 2020 election but were certainly more pronounced. Our survey data is limited in the inferences that can be made about the effects of calling into question the integrity of the electoral system on political engagement and participation. However, it is clear that Millennials were not immune to such narratives. Future research should carefully consider these questions.

Millennials have come a long way from the political slackers they were purported to be early in their political lives. Although more of a stereotype than based in fact, Millennials were less likely to engage with "duty-based" forms of participation, like voting (Dalton 2016). And while their turnout rate still slightly lags behind older adults, their formal participation in the political system has increased from the 2016 election to the 2020 election. Furthermore, our survey data indicates they *feel* slightly more engaged than older adults. Looking to the future, Millennials express a desire for greater ease in voting and fewer obstacles to political participation. They also continue to be focused on political representation and are looking for politicians and parties that better represent their interests. Despite their increased engagement, an undercurrent of dissatisfaction with the political system remains among some Millennials. We unpack this in the next section.

Desire for Political Change

When asked about opinion on changes to the political system, most Millennials express a desire for change. In 2016, 52 percent of Millennial respondents said they wanted "gradual change" to the system while 28 percent expressed a desire for "revolutionary change." Older adults were similar: 49 percent said they want "gradual change" while 33 percent said "revolutionary change" was needed. In 2020, Millennials and older adults exhibited continued and rather equal desire for change—46 percent of Millennials and 44 percent of older adults say gradual change is needed. While differences in attitudes about political change between Millennials and older adults are evident when looking at age cohorts as a whole, examination of race and ethnic subgroups reveals that Millennials in 2016 looked most similar not to other Millennials but to older adults of their race or ethnicity.

In 2016, 42 percent of Millennial Blacks and 43 percent of older adult Blacks said "I think our political system needs revolutionary change." The same sentiment was expressed by 30 percent of Millennial whites and 35 percent of older adult whites. Among Latinos, 24 percent of both Millennial and older adult groups expressed a need for

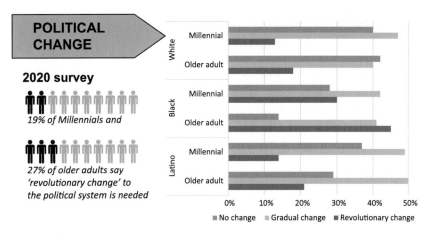

Fig. 11.5. Political Change and Millennials
Source: Derived with data collected from authors' conducted surveys.

revolutionary change. However, more divergence occurred in 2020 among Millennial and older adult subgroups. As shown in figure 11.5, 30 percent of Millennial Blacks and 45 percent of older adult Blacks said the same in 2020. Among whites and Latinos, fewer Millennials cited a desire for revolutionary change. This sentiment prevailed among 13 percent of Millennial whites and 14 percent of Millennial Latinos, compared to 18 percent and 21 percent of white and Latino older adults, respectively.

Given the timing of the surveys in the weeks after the presidential election, it is difficult to determine the reference point for respondents in answering questions about political change. Was the evaluation of political change made of the system now (postelection) or the system in the past (preelection)? The survey question asked in 2020 gave a more specific evaluation frame—*How much change do you think has happened to the political system in the past four years?* Millennials were split in their evaluation of the past four years: 46 percent cited positive change while another 46 percent identified negative change. Eight percent said there was "no change" at all. However, the highest percentage of Millennials—34 percent—said there was "a great deal of negative change," compared to 22 percent of Millennials that cited "a great deal of positive change." A total of 70 percent of older adults said that there was positive change over the past four years: 26 percent "a great deal," 25 percent "some," and 19 percent "a little." Only 15 percent of older adults said there was "a great deal of negative change" in the past four years.[3]

POLITICAL SYSTEM EVALUATION

Millennial Evaluation of Change in Past 4 Years

In 2020, Black Millennials said:

20%
there has been 'a great deal of negative change'

28%
'the system is rigged against people like me'

	White	Black	Latino
A great deal of positive change	30%	23%	25%
Some positive change	31%	16%	27%
A little positive change	17%	19%	21%
A great deal of negative change	11%	20%	15%
Some negative change	3%	7%	7%
A little negative change	3%	3%	0%
No change	5%	12%	5%

Fig. 11.6. Political System and Millennials
Source: Derived with data collected from authors' conducted surveys.

As we have seen throughout this chapter, Millennials are not a monolithic group. Their evaluation of the political system displays this diversity. As shown in figure 11.6, among Millennials, more whites cite positive change: 30 percent of Millennial whites say there has been "a great deal of positive change" in the past four years, compared to 23 percent and 25 percent of Millennial Blacks and Latinos, respectively. Black Millennials exhibit the most dissatisfaction with 20 percent saying there has been "a great deal of negative change," compared to 11 percent of white Millennials and 15 percent of Latino Millennials. Another 12 percent of Black Millennials say there has been "no change," compared to only 5 percent of white and Latino Millennials.

Negative sentiment about the political system among Black Millennials is further evidenced in responses to the following question: *How much do you agree with this statement? Our system is rigged against people like me.* Twenty-eight percent of Black Millennials say they "strongly agree" with this statement while another 39 percent say they "somewhat agree." In comparison, only 25 percent of Latino and white Millennials say they "strongly agree" the system is rigged against them. Underscoring that this sentiment is particularly acute among young Blacks are the responses from older adult Blacks: 17 percent of older adult Blacks "strongly agree" the system is rigged against them while 48 percent of this subgroup say they "somewhat agree."

Feeling that the system is rigged against them is associated with poorer political engagement among Black Millennials. Among Black Millennials who say they "strongly agree" the system is rigged against them, 33 percent did not vote in 2020 and 36 percent say they do not feel engaged in the political system. Voting rates were equally low among Latino Millennials who feel the system is rigged against them, but not among white Millennials. In the same vein, 43 percent of Black Millennials who cited a need for "revolutionary change" to the political system did not vote in 2020. This implies that negative experiences and evaluations about the political system are associated with depressed political participation among minority Millennials. On the other hand, can positive evaluations boost participation and engagement among Millennials, minority Millennials in particular?

Circling back to the question of change in the past four years, we find associations between attitudes about change and voting in the 2020 election. As shown in figure 11.7, among Millennials who said they voted in 2020, the majority evaluated the past four years positively: 28 percent cited "a great deal of positive change" in the past four years, 27 percent said there was a "some positive change," another 18 percent said there was "a little positive change." Among older adults who voted in 2020, the largest group—35 percent—said there was "a great deal of negative change" in the past four years; only 22 percent of older adults who voted said there was a "great deal of positive change." Again examining race and ethnic minority subgroups of Millennials, we find that 32 percent of white Millennials, 26 percent of Black Millennials, and 26 percent of Latino Millennials who voted in 2020 said there was "a great deal of positive change" over the last four years. In contrast, 29 percent of white older adults, 12 percent of Black older adults, and 22 percent of Latino older adults said the same. Rather, higher percentages of older adults who voted in 2020 said there has been "a great deal of negative change": 30 percent of white older adults, 49 percent of Black older adults, and 29 percent of Latino older adults. Only 11 percent and 12 percent of white and Latino Millennial voters, respectively, said the same while 23 percent of Black Millennial voters evaluated the past four years as having "a great deal of negative change."

It is clear that a desire for political change has not substantially waned among Millennials over the past four years. However, Millennials look more like the older adults of their respective race and ethnic subgroups than they do to members of their generational cohort. In other words, it appears that when it comes to a desire for change, race and ethnic group identity may have a stronger impact than the Millennial generation identity. It remains to be seen how much of this effect is durable and how much is cyclical. It may be that changing political winds and the (in)effectiveness of proposed and enacted policies could

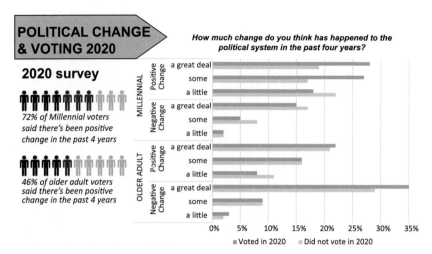

Fig. 11.7. Political Change and Millennials
Source: Derived with data collected from authors' conducted surveys.

impact the desire for and degree of change, especially among race and ethnic subgroups who often feel left out of the political process.

Concluding Thoughts on Millennials—Democratically Motivated or Disenchanted?

The years 2016–20 were eventful for the country at-large, but certainly for the Millennial generation more specifically. As the largest adult cohort, this generation is poised to take over the political, economic, and social levers of the country. What do their (changing) political attitudes and their interest in and engagement with politics say about what we may expect from their leadership in years to come? We know that the Millennial generation shares a unique identity or generational persona that is important for understanding their viewpoints. This identity is rooted in shared experiences that are based on broad cultural shifts resulting from social, economic, and political events that occurred during this group's impressionable years. These include the rapid spread of technology, the rapid pace of globalization, and the racial and ethnic diversity present within their own cohort. In addition, Millennials experienced the attacks of September 11, 2001 and the ensuing war on terrorism, extreme levels of partisanship and gridlock within governing institutions, and the Great Recession. All of these factors have had an indelible influence on their perspectives. However, we also know that Millennials are not monolithic, and while their attitudes are affected by a broad set of formative factors and experiences, they are also influenced by other group identities, as well as aging. While it is too early to evaluate with any certainty how the Millennial identity will ultimately interact with other identities, and how life cycle effects will play out, two snapshots in time (2016 and 2020) provide us with insights.

We employed two data sets that surveyed a nationally representative sample of Millennials following the presidential elections of 2016 and 2020 about their political attitudes and habits of political participation. While our surveys do not involve the same panel of respondents, and thus cannot yield causal inferences, they do offer a snapshot of political beliefs and behaviors that provide us with some first-of-its-kind insights into attitudinal preferences and changes to those preferences for this cohort. In 2016, Millennials were still recovering from the disproportionate effects they encountered as a result of the Great Recession. Furthermore, they were figuring out how to deal with the disappointment of their preferred presidential candidate, Bernie Sanders, being defeated in the Democratic Party primary race. In addition, they faced a looming choice in the presidential general election—turning out to vote for Hillary Clinton, the person responsible for defeating Sanders, or supporting a political neophyte, Donald Trump, who promised to disrupt the political system. The choices and what they represented with respect to Millennial political behavior provided an important backdrop for our study. Moving forward to 2020, Millennials faced a new set of issues. In addition to living through four years of a Trump presidency, they were also now dealing with the effects of another economic hardship brought on by the COVID-19 pandemic, as well as a social reckoning with racism and police brutality. These were likely important factors in the changes we observed in our 2020 survey.

First, our survey results show that Millennials have remained fairly liberal across the four-year time span surveyed. In 2016, all racial and ethnic subgroups of Millennials were more liberal than older adults of similar subgroups. However, we observed some change in this among white Millennials. In 2020, the percentages of liberal and conservative Millennials, respectively, were similar in percentages to their older adult counterparts. In 2020, Black and Latino Millennials remained more liberal than their older adult counterparts.

Our survey findings also indicated that a plurality of Millennials identify with the Democratic Party. This was true for both 2016 and 2020. However, we did observe some changes in party affiliation among Millennial subgroups in 2020. About a quarter of white Millennials affiliated with the Democratic Party in 2016, but in 2020, this number had risen to just over half. In contrast, there was a decline in Democratic Party affiliation among Black (26%) and Latino (19%) Millennials. Our survey questions do not allow us to specifically pinpoint the reasons behind changes in party affiliation among Millennial subgroups. However, we should note that a number of Black and Latino Millennials removed their party affiliation altogether, opting instead to identify as political independents. And even though there was some increase in Republican Party affiliation among minority Millennials, these numbers remain relatively small. Still, it is of note that during the period that encompasses the Trump presidency, we observed a decline in Democratic Party affiliation among its most traditionally ardent party supporters. More analysis and trend data are needed to better tease out these effects among young minority Millennials, but it is a cautionary note for the Democratic Party that Millennials may be more malleable in their party allegiances.

Despite the changes we see in Millennial party affiliation, this cohort largely came out in support of Joe Biden in the 2020 presidential election. Seven-in-ten white and Black Millennials and more than five-in-ten Latino Millennials said they voted for Joe Biden in 2020. There was an increase in support for Joe Biden among white Millennials (69%), compared to their support for Hillary Clinton (47%) in 2016. Conversely, we observed a drop in support for Biden, compared to Clinton, among Black (87% versus 71%) and Latino (64% versus. 53%) Millennials. These numbers, taken along with changes in party affiliation, warrant further scrutiny. While party affiliation and vote choice do not always align (especially for Millennials—a cohort less prone to affiliate with a political party), Republican (Trump) gains among Black and Latinos were the subject of numerous media headlines in 2020 election postmortems. Our nonprobability survey of self-reported voting, as well as the scope of our questions, limits our ability to draw conclusions about the reasons for these changes. However, we do know that some racial and ethnic minorities (including Millennials) were drawn to Donald Trump's more stringent immigration policies and his tough stance against the spread of communism (Nagesh 2020; al-Gharbi 2020). While much of his campaign rhetoric distorted the truth about these and other issues, his positions resonated with segments of the electorate that warrant further examination. It will also be important to track whether some Millennials were drawn to the candidacy of Donald Trump due to durable changes in their ideology or party affiliation, or if it had more to do with the uniqueness of the candidate.

Party affiliation and vote choice are likely reflections of how individuals feel about the broader political climate, specifically how well they engage with the political system and their desire for political change. When we queried Millennials in 2015 about whether they felt engaged with the political system, we were surprised that they expressed engagement at similar levels as older adults (about one-third of respondents). While the percentage is fairly low, it is in line with the general population. Therefore, stereotypes painting Millennials as less engaged were not accurate. In 2020, we asked again about feelings of engagement. There was a marked increase, in fact a doubling among both Millennials and older adults in terms of feeling engaged with the political system. In 2020, most frequently Millennials note that being more involved in the political system is dependent on having better political representation and politicians who are trustworthy, honest, and accountable. It is likely that Donald Trump and his brand of politics contributed to both increased levels of political engagement among Millennials (as evidenced by their increased voter turnout in 2018 and 2020) and sentiments about factors that could keep them engaged.

Millennials express a strong desire for political change. This general sentiment has not changed significantly during the four-year span between our surveys. However, there is some difference in the type or rate of change they prefer. Over 4-in-10 Millennials express a preference for gradual or incremental change to the political system, while two-in-ten prefer rapid or revolutionary change. What is interesting is that in 2016, preferences for revolutionary political change among Millennials were higher and more in line with older adults in their respective racial and ethnic subgroups. In 2020, there was a drop in desire for revolutionary change among all Millennial subgroups. Despite the decrease in support for revolutionary change, about a third of Black Millennials still expressed a preference for this type of action. The limitations of our survey do not allow us to conclude with any certainty why fewer Millennials now prefer revolutionary change compared to 2016. However, we can speculate that the outcome of the 2020 presidential election may have contributed to our findings. Millennials, having been witness to what the chaotic presidency of Donald Trump entailed, may have concluded that an incremental approach is the best way to bring about political change. This, of course, does not preclude specific areas where Millennials prefer more rapid or revolutionary political change than others. One example may be that many young Black people want to see more rapid and drastic action taken with respect to police brutality, while they may not express the same urgency for change in other policy areas. Future work should examine in more detail how Millennials think about political change in specific policy domains.

In a question related to political change, we probed our survey respondents about whether they felt the system was rigged against people like them. Not surprisingly, we found that about 1-in-3 Black Millennials strongly agree that this is the case. This compares to about a quarter of white and Latino Millennials who also strongly agree with this sentiment. We also found that Black Millennials who feel that the system is rigged against them were less likely to be politically engaged. A third of Black Millennials who strongly agreed that the system is rigged against them did not vote in the 2020 election. A similar percentage of Black Millennials who expressed a need for revolutionary changes in the political system also did not vote in the 2020 election. These findings raise questions about how Millennials, particularly Black Millennials, will view the state of American democracy in a post-Trump era. For example, it remains to be seen how Millennials respond to Republican-sponsored bills in 43 states to increase voter restrictions. Will they largely view these bills as necessary to protect election integrity or as further infringements upon the right of every citizen to vote? The diverse makeup of the Millennial generation could serve as an important bellwether for how political parties and political institutions respond to the preferences and demands of a rapidly changing society.

There is much left to explore regarding the political attitudes and levels of engagement among the Millennial generation. This chapter, which relies upon the results of two surveys conducted at the bookends of the Trump presidency, serves as a first cut in presenting changes that have occurred as this cohort ages. However, we are careful not to draw definitive inferences because our survey does not include a panel of respondents who were queried across time. Rather, our findings offer snapshots of the Millennial generation that can serve as important baselines for further analysis. A crucial question left to answer (among many) is whether the 2020 election was unique in the level of turnout and engagement we saw from the Millennial generation. Will the next presidential election match this? Our survey does not provide enough information to answer this question. However, we know that Millennial voter turnout in 2022 was consistent with mid-term election turnout in 2018—about 38% (U.S. Census Bureau 2018, 2020). This question is best addressed by having more data points across election years in order to make substantive comparisons.

At the beginning of this chapter, we posed the question: Are Millennials politically motivated or disenchanted? A clear answer to this question was not evident in 2016 and continues to be nuanced in 2020. In both 2016 and 2020, Millennials reported a distrust in political institutions, a desire for political change, and a sense that the system was rigged against them. While these sentiments varied across the two time spans and among Millennial subgroups, there is a level of disenchantment that may either be improved or exacerbated, depending on how this cohort comes out on the other side of pandemic and whether issues of racial injustice are addressed in any meaningful way. On the other hand, there is optimism as a result of Millennial voter turnout levels in 2018 and 2020. Were high turnout rates a result of general and persistent engagement with the political system or were Millennials largely motivated by the election (and potential reelection) of Donald Trump? Again, only time will tell how the motivated/disenchanted debate will ultimately play out, and how the Millennial generation identity will further interact with group identities and life cycle effects to help settle this debate.

NOTES

1. This question was not asked in the 2016 election.
2. The higher rate of self-reported voting may indicate bias in our survey data toward individuals who are more civic minded.
3. This question was not asked in the 2016 survey.

REFERENCES

al-Gharbi, M. 2020. "White Men Swung to Biden. Trump Made Gains with Black and Latino Voters. Why?" *Guardian*, November 14. https://www.theguardian.com/commentisfree/2020/nov/14/joe-biden-trump-black-latino-republicans

Andrews, T. M. 2016. "It's Official: Millennials Have Surpassed Baby Boomers to Become America's Largest Living Generation." *Washington Post*, April 26. https://

www.washingtonpost.com/news/morning-mix/wp/2016/04/26/its-official-mille nnials-have-surpassed-baby-boomers-to-become-americas-largest-living-gener ation/?noredirect=on&utm_term=.7d719c78266e

Baker, R., J. M. Brick, N. A. Bates, M. Battaglia, M. P. Couper, J. A. Dever, K. J. Gile, and R. Tourangeau. 2013. "Summary Report of the AAPOR Task Force on Non-Probability Sampling." *Journal of Survey Statistics and Methodology* 1 (2): 90–143. https://doi.org/10.1093/jssam/smt008

Battaglia, M. 2008. "Nonprobability Sampling." In *Encyclopedia of Survey Research Methods*, edited by P. J. Lavrakas, 524–37. Thousand Oaks, CA: Sage.

Campbell, A., P. E. Converse, W. E. Miller, and D. Stokes. 1960. *The American Voter*. New York: Wiley.

Campbell, W. K., S. M. Campbell, L. W. Siedor, and J. M. Twenge. 2015. "Generational Differences Are Real and Useful." *Industrial and Organizational Psychology* 8 (3): 324–31. https://doi.org/10.1017/iop.2015.43

Center for Information and Research on Civic Learning and Engagement (CIRCLE). 2018. *Election Night 2018: Historically High Youth Turnout, Support for Democrats*. November 7. https://circle.tufts.edu/latest-research/election-night-2018-historic ally-high-youth-turnout-support-democrats

Center for Information and Research on Civic Learning and Engagement (CIRCLE). 2020. *2016 Election Center*. October 17. https://circle.tufts.edu/2016-election-ce nter

Cilluffo, A., and W. Fry. 2019. "Gen Z, Millennials, and Gen X Outvoted Older Generations in 2018 Midterms." Pew Research Center, May 29. https://www.pewrese arch.org/fact-tank/2019/05/29/gen-z-millennials-and-gen-x-outvoted-older-gen erations-in-2018-midterms/

Collins, S. 2020. "Why the Covid-19 Economy Is Particularly Devastating to Millennials, in 14 Charts." *Vox*, May 5. https://www.vox.com/2020/5/5/21222759/covid -19-recession-millennials-coronavirus-economic-impact-charts

Cramer, R., F. R. Addo, C. Campbell, J. Choi, B. J. Cohen, C. Cohen, W. R. Emmons, M. Fowler, T. Garon, C. Hancock, L. Hipple, J. Hodgson, A. H. Kent, S. McKernan, V. E. Medenica, G. Melford, B. Miller, I. Rademacher, C. Ratcliffe, L. R. Ricketts, T. Shanks, W. Whistle, and Y. Zhang. 2019. *The Emerging Millennial Wealth Gap*. New America, October. https://d1y8sb8igg2f8e.cloudfront.net/docu ments/The_Emerging_Millennial_Wealth_Gap_4y0UuVQ.pdf

Dalton, R. J. 2016. *The Good Citizen*. 2nd ed. Los Angeles: CQ Press.

Dimock, M. 2019. *Defining Generations: Where Millennials End and Generation Z Begins*. Pew Research Center Fact Tank, January 17. https:// www.pewresearch.org/fact-tank/2019/01/17/where-millennials-end-and-generation-z-begins/

Edsall, T. B. 2018. "The Deepening 'Racialization' of American Politics." *New York Times*, February 27. https://www.nytimes.com/2019/02/27/opinion/trump-oba ma-race.html

Fisher, D. R., and S. M. Rouse. 2022. "Intersectionality within the Racial Justice Movement in the Summer of 2020." *Proceedings of the National Academy of Sciences* 119 (30).

Frazee, G. 2020. "Millennials Report More Stress Than Older Americans during Pan-

demic." *PBS News Hour*, August 4. https://www.pbs.org/newshour/health/millen
nials-report-more-stress-than-older-americans-during-pandemic

Frey, W. H. 2018. *The Millennial Generation: A Demographic Bridge to America's Diverse Future*. Brookings Institution, January 18. https://www.brookings.edu/research/millennials/

Fry, R. 2018. *Millennials Approach Baby Boomers as America's Largest Generation in the Electorate*. Pew Research Center, April 3. https://www.pewresearch.org/fact-ta
nk/2018/04/03/millennials-approach-baby-boomers-as-largest-generation-in
-u-s-electorate/

Fry, R. 2020. *Millennials Overtake Baby Boomers as America's Largest Generation*. Pew Research Center, April 28. https://www.pewresearch.org/short-reads/2020/04/28
/millennials-overtake-baby-boomers-as-americas-largest-generation/

Galston, W. A., and C. Hendrickson. 2016. *How Millennials Voted This Election*. Brookings Institute, November 21. https://www.brookings.edu/blog/fixgov/2016/11/21
/how-millennials-voted/

Garcia-Rios, S., F. Pedraza, and B. Wilcox-Archuleta. 2019. "Direct and Indirect Xenophobic Attacks: Unpacking Portfolios of Identity." *Political Behavior* 41:633–56.

Holbein, J. B., and D. S. Hillygus. 2020. *Making Young Voters: Converting Civic Attitudes into Civic Action*. Cambridge: Cambridge University Press.

Kennedy, C., A. Mercer, S. Keeter, N. Hatley, K. McGeeney, and A. Gimenez. 2016. *Evaluating Online Nonprobability*. Pew Research Center, May 2. https://www.pew
research.org/methods/2016/05/02/evaluating-online-nonprobability-surveys/

Kent, A. H. 2020. *Three Reasons Millennials May Face Devastating Setback from COVID-19*. Federal Reserve Bank of St. Louis, May 21. https://www.stlouisfed.org/on-the
-economy/2020/may/three-reasons-millennials-may-face-devastating-setback
-covid19

Lopez, M. H., L. Rainie, and A. Budiman. 2020. *Financial and Health Impacts of COVID-19 Vary Widely by Race and Ethnicity*. Pew Research Center, May 5. https://
www.pewresearch.org/fact-tank/2020/05/05/financial-and-health-impacts-of-co
vid-19-vary-widely-by-race-and-ethnicity/

Maniam, S., and S. Smith. 2017. *A Wider Partisan and Ideological Gap between Younger, Older Generations*. Pew Research Center, March 20. https://www.pewresearch
.org/fact-tank/2017/03/20/a-wider-partisan-and-ideological-gap-between-young
er-older-generations/

Molyneux, G., and R. Teixeira. 2010. *The Generation Gap on Government: Why and How the Millennial Generation Is the Most Pro-Government Generation and What This Means for Our Future*. Center for American Progress, July 25. https://www.am
ericanprogress.org/article/the-generation-gap-on-government/

Nagesh, A. 2020. "US Elections 2020: Why Trump Gained Support among Minorities." *BBC News*, November 22. https://www.bbc.com/news/world-us-canada-549
72389

Parker, K., N. Graf, and R. Igielnik. 2019. *Generation Z Looks a Lot Like Millennials on Key Social and Political Issues*. Pew Research Center, January 17. https://www.pe
wresearch.org/social-trends/2019/01/17/generation-z-looks-a-lot-like-millennia
ls-on-key-social-and-political-issues/

Parker, S. 2022. "Young, Black Americans are Turning to the GOP—which Needs Them to Survive." *New York Post,* November 24. https://nypost.com/2022/11/24/young-black-americans-are-turning-to-the-gop-which-needs-them-to-survive/

Pew Research Center. 2015. *A Different Look at Generations and Partisanship.* April 30. http://www.people-press.org/2015/04/30/a-different-look-at-generations-and-partisanship/

Pew Research Center. 2018. *The Generation Gap in American Politics.* March 1. https://www.pewresearch.org/politics/2018/03/01/the-generation-gap-in-american-politics/

Pew Research Center. 2019. *Trust in Government by Generation.* April 10. https://www.pewresearch.org/politics/chart/trust-in-government-by-generation/

Pew Research Center. 2020. *Faith among Black Americans Dataset.* https://www.pewresearch.org/religion/dataset/faith-among-black-americans/

Pew Research Center. 2022. *Public Trust in Government: 1958–2022.* June 6. https://www.pewresearch.org/politics/2022/06/06/public-trust-in-government-1958-2022/

Roosevelt Institute. 2013. *Government by and for Millennial America.* http://rooseveltinstitute.or/government-by-and-millennial-america-3/

Ross, A. D., and S. M. Rouse. 2015. "Economic Uncertainty, Job Threat, and the Resiliency of the Millennial Generation's Attitudes toward Immigration." *Social Science Quarterly* 96 (5): 1363–79. https://doi.org/10.1111/ssqu.12168

Ross, A. D., S. M. Rouse, and W. Mobley. 2019. "Polarization of Climate Change Beliefs: The Role of the Millennial Generation Identity." *Social Science Quarterly* 100 (7): 2625–40. https://doi.org/10.1111/ssqu.12640

Ross, A. D., and S. M. Rouse. 2020. "(Young) Generations as Social Identities: The Role of Latino*Millennial/Generation Z in Shaping Attitudes about Climate Change." *Political Behavior* 44:1105–24.

Rouse, S. M., J. McDonald, R. N. Engstrom, M. J. Hanmer, R. Gonzàlez, S. Lay, and D. Miranda. 2022. *Citizens of the World: Political Engagement and Policy Attitudes of Millennials across the Globe.* New York: Oxford University Press.

Rouse, S. M., and A. D. Ross. 2018. *The Politics of Millennials: Political Beliefs and Policy Preferences of America's Most Diverse Generation.* Ann Arbor: University of Michigan Press.

Sewell, D. 2020. "Millennials and Boomers: Pandemic Pain, by the Generation." *Washington Post,* July 13. https://www.washingtonpost.com/lifestyle/food/millennials-and-boomers-pandemic-pain-by-the-generation/2020/07/13/3e6b0df2-c4d7-11ea-a825-8722004e4150_story.html

Tam Cho, W. K., J. G. Gimpel, and T. Wu. 2006. "Clarifying the Role of SES in Political Participation: Policy Threat and Arab American Mobilization." *Journal of Politics* 68 (4): 977–91.

Teixeria, R., W. H. Frey, and R. Griffin 2015. *State of Change: The Demographic Evolution of the American Electorate, 1974–2060.* Center for American Progress, February 24. https://www.americanprogress.org/issues/democracy/reports/2015/02/24/107261/states-of-change/

U.S. Census Bureau. 2018. November. Current Population Survey.

U.S. Census Bureau. 2022. November. Current Population Survey.

Verba, S., and N. H. Nie. 1972. *Participation in America: Political Democracy and Social Equality*. New York: Harper & Row.

Verba, S., K. Schlozman, and H. Brady. 1995. *Voice and Equality: Civic Voluntarism in American Politics*. Cambridge: Harvard University Press.

Wolfinger, R., and S. J. Rosenstone. 1980. *Who Votes?* New Haven: Yale University Press.

12 | Generational Shifts Change Politics in Florida

Susan A. MacManus and Anthony A. Cilluffo

Older people are a crucial voting bloc in Florida, a haven for retirees. . . . In Florida, Mr. Trump won by 17 points among voters 65 and older in the 2016 election. But a recent *New York Times*/Siena College poll of likely voters in Florida showed a tight contest this time around within that age group.
—Patricia Mazzei and Thomas Kaplan,
New York Times, October 13, 2020

A generation more familiar with TikTok, Instagram and Xbox has the potential to make the difference in Florida's toss-up presidential race between two 70-somethings.
—Mary Ellen Klas, *Miami Herald*, October 26, 2020

Journalists from two well-respected newspapers based their 2020 election projections (above) on *age*: one on Florida's retirees, the other on the state's growing younger generations. Certainly, Florida has long been known (and still is) as a retiree haven and a state where older voters, with their traditionally higher turnout rates, have dominated politics.

But, as we show in this chapter, that description of the Sunshine State is far too simplistic. Florida's population and voter demographics have changed significantly, shifting voter attitudes and behavior across generations. As evidence, we offer the results of the 2016 presidential election, the 2018 governor's race, and the 2020 presidential contest, revealing the complexities of generational-focused campaign approaches and consequent turnout rate differentials. Recent elections show that it is nearly impossible to win the state while ignoring differences between and *within* generations.

At first glance, generational change may appear to threaten Florida's status as a swing state with younger generations increasing in number and impact. However, the Baby Boomer generation will continue to influence campaigns and elections; it's a phenomenon that may persist longer in Florida than many other states due to recent projections of higher retiree in-migration.

Rapid Population Growth Yields a More Diverse State

Florida's rapid population growth in recent years has changed its electorate to a remarkable degree. Much of the growth has been driven at different points in time by large numbers of people migrating from other parts of the country, notably the Northeast and Midwest (retirees), other southern states (younger people), and countries in Latin America (Latinos), the Caribbean (Blacks), and Asia. It is important to note, however, that broad labels (Black, Hispanic, Asian) mask country-of-origin-based cultural and political diversity,[1] especially in Florida.

Between 2000 and 2019, the white (non-Hispanic) population sharply declined from 64 percent to 53 percent, while nonwhite populations grew, notably Hispanics from 17 percent to 26 percent (see fig. 12.1). Projections are that by 2030, Hispanics will make up 30 percent of Florida's population, and by 2040, Florida will be a majority non-white state.

Over time Florida has evolved from a one-party state (Democratic) into one of the nation's most partisan-competitive swing states. In the five statewide elections prior to 2020 (two presidential, three gubernatorial), the winner was decided by a mere 1 percent (0.5% in the 2018 governor's race). Heading into the 2020 election, Democrats were 37 percent of all registered voters and Republicans 36 percent—the closest they have ever been. The other 27 percent were registered as No Party Affiliation (NPA) or with a minor party. But these figures mask important generational differences that are critical to understanding Florida's changing politics.

Generations in Florida

The generational approach to studying campaigns has grown in popularity, largely as a result of the increasingly sharper dividing lines

Florida Resident Population by Race and Ethnicity

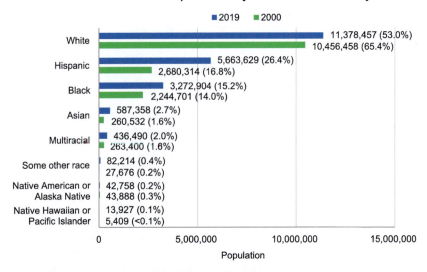

Fig. 12.1. Racial and Ethnic Diversity in Florida. (*Note:* All categories except Hispanic are non-Hispanic; Hispanics are of any race.)
Source: Data for 2000 from U.S. Census Bureau, "Hispanic or Latino Origin by Race," Table P007, 2000 Decennial Census Summary File 3; data for 2019 from U.S. Census Bureau, "Hispanic or Latino Origin by Race," Table B03002, 2019 1-year ACS file.

between younger and older generations.[2] Our definition of *generation* is the same as that of the Pew Research Center (Dimock 2019), which bases generational classification on birth years; it includes the emerging Gen Z.

In 2020, for the first time, Florida's three youngest generations—Gen X, Millennial, and Gen Z—together comprised more than half (55%) of Florida's registered voters[3] (see fig. 12.2). Among the three older generations, registration drop-off was greatest among those from the Silent and Greatest generations (all ages 75 or older) due to higher mortality rates. The fall-off was lower among Baby Boomers, who remain the largest generation in the Florida electorate. While the *number* of Baby Boomers registered to vote increased slightly between 2015 and 2020, their *share* of the electorate fell for the first time in decades, but less sharply than nationally. A spurt of Baby Boomer in-migration from other states helped offset the normal mortality rate seen in the Boomer population nationally (Fry 2020).

COVID-19 sparked higher in-migration of Baby Boomer retirees from other states, most notably New York. This may mean that Florida's

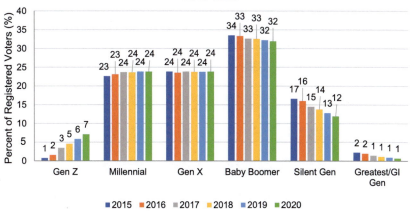

Fig. 12.2. Gen Z Is Increasing as a Share of Florida's Registered Voters, while Silent and Greatest Generation Are Falling. (*Note:* See text and table 12.1 for generation age definitions.)
Source: Authors' analysis of Florida Division of Elections, Florida Voter Registration System: July 2015, August 2016, August 2017, August 2018, September 2019, June 2020.

Baby Boomer generation will dominate the state's politics a little longer than in other states, although the generation's political leanings may change. At the same time, COVID-19 also attracted more young people (Millennials) to Florida because of its jobs, recreational amenities, and cheaper housing (Riccardi and Schneider 2021). However, there is some doubt about whether the young in-migrants' moves will be as permanent as those of newly arrived Baby Boomers.

Racial and Ethnic Diversity of Florida's Voters by Generation

In Florida, racial and ethnic diversity is significantly higher among the three youngest generations of registrants (see fig. 12.3). A majority of Gen Zers and a near-majority of Millennials are nonwhite as a result of the in-migration of Latinos, people from the Caribbean, and Asians. These immigrants are younger, with higher birth rates than non-Hispanic whites. In sharp contrast, non-Hispanic whites make up more than three-quarters of the Greatest and Silent generations' registrants. From a political perspective, it is generally assumed that growing up with people from more diverse backgrounds (racial, eth-

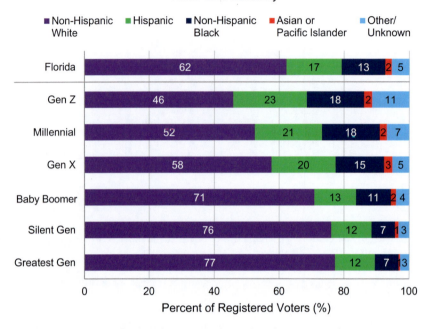

Fig. 12.3. A Majority of Florida's Gen Z Registered Voters Are Nonwhite. (*Note:* See text and table 12.1 for generation age definitions. "Other/Unknown" includes American Indian or Alaskan Native, other races, multiracial, and unknown.) *Source:* Authors' analysis of Florida Division of Elections, Florida Voter Registration System, June 2020.

nic, religious, sexual preference, family structure, socioeconomic, political) has made younger generations more socially liberal than older generations.

Increased diversity has not been limited to younger generations. The share of nonwhite registered voters has increased among *all* generations since 2015 (see fig. 12.4). Change has been fastest among the oldest and youngest generations. Growth in the proportion of Hispanic and other racial group registrants has outpaced that of Blacks. In fact, the Black *share* of registrants *fell* for every generation except the Greatest generation.

In-migration and generational replacement have created a more racially and ethnically diverse electorate. Many of these changes are happening nationally and in some other states, but Florida stands out

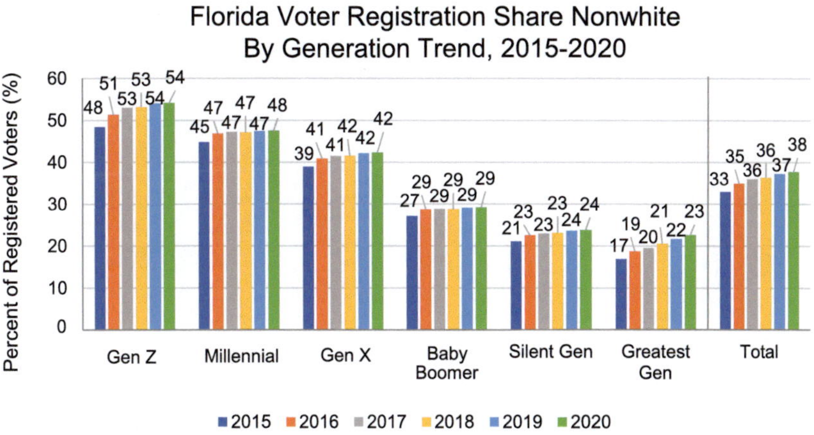

Florida Voter Registration Share Nonwhite By Generation Trend, 2015-2020

Fig. 12.4. Share of Nonwhite Registrants Has Increased for Every Generation Since 2015. (*Note:* See text and table 12.1 for generation age definitions.)
Source: Authors' analysis of Florida Division of Elections, Florida Voter Registration System: July 2015, August 2016, August 2017, August 2018, September 2019, June 2020.

for the speed of the transformation. These changes predictably have led to differences in party preference across generations.

Party Preferences Differ by Generation

"Most people's basic outlooks and orientations are set fairly early on in life . . . generations carry with them the imprint of early political experiences," concluded a major analysis of nearly two decades of Pew Research Center's political polling (DeSilver 2014). The study found that voters who came of age during the Bill Clinton, George W. Bush, and Barack Obama presidencies tended to vote more Democratic, while voters who came of age during the Gerald Ford, Jimmy Carter, Ronald Reagan, and George H. W. Bush presidencies tended to vote more Republican (Pew Research Center 2011). More recently, there has been a rise in voters registering as independents nationally and in Florida, particularly among young voters.

As recently as 1994, 9 percent of Florida voters did not choose a party; today, more than a quarter of Florida voters are not formally registered with a political party (MacManus and Cilluffo 2021, 41–42). Millennials and Gen Zers are more than twice as likely as members of the Silent or Greatest generations to register as NPA (see fig. 12.5).

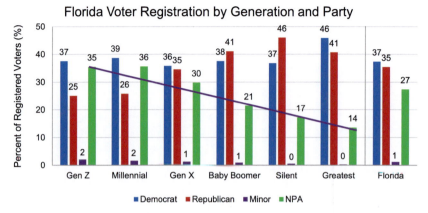

Fig. 12.5. Millennials, Gen Zers Most Likely to Register Without a Party Affiliation. (*Note:* Share of each generation registered with a minor party is shown but not labeled. NPA means "No Party Affiliation." See text and table 12.1 for generation age definitions.)

Source: Authors' analysis of Florida Division of Elections, Florida Voter Registration System, June 2020.

Many do so because of disillusionment with both parties' inability to resolve pressing problems, general dissatisfaction with public officials, or little knowledge of government (Pew Research Center 2019a).

Younger people also tend to be more alienated by highly negative campaigns than older voters. NextGen, a well-funded progressive group engaged in mobilizing young voters, purposively avoids any mention of Republicans or Democrats in campaign paraphernalia and talking points because "when [young] people see the label of a party on it, they immediately take a step back" (Catanese 2018).

The party registration changes seen among Florida's generations over a five-year period (2015–20) mirror a national trend—a widening generational and racial and ethnic divide between the two major parties' registrants. In other words, the two parties are becoming more "age and racially and ethnically bound." By 2020, a majority of Florida's Republicans were Baby Boomers or older (53%) and less racially and ethnically diverse than Democratic registrants, a majority of whom were GenXers and younger (55%) (see fig. 12.6).

While a sizable share of Florida's younger generations register as NPAs, they have leaned more Democratic in their vote choices *when* they vote. At least since 2008, a majority of voters ages 18 to 29 have voted for the Democratic candidate in presidential races—2008 (Obama

Florida Voter Registration by Party and Generation

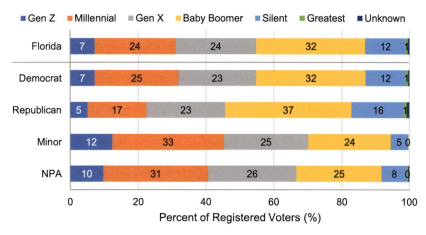

Fig. 12.6. Millennials Are a Plurality of NPA and Minor Party Registrants; Boomers Are a Plurality of Both Major Parties. (*Note:* Share of each party affiliation for whom age is unknown is shown but not labeled. NPA means "No Party Affiliation." See text and table 12.1 for generation age definitions.)
Source: Authors' analysis of Florida Division of Elections, Florida Voter Registration System, June 2020.

61%), 2012 (Obama 66%), 2016 (54% Clinton), and 2020 (60% Biden)—and in gubernatorial races since at least 2014—2014 (Charlie Crist 51%) and 2018 (Andrew Gillum 61%). Significantly, support from younger voters was stronger for the two Black candidates—Obama for president and Gillum for governor. These two candidates were much more appealing and effective in their messaging to these younger, more diverse voters.

Generational Shifts Necessitate More Targeted Outreach Strategies

A closer look at history shows that each generation is shaped to a certain degree by major national events (wars, economic crises, social movements), presidencies, local crises (shootings, natural disasters, business closings), and technological innovations occurring during their early lives (see table 12.1). Familiarity with the context in which each generation came of voting age is essential to effectively frame messages targeted to them. (For more on generational differences in lifetime political attitudes, see Laura Stoker, chap. 2, this volume.)

TABLE 12.1. Today's Living Generations and Their Early Political Experiences

Generation	Born	Age in 2020	Major Events	Presidents[a]
Greatest Generation	Before 1928	93+	Great Depression, New Deal, World War II	F.D. Roosevelt (D)
Silent Generation	1928–1945	75–92	Postwar Happiness, Era of Conformity, Korean War	Truman (D); Eisenhower (R)
Baby Boomer	1946–1964	56–74	Civil Rights Movement, 1960s Youth Culture— Save the World Activism, Drugs, Free Love, Vietnam War	Kennedy (D); Johnson (D); Nixon (R); Ford (R); Carter (D)
Generation X	1965–1980	40–55	MTV, 24-Hour News, Latch-Key Kids, Transition to Computers, AIDS	Reagan (R); G.H.W. Bush (R); Clinton (D)
Millennial	1981–1996	24–39	9/11, Social Media, Iraq and Afghanistan Conflicts, Great Recession, BP Oil Spill, Cyber-Security Concerns	G.W. Bush (R); Obama (D)
Generation Z	After 1996	23 and younger[b]	Brexit, #BlackLivesMatter, #MeToo, #NeverAgain (Parkland School Shooting), Cancel Culture, COVID-19, George Floyd Protests	Obama (D); Trump (R); Biden (D)

Source: Generation birth years and ages from Dimock (2019). Major events and presidents from authors' analysis.

[a]Indicates the president at the time a member of the generation turned 18 years of age.

[b]The youngest members of Generation Z are children. No chronological endpoint has been set for this group.

The growing diversity *within* Florida's younger generations—race/ethnicity, issue priorities, ideology—has made both message micro-targeting and the selection of the best means of communicating to them more challenging—much more so than for older voters. A national Pew Research survey found sharp generational differences in sources of political news. Specifically, 71 percent of adults ages 18 to 29 often get their news from a smartphone, computer, or tablet, while only 16 percent often get news from television. Among Americans ages 65 and older, 68 percent often get news from television, while 48 percent receive news from a digital source (Shearer 2021).

Campaigns must also be sensitive to generational differences in levels and forms of political engagement. Younger Floridians are more actively engaged in politics but are *more issue than partisan driven—* protesting, participating in boycotts, signing petitions, canvassing door-to-door, waving signs, and so forth. (For more on the activism of Gen Zers, see Robin Boyle-Laisure, chap. 8, this volume.) By contrast, older Floridians are more likely to give money and time to campaigns, be loyal to a political party, and vote.

Statewide Elections in Florida: Increasingly "Young vs. Old" Battles

Age differences among voters in their voting patterns are a recent phenomenon nationally.[4] As noted by the Pew Research Center (2011), the 2000 election had virtually no evidence of age differences. But it was already observable in Florida, a state with a unique age profile. With each subsequent Florida statewide election, the widening generational divide has led campaigns and the media to cast issues and candidates in "young vs. old" terms, but more recently in generationally specific language—"Millennials (or just Gen Z) vs. the Baby Boomers."

Obama Wins Florida's Young Voters by Historic Margins in 2008 and 2012

Barack Obama won Florida twice on the path to winning the 2008 and 2012 presidential elections. His historic candidacy, relative youth and energy, and message of hope and change were strong motivators, particularly for younger voters (Keeter, Horowitz, and Tyson 2008). He won voters ages 18 to 29 (mostly Millennials in both elections) by historic margins: more than 24 percent in 2008 and more than 34 percent in 2012. The candidate-driven Millennials gravitated toward Obama, while they struggled to identify with either John McCain or Mitt Romney. Although Obama won large majorities among young voters, they formed relatively small portions of the electorate. Voters younger than age 30 were 15 percent of the electorate in 2008, and 16 percent in 2012 (see table 12.2).

TABLE 12.2. Much Larger Age Gap in Share of Actual Voters in 2020 Presidential Election

Age	2008			2012			2016			2020		
	% of Voters	McCain (R)	Obama (D)	% of Voters	Romney (R)	Obama (D)	% of Voters	Trump (R)	Clinton (D)	% of Voters	Trump (R)	Biden (D)
18–29	15	37	61	16	32	66	17	36	54	14	38	60
30–44	25	49	49	23	46	52	23	39	54	20	50	48
45–64	37	47	52	37	52	48	38	56	43	34	54	45
65 and older	22	53	45	22	58	41	21	57	40	32	55	45

Source: Florida exit polls for each election year, as reported by CNN.

Although Obama did very well with young Florida voters, his wins relied upon older generations. In 2008, he won or split every age group younger than age 64 and kept McCain's margin down among seniors. Obama was widely seen as a better choice for economic recovery: a majority of Florida voters who were worried about economic conditions voted for him.[5] His path was harder in 2012, as an incumbent running on a record of a sluggish economic recovery. Romney did far better than McCain among voters ages 45 and older (Baby Boomers and older). Yet Obama's strength with young voters (Gen X and younger) was enough to narrowly win the state.

Clinton's Florida Loss in 2016 Partially Due to Failing to Energize Younger Voters

In 2016 Millennials preferred Bernie Sanders in the primary by an almost 2–1 margin.[6] Although Hillary Clinton won the primary, young voters—particularly young, college-educated progressives—never fully embraced her. Her potential to break the gender glass ceiling was not as much of a motivator as Obama's opportunity to be the first Black president. According to one Florida Millennial voter, "We look at the things [Clinton has] done and from that we cannot support her even if Sanders supports her" (Lemongello 2016).

Donald Trump easily won the five-way race in the state's Republican primary in 2016, even beating Marco Rubio in his home state. Age-based differences were clearly evident. Republicans ages 18 to 29 were nearly evenly split between Trump (36%) and Rubio (34%). Trump's lead was much larger among older Republican voters. Many young Republicans struggled to unite behind their party's candidate after the primary. According to the president of a Young Republicans club, "How do we support a racist, how do we support someone who says horrible things about people, when that's just not what we believe?" (Dart 2016).

Outreach in the general election followed generational lines. Democratic outreach had an unprecedentedly strong focus on young voters. President Obama, who was more popular with young people than Clinton, campaigned on her behalf on Florida college campuses, including the University of North Florida, Miami Dade College, and the University of Central Florida. Trump focused largely on older voters, including mega-rallies in Ocala (near The Villages retirement community), Lakeland, and Miami.

While younger voters formed a larger share of the electorate (17%) in 2016, Clinton fared worse among Millennial voters than had Obama. Meanwhile, Trump replicated and expanded Romney's strength among Baby Boomer and older voters. Increased turnout and enthusiasm from older white voters carried Trump to his narrow statewide win.

Gubernatorial Election 2018: Younger Voters More Impactful

Voter interest was at historic levels heading into the 2018 midterm election, following the first two years of the Trump administration (Pew Research Center 2018). Turnout was the highest it had been since 1994 for several reasons—close races for governor and U.S. senator, a chance to cast a referendum on Trump, and several controversial proposed constitutional amendments on the ballot.

The race for governor (an open seat) drew the most attention. Andrew Gillum, the 38-year-old Black mayor of Tallahassee and a national progressive hero, won the Democratic nomination in a crowded field of better known, well-financed white candidates. He stood to make history as Florida's first Black governor. Gillum's strategy of targeting minorities and young voters was perceived by some Democrats as risky (based on their low turnout rates in midterm elections). But he cited the need "to move more of our voters who typically don't participate in midterm elections" (Capitol News Service 2018). Many of his early rallies were at college campuses including Florida A & M University, a historically Black university where he was once student body president. His "Bring It Home, Florida" campaign focused on progressive priorities: raising the minimum wage, increasing pay for teachers, expanding Medicaid, and reforming the criminal justice system.

Republican Ron DeSantis, who emerged as the Gillum's general election opponent, embraced the traditional GOP positions (such as supporting school choice), relied upon a high-profile endorsement from Trump, and depended on high turnout of older white voters. He also attacked Gillum's policies as "socialist" and his time as mayor as corrupt.[7]

Generational fault lines were clear in the result. Gillum won 61 percent of the votes cast by people younger than 45, but they were only 25 percent of the electorate (compared with 40% in 2016). DeSantis won 54 percent of those 45 and older, which was enough to eke out a narrow victory.[8] The race was so close (0.5%) that a mandatory recount was required.

The 2018 election marked a generational changing of the guard in statewide politics. For the first time, the governor, lieutenant governor, and the Florida cabinet (commissioner of agriculture and consumer services, chief financial officer, and attorney general—each separately elected statewide) were all Gen Xers. Their successes and Gillum's near success fueled a sharp increase in younger candidates running for Congress and the state legislature in 2020.[9] (For more on the changing generational composition of elected officials in the 2018 election nationwide, see Sally Friedman, Emily Matott, and Andrew McMahon, chap. 14, in this volume.)

The 2020 Presidential Election: Candidates' Age and Race Tamp Down Young Turnout

Heading into the 2020 election, political interest stood at a record high. Politics was constantly in the news during Trump's presidency (not least because of his Florida residency). Many Floridians were eager to vote—to either support or oppose the president. *Generational schisms were once again front and center.*

The Democratic primary pitted Bernie Sanders against an establishment favorite, Joe Biden. Sanders again drew strong youth support, while Joe Biden struggled with that demographic. Many young progressives believed he was not liberal enough and had been in politics too long to represent the future. Biden was popular with older Democrats, who were most concerned with choosing a candidate who could defeat Trump. The generational split led *FiveThirtyEight* (a popular political website) to speculate that "age might be the most important fault line in the 2020 Democratic primary" (Bacon 2020). The results of the March 15 primary were similar to 2016—younger voters preferred Sanders, while older Democratic voters strongly favored Biden and turned out at a much higher rate.

Issues. The context of the 2020 general election is crucial to understanding generational issue priorities and voting cues (see fig. 12.7). The COVID-19 pandemic upended normal lives for all Americans, but it affected people of different ages in different ways. Young adults and people with less formal education were more likely to have lost a job in the shutdown, raising economic security concerns (Gould and Kassa 2020). Older Floridians were at greater risk from the virus itself, raising personal security concerns (CDC 2023). These cross-cutting concerns led to

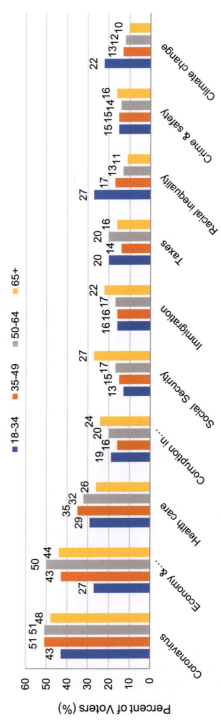

Which of the Following Issues Was the Most Important to You in the 2020 Election? (Top Three Shown)

Legend: 18-34 | 35-49 | 50-64 | 65+

Categories: Coronavirus, Economy &…, Health care, Corruption in…, Social Security, Immigration, Taxes, Racial inequality, Crime & safety, Climate change

Y-axis: Percent of Voters (%)

Fig. 12.7. Younger Voters More Likely to Say Racial Inequality, Climate Change Were Their Most Important Issues in Election. (*Note*: Data are national, not Florida specific.)

Source: Seven Letter Insight, "2020 Voter Priorities Survey," conducted Nov. 10–19, 2020, available at https://www.politico. com/f/?id=00000175-f4af-d692-a975-fcff0b650000

intergenerational differences: young adults were more likely to say the pandemic was a major economic threat to their personal situation than a health threat, while older adults were more likely to say it was a major health threat to them, over an economic threat (Jones 2020).

After the killing of George Floyd by a Minneapolis police officer, racial and social justice became top issues in the campaign and evoked activism among the young and minority communities (Parker, Horowitz, and Anderson 2020). Many expected Florida's Gen Zers and Millennials, who had mobilized to push for gun control after the Parkland school shooting, to be even more active in the 2020 election cycle. As it turned out, these young activists were more motivated by issues than by any candidate—gun control, racial injustice, criminal justice reform, and climate change. It was not surprising when March for Our Lives, the Gen Z-led activist organization created after the Parkland school shooting, announced a strategy of mobilizing young voters based on policies, without endorsing any candidate (Alemany 2020).

Other election issues were more perennial ones. The last TV ads for both campaigns in Florida focused on issues dear to Baby Boomers—Social Security and Medicare. Each candidate accused the other of endangering the old-age safety net (Nicol 2020; Corasaniti 2020). The Biden campaign believed it could make inroads into the Florida senior vote, particularly older women, by attacking Trump for his poor handling of COVID-19 and his "unpresidential" demeanor. The Trump campaign accused Biden of promoting socialism, hoping to scare seniors with a memory of the Cold War or dictatorial politics in a country they had fled.

Biden easily won Gen Z and the youngest Millennials; those ages 18 to 29 preferred him by 60 percent to 38 percent (see table 12.2). Older Millennials and Gen X, however, shifted to Trump more so than in 2016. This shift among older Millennials was most evident among those ages 30 to 39. In 2016, only 38 percent of that age group voted for Trump; in 2020, 50 percent did. Fears over another economic shutdown likely led some older Millennials—laden with student loan debt, employed in service sector jobs, or just starting their careers and families—to prefer Trump. (For more on political engagement and opinions of Millennials nationwide between 2016 and 2020, see the original survey data in Ashley Ross and Stella Rouse, chap. 11, this volume.)

Voting patterns among older voters, especially Baby Boomers, did not change as much, although there was a slight move toward Biden relative to Clinton. Biden's better performance among older Floridians

Florida 2020 Election Turnout by Generation

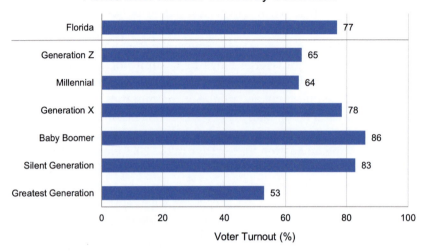

Fig. 12.8. As in Previous Elections, Turnout for Younger Generations in 2020 Lagged Older Generations. (*Note:* See text and table 12.1 for generation age definitions. Turnout figures differ from official figures due to differences in how counties report individual voter history to the state Division of Elections.) *Source:* Authors' analysis of Florida Division of Elections, Florida Voter Registration System, January 2021 extract.

may have been due to effective ads from the Biden campaign attacking Trump's offensive behavior (an important issue for older women), and the pandemic-driven in-migration of more politically liberal retirees from the Northeast.

In spite of increases in their share of Florida *registrants*, younger voters' share of actual *voters* shrank significantly compared with the 2016 presidential race. In 2016, 40 percent of Florida voters were younger than 45; in 2020, it was 34 percent (see table 12.2). The result was disappointing to the Biden campaign, which had anticipated much higher turnout rates among younger generations. While the turnout rate of Gen Zers and Millennials did go up slightly, it went up much more among older voters (see fig. 12.8).

Young Voter Mobilization Problems. In general, mobilization of younger voters was made much more difficult due to pandemic limits on in-person campaigning and the rise of new social media sources unfamiliar to older campaign strategists and party activists. But the warning signs of impending turnout problems were already there in early fall. Research conducted for the Advancement Project's Young Voters of Color Get Out the Vote campaign, including focus groups in Florida, found that young minority voters between ages 18 and 24 were "widely pessimistic and personally grappling with our country's mounting challenges. Few seem inspired by or engaged in the current political climate" (Turner and Kam 2020). They had little enthusiasm for the 2020 presidential candidates, especially "two old white men." In the end, Biden's small vote gains among older voters were not enough to offset the loss of votes from the larger-than-ever pool of young registrants, heavily targeted by the Biden campaign. Trump won Florida by 3.4 percent—considered a Florida landslide in a state known for 1 percent margin-of-victories.

Many Florida Democrats blamed Biden's loss on a badly run campaign that was ineffective in reaching and *mobilizing* Latinos, Blacks, women, and younger voters in the middle of a pandemic. They pointed to demographic data that were out-of-date and not sliced thinly enough to yield meaningful messages or successful GOTV. They blamed Biden campaign consultants at the national level for failing to realize the complexity of intra- and intergenerational differences among Florida voters and the political diversity of Florida's Latino and Asian populations. Moreover, poor internal polling led to false expectations about vote preferences and turnout rates of different generations of Latinos, Blacks, and women.

But what incensed Florida Democrats the most was the Biden campaign's prohibition against face-to-face, in-person registration drives, campaign events, and door-to-door canvassing once COVID-19 hit. (Republicans were not constrained by any such strict no-contact instructions from the Trump campaign.) Black leaders pointed to the vital need to engage in such activities to turn out Black voters, especially young Black voters. Latino Democratic campaign workers and volunteers complained about failures to recognize country-of-origin differences among Latino voters and to devise a counter argument to the Republicans' "antisocialism" rallying cry that created a large, high-turnout coalition of Cubans, Venezuelans, Nicaraguans, Colombians, and Hondurans of all ages. Vietnamese voters were also moved by the antisocialism message and heavily supported Trump.

Florida Democrats were stunned by exit polls showing higher-than-expected votes for Trump from older Millennials, male and female Latinos (including Puerto Ricans—traditionally Democratic leaning), and Black men. Biden did make some inroads with college-educated white women, suburban women with children, and older women—although considerably less than Democrats had expected in the "Year of the Woman," the 100th anniversary of women's suffrage. In Florida, as elsewhere, Black women were the strongest Biden supporters. But nothing Democrats or the Biden campaign did would close the generational turnout gap between younger and older voters.

The COVID-19 pandemic exacerbated youth turnout concerns. In the past, campaigns went to college campuses to register and rally young voters. Such high visibility events show energy and help with engagement, but were not possible during the pandemic. Many Florida colleges and universities were operating mostly online in the fall 2020 semester; in-person events were often prohibited. Campaigns turned to social media and popular apps to encourage young people to register, make a voting plan, and vote (Bennett 2020).

It was easier said than done: "The country kind of came to a shut down and we were like, 'What do we do next?'" lamented one young volunteer (Associated Press 2020). Other college-age campaign staffers found social media to be no substitute for in-person contacts. "I feel texting is super important," said the president of the Florida Federation of Young Republicans. "But you can't negate the fact that talking to a voter face-to-face is the most powerful way of getting them to vote" (Evans 2020). Neither were impersonal texts nor phone calls using uninspiring scripts a substitute for in-person contacts. One young Democratic staffer charged with ramping up young voter turnout said many he called told him they equated those GOTV tactics as a form of "telemarketing"—annoying, invasive of their privacy, and easy to avoid.

In hindsight, Democrats' problems began at the registration stage. When COVID-19 hit in March 2020, both parties halted their in-person outreach in the immediate aftermath of state-ordered shutdowns. Republicans quickly resumed in-person registration and door-to-door canvassing, while Democrats kept their outreach online, fearful of COVID-19 and of contradicting the Biden campaign's message on the pandemic. During that time, Florida Republicans registered thousands of voters, narrowing the gap between Democrat and Republican registrants to less than 1 percent, the closest it had ever been (King 2020). The Biden campaign resumed in-person canvassing only in October, just a little more than a month before Election Day (Peoples 2020). The registration deadline for the election (October 5) had come and gone by then. Too little, too late.

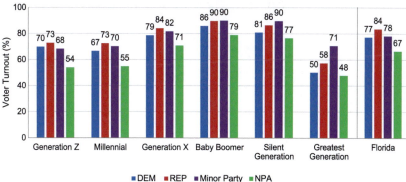

Fig. 12.9. Higher Turnout for Republicans Across Every Generation. (*Note:* See text and table 12.1 for generation age definitions. Turnout figures differ from official figures due to differences in how counties report individual voter history to the state Division of Elections.)
Source: Authors' analysis of Florida Division of Elections, Florida Voter Registration System, January 2021 extract.

Younger Generations' Turnout Rate Differentials: Party, Race, Gender

The difficulties of mobilizing the *larger-than-ever pool of younger regis-trants*—a key to a Biden victory—were blatantly apparent in postelection analyses of turnout rates.

Party. Shocking to Democrats was the fact that Republicans turned out to vote at higher rates than Democrats across *every* generation, including Gen Z and Millennial (see fig. 12.9). Republicans had targeted younger voters by framing their vote choice as lockdown (Biden) or jobs (Trump). Democrats posed the choice as either racial equality[10] (Biden) or systemic racism (Trump), but Democrats' GOTV strategies failed to deliver their message as effectively as Republicans did theirs. Less surprising was that across all generations, voters registered as NPA had substantially lower turnout than voters with any party affiliation (even a minor party). Neither candidate appeared any better to them than the other at improving their lives economically or safeguarding their health.

Race. Turnout differences were also evident by race and ethnicity (see fig. 12.10). For non-Hispanic whites, the turnout was relatively high among all generations. Among Gen Zers and Millennials, Hispan-

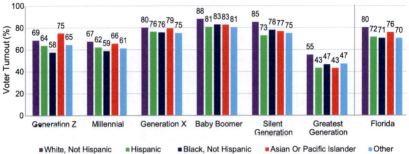

Fig. 12.10. Hispanic Turnout Higher than Black Turnout Among Younger Generations, Opposite for Older Generations. (*Note:* See text and table 12.1 for generation age definitions. Turnout figures differ from official figures due to differences in how counties report individual voter history to the state Division of Elections.)

Source: Authors' analysis of Florida Division of Elections, Florida Voter Registration System, January 2021 extract.

ics voted at a higher rate than Blacks. For the Baby Boomer and older generations, the opposite pattern was true.

Some attribute the Hispanic turnout edge to rapid increases in educational attainment levels among young Hispanics. Nationally, Hispanics have largely caught up to and surpassed Blacks in high school graduation and college enrollment rates (Gramlich 2017). The same reason is often offered for high turnout of Asian and Pacific Islanders among Gen Zers, Millennials, and Gen Xers.

Aside from educational gains, the Republicans' antisocialism message in 2020 strongly resonated with Latinos of all generations whose family heritage was linked to socialist countries they had escaped. Fearing the rise of socialism in the United States, they turned out to vote (mostly for Trump) in record numbers (Ordonez 2020; Mazzei 2020).

Among older generations, Blacks, especially Black women, were a larger share of registrants and turned out at higher rates than Latinos. Voting is a high priority of Black voters—a civil right for which they have fought hard. Black churches in Florida have long played an important role in mobilizing the Black vote through "Souls to the Polls" events held on the Sunday prior to Election Day.

Gender. Women of every generation turned out at a higher rate

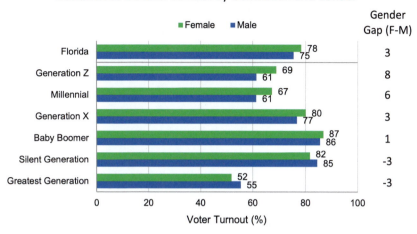

Fig. 12.11. Turnout Gender Gap Largest for Youngest Generations. (*Note:* See text and table 12.1 for generation age definitions. Turnout figures differ from official figures due to differences in how counties report individual voter history to the state Division of Elections.)
Source: Authors' analysis of Florida Division of Elections, Florida Voter Registration System, January 2021 extract.

than men. The gender gap was widest among Gen Zers and Millennials (see fig. 12.11). Younger women were 7 percentage points more likely to vote than men. The gap was also widest among young persons of color. A major reason for this differential is that young minority women are much more likely to go to college and graduate than minority men (U.S. Census Bureau 2020). Biden's strongest support came from Black women who applauded his choice of Kamala Harris (an Alpha Kappa Alpha[11]) for his vice presidential running mate more than did Black men.

The Big Takeaway

Younger generations are more likely to be inspired to vote by issues or a candidate (either for or against) than simply a party label, but they also need more careful targeting—both in messaging and the delivery of messages through relevant communication mechanisms. The rise of younger generations makes this more urgent for both candidates and political parties.

Obama's historic candidacy and effective campaign turned out young voters, while the coronavirus and message-targeting failures found his vice president, Joe Biden, struggling to do so 12 years later when younger registrants were a larger share of the electorate. *The growing diversity among the younger, rising generations makes effective micro-targeting much more difficult, but in a constantly changing state, it is also more imperative.*

A Look Forward

Florida's rapid demographic changes have made the state more diverse in race and ethnicity as well as in age. The effect is already evident to the major political parties as they struggle to appeal to younger voters. Younger voters are increasingly likely to register without a party affiliation and thus are more driven to turn out to vote not by party label but rather by a candidate's diversity and ability to inspire and speak to them more genuinely in terms they understand and through communication venues they use.

At the same time, it is not clear that demographics is destiny. Florida Republicans have managed to maintain or expand their hold on state offices, even when facing demographic headwinds. But Florida Democrats remain confident the state's rapid demographic changes and the growing size and diversity of the Gen Z and Millennial generations will soon give them an advantage in statewide elections. Unfortunately for them, the 2022 Florida elections did not reveal this as Republican Governor Ron DeSantis won handedly as did his party.

Also unclear is how—or if—the two major parties can regain their relevance with younger voters. Recruiting and supporting younger candidates and promoting policies important to younger people are likely keys to enticing them back, but campaign strategists must find communication tools and messaging that will work with younger generations. One thing is certain: ignoring them is a sure-fire design for long-term trouble.

Generational replacement is slowly eroding the number and impact of older voters. One exception in Florida is the Baby Boomer generation. While declining nationally, this generation will continue to exert its influence in Florida because the state remains a top destination for retirees. This in-migration means that the state's Baby Boomer generation will likely be a force in state politics longer than elsewhere.

Finally, generational change may affect Florida's status as a swing state. According to one school of thought, based on the 2020 election and Republican gains at every level, Florida has become a red state. A second view, based on demographic projections of a larger young, more diverse, and more progressive electorate, is that Florida will keep its swing state status. This second view, taken together with the poorly run campaign by Democrats in 2020, is more convincing, although the 2022 elections question this.

NOTES

1. Among Florida Hispanics, the top countries of origin in order are Cuba, Puerto Rico, Mexico, Colombia, the Dominican Republic, Venezuela, Honduras, and Nicaragua. Non-Cubans outnumber Cubans. A majority are registered as Democrats or NPAs. Florida's Black population has become more diverse with an influx from Haiti, Jamaica, Trinidad and Tobago, and the Dominican Republic. The state's smaller, but growing, Asian population is very diverse, in order, from India, the Philippines, China, Vietnam, Korea, Pakistan, and Japan. MacManus (2018).

2. Parts of this section are adopted from MacManus et al. (2019), chapter 1; MacManus (2018), October 2.

3. Authors' analysis of Florida Division of Elections, Florida Voter Registration System, June 2020.

4. Parts of this section are adopted from MacManus et al. (2019), chapter 4.

5. Florida 2008 exit poll, as reported by CNN.

6. Florida 2016 Democratic primary exit poll, as reported by CNN.

7. Gillum was accused by the Florida Ethics Commission of accepting a gift of over $100 from a lobbyist without reporting it. After the election, he paid a $5,000 fine.

8. Florida 2018 exit poll, as reported by CNN.

9. In 2020, 177 women filed to run for Congress, the state Senate, and the state House. Of those, 47% were women of color. Many were first-time candidates—mostly Millennials or Gen Xers.

10. Two Biden campaign videos (30 and 60 second) targeting Generation Z featured a young Black female college student making a Black Lives Matter poster following the death of George Floyd. While drawing, she discusses how the Black Lives Matter movement "has grown to be more than a protest against police brutality to include systematic racism and economic injustice" (Call 2020, September 1). The video spots first appeared during the 2020 MTV Video Music Awards.

11. A Black sorority whose members and alums are strongly connected via a powerful national network. They hold many leadership posts in their communities and are very effective at registering and turning out Black voters.

REFERENCES

Alemany, J. 2020. "Power Up: March for Our Lives Wants to Rally Young People to Vote—for Policies." *Washington Post*, August 6. https://www.washingtonpost.com/politics/2020/08/06/power-up-march-our-lives-wants-rally-young-people-vote-policies/

Associated Press. 2020. "Voting Groups Scramble to Reach College Students in Pandemic." *Tampa Bay Times*, August 30. https://www.tampabay.com/florida-politics/elections/2020/08/30/voting-groups-scramble-to-reach-college-students-in-pandemic/

Bacon, P., Jr. 2020. "Why Younger Democrats Are Overwhelmingly Rejecting Biden." *FiveThirtyEight*, February 28. https://fivethirtyeight.com/features/young-democrats-have-rejected-biden-and-it-could-cost-him-the-nomination/

Bennett, B. 2020. "Get-Out-the-Vote Effort Goes Digital for COVID-19 Pandemic." Southern Poverty Law Center, April 11. https://www.splcenter.org/news/2020/04/11/get-out-vote-effort-goes-digital-covid-19-pandemic

Call, J. 2020. "Tallahassee Student Featured in Joe Biden Commercial for Gen Z." *Tallahassee Democrat*, September 1. https://www.tallahassee.com/story/news/politics/2020/09/01/tallahassee-student-takes-center-stage-joe-biden-commercial-gen-z-adrianna-williams-trump/5678302002/

Capitol News Service. 2018. "Gillum Launches Last Minute Bus Tour ahead of Primary." *WCTV* (Tallahassee, FL), August 20. https://www.wctv.tv/content/news/Gillum-launches-last-minute-bus-tour-ahead-of-primary-491296611.html

Casey, N., and P. Mazzei. 2020. "After a Big Trump Win, 'It's Hard to Argue Florida Is a True Swing State.'" *New York Times*, November 5. https://www.nytimes.com/2020/11/05/us/florida-election-swing-state.html

Catanese, D. 2018. "Will Young People Make the Difference in Florida?" *U.S. News & World Report*, October 10. https://www.usnews.com/news/the-run/articles/2018-10-10/will-young-people-make-the-difference-in-florida

CDC. 2023. "COVID-19 Risks and Information for Older Adults." Retrieved from https://www.cdc.gov/aging/covid19/index.html#:~:text=The%20risk%20increases%20with%20age,very%20sick%20from%20COVID%2D19

Corasaniti, N. 2020. "Trump Targets Older Voters with an Ad Focusing on Social Security and Medicare." *New York Times*, September 15. https://www.nytimes.com/2020/09/15/us/elections/trump-targets-older-voters-with-an-ad-focusing-on-social-security-and-medicare.html

Dart, T. 2016. "'How Do We Support a Racist?' Young Republicans Grapple with 2016 Election." *Guardian*, September 28. https://www.theguardian.com/us-news/2016/sep/28/millennial-voters-young-republicans-trump-2016-election

DeSilver, D. 2014. "The Politics of American Generations: How Age Affects Attitudes and Voting Behavior." Pew Research Center, July 9. https://www.pewresearch.org/fact-tank/2014/07/09/the-politics-of-american-generations-how-age-affects-attitudes-and-voting-behavior/

Dimock, M. 2019. "Defining Generations: Where Millennials End and Generation Z Begins." Pew Research Center, January 17. https://www.pewresearch.org/fact-tank/2019/01/17/where-millennials-end-and-generation-z-begins/

Evans, Dan. 2020. "Motivating Young Voters Is a Priority in 2020 Election. Why Is It

So Hard?" *Miami Herald*, October 28. https://www.miamiherald.com/news/polit
ics-government/state-politics/article246774327.html

Florida Legislature, Office of Economic and Demographic Research. 2020. *Demographic Overview & Population Trends*. January 28. http://edr.state.fl.us/Content
/presentations/population-demographics/DemographicTrends_1-28-20.pdf

Fry, R. 2020. "Millennials Overtake Baby Boomers as America's Largest Generation."
Pew Research Center, April 28. https://www.pewresearch.org/fact-tank/2020/04
/28/millennials-overtake-baby-boomers-as-americas-largest-generation/

Gould, E., and M. Kassa. 2020. "Young Workers Hit Hard by the COVID-19 Economy." Economic Policy Institute, October 14. https://www.epi.org/publication
/young-workers-covid-recession/

Gramlich, J. 2017. "Hispanic Dropout Rate Hits New Low, College Enrollment at
New High." Pew Research Center, September 29. https://www.pewresearch.org
/fact-tank/2017/09/29/hispanic-dropout-rate-hits-new-low-college-enrollment
-at-new-high/

Jones, B. 2020. "Younger Americans View Coronavirus Outbreak More as a Major
Threat to Finances Than Health." Pew Research Center, April 7. https://www.pe
wresearch.org/fact-tank/2020/04/07/younger-americans-view-coronavirus-outb
reak-more-as-a-major-threat-to-finances-than-health/

Keeter, S., J. Horowitz, and A. Tyson. 2008. *Young Voters in the 2008 Election*. Pew
Research Center, November 13. https://www.pewresearch.org/2008/11/13/you
ng-voters-in-the-2008-election/

King, M. 2020. "Florida Republicans Narrow Voter Registration Gap with Democrats to
Historic Low." *ABC Action News—WFTS Tampa Bay*, October 18. https://www
.abcactionnews.com/news/local-news/florida-republicans-narrow-voter-registr
ation-gap-with-democrats-to-historic-low

Klas, M. E. 2020. "Young Florida Voters Are Registering in Higher Numbers." *Miami
Herald*, October 23. https://www.miamiherald.com/news/politics-government
/election/article246576668.html

Lemongello, S. 2016. "Sanders Supporters Not Ready to Back Clinton." *Orlando Sen-
tinel*, June 8. https://www.orlandosentinel.com/politics/os-bernie-sanders-supp
orters-future-20160608-story.html

MacManus, S. A. 2018. "Florida's Changing Electorate: More Racially/Ethnically and
Age Diverse." *The Journal*, James Madison Institute, October 2. https://www.jam
esmadison.org/floridas-changing-electorate-more-racially-ethnically-and-age
-diverse/

MacManus, S. A., and D. J. Bonanza. 2015. "Florida's Two 'Super-Sized Generations'—
the Boomers and the Millennials." *Sayfie Review*, September 15. https://www.say
fiereview.com/featured_column?column_id=55

MacManus, S. A., and A. A. Cilluffo. 2021. "Demographic Change." In *A Divided
Union: Structural Challenges to Bipartisanship in America*, edited by D. Moreno, E.
Gamarra, P. E. Murphy, and D. Jolly. New York: Routledge.

MacManus, S. A., A. Jewett, D. J. Bonanza, and T. R. Dye. 2019. *Politics in Florida*. 5th
ed. Orlando: Florida Institute of Government.

Mazzei, P. 2020. "In Miami-Dade County, Younger Cuban Voters Offer Opening for
Trump." *New York Times*, October 25. https://www.nytimes.com/2020/10/25/us
/miami-cuban-trump-biden.html

Mazzei, P., and T. Kaplan. 2020. "Biden Aims to Erode Trump's Support among Older Voters in Florida." *New York Times*, October 13. https://www.nytimes.com/2020/10/13/us/politics/joe-biden-florida-voters.html

Nicol, R. 2020. "Mike Bloomberg-Backed Ad Calls on Florida Seniors to Ditch Donald Trump." *Florida Politics*, October 14. https://floridapolitics.com/archives/374404-bloomberg-ad-seniors-trump

Ordonez, F. 2020. "With Warnings of Socialism, Trump Seeks to Boost Support among Young Florida Latinos." National Public Radio, September 24. https://www.npr.org/2020/09/24/916067522/with-warnings-of-socialism-trump-seeks-to-boost-support-among-young-florida-lati

Parker, K., J. M. Horowitz, and M. Anderson. 2020. "Amid Protests, Majorities across Racial and Ethnic Groups Express Support for the Black Lives Matter Movement." Pew Research Center, June 12. https://www.pewsocialtrends.org/2020/06/12/amid-protests-majorities-across-racial-and-ethnic-groups-express-support-for-the-Black-lives-matter-movement/

Peoples, S. 2020. "After Pandemic Delay, Biden Launching In-Person Canvassing." Associated Press, October 1. https://apnews.com/article/election-2020-virus-outbreak-joe-biden-donald-trump-elections-1e4e392fff3fed0a7925ef9cd9ca33e1

Pew Research Center. 2004. "Bush Ratings Rise Even as Iraq Concerns Continue." April 26. https://www.pewresearch.org/politics/2004/04/26/bush-ratings-rise-even-as-iraq-concerns-continue/

Pew Research Center. 2011. "The Generation Gap and the 2012 Election." November 3. https://www.pewresearch.org/politics/2011/11/03/the-generation-gap-and-the-2012-election-3/

Pew Research Center. 2018. "Voter Enthusiasm at Record High in Nationalized Political Environment." September 26. https://www.pewresearch.org/politics/2018/09/26/voter-enthusiasm-at-record-high-in-nationalized-midterm-environment/

Pew Research Center. 2019a. "Political Independents: Who They Are, What They Think." March 14. https://www.pewresearch.org/politics/2019/03/14/political-independents-who-they-are-what-they-think/

Pew Research Center. 2019b. "Social Media Fact Sheet." June 12. https://www.pewresearch.org/internet/fact-sheet/social-media/

Riccardi, Nicholas, and Mike Schneider. 2021. "Young Adults' Relocations Are Reshaping Political Geography." Associated Press, April 25. https://apnews.com/article/health-census-2020-business-government-and-politics-immigration-cbc10b35e47a331515cce18abc9dcddc

Shearer, Elisa. 2021. "More Than Eight-in-Ten Americans Get News from Digital Devices." Pew Research Center, January 12. https://www.pewresearch.org/fact-tank/2021/01/12/more-than-eight-in-ten-americans-get-news-from-digital-devices/

Turner, J., and D. Kam. 2020. "Backroom Briefing: Trump? Biden? No, the Issues." News Service of Florida, October 6.

U.S. Census Bureau. 2020. *Educational Attainment in the United States: 2019*. Table 1. Educational Attainment of the Population 18 Years and Over, by Age, Sex, Race, and Hispanic Origin: 2019. March 30. https://www.census.gov/data/tables/2019/demo/educational-attainment/cps-detailed-tables.html

13 | How They Govern

Do Millennial Mayors Bring a Generational Perspective to Their Activities?

Sally Friedman, Michael A. Armato,
and Emily R. Matott

> Love 'em or hate 'em, this much is true: one day soon,
> millennials will rule America. . . . Their startups have
> revolutionized the economy, their tastes have shifted the
> culture, and their enormous appetite for social media has
> transformed human interaction. American politics is the next
> arena ripe for disruption.
> —Charlotte Alter, "How Millennial Leaders
> Will Change America." *Time*, January 23, 2020

> Young leaders—like Holyoke, Mass., Mayor Alex Morse
> who was 22 years old when he took office—are injecting
> cities with a new energy.
> —Caroline Cournoyer, "Millennials in the
> Mayor's Seat." *Governing*, January 2013

The quotations above are indicative of a recent spate of articles (Alter 2020; Bloomberg Cities Staff 2018; Small 2018) cataloging the impact that Millennial leaders (in this case mayors) are beginning to have on politics. As Charlotte Alter notes, Millennials are said to have made a difference in many arenas of life; it makes demographic sense that they are now coming of age to occupy positions of institutional power. As the chief elected officers of their cities, mayors have notable influence over all manner of political life, from the political agenda to the nature of budgets to the engagement of citizens (Ammons and Newell

1989; Flanagan 2004; Stein 2003). Because of their youth, they also have the potential to infuse the political arena with enthusiasm and energy.

Each of the quotes above tells a key piece of the story. Taken together, though, and as has been described in other chapters of the book, the two quotes reflect a common source of conflation in the generations literature. Each directs our attention to different demographic characteristics of mayors, the first focusing on generation (Millennials) and the second on the youth (regardless of actual birthdate) of the mayor. While the main variable of interest here is of course the "Millennial-ness" of the mayor, the mayor's youth also impacts a mayor's activities, including their presentation to constituents and in some cases constituent reactions. For each of these mayors as we describe below, age as well as generation is part of the story.

But are Millennials really that different? Is it something about the "Millennial persona" (Rouse and Ross 2018) that is telling or is the main variable of relevance the age of the mayor—do young mayors, regardless of generation, put a unique stamp on their activities? As Caroline Cournoyer suggests in her description of Mayor Alex Morse, is it the youth of these mayors, as much as their generational status, that leads to "injecting cities with a new energy"? Literature on other "identity" characteristics—race, gender—suggests that the demographic character of politicians has the potential to impact their behavior. What of Millennials?

This chapter takes a first cut at answering these kinds of questions by providing an in-depth case study of the activities of several Millennial, as compared to non-Millennial, mayors. That is to say, the recent spate of articles on Millennial mayors points to the differential impact of generation. What these studies lack is an analysis comparing these mayors to their non-Millennial counterparts. How do we know that Millennials (or for that matter simply mayors who are young) do things differently without also focusing on the activities of their older colleagues? Using U.S. Census data to match cities on a variety of demographic and political characteristics, we conduct a qualitative comparative case study (most similar systems design) of matched pairs, the key difference focusing on Millennial versus non-Millennial mayors.

Though exploratory, this chapter and its qualitative research design seeks to add to the literature in several ways. As the good work in this volume exemplifies, much of the work on generations focuses on quantitative analysis. In turn, a qualitative approach has the potential to highlight the multifaceted experience of what it means to be a Millennial, and it provides a holistic picture of demographic and other influences. The profiles of the mayors described here are an attempt to show not only that generation (and relative youth) matter but that these interact with other socializing influences. Quantitative work may productively sort out the impact of each of these variables; a qualitative approach can focus on their interconnections.

Additionally, most work on generations focuses on the mass public. This paper is clearly an effort to turn attention to Millennials (and non-Millennials) who have made it to the level of political elites.

Given their young age, it is clear that all the Millennial mayors were quite the overachievers; in comparison with their non-Millennial counterparts, they were more likely to combine traditional economic development with social justice concerns, and they were more likely to reach out to Millennials. Age (or the lack of it) was brought up frequently about most of these mayors, though obviously not enough to upend their careers.

At the same time, there are similarities between the Millennial and non-Millennial mayors. Some of the non-Millennials engaged in the same kinds of activities as did the Millennials; other characteristics of the mayors mattered; and the needs and character of each city conditioned the activities of all mayors. That said, findings overall do show a "Millennial" imprint.

The Role of Generations and the Views of Millennials

Do Millennial mayors bring a different perspective to politics? Proponents of generational theory, focusing on the importance of one's formative years and socializing experiences, suggest they should (Dalton 2016; Dimock 2019; Mannheim [1926] 1952); see other chapters in this volume).

Here we focus on the number of ways "Millennial" status can make a difference, including the issues they are said to prioritize and their often-cited emphasis on diversity and inclusive participation, specifically including fellow Millennials. Because age (or the lack of it) is also an integral part of the story of these mayors, we also focus more specifically on ways these younger mayors have had to counter campaign tactics pointing up their relative inexperience. Acknowledging the unique place of these mayors as chief executives of their cities operating under a number of contextual constraints (Gerber and Hopkins

2011), we nonetheless hypothesize that Millennial mayors, as products of their generation, fit the descriptions associated with Millennials in the mass public.

In terms of issues, most agree that Millennials, because of their connection to the economic recession of 2007–8 and subsequent economic conditions, including difficult employment situations, student debt, and rising income inequality, will care about economic issues. Additionally, the demographic diversity of the generation implies a generation promulgating tolerance for diverse views and groups (Rouse and Ross 2018), standing for equality more generally, and supporting liberal politics (Fry 2018; Rouse and Ross 2018).

Elli Denison, director of research for the Center for Generational Kinetics, a Texas-based consulting firm that specializes in generational research, said Millennials have grown up with diversity and celebrate it: "They really value that. They look at a group of people and think 'Oh, dear, we all look the same'" (Campbell et al. 2016).

A final issue that Millennials are said to be particularly concerned about is climate change; they place a higher priority on the issue and are more likely to attribute the cause to man-made activity (Ballew et al. 2019; Funk and Tyson 2020).

Finally, "young Americans subscribe to a range of values and behaviors that should benefit the democratic process. They are more supportive of autonomy and social solidarity as norms of citizenship and more supportive of participation beyond elections" (Milkman 2017). Dalton (2016, 178) suggests that young people prefer participation that is "direct, action-oriented, and collective" (his concept of engaged citizenship). And Millennials' preferred style of leadership is thought to include similar participatory qualities, such as "communication, relationship-building and empowerment" (Business.com 2020), as well as considerable collaboration (Fore 2012).

For purposes of this chapter, we narrow the scope. Do Millennials focus on different issues? While most or all mayors may find it expedient to prioritize some version of traditional economic development, a Millennial imprint suggests that these mayors would simultaneously focus on a broader range of social justice issues as well. Similarly, it makes sense that most or all mayors would find it in their interests to encourage some degree of citizen participation. We expect Millennial mayors to be even more likely to do so and to particularly reach out to others in the Millennial cohort. Finally, and from a different perspective, we examine the degree that age was raised, most often as a concern but sometimes as a plus, as these mayors campaigned and developed their governing styles.

Research Design

Consistent with generational theory, are Millennial mayors likely to bring the perspective of their generation to their work as mayor? The above section has shown that Millennials on average are often characterized as more tolerant of differences, interested in a variety of social-justice-related concerns, and value inclusionary practices. What about the elite level of politics?

Given the potential for descriptive representation of others in their age cohort, we hypothesize that Millennial politicians will include social justice concerns in their activities and will strongly encourage civic engagement. We expect their political focus to reflect the experiences of their generation as well as what Millennials want the future to look like.

To take a first cut at these questions, we used census data (collected in 2019) to select pairs of reasonably comparable cities (populations over 30,000), a major difference being the age of the current mayor. Thus, given similar demographics and presumably reasonably similar issues confronting the government (most similar systems design), what can be said about the actions of Millennial (born after 1980) versus older mayors. (See Tolleson-Rhinehart [2001] for a similar research design comparing the behaviors of male and female mayors.)

Table 13.1 displays the characteristics of the matched pairs of cities (four pairs of cities were most similar) that resulted from our examination of census data. These pairs include a variety of contexts: South Bend and Bloomington, Indiana; Fall River and New Bedford, Massachusetts; San Bernardino and Stockton, California; and Richmond and Newport News, Virginia.

The census figures displayed in table 13.1 show reasonable comparability between the cities as well as a significant diversity of the contexts in which mayors operated. Fall River and New Bedford—post-industrial cities that had experienced notable economic downturns—are pretty well matched in terms of overall population, poverty rates, and key industries, though New Bedford has a notably larger minority community (mostly comprised of non-white Latinos). Similarly, South Bend and Bloomington—cities with a strong college presence—compare well

TABLE 13.1. Characteristics of Cities and Mayors

	Indiana		Virginia		Massachusetts			California
	South Bend	Bloomington	Richmond	Newport News	Fall River	New Bedford	Stockton	San Bernardino
Mayor	Peter Buttigieg	Mark Kruzan John Hamilton	Levar Stoney	McKinley L. Price	Jasiel Correia II	Jon Mitchell	Michael D. Tubbs	R. Carey Davis John Valdivia
Birth Year	1982	1960 Before 1980	1981	1949	1991	1969	1990	1952 or 1953 1975
Mayoral Term	January 2012 to 2020	January 2004 to 2016 January 2016 to 2024	December 2016–2020	July 2010 to June 2022	January 2016–2020	January 2012–2024	January 2017–2021	March 2014– December 2018 December 2018–2022
Population	101,928	83,636	220,892	180,719	89,258	95,125	304,358	215,252
Median Household Income	$37,441	$33,172	$42,356	$51,082	$39,328	$40,626	$48,396	$41,027
Families Below Poverty Level	20.20%	18.30%	18.70%	12.90%	17.50%	19.30%	18.60%	26.30%
White Alone (%)	53.90%	78.40%	40.00%	44.00%	78.00%	63.40%	21.20%	15.30%
Black (%)	26.00%	4.20%	47.90%	39.80%	4.90%	5.40%	11.10%	13.20%
Non-White Latino (%)	14.40%	4.20%	6.50%	8.60%	9.80%	20.00%	42.20%	64.30%
Asian (if notable) (%)	NA	9.60%	NA	NA	NA	NA	NA	NA

1st Major Industry (and percent)	Educational Service, Health Care, Social Assistant (28.3%)	Educational Service, Health Care, Social Assistant (38.6%)	Educational Service, Health Care, Social Assistant (26.7%)	Educational Service, Health Care, Social Assistant (23.1%)	Educational Service, Health Care, Social Assistant (27.3%)	Educational Service, Health Care, Social Assistant (26.5%)	Educational Service, Health Care, Social Assistant (22.7%)	Educational Service, Health Care, Social Assistant (20.9%)
2nd Major Industry	Manufacturing (17.5%)	Arts, Entertainment, Recreation (17.7%)	Professional, Scientific, Management (14.1%)	Manufacturing (13.4%)	Manufacturing (12.8%)	Retail (12.6%)	Retail (12.4%)	Retail (12.7%)
3rd Major Industry	Retail (11.2%)	Retail (10.9%)	Arts, Entertainment, Recreation (11.5%)	Retail (12.7%)	Retail (12.8%)	Manufacturing (12.1%)	Arts, Entertainment, Recreation (8.8%)	Transportation and Warehousing (10.5%)
4th Major Industry	Arts, Entertainment, Recreation (10.6%)	Professional, Scientific, Management (7.1%)	Retail (10.7%)	Arts, Entertainment, Recreation (10.6%)	Arts, Entertainment, Recreation (10%)	Arts, Entertainment, Recreation (9.7%)	Manufacturing (8.5%)	Professional, Scientific, Management (9.2%)

on overall population and poverty rates. South Bend does have notably more of a minority community, and the percentages of citizens involved in key industries differ somewhat.

In turn, Richmond and Newport News are two heavily Democratic cities with significant black populations, and both cities in 2022 had black mayors. With similar demographics, San Bernardino and Stockton are both in the rebuilding process after filing for bankruptcy. All mayors in this study happen to be Democrats, except for the two in San Bernardino. The results below are a "redacted" version of the approximately 100 pages of material we have compiled over the last year (see Friedman et al. 2019 and unpublished material available on personal communication). We have provided enough detail in what follows to demonstrate the variety of ways generation played a role in the activities of these mayors and the ways generation interconnected with other socializing influences.

In order to assess the differences in mayoral behavior, we use the public record. We review government and campaign websites, newspaper sources, and Twitter accounts to assess the activities of these mayors, and we set these activities in the larger context of the urban area each mayor represents. That said, in the spirit of Fenno's (1978) work on the presentational styles of politicians generally and members of Congress more specifically, we have tried to present descriptions from the point of view of each mayor—how they seek to present themselves to constituents. In what follows, we examine the activities of the Millennial mayors, subsequently comparing them to their non-Millennial counterparts.

The Millennial Mayors

As we know, a key advantage of qualitative work is thick description; in that regard, the backgrounds of the mayors (Millennial and non-Millennial) are fascinating and in some cases even inspirational. Three came from significant poverty or broken homes; at very young ages, all by any standards had accomplished a lot. Born in a tenement to immigrant parents (from the Caribbean), Jasiel Correia II, at age 23, became mayor of Fall River, Massachusetts, scoring an upset victory over the incumbent. As a high school student, he and his peers took the unusual step of drafting a "youth Bill of Rights" which subsequently became law, and he was honored as Fall River's youth of the year for work with a student substance-abuse organization. In college, he was elected as class president, later becoming an entrepreneur who formed a company that designed an app attempting to connect businesses with potential customers; and he was elected to a seat on the Fall River City Council at age 21 (Northern Star 2016).

Age 26 on his election as mayor of Stockton, California in 2016, Michael Tubbs was only a few years older than Correia. It was even thought that he "may be the youngest mayor ever in a city in the United States with a population exceeding 100,000" (Phillips 2017a). Raised by a single mother—Tubbs's father is in prison with a life sentence on charges including drugs and kidnapping (Hubert 2017)—Tubbs as a high school student participated in a national debate competition, his team arguing the benefits of universal health care (Reid 2018). After the debate, Tubbs had a chance to meet presidential candidate Barack Obama: "I looked at him, shook his hand and told him 'I'm next,'" said Tubbs (Reid 2018). Tubbs went on to earn two degrees from Stanford University and was elected to the Stockton City Council before running for and winning the mayoralty (Carpizo 2016).

As is reasonably well known from his 2020 presidential campaign, Pete Buttigieg, born in South Bend, Indiana, was an undergraduate at Harvard University. "He went on to become a Rhodes scholar [at Oxford], work on a presidential campaign, join the military and be elected mayor all before he turned 30" (Peters 2019). From 2007 to 2010, "Buttigieg worked as a consultant for McKinsey & Company, specializing in economic development, business, logistics, and energy initiatives for government and private sector clients" (Ballotpedia), and having served as an intelligence officer in the Naval Reserve, he was deployed to Afghanistan for six months during his first term in office (Zeleny 2019). He was elected mayor in 2011, receiving almost three-fourths of the vote (Sloma 2011).

In turn at age 35, the oldest of the Millennial mayors considered here, Levar Stoney in 2016 became mayor of Richmond, Virginia. He was "reared by a grandparent, a single-parent home. 'There's nothing special about my circumstances'" (Schapiro 2016). A product of Virginia public schools, he participated in the free and reduced fee lunch program and was the first in his family to earn a high school diploma (Stoney Official Mayor Biography). He went on to become the first in his family to attend college and was the first African American man elected student-government president of his university (Kruszewski 2018). "My father was a high school janitor. He cleaned bathrooms and mopped floors," Stoney said. "My worst day isn't as hard as the job that he had" (Kruszewski 2018).

Thereafter Stoney was clearly on a fast track to success as he became active in Virginia's Democratic Party politics, serving "as Executive Director of the Democratic Party of Virginia . . . and key player in Obama's victory in the state," "as Deputy Campaign Manager for Governor [Terry] McAuliffe's successful campaign," and he "was appointed by McAuliffe as Secretary of the Commonwealth of Virginia, the first African-American to hold the post and the youngest member of the governor's cabinet" (Stoney Official Mayor Biography).[1]

Thus, at notably young ages, all these Millennials had accomplished a lot, and as a first cut, there are a number of ways the activities of these Millennial mayors conform to expectations about generation and also about age. A "Millennial" imprint shows up when we examine the issues they focus on and their participatory styles. We see also for these mayors the tendency of the young to innovate, and from a different viewpoint, all found themselves questioned about their relative youth. As a first cut, the activities of these mayors in many ways conform to expectations.

Consistent with stereotypes of the energy and enthusiasm of youth, all four Millennial mayors introduced new programs and initiatives throughout their time in office. For example, for Mayor Stoney of Richmond, Virginia, the enthusiasm and energy focused on his vision of creative leadership, and for Mayor Tubbs (Stockton, California) the focus came to center on the benefits of programs of universal basic income in and of its own right but, in his view, such a program would have the added benefit of completely upgrading the image of his city:

> Mayor Stoney: When the mayor sees the tortoise-colored shell [from a ceramic tortoise given to him as a present], it reminds him what makes a strong politician. "Good leaders stick their necks out in a time of crisis," he said. (Belletti 2018)

> Mayor Stoney: If we don't think ambitiously, and creatively, about how investments today can pay big dividends tomorrow, then we are little more than caretakers of the way things are, de facto defenders of the status quo. (Richmond Virginia Mayor Blog 2018)

> Mayor Tubbs: "I became very bullish on the idea [of universal basic income], because I recognized the opportunity to not just

tell a story of basic income but also a story of Stockton that was nuanced and rooted in the folks who make our community. . . . I thought having Stockton centered for once as a possible solution would be inspiring for the city and also for the nation—because there are so many cities like Stockton . . . now when you mention Stockton people say, 'Oh, the city that is doing basic income,' which is a much better designation than the city that is miserable or bankrupt." (Kaufmann 2020)[2]

Also consistent with expectations, these mayors (here all Democrats) in general fall on the progressive end of the political spectrum. What that means for our purposes is that while all focus on the kinds of traditional economic development concerns often associated with big-city mayors, they also are likely to link those concerns to a broader social justice focus.

For starters, the economy, and particularly the creation of new jobs, were a core focus of these mayors, and our earlier writings are filled with examples of the many ways all these mayors encouraged economic development:

From Mayor Buttigieg: "This election is about jobs. . . . I'm the only candidate who has been involved in multibillion dollar decisions in the private sector, with some of the world's top firms." (Parrott 2011)

From Correia: "In the next month we will reveal the details of our new economic development office. Over the last several months, we have been testing the city's capability to provide high quality economic growth results across a variety of areas including big and small business growth, job creation, small business lending, and housing. And I'm happy to report that we have seen success through the new office of economic development that is poised to bring about the next generation of economic development in our region." (Correia 2018)

From Tubbs: "We look forward to working in partnership with Amazon filling all those jobs with Stocktonians." (Phillips 2017c)

And from Stoney: "In the 2016–2017 fiscal year alone, the administration has helped create over 2,400 new jobs and has attracted 37 new businesses to the Richmond area." (Official RVA Website)

Yet, while these statements point up a very traditional, development-oriented approach, most of these mayors mixed their economic priorities with aspects of progressive regimes, often interrelating these priorities. Mayor Correia notably did so during his 2018 State of the City Address, connecting the issue of economic development with public safety and education in Fall River (Correia 2018). Mayor Stoney announced, "All four of my major budget priorities: public education, public safety, core services and community wealth building (focused on alleviating poverty) were all adopted and funded by City Council" (Richmond Virginia Mayor Blog 2017). Mayor Tubbs used a 2017 op-ed to highlight his core policy interests, economic development, housing and homelessness, crime and safety, and education (Tubbs 2017), and he reiterated these interrelated themes during his reelection campaign (Stockton Record Staff 2020). Finally, though more of a traditional development mayor than the other Millennials, Mayor Buttigieg related his focus on the economy to broader issues, for instance promoting a minority and women's owned business enterprise program (US State News 2012) and issuing an executive order establishing a new diversity and inclusion initiative for the city (Vivian 2016).

Relatedly, three of the four mayors made education a priority. For example:

Mayor Correia: "Education for All [initiative] will focus on educating youth and adults in the traditional ways in classrooms as well as utilizing on the job training." (Correia 2017)

Mayor Stoney: "[I] proposed the largest ever single year funding increase for education, and now $170 million will be allocated for Richmond Public Schools providing needed cost of living increases for school personnel and long overdue increases in teacher salaries." (Richmond Virginia Mayor Blog 2017)[3]

From a different perspective, and also in line with expectations, these mayors rank high on the participatory end of any scale. That is to say, it is easy to find each of them out and about interacting with constituents and generally encouraging citizen input (see also Armato and Friedman 2015). They also consistently used their participatory platform to connect with young people, and several reached out specifically to Millennials.

For example, Mayor Stoney noted that he had "visited nearly every school, every police precinct, held Mayor's Community Office Hours in every district and participated in more than 150 community events" (biography on mayor's website). Buttigieg regularly hosted a "mayor's night in," developed a mayor's youth task force, and encouraged a variety of mentoring programs throughout the area (Blasko 2013). In addition to his efforts on education cited above, Correia along with Stoney and Buttigieg pointed to their administration's efforts to attract Millennials to their cities (Commonwealth Times Staff 2016; Gagne 2016). And Mayor Tubbs was described as having "invigorated a legion of young followers who bring with them the promise of vitality as he works to unite a city and vows to work to solve longstanding issues of homelessness, poverty and crime" (Stockton Record Staff 2016).

It is worth noting that all these mayors, in one way or another, reached out to young people in general; with the exception of Mayor Tubbs, three also reached out to Millennials.

Turning to electoral politics, age surfaced as an issue in campaigns, and particularly early in the governing tenure of at least three of these mayors (Parrott 2011; Northern Star 2016). Mayor Stoney, the oldest of these Millennials, may be the exception. Some countered with examples of their experience even at a young age, or noted, as Buttigieg did, the advantages of running as a young candidate. Mayor Buttigieg also noted, "When you run for office in your 20s, your face is your message. You are going to be the candidate of new ideas, technology and innovation. Even if you don't have any new ideas and don't like technology" (Alter 2020).

Similarly, in an interview shortly after his first election, Mayor Correia touted the energy and optimism he, as a young person, could bring to the campaign (Fitzpatrick 2016). He noted his willingness to get out there to work with the people, including working with snow removal crews (Siefer 2018), and he noted his skill as a good listener as a way to show people he was ready for the job: "I love to listen. I like to talk, too, but I like to hear different perspectives." He added that he sat at a conference table for the interview rather than behind his mayoral desk. "This is my preferred atmosphere," he said. In meetings, he often asks for input from those who aren't speaking up because they might have insights or objections that can turn the conversation in a new direction (Fitzpatrick 2016). "Most people, after they meet me or after a couple of meetings, they don't underestimate me anymore" (Fitzpatrick 2016).

But in terms of questioning the readiness of a young leader, the harshest dialog was reserved for Tubbs. The incumbent mayor prior to

Tubbs, and Tubbs's opponent in the 2016 election, said, "He needs to spend more time and get his hands dirty and put more time into the community, maybe hire a few people, pay a few more bills, go through a few more struggles and then he'll be ready" (Phillips 2016). Some constituents followed suit, even asking the 67-year-old vice mayor to "help the boy" (Phillips 2017b). And, while running for reelection, a septuagenarian opponent criticized Mayor Tubbs, insisting, "What does a kid out of high school and four years of college know about running a billion-dollar business" (Phillips 2019).

Thus, in many ways on its face the activities of these mayors conform to expectations about Millennials in the mass public (as well as about age), and the qualitative analysis demonstrates the variety of ways—the energy they bring to the job, the focus on issues, the participatory governing style, and the role age played in the campaigns—that generation can matter. Perhaps Mayor Buttigieg expresses it best, saying "I never set out to be a Millennial mayor." But his youthfulness quickly became a useful symbol: "Your generation becomes part of the story and your face becomes part of the message." He says the same month he got in the race "because the city was struggling, *Newsweek* declared South Bend one of 'America's Dying Cities.' 'Where it made a difference that I was a young candidate is that running for office is an act of hope—it's only something you do if you believe it makes a difference'" (Small 2018).

The Non-Millennial Mayors

But what of the non-Millennial counterparts? Table 13.2 presents a rough comparison of the Millennial and non-Millennial mayors on a number of the dimensions of interest. On balance, at least for this sample, the older mayors are more likely to be traditionally development-oriented, placing a higher priority on the economy in its own right. The non-Millennial group is less likely to reach out to Millennials in particular. Both sets of mayors share commonalities: all have engaged in notable initiatives; all significantly interact with constituents, including young people; and non-Millennials do their share of interacting with technology. Our case studies demonstrate the importance of individual socialization and the role of the larger political and economic context.

In three of our four comparisons (the cities in Massachusetts, Virginia, and California), the non-Millennial mayor was more likely to be

TABLE 13.2. Mayor Activities: Millennial and Non-Millennial Mayors

Mayor Activities	Millennial Mayors	Non-Millennial Mayors	Number of Mayors
Activist mayor	all Millennials	Mitchell, Hamilton, Davis	4 Millennials, 3 non-Millennials
At least one large-scale initiative	all Millennials	all non-Millennials	4 Millennials, 6 non-Millennials
Prioritized traditional economic development*	Buttigieg	Mitchell, Price, Davis, Valdivia	1 Millennial, 4 non-Millennials
Combined focus on economic development with broader issues*	all Millennials	Mitchell, Hamilton, Kruzan	4 Millennials, 3 non-Millennials
Reach out to constituents	all Millennials	all non-Millennials	4 Millennials, 6 non-Millennials
Reach out to youth	all Millennials	all non-Millennials	4 Millennials, 6 non-Millennials
Reach out to Millennials	Buttigieg, Correia, Stoney	Price, Kruzan	3 Millennials, 2 non-Millennials
Used technology to encourage participation	Buttigieg, Correia	Mitchell, Hamilton, Price	2 Millennials, 3 non-Millennials
Questioned about age in campaign	Buttigieg, Correia, Tubbs	none	3 Millennials, 0 non-Millennials
Highlighted experience even though young	all Millennials	none	4 Millennials, 0 non-Millennials

development oriented, focusing on economic priorities with less reference to social justice or quality of life concerns. While Mayor Tubbs of Stockton was focusing on universal basic income and worrying about stemming poverty and homelessness, his San Bernardino counterparts, R. Carey Davis and John Valdivia (elected in nominally nonpartisan elections, but both identifying as Republicans), took a more traditional approach, placing more emphasis on attracting new businesses and jobs. Elected in 2014, Davis holds a master's in business administration and had a career in the financial and accounting sectors (Ballotpedia), and he "got involved in city politics . . . when he studied financial statements and concluded that years of excessive spending . . . left a clear trail of bad decisions leading up to the city's 2012 bankruptcy filing" (Yarbrough 2014).

> Davis' (reelection) campaign has centered on his work helping San Bernardino exit bankruptcy. At forums, he has touted recent city and Police Department hires, low crime statistics and outside investment in the community. (Whitehead 2018a)

> Davis credited the city's economic development team with bringing in 2,566 new business licenses over the last year and lowering the unemployment rate from 10.2 percent to 7.3 percent. (Hagen 2016)

He was defeated in 2018 by City Councilmember John Valdivia, who said,

> "We'll be pushing really hard on being pro-growth, pro-development, pro-safety and pro-business." (Whitehead 2018c)

Three thousand miles across the country, Mayor Jon Mitchell in New Bedford, Massachusetts, advocated for the same kind of broad and interrelated priorities as his Fall River counterpart, Mayor Correia, but his activities began with a focus on the economy. Raised in New Bedford, Mitchell received a law degree from George Washington University, made a name for himself as a prosecutor in the District of Columbia and Boston (Mitchell Official Mayor Biography), and has served as mayor since 2011. The title of his inaugural speech, "Poised for Progress," set the tone as Mitchell described the importance of "growing jobs and effectively competing in the global economy, keeping our neighborhoods safe and thriving, delivering efficient government services, and building a first-rate school system" (Mitchell 2012).

Thereafter, "as mayor, Jon has sought to reestablish New Bedford as one of the leading cities in the Northeast. He has moved aggressively to reform the city's schools, modernize the port, solidify the downtown as the economic and cultural center of Southeastern Massachusetts, and to elevate the quality of life in every neighborhood." He has even become known as a leader as he has been profiled in a statewide magazine (Mohl 2016); he has given speeches to national organizations on how to run smart cities; and he has chaired the National Council of Mayors' Task Force on Environmental Concerns (Mitchell Official Mayor Biography).

Yet as a matter of emphasis, Mitchell is more likely to frame his actions first and foremost in terms of growing the economy—in contrast to Correia's focus on quality of life. Both mayors take action on both fronts, and both cite the synergistic connections between the many avenues of their activities.

But while Correia talked about the interrelated priorities of a good economy and education, Mitchell explained in his first inaugural address that "our starting point will be to support our existing businesses, as well as to protect our fishing industry from unfair regulations. But to bring new business here, our economic strategy must play to our natural competitive advantages" (Mitchell 2012).[4]

Similarly, McKinley Price, mayor of Newport News, Virginia, concentrated first and foremost on the economy. A career dentist, Price accumulated a record of activism in the community, working to ease racial tensions and serving on a number of local boards, statewide commissions, and in volunteer positions to help underprivileged youth. He became mayor (a part-time position in a council-manager form of government) at age 61. For starters, and given the significance of the shipbuilding industry for the city, the Price administration has promoted a major expansion of the shipbuilding school, a 90,000-square-foot building anchoring a six-acre mixed-use development (Rockett 2013). Businesses, including a Walmart superstore, have come to the area (Paitsel 2013). And plans are in the works to significantly revitalize the City Center District (Newport News Virginia Website 2016).

As somewhat of a side note to this project, it is interesting to note the Stoney (Millennial) and Price (older) comparison. Both African American, the two men were socialized in very different contexts with respect to the civil rights movement of the 1960s. For instance, Price would describe a teenage experience of being the only African American student to attend a math summer camp for honors' students. "'I was called names all day.' Similarly, as a young married man initially living in a mostly white neighborhood, Price noted, "We did not feel accepted there. We had to replace our picture window several times" (Lawlor 2010). He later recalled being delighted seeing his daughter able to play with white children, though she was barred from an apparently whites-only swimming pool, even after the civil rights movement was in full swing (Lawlor 2010).

Further, both sought to become active in their communities (Price through service on boards and commissions and Stoney through electoral and party politics), and both currently serve as mayors of cities with large percentages of African Americans (upwards of 40%). Yet the styles of the two mayors are notably different. Price takes an incremental approach—he wants to see change, but he does not want to rock the boat—in contrast to Stoney's wanting to often go for a bigger vision. In contrast to Stoney's search for "creative leadership," Price notes his incremental and collaborative approach means he encourages participation: "'I'm not a 'follow me over the hill' kind of leader,' says Price, but a leader by example. His role is to do what he does best: listen well and be patient. Recognize problems, use his contacts to argue for an issue, help find solutions and negotiate compromises. Facilitate. Encourage people that, 'If you participate, this can happen'" (Daily Press Staff 2010).

Price also seems more likely to deal with racial issues by seeking community dialog and advancing opportunities for underserved youth (in contrast to Stoney's focus on poverty and housing with less of a direct focus on race).[5]

Finally, in Bloomington (matched with South Bend), Mayors Kruzan (2003–15) and Hamilton (2015–present) overlapped with Mayor Buttigieg's mayoralty in South Bend. Both were long-time progressives with strong local roots. After receiving a law degree from Indiana University, Kruzan had been a long-time Indiana state legislator, with particular interests in the environment, a variety of additional progressive causes, and a desire to protect the "eclectic nature" of the city (Erdody 2014). In turn, and with particular interests including education and housing for the homeless, Hamilton had served in a variety of capacities in government and the nonprofit sector, having headed two state agencies, having served as a Monroe County Community School Corporation school board member and on the Bloomington Commission on Sustainability (Erdody 2015). Thus, "As a longtime progressive . . . Hamilton said he would continue the tradition handed down from progressive mayor to progressive mayor," and he would seek to "deliver a better Bloomington to the next generation" (Bunn 2015).

Consistent with this progressive nature, both of these mayors emphasized the kinds of interrelated priorities expressed by the Millennial mayors. Thus, "one of Kruzan's hallmarks has been expanding the definition of economic development and equating it with quality of life. He separated economic development into its own office and added positions for arts, small business, and sustainability—and he reached out to social services agencies as economic developers" (Banta 2016). During his time in office, he oversaw the opening of the B-line trail, as a means to promote the use of more outdoor activities, helping downtown businesses in the process (Gabrick 2011). And he was a staunch promoter of expanding the downtown arts scene (City of Bloomington 2006a).

Similarly, Hamilton, in his first day in office, said his administration would focus on three interrelated priorities: "maintaining a strong local economy, establishing affordable housing for all, and supporting public education" (Lane 2016). According to Hamilton's website, "He is focused on improving the economy—helping it become more equitable, so Bloomington works for people from all walks of life; more sustainable, so we are building a better future with today's efforts; and more productive, so we can help build value for all to share." His administration has developed pilot programs to expand affordable housing (City of Bloomington 2016b), to develop solar energy (City of Bloomington 2019), and to boost the local arts scene (City of Bloomington 2020).

If anything, as a matter of degree, it was Millennial Mayor Buttigieg that was most focused on economic development, and he was least likely to focus on other issues. He campaigned first and foremost on the importance of revitalizing and diversifying the economy. "We've got a lot of supporters, we've got a big tent and the important thing is we have a big tent because we've laid out a forward looking agenda for the South Bend economy" (Peterson 2011). South Bend "needs to recognize that the days of Studebaker and Bendix are over, and advance an economic development plan that emphasizes diversity within the local economy" (Blasko 2011).

Mayor Buttigieg further argued that a good economy would bring about additional benefits. "If we can tackle vacant and abandoned houses, we will see an impact in the crime rate. . . . If we can provide more meaningful job opportunities, we'll see an impact in the crime rate" (Allen 2011). "I ran on a platform of economic development, and part of how you show that you have a healthy economy is you show that workers are treated fairly. . . . We need to make a statement that workers should not have to fear for their jobs for reasons that have nothing to do with their performance" (Allen 2012). Regarding immigration concerns, the mayor observed, "I don't always get involved in national issues. I'm usually concentrating on local issues like potholes. This is one that when they get it right I think our community will feel the difference, our economy will feel the difference and our neighborhoods will be better off" (Blake 2013).

From a different perspective, it is important to note that most of these non-Millennial mayors were reasonably participatory, with that participation including reaching out to young people. It appears though that it is the Millennials who are most likely to explicitly reach out to Millennials; only Price (Ress 2016) and Kruzan (Hren 2014) were likely to do the latter, and they seem to have done so only through spokespeople.

Thus, New Bedford's Mayor Mitchell certainly encourages robust citizen participation, and he can often be found out and about in the community. "Mitchell's understated manner can make attendees at his annual State of the City address unsure of whether to laugh at the mayor's puns. The dry humor is familiar at business ribbon-cuttings, budget press conferences, and community events across New Bedford, at campaign handshake events and even in the infomercial Mitchell made with his grandmother to encourage residents to recycle" (Lawrence 2015). Additionally, Mitchell's monthly office hours are often held at local restaurants (South Coast Today Staff 2019), and his administration modernized technology to make it easier for citizens to inform the city of community problems (Dunlop 2019).

Similarly, Mayor Davis (San Bernardino) has reached out to constituents by promoting the importance of literacy as a contributor to a sustainable society (San Bernardino Sun Staff 2015) and the importance of families including their children in outdoor activities (Hagen 2016). In turn, as described above, Mayor Price has engaged in a number of efforts to better the conditions of underserved youth. Neither of these or the other non-Millennial mayors seemed to have particularly included Millennials or young professionals in their explicit efforts.

The activities of Mayor Hamilton in Bloomington particularly stand out. He has emphasized transparency in government and has worked toward modernizing technology to ensure residents know what the city government is doing (Hamilton Official Mayor Biography). Among other activities, he has instituted a "mayor at the market" program, helping citizens connect (City of Bloomington 2016a), and in an innovative move, he has initiated a program where high school students contribute to the budgetary process: "Hamilton speaking at a forum for high school students answered the Young Democrats' question about inclusive policies by highlighting the city's ongoing youth participatory budgeting program. He said the city council approved $15,000 to be used in 2019 according to the wishes of a group of teenagers" (Christian 2019).

Thus, some non-Millennial mayors have pretty broad-gauged agendas, and some certainly encourage citizen participation, though not particularly of Millennials.

Conclusion

So, what have we learned about Millennial and non-Millennial mayors? At the level of the mass public, considerable literature suggests that Millennials often have different priorities and interests. Here we hypothesized that the Millennial mayors would combine a focus on social justice concerns with traditional economic priorities and that they would encourage citizen participation, particularly including young people and Millennials. We were also interested in how they and their constituents thought about their age.

Acknowledging the exploratory nature of our study (comparing mayors in a small yet diverse group of cities), we suggest that these characterizations of Millennials in the mass public can carry over to the elite level as well. We also note the nuance and detail provided by the qualitative research design, reminding us of the diversity of governing styles and the variety of issues that mayors address as they relate to their micropolities. It may come as no surprise that these mayors focus on the economy or interact with constituents. But the qualitative focus exemplifies the reality of mayoral activities. We recommend more use of this type of qualitative design in the future of generational studies.

So do generations matter? Are Millennial mayors different? At least in this sample, the answer becomes a qualified yes. In a way that is easy to underappreciate, the mayors described here can easily point to significant accomplishments at notably young ages. They provide important reminders that age need not correlate with inexperience.

Also, it happens to be the case that the Millennial mayors profiled here all represent "marginalized" groups (as African Americans, ethnic minorities, or, in Buttigieg's case, as a gay man). While this in some ways complicates our research design—all except one (Price) of the non-Millennial mayors are white—it reminds us of two important points. First, the often-noted diversity of the Millennial generation is alive and well here. As more Millennials obtain high levels of political office, we can expect to see more diversity in the backgrounds of the leaders who achieve those offices. Second, and as a consequence, it is perhaps a sign of the times signaling greater public acceptance that these mayors have achieved public office in the first place, for example, Buttigieg first publicly announcing his homosexuality during his 2015 reelection campaign (Peters 2019).

In terms of policies, too, these mayors tend to bring a "Millennial" perspective to their jobs. As illustrated by Mayor Tubbs, the Millennial mayors we examined melded a focus on traditional economic concerns with the social-justice orientations for which Millennials are known. The mayors sought to build the economies of their cities by bringing in jobs, by encouraging development, and by seeking assistance from state governments. The Millennial mayors, though, were as likely to meld economic priorities with more social-justice oriented concerns, viewing economic development as part of a broader agenda. Mayor Buttigieg was somewhat of an exception—he showed more concern for the economy in its own right; however, he also was quick to note that in his view a better economy would bring broader social benefits.

At the same time as these case studies show the impact of generation, a number of other factors are relevant to the story. Millennial and non-Millennial mayors often engaged in similar activities. Additional background characteristics, including race, ethnicity, and partisanship as well as personal experiences matter, as does the context of the larger environment—a mayor of most college towns might be expected to take reasonably progressive stances. Further it would be unfair to over-stereotype both Millennials and non-Millennials. For example, Mayor Buttigieg appears to be economically more conservative than Tubbs, and non-Millennial John Hamilton put quite a bit of stock in connecting with young people.

Finally, given what we know about the formative experiences of Millennials, these mayors appear to not "represent" the views of their generations as much as one might expect. They focus on economic issues more because of their role as mayors of large cities rather than as an outgrowth of their own socialization. They are more likely to focus on economic issues as part of a broader agenda, but they do not necessarily go out of their way to point up issues of diversity and inclusion. And issues, including climate change and the environment, are not necessarily front and center on their agendas. Millennial status matters, but we see its limitations too as mayors face the constraints of their job. Finally, the ways Millennial mayors encourage participation do not seem to differ from what the non-Millennials are doing.

As we consider the ways generation (in this case Millennial status) matters, a number of cautions and questions arise. While we argue that much of our evidence supports a generational hypothesis, we recognize that "causality" is hard to pin down. Indeed, it is the thick description provided by qualitative analysis that helps us situate the activities of these mayors in a broader economic and political context.

That said, some intriguing questions remain. Are there underlying differences between our comparison cities that our research design—based as it is on matching cities via demographic characteristics—might not pick up? Is there something about the kinds of cities that have elected Millennial mayors that differentiate them from other cities? How do our findings generalize to a larger set of cities?

In the end, do Millennial mayors bring a "Millennial" perspective to their activities? We think the case studies described here suggest at least a qualified yes.

NOTES

1. Pete Buttigieg (South Bend) left office in December 2019 and served as of 2021 as U.S. Secretary of Transportation. Michael Tubbs (Stockton) was defeated in his 2020 reelection bid (Chabria 2020). In a different vein altogether, Mayor Correia (Fall River) has faced a variety of criminal charges over his time in office. In 2018, he was charged with fraud due to his app (Farzan 2018). He subsequently survived a 2018 recall (Crimaldi 2019), but thereafter he has been convicted of "extorting marijuana vendors and defrauding investors" (DOJ 2021). He is currently serving time in jail. As of June 2021, the situation for the other mayors is as described in the text.

2. Mayors Buttigieg and Correia similarly instituted new initiatives (Friedman et al. 2019).

3. See also Tubbs 2017.

4. In New Bedford, though Mayor Mitchell's efforts began with economic development, there is no doubt his focus included a broad agenda tackling education and environmental concerns.

5. All the non-Millennial mayors encourage some degree of citizen participation, and all are involved in some way with young people. In addition to the generally participatory activities of Mitchell, Hamilton, and Davis described above, Kruzan encouraged people to sit on city boards and commissions (Banta 2016), Price encouraged citizens to participate to help solve community issues (Daily Press Staff 2010), and Valdivia regularly sends out constituent surveys (Whitehead 2018b). With respect particularly to youth, in addition to the examples described in the text, the other mayors were also involved: Kruzan (City of Bloomington 2006b), Valdivia (Mayor John Valdivia 2019), Mitchell (City of New Bedford 2014), Price (Lawlor 2011).

REFERENCES

Allen, K. 2011. "Mayoral Hopefuls Share Safety Plans." *South Bend Tribune*, October 19.

Allen, K. 2012. "Mayor Listens to Residents at 'Night Out'." *South Bend Tribune*, February 1.

Alter, C. 2020. "How Millennial Leaders Will Change America." *Time*, January 23. https://time.com/5770140/millennials-change-american-politics/

Ammons, D., and C. Newell. 1989. *City Executives Leadership Roles, Work Characteristics, and Time Management*. Albany: State University of New York Press.

Armato, M., and S. Friedman. 2015. "The Civically Oriented Activities of Big City Mayors." In *Civic Education in the 21st Century: A Multidimensional Inquiry*, edited by Michael T. Rogers and Donald M. Gooch, 215–47. Lanham, MD: Lexington Books.

Ballew, M., J. Marlon, S. Rosenthal, A. Gustafson, J. Kotcher, E. Maibach, and A. Leiserowitz. 2019. "Do Younger Generations Care More about Global Warming?" Climate Communications, Yale, June 11. https://climatecommunication.yale.edu/publications/do-younger-generations-care-more-about-global-warming/

Ballotpedia. N.d. "Pete Buttigieg." https://ballotpedia.org/Pete_Buttigieg

Ballotpedia. N.d. "R. Carey Davis." https://ballotpedia.org/Carey_Davis

Banta, M. 2016. "Mayor Kruzan Reflects on Reaching the End of the Road." *Herald Times*, January 1. https://www.heraldtimesonline.com/story/news/local/2016/01/01/mayor-kruzan-reflects-on-reaching-the-end-of-the-road/117596932/

Belletti, S. 2018. "Richmond Mayor Sees a City 'Ready to Turn the Page'." March 15. https://apnews.com/article/cbe7624f2ac44a5184723232cddc3bde

Blake, B. 2013. "Dozens Rally for Immigration Reform." *South Bend Tribune*, June 15.

Blasko, E. 2011. "Dem Mayoral Candidates Attend IUSB Forum." *South Bend Tribune*, April 10.

Blasko, E. 2013. "Student Task Force to Address Youth Concerns." *South Bend Tribune*, December 18.

Bloomberg Cities Staff. 2018. "7 Millennial Mayors to Watch." *Bloomberg Cities*, May 31. https://bloombergcities.medium.com/7-millennial-mayors-to-watch-c85e207995d3.

Bunn, R. 2015. "Hamilton Spells Out His Campaign Platform." *Herald-Times*, February 20. https://advance-lexis-com.felix.albright.edu/api/document?collection=news&id=urn:contentItem:5FBJ-GVW1-DYNS-326W-00000-00&context=1516831

Business.com Staff. 2020. "Millennials and Modern Leadership Styles." May 7. https://www.business.com/articles/leadership-styles-millennials/

Campbell, E., N. Griffin, and A. Reece. 2016. "What You Need to Know about Millennials and Politics." *Cronkite News*, August 24. https://cronkitenews.azpbs.org/2016/08/24/need-to-know-millennials-and-politics/

Carpizo, A. 2016. "Mentor Program Teaches Kids 'My Life Matters'." *Stockton Record*, May 27, 3.

Chabria, A. 2020. "Election 2020: Stockton May Not Reelect Mayor Michael Tubbs." *Los Angeles Times*, November 6.

Christian, K. 2019. "City Candidates Discuss Inclusivity, Guns at North's Election Forum." *Hoosier Times*, April 18. Https://Www.Hoosiertimes.Com/Herald_Times

_Online/News/Local/City-Candidates-Discuss-Inclusivity-Guns-At-North-S-Elec tion-Forum/Article_C4a25408-27f6-58a9-97eb-46650c79371b.Html

City of Bloomington. 2006a. "Mayor Kruzan Invites Public to City Vision." Press release, April 3. https://bloomington.in.gov/news/2006/04/03/2407

City of Bloomington. 2006b. "City Caps Off Be Beautiful Bloomington Month with Arbor Day Celebration." Press release, April 28. https://bloomington.in.gov/ne ws/2006/04/28/1463

City of Bloomington. 2016a. "Mayor Hamilton Announces Mayor at the Market." Press release, March 31. https://bloomington.in.gov/news/2016/03/31/2389

City of Bloomington. 2016b. "Mayor John Hamilton Announces Affordable Housing Initiatives." Press release, August 18. https://bloomington.in.gov/news/2016/08 /18/2409

City of Bloomington. 2019. "Mayors Hamilton, Buttigieg among Five Indiana May- ors for Solar Energy." Press release, July 25. https://bloomington.in.gov/news/20 19/07/25/4155

City of Bloomington. 2020. "Applications Sought for 2020 Recover Forward Grants for the Arts." Press release, September 3. https://bloomington.in.gov/news/2020 /09/03/4566

City of New Bedford. 2014. "City of New Bedford Launches 2014 Learn and Serve Summer Youth Program." Press release, June 18. http://s3.amazonaws.com/new bedford-ma/wp-content/uploads/sites/3/20191219193828/061814_Learn_and _Serve_Summer_Youth_Program.pdf

City of Richmond, Virginia. N.d. "Economic Development: Community Wealth Building." https://www.rva.gov/index.php/economic-development/community -wealth-building

Commonwealth Times Staff. 2016. "One for the Ages: How a Team of Millennials Helped Elect RVA's Youngest Mayor." *Commonwealth Times*, December 5. https:// commonwealthtimes.org/2016/12/05/one-ages-team-millennials-helped-elect -rvas-youngest-mayor/

Correia, J. 2018. Fall River State of the City Address. Available at https://www.youtu be.com/watch?v=Pr2hrROw4XA&ab_channel=NewBedfordGuide

Cournoyer, C. 2013. "Millennials in the Mayor's Seat." *Governing*, January. https:// www.governing.com/archive/gov-millennial-mayors.html

Crimaldi, L. 2019. "Correia Remains Fall River Mayor in Election Stunner." *Boston Globe*, March 12. https://www.bostonglobe.com/metro/2019/03/12/correia-rema ins-fall-river-mayor-election-stunner/0YA2M7nQxNNJNIMxc9nu3K/story.html

Daily Press Staff, 2010. "2005 Citizen of the Year: McKinley Price." *Daily Press*, Febru- ary 12. https://www.dailypress.com/news/newport-news/dp-coy-2005-mckinley -price-story.html

Dalton, R. J. 2016. *The Good Citizen: How a Younger Generation Is Reshaping American Politics*. Los Angeles: CQ Press.

Department of Justice. 2021. "Former Fall River Mayor Convicted of Extorting Mari- juana Vendors and Defrauding Investors." May 14. https://www.justice.gov/usao -ma/pr/former-fall-river-mayor-convicted-extorting-marijuana-vendors-and-de frauding-investors

Dimock, M. 2019. *Defining Generations: Where Millennials End and Generation Z Begins*. Pew Research Center, January 17. https://www.pewresearch.org/fact-ta nk/2019/01/17/where-millennials-end-and-generation-z-begins/

Dunlop, K. 2019. "Fixing Potholes in the Digital Age: There's an App for That in New Bedford." *South Coast Daily*, June 16. https://www.southcoasttoday.com/story/ne ws/2019/06/16/fixing-potholes-in-digital-age/4896329007/

Erdody, L. 2014. "Bloomington Mayor Mark Kruzan Not Seeking a 4th Term." *Herald Times*, November 19. https://www.heraldtimesonline.com/story/news/local/20 14/11/19/bloomington-mayor-mark-kruzan-not-seeking-a-4th-term/47521411/

Erdody, L. 2015. "John Hamilton Files Candidacy for Bloomington Mayor." *Hoosier Times*, January 13. https://www.hoosiertimes.com/herald_times_online/news/lo cal/john-hamilton-files-candidacy-for-bloomington-mayor/article_a5b69db7-e6 e8-51e3-b615-c7c133491498.html?redir=0

Farzan, A. 2018. "Elected Mayor at 23 in Struggling Fall River, Jasiel Correia Had the Makings of a Rising Star." *Boston.com*, October 8. https://www.boston.com/news /politics/2018/10/12/fall-river-mayor-jasiel-correia-rising-star-arrest-federal-ch arges/

Fenno, R. 1978. *Homestyle: House Members in Their Districts*. Boston: Little, Brown.

Fitzpatrick, E. 2016. "Young Mayor Isn't Gun-Shy about Fall River's Future." *Providence Journal*, January 10.

Flanagan, R. 2004. *Mayors and the Challenge of Urban Leadership*. Lanham, MD: University Press of America.

Fore, C. 2012. *Next Generation Leadership: Millennials as Leaders*. Minneapolis: Capella University.

Friedman, S., M. A. Armato, and R. Matott. 2019. "How They Govern: Do Millennial Mayors Bring a Generational Perspective to Their Activities?" Paper presented at the Northeastern Political Science Association Conference, Philadelphia.

Fry, R. 2018. *Will Millennial, GenX Voters Match Older Generations in 2018 Turnout?* Pew Research Center, June 14. https://www.pewresearch.org/fact-tank/2018/06 /14/younger-generations-make-up-a-majority-of-the-electorate-but-may-not-be -a-majority-of-voters-this-november/

Funk, C., and A. Tyson. 2020. *Millennial and Gen Z Republicans Stand Out from Their Elders on Climate and Energy Issues*. Pew Research Center, August 24. https://www .pewresearch.org/fact-tank/2020/06/24/millennial-and-gen-z-republicans-stand -out-from-their-elders-on-climate-and-energy-issues/

Gabrick, J. 2011. "B-Line Trail Opens in Bloomington." *Indiana Public Media*, September 9. https://indianapublicmedia.org/news/bline-trail-opens-bloomington .php

Gagne, M. 2016. "Millennials Speak of Generational Needs at Fall River Forum." *Herald News*, April 6.

Gerber, E., and D. Hopkins. 2011. "When Mayors Matter: Estimating the Impact of Mayoral Partisanship on City Policy." *American Journal of Political Science* 55 (2): 326–39.

Greenblatt, A. 2015. "Millennial Generation." *CQ Researcher* 25: 553–76. http://library .cqpress.com/

Hagen, R. 2014. "San Bernardino Plan Aims to Dampen Crime in Short- and Long Term." *San Bernardino Sun*, April 2. https://www.sbsun.com/2014/04/02/san-ber nardino-plan-aims-to-dampen-crime-in-short-and-long-term/

Hagen, R. 2016. "Mayor Carey Davis State of City Speech Channels 'San Bernardino

Strong'." *San Bernardino Sun*, April 22. https://www.sbsun.com/2016/04/22/may or-carey-davis-state-of-city-speech-channels-san-bernardino-strong/

Hamilton Official Mayor Biography. N.d. https://bloomington.in.gov/mayor#:~:text =Mayor%20Hamilton%20was%20born%20in,University%20Maurer%20School %20of%20Law

Hren, J. 2014. "Bloomington Leaders Balancing Development with Uniqueness." *Indiana Public Media*, November 21. https://indianapublicmedia.org/news/deba te-balance-development-kirkwood-uniqueness-75031.php

Hubert, C. 2017. "Michael Tubbs, One of America's Youngest Mayors, Aims to Lift His Hometown of Stockton." *Sacramento Bee*, April 12.

Kaufmann, G. 2020. "A Young Mayor Makes the Case for a Guaranteed Income." *The Nation*, August 16. https://www.thenation.com/article/archive/stockton-californ ia-michael-tubbs-poverty-basic-income/

Kraus, J. 2004. "Generational Conflict in Urban Politics: The 2002 Newark Mayoral Election." *The Forum* 2 (3). https://doi.org/10.2202/1540-8884.1030

Kruszewski, J. 2018. "Mayor Levar Stoney: 7 (Somewhat) Unexpected Things about Being a Young, Single Mayor in Richmond." *Richmond Times Dispatch*, April 17. https://richmond.com/mayor-levar-stoney-7-somewhat-unexpected-things-abo ut-being-a-young-single-mayor-in-richmond/article_0c502c81-dd42-5337-9bcd -ecf21ab8f9d2.html

Lane, L. 2016. "Hamilton Hits Ground Running, Quotes Dr. Seuss." *Herald-Times*, January 2.

Lawlor, J. 2010. "Reserved Mayor Ready to Work." *Daily Press*, July 5.

Lawlor, J. 2011. "Newport News Releases Road Map to Fighting Gangs." *Daily Press*, September 26.

Lawlor, J. 2012. "Newport News Council Revives Anti-Gang Proposal." *Daily Press*, December 5.

Lawrence, M. 2015. "Mayor's Race: Jon Mitchell Takes Long View." *South Coast Today*, October 20. https://www.southcoasttoday.com/article/20151025/NEWS /151029571/

Mannheim, Karl. 1952. "The Problem of Generations." In *Karl Mannheim: Essays*, edited by Paul Kecskemeti. London: Routledge.

Mayor John Valdivia. 2019. "Today, We Had the Pleasure of Welcoming the Third Campus of the Options for Youth Charter School in San Bernardino [image attached] [status update]." Facebook, November 5. https://www.facebook.com/Ma yorJValdivia/posts/today-we-had-the-pleasure-of-welcoming-the-third-campus -of-the-options-for-youth/2584588234932818/

Milkman, R. 2017. "A New Political Generation: Millennials and the Post-2008 Wave of Protest." *American Sociological Review* 82 (1): 1–31. https://doi.org/10.1177/000 3122416681031.

Mitchell, J. 2012. "Poised for Progress." http://s3.amazonaws.com/newbedford-ma/wp -content/uploads/sites/3/20191219193958/Mayor_Speech_2012-1-2.pdf

Mitchell Official Mayor Biography. N.d. https://www.newbedford-ma.gov/mayor/bi ography/

Mohl, B. 2016. "Turning Around New Bedford." *Commonwealth Magazine*, October

10. https://commonwealthmagazine.org/economy/turning-around-new-bedford/

Newport News Virginia Website. 2016. "Local Group Invests $64 Million in Mixed-Use Portfolio in City Center at Oyster Point." July 15. https://newportnewsva.com/local-group-invests-64-million-in-mixed-use-portfolio-in-city-center-at-oyster-point/

Northern Star. 2016. "In Struggling Mill City, 24-Year-Old Mayor Seeks Turnaround." January 19.

Paitsel, N. 2013. "'Walmart {Super Store Close to Downtown} Grand Opening' Brings 340 New Jobs and a Million Dollars in Tax Revenue Annually." *Daily Press*, February 1. https://www.dailypress.com/news/dp-xpm-20130201-2013-02-01-dp-nws-walmart-supercenter-newport-news-20130201-story.html

Parrott, J. 2011. "Chamber Endorses Buttigieg for Mayor." *South Bend Tribune*, April 1, B3.

Peters, J. 2019. "Pete Buttigieg's Life in the Closet." *New York Times*, July 14.

Peterson, M. 2011. "SB Mayor's Race Goes 'Negative'." *South Bend Tribune*, April 29, A1.

Phillips, R. 2016. "Mayoral Candidates' Differing Styles on Display." *Recordnet.com*, June 8. https://www.recordnet.com/article/20160608/NEWS/160609716

Phillips, R. 2017a. "Tubbs Humbled by 'Huge Opportunity' Ahead." *Stockton Record*, January 1, A1.

Phillips, R. 2017b. "Protesters, Police Tangle Downtown in Latest Clash." *Stockton Record*, March 8, A1.

Phillips, R. 2017c. "Stockton Lands Amazon Facility—Venture to Generate 1,000 Jobs for Local Economy." *Stockton Record*, August 3, A1.

Phillips, R. 2019. "Never Too Old to Get Back in the Game—at 76, Ralph Lee White, Who Is Planning Town Hall on Violence, Says He's Running for Mayor." *Stockton Record*, June 5.

Reid, K. 2018. S. J. "Team Wins in NAACP Debate." *Stockton Record*, July 15.

Ress, Dave. 2016. "Here's How Newport News Is Trying to Woo Millennials: A Downtown Urban Waterfront." *Daily Press*, November 21. https://www.dailypress.com/news/newport-news/dp-nws-nn-council-advance-1119-20161118-story.html

Richmond Virginia Mayor Blog. 2017. "Mayor Levar M. Stoney's Statement on City of Richmond FY 2018 Budget." May 19. http://richmondvirginiamayor.blogspot.com/2017/05/mayor-levar-m-stoneys-statement-on-city.html

Richmond Virginia Mayor Blog. 2018. "Mayor Stoney Delivers Budget Proposal for FY2019/2020." March 6. http://richmondvirginiamayor.blogspot.com/2018/03/mayor-stoney-delivers-budget-proposal.html

Rockett, A. 2013. "New Apprentice School to Continue Shipbuilding Tradition in Newport News." *Daily News*, December 6. https://www.dailypress.com/news/newport-news/dp-xpm-20131206-2013-12-06-dp-nws-nn-apprentice-opening-20131207-story.html

Rouse, S., and A. Ross. 2018. *The Politics of Millennials: Political Beliefs and Policy Preferences of America's Most Diverse Generation*. Ann Arbor: University of Michigan Press.

San Bernardino Sun Staff. 2015. "San Bernardino Public Library Spotlights International Literacy Day." *San Bernardino Sun,* September 5. https://www.sbsun.com/2015/09/04/san-bernardino-public-library-spotlights-international-literacy-day/

Schapiro, J. 2016. "2016 RTD Person of the Year: Levar Stoney, Richmond Mayor-Elect." *Richmond Times Dispatch,* December 11.

Siefer, T. 2018. "Fall River's Lightning Rod." *Commonwealth Magazine,* April 10. https://commonwealthmagazine.org/politics/fall-rivers-lightning-rod/

Shalash, S. 2012. "Newport News Schools Recruiting Partners for STEM Initiative." *Daily Press,* March 29.

Sloma, T. 2011. "Pete Buttigieg Becomes Second Youngest Mayor in South Bend." *WNDU 9,* November 9.

Small, A. 2018. "What Millennial Mayors Are Doing for City Hall." *Bloomberg,* January 31. https://www.bloomberg.com/news/articles/2018-01-31/what-millennial-mayors-are-doing-for-city-hall

South Coast Today Staff. 2019. "Mayor Mitchell to Host Office Hours at Brigham Corner Seafood and Pizza." *South Coast Today,* May 28. https://www.southcoasttoday.com/story/news/2019/05/28/mitchell-to-host-office-hours/5044838007/

Stein, L. 2003. "Mayoral Politics." In *Cities, Politics, and Policy,* edited by John P. Pelissero, 148–68. Washington, DC: CQ Press.

Stockton Record Staff. 2016. "No. 2: Tubbs Is Elected Mayor in a Landslide." *Stockton Record,* December 30, A1.

Stockton Record Staff. 2020. "Primary Answers: Michael Tubbs, Mayor of Stockton." *Stockton Record,* March 1. https://www.recordnet.com/story/news/politics/2020/03/01/primary-answers-michael-tubbs-mayor/1609647007/

Stoney Official Mayor Biography. N.d. https://www.rva.gov/mayors-office/about

Tolleson-Rhinehart, S. 2001. "Do Women Leaders Make a Difference? Substance, Style, and Perception." In *The Impact of Women in Public Office,* edited by Susan J. Carroll. Bloomington: Indiana University Press.

Tubbs, M. 2017. "Stockton: Time to Reinvent." *Stockton Record,* May 14, A11.

United States Economic Development Administration. 2014. "U.S. Economic Development Administration Invests $200,000 to Aid Development of Critical Plans to Grow the Manufacturing, Commercial Fishing, and Tourism Sectors in New Bedford, Massachusetts." Press release, April 23.

US State News. 2012. "City of South Bend to Host Minority and Women-Owned Business Outreach Program." October 1.

Vivian, K. 2016. "Diversity and Inclusion Executive Order Issued by South Bend Mayor Pete Buttigieg." *95.3 MNC.com,* January 18. https://www.953mnc.com/2016/01/18/south-bend-diversity/

Whitehead, B. 2018a. "Here's What You Need to Know about San Bernardino Mayoral, City Council Candidates ahead of Election Day." *San Bernardino Sun,* May 27. https://www.sbsun.com/2018/05/27/heres-what-you-need-to-know-about-san-bernardino-mayoral-city-council-candidates-ahead-of-election-day/

Whitehead, B. 2018b. "Mayoral Candidates Lay Out Plans for Citizen Participation, Downtown Renaissance." *Redlands Daily Facts,* April 18, A6.

Whitehead, B. 2018c. "Valdivia Is on Verge of Taking Over Mayor's Post." *San Bernardino Sun*, November 8, A1.

Yarbrough, B. 2014. "Carey Davis Elected San Bernardino Mayor." *San Bernardino Sun*, February 14. https://www.sbsun.com/2014/02/05/carey-davis-elected-san-bernardino-mayor/

Zeleny, J. 2019. "Buttigieg Wields His Military Credentials: 'It's Not Like I Killed Bin Laden,' but It Was Dangerous." *CNN*, May 17. https://edition.cnn.com/2019/05/17/politics/buttigieg-military-service-2020/index.html

14 | The Language of Representation

How Millennial and Non-Millennial Legislators Present Themselves to Constituents

Sally Friedman, Emily R. Matott, and Andrew McMahon

> There's actually a millennial cohort! We live our best lives together, and do the work on behalf of young people who have not had a voice in this chamber. . . . I'm really excited because we all come from different backgrounds in terms of geography, upbringing, lived experience, race, ethnicity, but we're united based on our experiences in the same generation. What's also great is that there are a lot of Republicans who are also millennials. It's a wonderful time to be able to do bipartisan work on issues that are so important to folks in our generation.
> —Representative Lauren Underwood (D-IL)

The 2018 midterm elections saw a record number of Millennials (for purposes of this chapter members of Congress born between 1981 and 1995) entering Congress (Dimock 2019).[1] Going from 5 to 26 members, "Millennials in Congress just went up by 420%" (Morrow 2019). Additionally, these Millennials included a distinguished group in the House of Representatives, among them Ilhan Omar (the first Somali woman to serve), Lauren Underwood (the youngest black woman thus far elected), and Alexandria Ocasio-Cortez and Dan Crenshaw (the latter two having achieved national reputations including for their ideology). Of these Millennial members of Congress, 6 are women and 8 are minorities, with several members being minority women. It is then an interesting time to see, as Rep. Underwood quoted above suggests, whether this new group of legislators indeed governs differently.

From the scholarly literature on Congress, we know of the many influences on legislative behavior, including constituency, party, and a member's own background. We also know that demographic identities, including race and gender, can impact many aspects of legislative behavior (Dittmar et al. 2018; Gross 2011). Due to specific historical circumstances and socializing experiences, does it also make a difference if a legislator is a member of a particular generation (in this case, Millennials)?

Hypothesizing that it can, we take a crack at applying the available knowledge on Millennials as a generational cohort (compared to their non-Millennial counterparts) to the topics and language that the House members elected in 2018 use across various channels of representation. We apply the latest in web scraping technology/content analysis (Grimmer 2013), analyzing a diverse set of data sets (legislator press releases, tweets, website biographies, and bills sponsored) to examine legislator communication across a wide range of representational activities.

The findings are a mixed bag. Does generation (here Millennial status) make a difference? The answer depends on what it means for a generation to in fact make a difference. If one expects to be hit over the head with a Millennial identity in this data set, expectations are not borne out. Null findings and even numbers pointing in directions opposite to those hypothesized are apparent in the tables below, and the small number of cases, especially for Republican Millennials, add to the difficulty of interpreting the data. That said, throughout there are indeed indications of a Millennial imprint; in most of our tables, there are ways in which some Millennials do things differently than non-Millennials. Given all the potential influences on the activities of members of Congress, and given the difficulty of capturing a generational effect (see, for example, other chapters in this volume), we think the data shown here provides evidence of a Millennial effect. As in the preceding chapter on the impact of Millennial mayors (Friedman, Armato, and Matott, chap. 13, this vol.), we answer the question of whether Millennials do things differently (in this case, communicate with constituents) with a qualified yes.

This chapter seeks to make a couple of contributions to the study of generational analysis. Methodologically, the web scraping technology employed here allows for an examination of incredibly large amounts of information, more substantively allowing us to look at a diverse set of legislator activities. The use of this technology also helps us focus on the words and topics legislators focus on, thus probing a nuanced aspect of ways generational cohorts can become relevant. Differently, the paper is also one effort to apply and extend what we know about Millennials at the mass level of politics to the elite level and to build on the literature on Congress by connecting a generational focus to tried-and-true activities of legislative representation. The findings have implications for the future as generational replacement means more Millennials will come to occupy positions of political power.

Literature and Hypotheses

Building an expected conceptual understanding of how Millennial members of Congress may differ, through their language and communications, in their approach from other members must be built upon a two-way perspective. It is rooted in both the approaches of congressional representation spanning seven decades of evolving theory and in social scientific research on the role of generations generally and the Millennial cohort in particular.

As it is considered to be the "first" branch of government, members of the U.S. Congress are particularly tasked with "representing" the will of the people, and political scientists have pointed up the myriad ways members of the legislative branch engage in these representational activities. For starters, there is the distinction between descriptive (demographic) and substantive representation (Pitkin 1967). Descriptively, it is often argued that legislators should demographically mirror the population characteristics of a nation in order to enhance citizen perceptions of fairness and legitimacy and to hold out possibilities for role models for future generations.

Substantively, members engage in a wide variety of activities including representing the issue positions of constituents (Miller and Stokes 1963; Grimmer 2013), engaging in a surprising number of local- and district-oriented activities (Fenno 1978), and, particularly given modern-day political polarization, members of Congress need increasingly to publicize their partisanship to their constituents and make decisions as to how much to go along with their national parties (Barber and McCarty 2015; Lee 2016).

But where do Millennials fit into this picture? Do the increasing number of Millennials entering Congress—and the potential of the even greater increases to come—bring, as Rep. Underwood (quoted at the top of this chapter) believes, a different perspective to their representational activities? Given the plethora of work on the importance of generations, including the diverse set of chapters in this volume, we think generation potentially impacts the ways members of Congress will view their jobs.

Following the categories of representation described above, we examine aspects of the activities of Millennials. In terms of issue priorities, we focus on a set of issues that either have been described as important to Millennials on the basis of academic and popular surveys of mass public opinion or issues that simply seem to be associated with the Millennial persona. All things considered, do Millennials at the elite level of politics bring these concerns forward as a key part of their political agenda?

For starters, the formative experiences of Millennials were centered in part on the economic recession of 2007–8, including the possibilities for increased unemployment or underemployment, as well as increasing student debt (Greenblatt 2015; MacManus and Cilluffo, chap. 12, this vol.). When asked about what they see as the most important issues facing their age group or generation, economic issues rate high (Rouse and Ross 2018). More specifically, while the economy has been among the highest priorities for both Millennials and non-Millennials, the specific economic foci of these groups differ somewhat as it makes sense that unemployment is of greater concern for Millennials and the cost of entitlement programs is of greater concern to non-Millennials (Rouse and Ross 2018). Income inequality is equally important to both groups, though clearly it is an issue often particularly promulgated by young people, as evidenced by their support for Bernie Sanders' 2016 and 2020 presidential campaigns (Higgons 2019). Not surprisingly, student debt was also a higher priority for Millennials than non-Millennials (Rouse and Ross 2018).

With these economic issues and related themes running through the narrative of the Millennial experience, we expect that Millennial legislators will in turn bring a higher level of scrutiny to these topics in their legislative communications. To be certain, the economy is a large portion of what legislators talk about in general and so our hypothesis here is that specific economic concerns (e.g., unemployment, income inequality) will be more frequent for Millennials than non-Millennials. General commentary on the state of the economy will not differ across groups.

In terms of foreign policy, it has been argued that Millennial socialization has been influenced on the one hand by the events of 9/11 and on the other by trends promoting globalization (Rouse and Ross 2018).

As Stella Rouse and Ashley Ross describe, "The attitudes of Millennials about foreign policy therefore, may have as much, if not more, to do with the collective effects of globalization as with the narrower scope of the 9/11 attacks and the wars in the Middle East. Overall, Millennials are less likely to embrace an adversarial position (compared to other cohorts) when it comes to dealing with other countries; they believe more in diplomacy and international cooperation than resorting to military force" (Rouse and Ross 2018, 107). We hypothesize here that Millennials in Congress will therefore focus more on terrorism and be more supportive of international institutions (here, NATO).

Additionally, climate change is said to be more important to Millennials than their older counterparts in the mass public. Though, according to Rouse and Ross (2018), only 5 percent of Millennials thought climate change was the most important issue facing their age and generation, other "surveys indicate that Millennials—sometimes described as the 'greenest generation'—take the issue of climate change seriously" (Greenblatt 2015). A recent Gallup poll (Reinhart 2018) found that younger Americans were more likely to worry "a good deal" or a "fair amount" about it, and a recent set of surveys conducted by researchers at Yale University suggests that climate issues could be a greater priority for the Millennial generation in determining their presidential vote (Ballew et al. 2019). It is also thought that Republican Millennials particularly differ from their older cohorts in the extent to which they focus on the issue and believe its causes are man-made (Funk and Tyson 2020).

Millennials in the mass public are described as more liberal than their older counterparts (Pew 2018; Ross and Rouse, chap. 11, this vol.). But representation goes well beyond issues. We hypothesize that Millennial legislators will be less attuned to partisan politics and consequently be more bipartisan in their communications than their non-Millennial counterparts. By a number of accounts, the younger generation is described as disaffected from the political world, particularly traditional political institutions (Greenblatt 2015; Pew 2014). "It has been a period during which Americans, especially Millennials, have become more detached from major institutions such as political parties, religion, the military and marriage" (Fry et al. 2018) and the media (Fingerhut 2016). They have also been described as more politically independent (see Stoker, chap. 2, and MacManus and Cilluffo, chap. 12, this vol.). Millennials are said to seek practical solutions to problems regardless of where those solutions come from and demonstrate flexibility in their approach to problem solving (Diggles 2014; Ermidis 2017). The implication is that Millennials in Congress will be less likely to attend to the work of political parties and to value bipartisanship more in their political communications. In terms of our words and phrases demonstrating partisanship (see appendix), we hypothesize that Millennial legislators might eschew the views of party leaders more, use words indicating partisanship to a lesser degree, and point up to an even greater extent than other legislators the need for bipartisanship and bipartisan solutions to social problems.[2]

Finally, we expect Millennial members of Congress to be more concerned with issues of diversity and inclusion given the demographic diversity of the generation along with the tendency of the generation to emphasize diversity-related issues (Greenblatt 2015; Parker 2019). We hypothesize that the differences between the Millennial generation and non-Millennials will translate into different language choices, including a higher proportion of words and phrases associated with their identities.

Some caveats are in order. Demographics clearly have been shown to matter in studies of representation, but not all the time and not under all conditions. Regardless of the influence of identity characteristics, other factors matter too—including the need to represent all constituents, day-to-day events, and partisanship. While we hypothesize Millennials should bring different perspectives to their jobs, the broader demands of the representational role should also matter.

Research Design

As the literature on Congress has examined the impact of identity characteristics including race and gender, this chapter takes a generational approach to the analysis of one cohort of freshman legislators. We compare the language that Millennial members of Congress use to describe their representational activities with that of their older counterparts, both groups of legislators elected for the first time in 2018. Thus, we examine the impact of Millennial vs. non-Millennial status on the language freshman legislators use to present themselves to constituents. Through web scraping (the collection of large amounts of data from open-source websites using automation) the content analysis of a number of diverse data sources, we examine the words and groups of words Millennial and non-Millennial freshmen use to characterize the types of representational activities described above—descriptive representation, their issue priorities, partisanship, and some of their constituency-oriented activities.

With the context of the 2018 election held constant, we took advantage of the latest in modern technology and innovative trends in content analysis to web scrape (see, for example, Grimmer 2013) four different data sets (press releases, official Twitter accounts, website biographies, and sponsored bills), each designed to capture a specific aspect of the language legislator's use when presenting their activities to constituents. As Grimmer (2013) describes press releases, "Press releases are one of the most important tools legislators use to present work to constituents. They serve as a communication tool used by all (or at least most) legislators, and as a source of data, they provide systematic information on what legislators do—the meetings they hold; the events/issues they are concerned about and the actions they take on the job" (Grimmer 2013, 29). Cumulatively, these data sets offer a large body of content sources to analyze for differences between Millennial and non-Millennial freshman legislators.

These data sources have a couple of other advantages. They provide systematic sources for Congress member's activities, and they are used by all (or at least most) legislators. At the same time, legislators have considerable leeway in their focus. As Grimmer notes in his study of Senate press releases, "Press releases are also useful for studying legislators' expressed priorities because there are no formal constraints on what [legislators] can say in their press releases other than the usual separation between the senators' legislative work and campaigning" (Grimmer 2013, 32). To the extent that these data sources point up issues that are most important to individual legislators, different generations of legislators should be more likely to put a different slant on this material. Collectively the data sets offer a comprehensive examination of the important communication tools of modern politicians and offer a diverse set of circumstances under which they might offer opinions, positions, and locutions on any number of topics.

In all these ways, the question of interest compares the 20 Millennial legislators first elected in 2018 to their 66 non-Millennial counterparts. We expect Millennial legislators, as described above, to be more likely to focus on their generation (fellow Millennials). We also expect Millennial legislators, if they are consistent with what Millennials at the level of the mass public do, to focus on issues thought to be of greatest interest or importance to Millennials and to be more likely to promote bipartisan solutions. (Expectations are less clear about differences in constituency service activities—perhaps Millennials engage more in efforts to form more inclusive coalitions or perhaps all freshman legislators need to make such engagement a critical part of their job as they focus on reelection—since these activities are an important part of a legislator's job and since all these data sets are replete with examples of these activities, we wanted to keep them as part of the study.)

Technically, we web scraped this data via R and we used R-studio to work through our scraped data and analyze its content. The web scraping process allows automation to collect the relevant data from open-source internet pages (e.g., legislator press releases) into files that can be statistically analyzed. The most critical issue in doing this kind of content analysis is developing a set of words and phrases (and, by proxy, larger ideas) by which to examine the data, in this case the operationalization of the representational activities described above. We accomplished this task via consulting expert colleagues and by examining the press releases themselves for the words and phrases members of Congress themselves used (Grimmer 2013). While there is an ad hoc nature to this kind of work, based on examination of the data, it appears the words and, for our purposes, groups of words, we derived (see appendix) seem like a reasonable starting point.[3]

We began with descriptive representation—how likely are Millennial (and non-Millennial) legislators to use specific words signifying generations, e.g., Millennial, Baby Boomer, the word "generation," and how does their usage compare with non-Millennials? Relatedly, are Millennials more likely to focus on the language of diversity and inclusion, such as referring to categories including race, gender, and LGBTQ? The groups of issue words (substantive representation) we flagged were designed to capture the issues that have been most associated with Millennial socialization, including education/student debt, aspects of the economy, climate change, and some foreign policy issues. Finally, as is said of the mass public, are Millennials in the context of Congress less attuned to partisanship?

All told, the data set reflects the latest in modern technology, including covering about 10,500 press releases, roughly 95,000 tweets, over 1,500 bills sponsored, and the website biographies of 86 members of Congress.[4]

In the next sections, we present tables comparing the language used by Millennial and non-Millennial freshmen on the various representational categories. Before going further, though, two clarifying points are in order. First, it is important to verify that this group of Millennial legislators is reasonably similar on some key demographic and electoral characteristics to their non-Millennial counterparts (table 14.1). There are some differences between Millennial and non-Millennial legislators. Compared to non-Millennial legislators, a smaller percentage (43% to 60%) of Millennial Democrats are women, the districts of Millennial Republicans are a little better off and notably less rural than non-Millennial Republicans, and Republican Millennials come out a little less conservative on the DW Nominate score measure commonly used to describe ideology in legislative politics. On a scale where closer to -1 indicates more liberal stands, Millennial Democrats come out just about as liberal as their non-Millennial counterparts; Republican Millennials are a little less conservative. On balance, though, there are more similarities than differences, the differences seem a matter of degree, and a number of the standard deviations are large enough to demonstrate considerable variation around these averages.[5]

Second, do Millennial and non-Millennial legislators differ in these types of activities? For instance, are Millennial legislators more likely to communicate with constituents via social media/Twitter and therefore less likely to use more traditional means such as press releases? Are Millennials, as younger legislators and as potentially newer to the political process, less likely to sponsor bills?

Table 14.2 suggests party differences—Democrats are more likely to come out higher on all these activities—but there are no particular differences between Millennials and non-Millennials. As distributions are skewed, the median seems a more appropriate measure of central tendency. By this measure, Millennials of both parties put out a few more press releases; Millennials of both parties are less likely to tweet; and there were no differences in bill sponsorship. In all cases, though, the differences are small, and as in table 14.1, standard deviations around the averages show considerable variation. We turn then to a discussion of the language Millennial and non-Millennial legislators use to describe the various representational categories.

We describe the findings displayed in each individual table (tables 14.3–14.5) below. While there are some differences between the groups that we think are important, the bottom line is that, reasonable hypotheses of difference notwithstanding, one might have expected these differences to be even larger. That is, the literature on the attitudes and beliefs of Millennials in the mass public leads to some pretty clear

TABLE 14.1. Demographic and Member Characteristics, Millennials and Non-Millennials, Elected 2018

District Characteristics		Democrat		Republican	
		Millennial	Non-Millennial	Millennial	Non-Millennial
Rural	Percent	7%	2%	0%	46%
Rural-Suburban	Percent	14%	10%	33%	29%
Suburban	Percent	57%	67%	67%	25%
Suburban-Urban	Percent	7%	17%	0%	0%
Urban	Percent	14%	5%	0%	0%
Per Capita Income	Mean	$36,319	$38,671	$33,350	$30,822
	Std. Dev.	$7,617	$10,264	$4,828	$4,847
Median Age	Mean	39	38	39.9	40.3
	Std. Dev.	3.4	3.5	4.1	4
% Millennials (ages 25–34)	Mean	14%	14%	13%	12%
	Std. Dev.	2.7	2.5	2	1.5
Race (percent White)	Mean	78%	74%	81%	83%
	St. Dev.	13.7	11.1	11.4	9.7
Race (percent Black)	Mean	8%	9%	9%	9%
	St. Dev.	5.9	9	6.8	8.1
Ethnicity (percent Hispanic)	Mean	18%	23%	14%	9%
	St. Dev.	18.7	23.1	13.2	7.7
2018 vote share, %	Mean	59%	57%	63%	58%
	Std. Dev.	11.3	8.7	18.6	4.9
Percent Legislators who are Female		43%	60%	0%	4%
Percent Legislators who are Black		29%	10%	0%	0%
Percent Legislators who are Hispanic		14%	17%	17%	0%
Ideology (DW Nominate Score)	Mean	−0.28	−0.32	0.46	0.53
	Std. Dev.	0.14	0.12	0.17	0.19
N		14	42	6	24

TABLE 14.2. Congressional Activities by Millennial and Party Status

	Democrat		Republican	
	Millennial	Non-Millennial	Millennial	Non-Millennial
Press Release				
Mean	155	148	69	80
Median	146	134	76	74
Standard Deviation	59	74	33	41
Min	70	59	27	7
Max	290	409	106	167
Tweets				
Mean	1021	1313	657	851
Median	995	1296	598	661
Standard Deviation	659	501	418	559
Min	105	460	293	275
Max	2502	2216	1438	2319
Bills				
Mean	28	25	12	14
Median	25	26	14	12
Standard Deviation	12	8	5	8
Min	13	10	4	4
Max	53	51	16	38
N	14a	42	6	24

a Rep Ocasio-Cortez doesn't use press releases.

expectations about how Millennials should be different. Writ large, these expectations do not jump out from a perusal of these tables. Percentages for Millennials are often similar to those for their non-Millennial same-party counterparts, and in a number of cases, results run against generational expectations.

That said, there are in each of the tables below some ways in which Millennials are in fact different. To make the strongest possible case, for each of the categories described below, we present data from the two sources that best make the argument for a Millennial effect, and we provide illustrative examples. Given the multitude of influences on this set of legislators along with the expected variation among characteristics of the legislators, a small but discernible impact of the Millennial members, even at this early stage of their inclusion in Congress, seems worth highlighting.

Descriptive Representation/Diversity

In table 14.3, we focus on descriptive representation. How likely are legislators to use generational words in their presentations to constituents? Are Millennial legislators more likely to directly use the word "Millennial?" Are they more likely to invoke the language of diversity or refer to traditionally underrepresented groups?

Table 14.3 presents for the press release and website biographical data percentages of some of the words and groups of words generational analysis would expect to be used more frequently by Millennial legislators.

First, words to describe specific generations were used quite sparingly in the press releases, nine times for Millennials, six times for Baby Boomers, and not at all for the Silent generation or Gen Z (the latter not shown). Similarly, the word "Millennial" showed up in only 22 tweets, one website biography, and none of the bills sponsored (which likely have a more issue-based focus).

Nonetheless, there are some interesting trends in the data. In the press releases, Millennial and non-Millennial Democrats used the word "Millennial" sparingly but in roughly equal percentages; though based on small numbers, 33 percent of Millennial Republicans ($N = 6$) did so compared to none of their older Republican counterparts. Democratic Millennials are a little more likely to include the word "Millennial" in their website biographies. It is clear though that these words are used infrequently, and the differences come down to usage by one or two representatives.

Of particular interest is the limited use of the word "Millennial" in the web biographies of these legislators. In a forum where one might expect members of Congress to highlight what is most important to them, these legislators are not jumping on the generational bandwagon to let their constituents know they represent a new generation and could therefore bring a different perspective to the legislature. Are they, even as they represent constituents of all ages, missing an opportunity to invoke a fresh kind of generational campaign strategy?

There are nonetheless a handful of clear statements expressing a "Millennial identity." Rep. Underwood (D-IL) let her constituents know she is the "the first woman, the first person of color, and the first Millennial to represent her community in Congress. She is also the youngest African American woman to serve in the United States House of Representatives" (website biography). Rep. Crenshaw (R-TX) also described himself as a Millennial when he "introduced H.R. 4559, the End-of-Year Fiscal Responsibility Act, to end the tendency of federal agencies to spend leftover money at the end of the fiscal year rather than returning it to the Treasury." He noted that as a "conservative Millennial," "I'm painfully aware of the potential consequences my generation faces if we fail to confront our over $22 trillion debt" (P.R. [press release] 9/27/2019). Former Representative Katie Hill (D-CA)—who subsequently resigned due to a scandal (Wire et al. 2019), and thus her press releases are not included in our overall tallies—nonetheless also "spoke like a Millennial" in the time she was in Congress. In cosponsoring a bill to "ensure unanticipated financial emergencies do not prevent low-income students from pursuing and completing higher education," Hill noted that "'as a Millennial in Congress who has been personally affected by the astronomical costs of higher education, I'm proud to introduce the CAMPUS Act with Representative Morelle, which will provide a safety net for low-income students who face emergency expenses that would otherwise force them to drop out'" (Morelle, P.R. 9/12/2019).[6] There were also occasional references to a generational identity:[7] "I can speak from personal experience, as a former first-generation student and now a mother of two young girls. It is a struggle to look past sticker prices to understand how much your family actually needs to earn, save, or borrow in order to afford a college degree" (Lori Trahan [D-MA], P.R. 10/29/2019). Others demonstrated a generational awareness by highlighting specific priorities: "Excited to represent Colorado and the Rocky Mountain West on the Select Committee on Climate. I hope to be a voice for my generation by advocating for bold, progressive solutions on climate change." #ActOnClimate—Rep Joe Neguse (Tweet 2/7/2019). "We often hear 'show me your budget, show me your values.' In the Budget Committee this week, we voted on a Dem proposal increasing spending caps, with no insight on how the money would be spent. 'Values' this shows? Endless spending at the expense of my generation."—Rep Crenshaw (Tweet 4/5/2019).

As a group, these legislators don't generally use generational words to describe their individual identities or their own formative experiences, and Millennials don't appear to focus on "generation" more than non-Millennials. Nonetheless, the few examples in the data set suggest

TABLE 14.3. Demographic Words by Millennial and Party Status, Biographies and Press Releases*

	Democrat		Republican				
Word/Phrase	Millennial	Non-Millennial	Millennial	Non-Millennial	Frequency by Member	Frequency by Bio or PR	Percent of Bio or PR
Bios							
Generation	21%	21%	17%	38%	22	22	26%
Baby Boomer*	0%	0%	0%	0%	0	0	0%
Millennial*	7%	0%	0%	0%	1	1	1%
Race	12%	14%	0%	0%	7	7	8%
Hispanic	7%	14%	0%	4%	8	8	9%
Gender	36%	45%	0%	21%	29	29	0%
LGBTQ+	7%	2%	0%	0%	2	2	2%
Poor*	0%	0%	0%	0%	0	0	0%
Low Income*	0%	0%	0%	0%	0	0	0%
Middle Class*	14%	0%	17%	0%	3	3	3%
Diversity Group	21%	19%	17%	0%	12	12	14%
Diversity*	0%	2%	17%	0%	2	2	2%
N	14	42	6	24			

PR

Generation	93%	100%	83%	92%	82	982	9%
Baby Boomer*	14%	7%	0%	0%	5	6	0%
Millennial*	7%	12%	33%	0%	8	9	0%
Race	71%	79%	83%	54%	61	251	2%
Hispanic	50%	76%	0%	13%	42	316	3%
Gender	93%	100%	100%	96%	84	4093	39%
LGBTQ+	64%	74%	0%	8%	42	155	1%
Poor*	57%	81%	17%	29%	50	142	1%
Low Income*	50%	48%	33%	13%	32	72	1%
Middle Class*	86%	74%	33%	25%	51	132	1%
Diversity Group	100%	100%	67%	83%	80	1520	14%
Diversity*	79%	88%	33%	21%	55	168	2%
N	14	42	6	24			

that some do focus on their Millennial identity or make it a point to reach out to focus on the identity of what they see as an important constituency group.[8]

Finally, are Millennial legislators more likely to invoke diversity-related topics more frequently than their older counterparts? Words and phrases we sought to analyze along these lines included the word (or groups of words) invoking "diversity" (see appendix). We also examined the propensity of Millennial legislators to "communicate" more in terms of a variety of "marginalized" groups, expecting Millennial legislators to focus more on "race," "Hispanic," "gender," "LGBTQ," and the "poor."

In table 14.3 (press releases and website biographies) there are no differences among Millennial and non-Millennial Democrats and a few differences between Republican Millennials and non-Millennials. In the press releases, Republican Millennials are somewhat more likely to communicate about "race," people who are "low income," and "diversity." The same is found in the biographies for "diversity" and "middle class." Though obviously based on small numbers of legislators (six Millennial Republicans), a pattern of difference emerges worthy of future investigation.

Substantive Representation

What about specific issues, and what about the relevance of party? Recall first that Millennials in the mass public are hypothesized to be less attuned to institutions including political parties. Therefore, as representatives in Congress they would be expected to be less ideological, less attentive to the activities of party leaders, and more bipartisan. According to the percentages of tweets and usage of the relevant words in their website biographies, there are hints that this may at times be the case (table 14.4).[9] Based on the tweets, Millennials of both parties are less likely to use the words in our ideology category. Democratic Millennials are somewhat less likely to refer to party leaders. In the biographical data, Millennials of both parties are less likely to invoke references to Democrats and Republicans (party words) as well as the variety of words in our partisan and ideological categories.[10]

Examples from the website biographies of a few of these legislators provide the spirit behind the hypotheses. A few Millennial legislators certainly present a nonpartisan problem-solving mold:

Bryan [Steil (R-WI] is a problem solver with extensive private sector experience who puts politics aside and focuses on issues impacting Wisconsin.

Andy [Kim (D-NJ)] is a dedicated public servant, who believes service is a way of life. He worked as a career public servant under both Democrats and Republicans, and served at the Pentagon, State Department, the White House National Security Council, and in Afghanistan as an advisor to Generals Petraeus and Allen.[11]

That said, the percentages in the tables remind us not to push this tendency too far. Several members of both parties hold positions at some level of party leadership, and the language of legislators, regardless of generation, can get pretty partisan.

Millennial Rep. Ilhan Omar:

In Georgia, where Brian Kemp oversaw the largest voter purge in history, poll closures correlate almost perfectly with high poverty areas across the state—where people are more likely to vote Democratic. (Tweet 2/26/2019)

Millennial Rep. William Timmons (R-SC):

There continues to be a lot of chatter about the President and Speaker Pelosi's "impeachment inquiry." I believe President Trump and his Administration are correct in calling out the Democrats on their . . . political show. I called the Speaker's announcement on September 25 "political theater," and what we have seen over the past two weeks has, unfortunately, confirmed that I was right. (Tweet 10/11/2019)

But what about differences in the language used on specific issues? Table 14.5 presents data from the press releases and bills sponsored data sets. In both data sets, party differences notwithstanding, we see some impact for Millennials. Party differences are relevant. To varying degrees, Democrats and Republicans emphasize different issues in

TABLE 14.4. Party and Constituency Words, Tweets and Biographies

	Democrat		Republican		Members using word or group of words (N)	Tweets or Bios (N)	Tweets or Bios (%)
	Millennial	Non-Millennial	Millennial	Non-Millennial			
Tweets							
Partisan Words	100%	100%	100%	100%	86	51,367	54%
Ideology Words	43%	50%	67%	79%	50	208	0%
Liberal and/or Conservative	0%	12%	67%	67%	25	72	0%
Pelosi and/or McCarthy	21%	24%	100%	96%	42	262	0%
Leadership Words	64%	86%	100%	96%	74	529	1%
Party Words (D and R)	100%	100%	100%	100%	86	51,367	54%
Bipartisan*	93%	100%	100%	100%	85	3,044	3%
Constituency Service Words	100%	100%	100%	100%	86	9,403	10%
N	14	42	6	24			

Bios

Partisan Words	14%	21%	17%	38%	21	21	24%
Ideology Words	12%	14%	0%	30%	14	14	16%
Liberal and/or Conservative	0%	0%	0%	25%	6	6	7%
Pelosi and/or McCarthy	0%	0%	0%	4%	1	1	1%
Leadership Words	0%	2%	0%	4%	2	2	2%
Party Words (D and R)	14%	21%	17%	38%	21	21	24%
Bipartisan*	0%	29%	0%	4%	12	12	14%
Constituency Service Words	29%	31%	50%	17%	24	24	28%
N	14	42	6	24			

TABLE 14.5. Issue Words by Millennial and Party Status, Press Releases and Bills Sponsored

Word/Phrase	Democrat		Republican		Members using word or group of words (N)	PR or Bills (N)	PR or Bills (%)
	Millennial	Non-Millennial	Millennial	Non-Millennial			
PR							
Economy							
Economic Issue Words	100%	100%	100%	100%	86	2,860	27%
Economic Issue Words No Economic	93%	100%	100%	83%	81	656	6%
Unemployment*	57%	64%	17%	58%	50	106	1%
Income Inequality*	14%	19%	0%	0%	10	20	0%
Education							
Education Issue Words	93%	100%	100%	100%	85	1870	18%
Education Issue Words No Education	93%	100%	83%	83%	80	712	7%
Student Debt Words	57%	52%	17%	13%	34	94	0%
Climate							
Climate Issue Words	93%	100%	83%	83%	80	1,243	12%
Climate Issue Words No Climate	93%	100%	83%	79%	79	1,190	11%
Foreign Policy							
Foreign Policy Issue Words	93%	100%	100%	100%	85	5,738	54%

Terrorism Words	86%	83%	100%	83%	73	411	4%
NATO*	14%	24%	17%	33%	21	44	0%
Marijuana							
Marijuana Issue Words	21%	31%	0%	13%	19	36	0%
Bills							
Economy							
Economic Issue Words	100%	95%	100%	83%	80	416	23%
Economic Issue Words No Economic	93%	79%	33%	54%	61	149	8%
Unemployment*	71%	62%	33%	13%	41	59	3%
Income Inequality*	7%	0%	0%	0%	1	1	0%
Education							
Education Issue Words	100%	100%	83%	92%	83	574	32%
Education Issue Words No Education	57%	81%	17%	38%	52	136	75%

their press releases. It is not surprising to note that Democrats are notably more likely to talk about issues such as climate change, income inequality, student debt, and marijuana.

But generation matters too. For Democrats in the press release data, it is often the case that non-Millennial legislators use "Millennial" words more often than the Millennials themselves. While all legislators focus on the economy and education (not a surprise), it is in fact non-Millennial Democrats who are more likely to use language including income inequality. It is also non-Millennial Democrats who are more likely to discuss unemployment, NATO, or marijuana.

The story is a little different for bills sponsored. There are a number of instances in table 14.5 where Democratic Millennials indeed invoke the issue categories expected of them more often than non-Millennials.[12] There are also indications in both the press release and bills sponsored data that Republican Millennials may indeed be using language in directions expected by Millennial theory. The caveat of small numbers notwithstanding, in the press release data this occurs in several places, including in the education, climate, and foreign policy categories. This is less the case with the bills sponsored data, but we see differences in the climate change and the foreign policy categories. In the case of the economic issue words and economic issue words sans the word economics, Republican Millennials talk less about economic issues when economics is not included.

Some examples from randomly chosen representatives make the point. Millennial Democrats are certainly among the representatives who focus on issues including student loans and climate change. For example, Millennial Rep. Colin Allred (D-TX) was among those proposing a Better Service to Borrowers Act (P.R. 6/27/2019), and Millennial Rep. Omar (D-MN) proposed an amendment to an Education and Labor bill to insure benefits to students over and above advantages to lenders and banks (P.R. 10/31/2019).

But non-Millennial Democrats also communicate about this issue. For example, along with a number of colleagues, Rep. Cindy Axne (D-IA) introduced the "Transform Student Debt to Home Equity Act" of 2019, which would "allow college graduates to roll federal student loan debt into a home mortgage through the purchase of a federally-owned vacant property" (P.R. 6/27/2019). Similarly, Representative Susie Lee (D-NV) "questioned Department of Education officials today on the troubling recent closures of dozens of for-profit colleges, as well as the department's mishandling of such closures at the expense of thousands of students" (P.R. 6/20/2019).

On climate change, Millennial Rep. Kim (D-NJ) announced the relaunch of a Democratic task force on national security that would be tasked with developing "policy solutions to complex challenges threatening our national security . . . from cyber warfare to global instability caused by climate change" (P.R. 9/18/2019). Joe Neguse (D-CO) introduced a "green government" resolution urging Congress to take steps to turn the U.S. Capitol green; he wanted Congress to take responsibility for climate change in the face of the inaction of the Trump administration (P.R. 11/14/2019).

Again, non-Millennial legislators do the same kind of work. "Rep. Lucy McBath (D-GA) and colleagues in the House of Representatives unveiled a new framework for a five-year, $760 billion investment to create an estimated 10 million jobs addressing some of the country's most urgent infrastructure needs, [setting] a path toward zero carbon pollution from the transportation sector, creating jobs, protecting our natural resources, promoting environmental justice and increasing resiliency to climate change. [and insuring] a transportation system that is green, affordable, reliable, efficient and provides access to jobs" (P.R. 1/30/2020). Similarly, Rep. Susie Lee (D-NV) and colleagues from Nevada introduced the bipartisan Colorado River Drought Contingency Plan Authorization Act. As Rep. Lee noted, "This bill is a good first step but I will continue fighting to make sure Congress takes more concrete action in fighting climate change and water shortages" (P.R. 4/3/2019).

From these examples, have Millennial issues, especially for Democrats, become mainstream? Have the issues associated with the formative experiences of Millennials—student debt, income inequality, climate change—gained enough traction in the popular press and within political parties so they are no longer unique to Millennials? The Sanders' campaigns of 2016 and 2020 certainly publicized many of the "Millennial" concerns and pushed segments of the Democratic Party to the left, as reflected in the 2020 Democratic Party platform: "The platform is created to uplift working people and write out the values that will guide our party for years to come." Sections on the party's website go further to point up the importance of "Building a Stronger, Fairer Economy," "Combating the Climate Crisis," and "Providing a World-Class Education in Every Zip Code" (DNC 2020).

So at least on the Democratic side, perhaps Millennials have already done their job, and by whatever process, the issues we associate with a Millennial identity have become mainstream. But what of Republicans? Small numbers notwithstanding, there are a number of places in the table including on education, climate, and terrorism where Republican legislators were more likely to take the "Millennial" perspective.[13]

Discussion and Speculation

So how do we interpret these findings? Rep. Underwood (quoted at the beginning of this chapter) perceives a notable impact for the Millennial generation. But, in reality, what would such an impact look like? The data displayed here certainly doesn't hit us over the head with the kind of generational effect described in the myriad of articles, tweets, and speculative writings that highlight how the Millennial generation is different. Percentage differences in the tables between Millennials and non-Millennials are not always large and not always in the direction expected by generational theory. Yet over and above the impact of one of the most important variables in the literature on Congress— political party—we do see something of a generational impact. Writ large and realizing the many other factors that explain congressional behavior, we see areas where Millennials differ from their non-Millennial counterparts. Democratic Millennials in particular appear to use "Millennial" language when sponsoring bills, and small numbers notwithstanding, Republican Millennials differ in at least one aspect in every table we have examined.

Additionally, this impact holds when we consider the notable variation in tried-and-true representational variables including constituency and the backgrounds of these legislators. The six Millennial Republicans in the data set represent diverse states: Ohio, Pennsylvania, South Carolina, Texas (2), and Wisconsin. Even more, the backgrounds and therefore many of the socializing experiences of these legislators differ. For example, Representative Timmons (SC) served as a member of the U.S. Army's Judge Advocate General's Corps and later as a state legislator, Rep. Steil (WI) had a background in nonprofits, and Rep. Gonzalez (OH) was a professional athlete who operated a small business upon the conclusion of his football career.

As with any given individual, the importance of generational identities can compete with other experiences.[14] Recall for example that Rep. Underwood (D-IL) noted on her website biography that she was the first woman, the first Millennial, and the first person of color to represent her Illinois district. Similarly, Millennial Rep. Omar (D-MN) let her constituents know that she was "the first African refugee to become a Member of Congress, the first woman of color to represent Minnesota, and one of the first two Muslim-American women elected to Congress" (website biography), and Max Rose (D-NY) emphasized a different aspect of his identity altogether: his status as a veteran (website biography).

Additionally, a number of political factors can operate to constrain a Millennial impact, beginning with the nature of a campaign for Congress itself. For example, while as a young person you can campaign on promises of hope for the future and as a fresh face (see Friedman, Armato, and Matott, chap. 13, this volume, on Millennial mayors), you are unlikely to win an election if you overfocus on themes that attract mostly voters of your generation. You likely need a broader appeal.

Two additional characteristics of modern-day politics could further blunt the Millennial impact, holding out the potential for a path to more "Millennial identity" politics in the future. In this era of party polarization, members of Congress are increasingly sticking together as party teams, and national parties are working harder to craft "party" messages trying to unify the troops (Lee 2016). Recruitment practices of the parties often lead to nominations of particularly polarizing members (Thomsen 2014), and a number of these legislators served in prior political positions where they had considerable time to learn the importance of toeing the party line. Add to this, the 2018 election (used as the baseline for this study) has been described as a referendum on a very polarizing president (Jacobson and Carson 2020).

While there are Millennial members of Congress, such as the ones highlighted in the introductory paragraphs of this chapter, who stand out as potential champions of the next generation of politicians and who may buck the party line, there are many more who are just beginning their careers in Congress. These legislators are often looking to make connections and allies, and it is through the party that they move forward, with good committee assignments, help with campaigns, and coalitions to pass laws. These members are less likely to diverge from a strict party line; such a choice offers them the best chance for a long and impactful career in the halls of the House.

Millennial members of the mass public may desire bipartisanship and decry governmental institutions, but by virtue of being recruited to run for office via polarized parties and subsequently running for office with a party label, the set of Millennial legislators described here may be atypical of their generational counterparts. We speculate that Millennial status could matter more in a less-partisan era.

Similarly, we speculate that a greater Millennial effect could come about when Millennials account for more of a critical mass within the institution of Congress. The pioneering work of Rosabeth Moss Kanter (1977) as long ago as the 1970s suggested that numbers matter. "Token" members of an organization might choose to play by organizational standards rather than attempt to make change, but reaching a critical mass could lead to a greater likelihood of changing an organizational culture. Thus, we speculate that as Millennials become a larger proportion of the membership of Congress, accumulating more seniority in the process, it is possible that a Millennial identity will become more central to a representative's presentation. The descriptive element of generation has started to appear, such as in the form of organizations like the Congressional Future Caucus (Millennial Action Project 2020b), but has yet to become enough of a descriptive element of legislative style as other "identity" characteristics such as gender or sexual orientation. While Millennials have achieved a critical mass within our society, they are significantly underrepresented in Congress. Thus, while the defining attributes of the Millennial generation can be measured writ large, they evade detection in the small, elite, and disproportionately older memberships of congressional bodies.[15]

All these factors—the variation in socializing experiences; the constituencies these legislators represent; the current popularity within the Democratic Party of issues associated with Millennials; the polarized nature of the political parties; and a lack of critical mass—notwithstanding, we come away, after perusing some fairly complicated data sets, arguing that, at least in limited ways, Millennials are making a difference.[16]

APPENDIX

As described in the research design section, the data used in this paper is based on web scraping a number of large data sets. We collected a list of words and phrases (cataloged below) based on a reading of a sampling from the data sources and input from colleagues. We refined these terms as we went along. Despite obvious subjectivity, we think this set of words and phrases captures interesting material and that our findings present a reasonable picture of the data.

The words and phrases compiled herein seemed in line with the literature on both the Millennial generation and the representational styles of members of Congress. Thus, for each of the representational categories described in the chapter (descriptive, issues, partisan, constituency-oriented), we developed a set of words and phrases indicative of each category, and developed hypotheses as to where we expected differences between Millennials and non-Millennials. For each representational category, we analyzed individual words, as well as combinations/groupings of words. Thus, tables 14.2–14.5 present data based on individual words (marked with an *) as well as combinations of words reflecting the larger category.

We use both individual words and larger groupings in the tables, and we took into account variations on particular words (e.g., singular and plural) as appropriate. The tables do not report all the words used.

We organize the description below by the categories of representation described in the text.

GENERATIONAL AND DEMOGRAPHIC WORDS

Generation: Generation, Silent Generation, Baby Boomer, Generation X, Millennial, Generation Z
Descriptive: Gender, LGBT, Poor, Low Income, Middle Class, Woman, Women, Native American, Indigenous, Asian
Race: African American, Black
Hispanic: Hispanic, Latina, Latino, Latinx
Diversity: Ableism, Bigot, Children of Color, Discrimination, Discriminatory, Diversity, Equality, Equity, Hate, Homophobia, Inclusion, Islamophobia, Men of Color, People of Color, Person of Color, Prejudice, Racism, Racist, Sexism, Sexual Orientation, Tolerance, Transphobia, White Supremacy, Women of Color, Xenophobia, Misogyny, Misogynist

ISSUE WORDS

Economy: Economy/Economics/Economical, Unemployment, Income Inequality, Top 1%, Workers Rights, Right to Work, Wealth Gap, Union Member, Paycheck, Labor Union, Universal Basic Income, Poverty
Education: Education, Tuition Free, Student Debt, Student Loan, Student Borrower, Standardized Test, Pell Grant, HR 3497,

Elementary and Secondary Education Act, Community College, College, College Affordability Act, Transform Student Debt to Home Equity Act, College Graduate, Free College

Student Debt: Student Debt, Student Loan, Student Borrower

Foreign policy: Afghanistan, Ally, Allies, Bilateral, China, Defense, EU, Europe, Iran, Iraq, Middle East, Multilateral, NATO, North Korea, Nuclear Weapon, Peace, Russia, Space Force, Terrorism, Terrorist, Torture, United Nations, War on Terrorism

Terrorism: Terrorism/Terrorist, Torture, War on Terrorism

Climate: Climate, Climate Change, HR 9, Renewable Energy, Natural Gas, Natural Resources, Carbon, Clean Energy, Climate Crisis, Energy Independence, Fuel Efficient, Global Warming, Greenhouse Gasses, Hybrid Vehicles, Conservation, Paris Climate Agreement, Paris A (to pick up Agreement and Accord), Planet, Electric Vehicles, Green New Deal, Nuclear Energy, Solar Energy, Hydro Energy, Wind Energy

Marijuana: Cannabis, Marijuana

PARTY AND CONGRESSIONAL WORDS

Partisan: Conservative, Democrat, Extremist, Liberal, Majority Leader, Minority Leader, Moderate, Party Leadership, Progressive, Radical, Republican, Senate Majority Leader, Speaker of the House, GOP, Right Wing, Left Wing, Bipartisan

Party: Democrat, Republican

Ideological: Liberal, Conservative, Libertarian, Extremist, Radical, Progressive

Leadership: Pelosi, McCarthy, McConnell, Schumer, Party Leadership, Senate Majority Leader, Speaker of the House, Majority Leader, Minority Leader

Constituency Service: Art Competition, Attended, District Office, Host, Hosted, Met With, Military Academy, Office Hours, Our District, Roundtable, Service Academy, Spoke With, Talked With, Tour, Toured, Town Hall, Visit, Visited, Was Honored

NOTES

1. Demarcations of generations are of course somewhat arbitrary; and quite a few of these Congress members were born in 1978 and 1979. All here are classified as non-Millennials.

2. To the extent that ideological words are used synonymously with partisan ones—for example, you're a liberal therefore you're a Democrat—we would expect Millennials to also be less likely to use ideological words in their communication. At the same time, current rhetoric across the political spectrum suggests the use of ideological words on all sides may be alive and well.

3. We did a fair amount of random checking as to the meaning of words that could be used in multiple contexts. Originally, for example, the word "diverse" was included in our "diversity" group, yet legislators used it in all kinds of ways, for example, to describe the diverse economies of their districts.

4. Some notes on data collection: we excluded several members who had served in office prior to 2018 but were elected in 2018 after a hiatus from serving as well as those who were "freshman" to their districts but not to Congress; our data covers the 116th Congress from its beginning in January 2019 and runs up to March 2020 (just prior to the onset of COVID-19); Rep. Jeff Van Drew (NJ) switched parties in December 2019 (Rogers et al. 2019), and we have coded him as a Republican, the party he joined. Although technically not a freshman, Conor Lamb is included in the data as he was only in office six months prior to the fall 2018 elections.

5. Especially for the Republican side, more work on the importance of district characteristics with relation to generation would be valuable based on able 14.1.

6. There are also examples, from Millennial and non-Millennials alike, focusing on the character of their constituents and the presence of Millennials—Josh Harder, P.R. 9/30/2019, and Ayanna Presley tweet, 2/15/2019.

7. More generally, the word "generation" was used more frequently than one might expect, in approximately 9% of the press releases, in 1% of the tweets, 6 bills sponsored (81 times in the bodies of the bills sponsored), and 22 website biographies. Skimming the content suggests that, for the most part, legislators used the word simply to describe a desire for good things to happen in the future. Sometimes though they invoked "generation" to describe long-standing roots in their districts.

8. In a few additional instances, legislators did use "generation" in a context with political implications, as Millennial Joe Neguse warning about the dangers of climate change to all generations (tweet 12/5/2019 and Andy Kim going out of his way to understand the needs of his Millennial constituents ((tweet 5/30/2019).

9. Table 14.4 also shows no differences in an orientation to constituency service; not surprisingly, word frequencies show a tendency for legislators to publicize these activities, but Millennial freshmen are not more likely to do so than their older counterparts.

10. Taken together, results in the other data sets are a mixed bag, with a few comparisons (especially in the press release titles) pointing in the expected direction; many cases of no difference, and some cases (bill sponsored bodies) contrary to the generational hypotheses. With reference to different subgroups, the PR data shows that white Republican men regardless of generation reference House party leaders Nancy Pelosi and Kevin McCarthy more than any other group.

11. There are similar examples in the other data sets.

12. Note here that we examined words in the body of each bill sponsored; the main subject of the bill need not be about the issue in question but the relevant Millennial words were used in some part of the justification for the bill. Note also there are fewer differences in the tweets and website biographies (data not shown).

13. Focus aside, and not surprisingly, party differences were apparent in solutions offered to the issues.

14. When looking at the usage of social issues words in the press releases by race, gender, party, and generation there are several findings that support this notion. For example, white Millennial men regardless of party were more likely to reference terrorism than any other groups. Across the different groups white Democrat Millennial women are more likely to reference education issues, while white Republican Millennial men are less likely to.

15. As an update, four of the Millennial legislators first elected in 2018—Abby Finkinauer (D-IA), Joe Cunningham (D-SC), Max Rose (D-NY), and Xochitl Torres-Small (D-NM)—lost their 2020 reelection bids, and Deb Haaland (D-NM) is now serving in the cabinet as the secretary of the interior. At the same time, 11 Millennials (born after 1980) serve as newly elected legislators in the 117th House (Millennial Action Project 2020), and Jon Ossoff (D-GA) is the first Millennial serving in the U.S. Senate, and in this context coverage has focused on his online activity (NBC News 2021; Robertson 2021).

16. We speculate, in line with one of the broader questions of this book, that this impact is due more to a generational effect than any effect of age. It is the socializing experiences of the Millennial generation (with respect for example to economic conditions or concerns about climate change) that affect their behavior. At the same time to the extent that subsequent generations (Gen Z; i-gen) will face similar sets of concerns, future generations may well share key aspects of the Millennial outlook.

We would like to acknowledge Professor Wendy Johnston (Adirondack Community College) for her getting us interested in generations; James McCulley for his insights on web scraping large data sets; Professor Michael Malbin for a particularly helpful set of comments; and Karyn Kalita, Christopher Khan, Farzin Shargh and Brian White for assistance at various stages of the process. You all did more than your share.

REFERENCES

2020 Democratic Party Platform. 2020. Accessed August 3, 2023, available at: https://www.presidency.ucsb.edu/documents/2020-democratic-party-platform

Ballew, M., A. Leiserowitz, C. Roser-Renouf, S. Rosenthal, J. Kotcher, J. Marlon, E. Lyon, M. Goldberg, and E. Maibach. 2019. "Climate Change in the American Mind: Data, Tools, and Trends." *Environment: Science and Policy for Sustainable Development* 61 (3): 4–18. https://doi.org/10.1080/00139157.2019.1589300

Barber, M., and N. McCarty. 2015. "Causes and Consequences of Polarization." In *Political Negotiation: A Handbook,* edited by J. Mansbridge and J. C. Martin, 37–90. Washington, DC: Brookings Institution Press.

Barberá, Pablo, and Gonzalo Rivero. 2015. "Understanding the Political Representativeness of Twitter Users." *Social Science Computer Review* 33 (6): 712–29.

Bekafigo, Marija Anna, and Allan McBride. 2013. "Who Tweets about Politics? Political Participation of Twitter Users during the 2011Gubernatorial Elections." *Social Science Computer Review* 31 (5): 625–43.

Cadigan, H. 2019. "Lauren Underwood Is Doing Her 30s Better Than Just about Anyone We Know." *Healthyish*, June 12.

Democratic National Convention. 2020. Party Platform. https://democrats.org/where-we-stand/party-platform/

DeSilver, D. 2018. "Millennials, Gen X Increase Their Ranks in the House, Especially among Democrats." Pew Research Center, November 21. https://www.pewresearch.org/fact-tank/2018/11/21/millennials-gen-x-increase-their-ranks-in-the-house-especially-among-democrats/

Diggles, M. 2014. "Millennials: Political Explorers—Third Way." March 20. https://www.thirdway.org/report/millennials-political-explorers

Dimock, M. 2019. "Defining Generations: Where Millennials End and Generation Z Begins." Pew Research Center, January 17. https://www.pewresearch.org/fact-tank/2019/01/17/where-millennials-end-and-generation-z-begins/

Dittmar, K., K. Sanbonmatsu, and S. Carroll. 2018. *A Seat at the Table: Congresswomen's Perspectives on Why Their Presence Matters.* Oxford: Oxford University Press.

Dvorsky, C. 2019. "Reps. Hill, Gooden, Gonzalez, Neguse to Lead Only Bipartisan Caucus for Young Members of Congress." June 20. https://www.millennialaction.org/press-archives/reps-hill-gooden-gonzalez-neguse-to-lead-only-bipartisan-caucus-for-young-members-of-congress

Ermidis, J. 2017. "Millennial Invasion! 4 Ways Millennials Are Changing the Way Sales Happen." Sales Force Research, December 15. https://www.salesforcesearch.com/blog/millennial-invasion-4-ways-millennials-changing-way-sales-happen/

Evans, J., and J. Hayden. 2019. *Congressional Communication in the Digital Age.* London: Routledge.

Fenno, R. 1978. *Home Style: House Members in Their Districts.* New York: Little, Brown.

Fingerhut, H. 2016. "Millennials' Views of News Media, Religious Organizations Grow More Negative." Pew Research Center, January 4. https://www.pewresearch.org/fact-tank/2016/01/04/millennials-views-of-news-media-religious-organizations-grow-more-negative/

Fry, R., R. Igielnik, and E. Patten. 2018. "How Millennials Today Compare with Their Grandparents 50 Years Ago." Pew Research Center, March 16. https://www.pewresearch.org/fact-tank/2018/03/16/how-millennials-compare-with-their-grandparent

Funk, C., and A. Tyson. 2020. "Millennial and Gen Z Republicans Stand Out from Their Elders on Climate and Energy Issues." Pew Research Center, June 24. https://www.pewresearch.org/fact-tank/2020/06/24/millennial-and-gen-z-republicans-stand-out-from-their-elders-on-climate-and-energy-issues/

Gray, E. 2019. "Get In, Millennials, We're Going to Congress." *Huffington Post*, January 22. https://www.huffpost.com/entry/millennials-going-to-congress_n_5c45f369e4b0bfa693c600e6

Greenblatt, A. 2015. "The Millennial Generation: Will Today's Young Adults Change American Society?" *CQ Researcher* 25: 553–76. http://library.cqpress.com/cqresearcher/cqresrre2015062601

Grimmer, Justin Ryan. 2010. *Representational Style: The Central Role of Communication in Representation.* Cambridge, MA: Harvard University Press.

Grimmer, J. 2013. *Representational Style in Congress: What Legislators Say and Why It Matters*. Cambridge: Cambridge University Press.

Grose, C. 2011. *Congress in Black and White: Race and Representation in Washington and at Home*. Cambridge: Cambridge University Press.

Higgons, K. 2019. "Why Millennials Want Bernie Sanders as President." *InsideOver*, August 17. https://www.insideover.com/politics/why-bernie-sanders-appeals-to -millennials.html

Huang, C., and L. Silver. 2020. "U.S. Millennials Tend to Have Favorable Views of Foreign Countries and Institutions—Even as They Age." Pew Research Center, July 8. https://www.pewresearch.org/fact-tank/2020/07/08/u-s-millennials-tend -to-have-favorable-views-of-foreign-countries-and-institutions-even-as-they -age/

Jacobson, G., and J. Carson. 2020. *The Politics of Congressional Elections*. Lanham, MD: Rowman & Littlefield.

Kanter, R. 1977. *Men and Women of the Corporation*. New York: Basic Books.

Lawless, J., S. Theriault, and S. Guthrie. 2018. "Nice Girls? Sex, Collegiality, and Bipartisan Cooperation in the US Congress." *Journal of Politics* 80 (4): 1268–82.

Lee, F. 2016. *Insecure Majorities: Congress and the Perpetual Campaign*. Chicago: University of Chicago Press.

Mann, T., and N. Ornstein. 2012. *It's Even Worse Than It Looks: How the American Constitutional System Collided with the New Politics of Extremism*. New York: Basic Books.

Millennial Action Project. 2020a. "About the CFC." https://www.millennialaction.org /congressional-future-caucus

Millennial Action Project. 2020b. "Millennials on the Rise in Congress." https://www .millennialaction.org/millennials-on-the-rise-in-congress

Miller, W., and D. Stokes. 1963. "Constituency Influence in Congress." *American Political Science Review* 57 (1): 45–56.

Morrow, S. 2019. "Millennials in Congress Just Went Up by 420%." January 4. https:// twitter.com/snmrrw/status/1081180694410350592

NBC News. 2021. "'A Generational Shift': Ossoff Reflects on Being the First Millennial Senator." January 20. https://www.wrcbtv.com/story/43206439/a-generation al-shift-ossoff-reflects-on-being-the-first-millennial-senator

Parker, K., N. Graf, and R. Igielnik. 2019. "Generation Z Looks a Lot Like Millennials on Key Social and Political Issues." Pew Social Trends, January 17. https://www .pewsocialtrends.org/2019/01/17/generation-z-looks-a-lot-like-millennials-on -key-social-and-political-issues/

Pew Research Center. 2014. "Beyond Red vs. Blue: The Political Typology." June 26. https://www.pewresearch.org/politics/2014/06/26/the-political-typology-beyo nd-red-vs-blue/

Pew Research Center. 2018. "The Generation Gap in American Politics." March 1. https://www.pewresearch.org/politics/2018/03/01/the-generation-gap-in-ameri can-politics/

Pitkin, H. 1967. *The Concept of Representation*. Berkeley: University of California Press.

R Core Team. 2021. "R: A Language and Environment for Statistical Computing." R Foundation for Statistical Computing, Vienna, Austria. https://www.R-project .org

Reinhart, R. 2018. "Global Warming Age Gap: Younger Americans Most Worried." Gallup Poll, May 11. https://news.gallup.com/poll/234314/global-warming-age -gap-younger-americans-worried.aspx

Robertson, D. 2021. "An Annotated Guide to Jon Ossoff's Extremely Online Twitter Feed." *Politico*, January 10. https://www.politico.com/news/magazine/2021/01 /10/jon-ossoff-old-tweet-twitter-imagine-dragons-456713

Rocca, M., and S. Gordon. 2010. "The Position-Taking Value of Bill Sponsorship in Congress." *Political Research Quarterly* 63 (2): 387–97. https://doi.org/10.1177/106 5912908330347

Rogers, A., K. Liptak, and Jim Acosta. 2019. "Jeff Van Drew, House Democrat Who Opposed Impeachment, Will Join Republican Party." *CNN*, December 19. https:// edition.cnn.com/2019/12/19/politics/jeff-van-drew-white-house/

Rose, M. 2018. Website Biography. Congress.gov.

Rosenthal, C. 2002. *Women Transforming Congress*. Norman: University of Oklahoma Press.

Rouse, S., and A. Ross. 2018. *The Politics of Millennials: Political Beliefs and Policy Preferences of America's Most Diverse Generation*. Ann Arbor: University of Michigan Press.

Russell, A. 2018. "U.S. Senators on Twitter: Asymmetric Party Rhetoric in 140 Characters." *American Politics Research* 46 (4): 695–723. https://doi.org/10.1177/153267 3X17715619

Schiller, W. 1995. "Senators as Political Entrepreneurs: Using Bill Sponsorship to Shape Legislative Agendas." *American Journal of Political Science* 39 (1): 186–203. https://doi.org/10.2307/2111763

Spiegelman, J. 2017. "Release: Millennial House Members in Georgia Announce Bipartisan Caucus." March 22. https://www.millennialaction.org/press-archives /press-release-millennial-house-members-announce-bipartisan-caucus

Straus, J., R. Williams, C. Shogan, and M. Glassman. 2016. "Congressional Social Media Communications: Evaluating Senate Twitter Usage." *Online Information Review* 40 (5): 643–59. https://doi.org/10.1108/oir-10-2015-0334

Swers, M. 2002. *The Difference Women Make: The Policy Impact of Women in Congress*. Chicago: University of Chicago Press.

Swers, M. 2014. *Women in the Club: Gender and Policy Making in the Senate*. Chicago: University of Chicago Press.

Tate, K. 2003. *Black Faces in the Mirror: African Americans and Their Representatives in the U.S. Congress*. Princeton: Princeton University Press.

Thomsen, D. 2014a. "Ideological Moderates Won't Run: How Party Fit Matters for Partisan Polarization in Congress." *Journal of Politics* 76 (3): 786–97. https://doi .org/10.1017/S0022381614000243

Thompson, D. 2014b. "Millennials' Political Views Don't Make Any Sense." *Atlantic*, July 15. https://www.theatlantic.com/politics/archive/2014/07/millennials-econ omics-voting-clueless-kids-these-days/374427/

Thrall, A., and E. Goepner. 2015. "Millennials and U.S. Foreign Policy: The Next Generation's Attitudes toward Foreign Policy and War (and Why They Matter)." Cato Institute, June 16. https://www.cato.org/publications/white-paper/millenn ials-us-foreign-policy-next-generations-attitudes-toward-foreign

Wire, S., C. Mai-duc, and J. Haberkorn. 2019. "Democratic Rep. Katie Hill to Resign amid Allegations of Improper Relationship with Staffer." *Los Angeles Times*, October 27. https://www.latimes.com/california/story/2019-10-27/rep-katie-hill-resig ns-amid-scandal

Contributors

Michael A. Armato, PhD, is Associate Professor of Political Science and the director of the public policy and administration program at Albright College. He is also the secretary of the New York State Political Science Association. He is interested in local politics and has been studying progressive political activism in the Hudson Valley since 2019. His work on this subject has appeared in the *Hudson River Valley Review*.

Leah Hutton Blumenfeld, PhD, has taught U.S. Government, Political Theory, Comparative Politics, and International Relations at Barry University since 2010. Her research interests include the international drug war, U.S.–Caribbean relations, political participation, and the status of women. She holds a doctorate in Political Science from Florida International University, a Bachelor's degree in Spanish with honors from Harvard University, and a Master's Degree in Latin American and Caribbean Studies from the University of Connecticut. Dr. Blumenfeld is a Past President of the Florida Political Science Association and has served on the Miami-Dade County Commission for Women since 2009. Her research has been published in the online journals *Gender Forum* and *Open Americas*.

Anthony A. Cilluffo is an economist who focuses on innovative data analysis and demographics. His research includes studies of the changing demographics of the U.S. South, the effects of population aging on state government budgets, patterns of U.S. income inequality over half a century, and numerous analyses of election results. He previously worked at Pew Research Center in Washington, DC. Cilluffo received his master in public affairs from Princeton University. He attended the General Course at the London School of Economics and completed his undergraduate education in economics and political science at the University of South Florida.

Jeffrey C. Dixon is Associate Professor in the Department of Sociology and Anthropology at the College of the Holy Cross. His current research focuses on worker insecurity, nonstandard work, neoliberalism, and the relationship among these phenomena. His research has appeared in such journals as *Social Forces, Public Opinion Quarterly, European Sociological Review,* and the *British Journal of Sociology.* He is also the coauthor of *The Process of Social Research* (2022, 3rd ed., with Royce A. Singleton Jr. and Bruce C. Straits).

Sally Friedman is Associate Professor of Political Science at Rockefeller College, University at Albany. Centered broadly around the concept of representation, her work focuses on a variety of areas in American politics. Her 2007 book *Dilemmas of Representation* (SUNY Press) provides an in-depth examination of the ways more nationalistic politics have impacted localistic home styles (sample from New York State members of Congress), and in the process focuses on the dilemmas and choices legislators face. More recently, her projects have been concerned with issues of identity, such as the campaign strategies of political candidates with disabilities, the off-the-bench speeches of female judges, and the partisanship of congressional press releases.

Andrew S. Fullerton is Professor of Sociology at Oklahoma State University. His research interests include work and occupations, political sociology, social stratification, and quantitative methods. His work has been published in journals such as *Social Forces, Social Problems, Sociological Methods & Research, European Sociological Review, Public Opinion Quarterly,* and *Social Science Research.* He is the coauthor of *Ordered Regression Models: Parallel, Partial, and Non-Parallel Alternatives* (2016, with Jun Xu). He is currently working on a book on categorical data analysis and several projects related to cross-national differences in job insecurity.

Robin Boyle-Laisure, JD, is Professor of Legal Writing at St. John's University School of Law in New York. In the early 1980s, she coauthored a legislative and administrative history of the War on Poverty programs. Since then, she attended Fordham Law School, practiced law in New York City, and joined St. John's University School of Law's faculty. She has written articles and book chapters on a range of topics, including federal statutes on human trafficking and the Violence Against Women's Act, emancipation laws, and an empirical study of the learning styles of Generation X.

Susan A. MacManus is a University of South Florida Distinguished University Professor Emerita in the Department of Government and International Affairs, School of Interdisciplinary Global Studies. MacManus received her MA from the University of Michigan and PhD from Florida State University. MacManus has authored or coauthored numerous publications on Florida politics, including *Florida's Minority Trailblazers: The Men and Women Who Changed the Face of Florida Government* (2017), *Politics in Florida* (2019, 5th ed.), *Young v. Old: Generational Combat in the 21st Century?* (1996), and *Targeting Senior Voters* (2000). From 1998 to 2015, she served as political analyst for WFLA News Channel 8 (Tampa's NBC affiliate). Since 2016, she has been the political analyst for ABC Action News (Tampa's ABC affiliate). She is a featured columnist on sayfiereview.com, a widely read Florida-based political website.

Whitney Ross Manzo is Assistant Professor of Political Science at Meredith College in Raleigh, NC and serves as Assistant Director of the Meredith Poll. She received her PhD in political science and methodology from the University of Texas at Dallas in 2014. Her scholarship focuses on gender and politics and issues of power and representation.

Emily R. Matott is a graduate student of American Politics and Political Theory at the Rockefeller College of Public Affairs and Policy, SUNY Albany. Her research interests include social movements, class and gender in politics, and queer theory. She has worked for the New York State Assembly and is a member of Lambda Pi Eta, the National Communication Studies Honor Society.

Scott L. McLean is Professor of Political Science at Quinnipiac University. He earned his PhD in political science from Rutgers University, with a focus on political philosophy and American politics. Professor McLean focuses his research and teaching on the intersection of political ideology, psychology, and political campaigns. His most recent work focuses on the politics of "swing state voters" in *Presidential Swing States: Why Only Ten Matter* (2018, 2nd ed.), edited by David Schultz. His political commentary has appeared in national and international media outlets such as NPR, CNN, Fox News Network, *The Hill, New York Times, Washington Post, Wall Street Journal,* Norway's *Verdens Gang,* and the London *Financial Times.* McLean's innovations in experiential learning in politics have been recognized in national media. He is the 2018 recipient of Quinnipiac University's Center for Excellence Award, the university's highest honor for teaching.

David B. McLennan is Professor of Political Science at Meredith College in Raleigh, NC and serves as Director of the Meredith Poll. He received his PhD in political communication from the University of Texas at Austin in 1990. He regularly comments on North Carolina and national politics for the media and biennially publishes the *Status of Women in North Carolina Politics*.

Andrew McMahon is a Budget Examiner with the New York State Division of the Budget and 2022–2023 State Academy of Public Administration (SAPA) Fellow. He is a graduate of the College of Emergency Preparedness, Homeland Security and Cybersecurity (BA '18) and the Rockefeller College of Public Affairs & Policy (MA '20). His research interests include social media, elections, national identity, and gender in politics. In 2018 he received the Presidential Research Award for Undergraduate Research from the University at Albany and in 2020 he received the Capstone of the Year Award from Rockefeller College.

Niall Guy Michelsen received his Bachelor's Degree in Anthropology from the University of Chicago in 1976. He received his MA in Political Science in 1985 and PhD in Political Science in 1990, both from the University of North Carolina at Chapel Hill. He taught at Roosevelt University in Chicago from 1989 to 2001 before moving to Western Carolina University as Department Head in 2001. He has been a faculty member holding several administrative positions including Associate Dean of the College of Arts and Sciences and Director of International Studies. His work has primarily been in the fields of international relations and comparative politics and the scholarship of teaching and learning. He is currently working on a book project on the topic of dropping the voting age to 16.

Kenneth W. Moffett is Professor of Political Science at Southern Illinois University Edwardsville, and is a coauthor of *Web 2.0 and the Political Mobilization of College Students* (2016) and of *The Political Voices of Generation Z* (2022), both coauthored with Laurie L. Rice. His research has appeared or is forthcoming in *American Politics Research*, the *Journal of Information Technology and Politics*, *Legislative Studies Quarterly*, *Social Science Computer Review*, *Social Science Quarterly*, and other journals. His research interests lie in American politics and policy, and include civic engagement among young adults.

Victoria E. Nash has a BA in Sociology at the College of the Holy Cross, is currently attending Suffolk University Law School, and is interested in inequality and immigration attitudes.

Bruce Peabody is Professor of Political Science at Fairleigh Dickinson University in Madison, New Jersey. He received his PhD in Government from the University of Texas at Austin and his BA in the College of Social Studies at Wesleyan University in Connecticut. He is the editor and author of several books including *Short Stories and Political Philosophy* (2019) and *Where Have All the Heroes Gone: Changing Conceptions of American Valor* (2017) (coauthored with Krista Jenkins). He has published over 30 scholarly articles and book chapters and dozens of short articles, academic book reviews, and publications written for a general audience. His work has been cited by or appeared in the *Washington Post, New York Times, Wall Street Journal, USA Today, Harvard Political Review,* and the Congressional Research Service.

Laurie L. Rice is Professor of Political Science at Southern Illinois University Edwardsville. She is coauthor of the book *Web 2.0 and the Political Mobilization of College Students* (2016) and *The Political Voices of Generation Z* (2022), both coauthored with Kenneth W. Moffett, and coeditor of *American Political Parties under Pressure: Strategic Adaptations for a Changing Electorate* (2018). Her research interests include political communication, the presidency, elections, and civic engagement and her work on these topics has appeared in such journals as *Presidential Studies Quarterly, Social Science Quarterly, Journal of Information Technology and Politics,* and *Social Science Computer Review.*

Ashley D. Ross is Associate Professor in the Department of Marine and Coastal Environmental Science at Texas A&M University at Galveston. She studies public perceptions, attitudes, and experiences in relation to policy and governance with a particular focus on natural hazards and disasters. Her research considers how political and social identities, among other personal attributes, affect attitudes toward climate change and disaster mitigation. Her current research explores how these identities as well as trust in science is associated with disparities in hazard information access, use, and interpretation. Ross is a faculty affiliate with the Institute for a Disaster Resilient Texas. She teaches graduate courses in environmental management, environmental conflict resolution, and research methods in coastal resources.

Stella M. Rouse is Professor and Director of the Hispanic Research Center at Arizona State University, specializing in the study of the institutional and behavioral components of identity politics. She is a leading Millennial generation scholar, and is the coauthor, with Ashley D. Ross, of *The Politics of Millennials: Political Beliefs and Policy Preferences of America's Most Diverse Generation* (2018).

David Schultz is Distinguished University Professor in the Departments of Political Science, Environmental Studies, and Legal Studies at Hamline University. He is also a professor of Law at the University of Minnesota and at the University of St. Thomas and an adjunct professor at Binghamton University. A four-time Fulbright scholar who has taught extensively in Europe and Asia, and the winner of the Leslie A. Whittington national award for excellence in public affairs teaching, David is the author of more than 45 books and 200+ articles on various aspects of American politics, election law, and the media and politics, and he is regularly interviewed and quoted in the local, national, and international media on these subjects including the *New York Times*, *Wall Street Journal*, *Washington Post*, *The Economist*, and National Public Radio. His most recent books are *Constitutional Precedent in US Supreme Court Reasoning* (2022), *Handbook of Election Law* (2022), and *Presidential Swing States* (2022). Prior to teaching, Professor Schultz served as a city director of planning, zoning and code enforcement, and as a housing and economic planner for a community action agency.

Laura Stoker is Associate Professor in the Department of Political Science at the University of California, Berkeley. Her research focuses on the development and change of political attitudes and behavior with a focus on family influences and generational change. She also writes on topics at the intersection of research design and statistics, including the optimal design of multilevel studies, problems of aggregation, and the estimation of cohort effects. She regularly teaches undergraduate and graduate courses on political psychology and research methods. Her publications have appeared in the *American Political Science Review*, *American Journal of Political Science*, *British Journal of Political Science*, *Electoral Studies*, and *Journal of Politics*. Stoker is the recipient of fellowships from the Center for Advanced Study in the Behavioral Sciences, Oxford University, and the University of Manchester. Stoker has served on the Board of Overseers of the American National Election Studies (2000–2002, 2019–present; Chair, 2000–2002) and the British National Election Studies (2014–16).

Index

Note: Page references in italics indicate illustrations and tables.

abolitionism, 186
abortion rights, 108
Above the Influence campaign, 144
Abramson, P. R., 14
accumulated heritage, 146
Achen, C. H., 51
adult-role theory, 285
affective polarization, 85, 185; African
    Americans and, 80n22; aging and,
    56–57; generational differences in,
    57–59; party hostility in, 67–68;
    period effects in, 59, 65; trends in,
    55–56, *56*
Affordable Care Act, 299
African Americans, 38–39, 303; affec-
    tive polarization and, 80n22; civil
    rights driven by students of, 216–17,
    220; in civil rights movement, 371;
    congressional woman as, 397; Demo-
    cratic identification by, 100, 320; Mil-
    lennial, 306–8; on political change,
    314–17; political system rigged and,
    322; as sorority members, 351n11;
    Souls to Polls by, 348; voting by,
    308–10
age: COVID-19 with different influence
    by, 341–43; demographics of, *69–70*;
    digital, 91, 214–15, 230–31, 233–34;
    heroes correlations with, 206n6;
    identifying, 17; immigrant families
    and, 78n4; midterm elections voting
    by, *242*; more conservative from
    advancing, 24; Pew Research vari-

ables of, 78n8; political socialization
    and, 38; presidential candidates race
    and, 341–47; in presidential elec-
    tions, *43*; presidential elections gap
    of, *338*; in Republican Party, 37;
    across subgroups, 78n9; 26th Amend-
    ment on minimum voting, 239; vot-
    ers in presidential election's gap by,
    338; voter turnout by, 251–53; voting,
    78n6; voting rates by, *240*; voting's
    minimum, 251–53; voting with low-
    ered, 243, 254–57
age cohorts: cohort groupings and, 42–
    44, 120–21; comparing, 88–89; Demo-
    cratic Party leaning, *106*; Gen Z in,
    90–91; marijuana support by, *149*;
    within Millennials, 129–32, *130*; par-
    tisanship and, 193–94; political dis-
    tinction of, 89; remembered events
    by, *98*; socialization in, 145–46
age group learning, 145–47
age-period-cohort (APC) model, 118; as
    accounting equation, 37; with ANES
    date, 42–46; debates on, 134; Demo-
    crats and Republicans in, *71–72*;
    independents in, *73*, 79n16; in-party
    ratings thermometer from, *74–75*;
    macro-political trends in, 41; out-
    party ratings thermometer from, *76–
    77*; party identification with, 44;
    Republican Party in, *71–72*; Stoker
    laying out, 2, 87; virtues of, 68; on
    women political leaders, 165–66

aging: affective polarization and, 56–57; conservatism prompted by, 24, 40, 152, 206n3, 306; Democrats influenced by, *47*, 47–48; in- and out-party ratings by, 56–57, *58*; Independents influenced by, 52–53, *54*; life-cycles in, 40; political consequences of, 40
Aigner-Clark, Julie, 186
air quality agenda, 218
Allred, Colin, 406
Alter, Charlotte, 355
Alwin, D. F., 146
Amaral, E. F. L., 122
American Journal of Political Science, 12
American National Election Studies (ANES), 122; APC model with data from, 42–46; presidential elections data used by, 78n5; secular realignment and, 34
American Political Science Review, 12
Anantharaman, Savitri, 226
ANES. *See* American National Election Studies
Anslinger, Harry, 141
anti-party sentiment, 67
antisocialism, 345, 348
APC. *See* age-period-cohort model
Armato, Michael, 6
Athey, S., 271, 273, 281, 289n22
ATT. *See* average effect of the treatment on the treated
Auerbach, Jonathan, 101
Austria, 256
average effect of the treatment on the treated (ATT), 268, 271, *272*
Axne, Cindy, 406

Baby Boomers: on civil rights movement, 214; in Florida, 330–31, 350; Gen X eclipsing, 45; on heroism, 200; as political generation, 97; political party identity by, 188; on socialization, 231; on social media, 156; tolerance by, 121
balance laws, gender, 174–76, *175*
Banuri, Mishka, 224
Barber, James David, 25

Bartels, L. M., 96, 165–66
battleground states, 261
Beatles, 11
behaviors: habitual, 248; legislative, 7; Millennial's voting, 319–20; reinforcement of, 38
belief stereotypes, 165
Better Service to Borrowers Act, 406
Biden, Joe, 86; climate movement advanced by, 218; Democrat's blame loss on, 345; election not recognized of, 313–14; on feeling thermometer, *102*; generational split on, 198; Gen Z support for, 102, 343; as heroic, 193; Millennials for, 309, 320; Millennials support for, 343; minority youth favoring, 87–88; older generation support for, 341; young voters key to victory of, 162
Big Green groups, 217, 224–25, 227
Bill of Rights, youth, 362
bin Laden, Osama, 183, 188
Black Lives Matter, 226; civil rights protests and, 195; cultural trauma and, 108; after Floyd death, 193, 229, 351n10; Gen Z and, 86; political leaders and, 195–96; prominence of, 64; social media used by, 229–30
Black Panther Party, 227–28
Boyle-Laisure, Robin, 5, 155
brain, neuroplasticity of, 215
Braungart, R. G., 97
Brown v. Board of Education (1954), 223
Burnham, W. D., 14
Bush, George W., 59, 101, 186
Buttigieg, Pete, 363, 365–68, 372, 376, 377n1

CAAs. *See* Community Action Agencies
Caldeira, G. A., 38
CAMPUS Act, 397
campus protest tactics, 223–24
carbon taxes, 215
Carpini, Delli, 14, 25–26
carpool system, 216
Carson, Rachel, 11
Carter, Jimmy, 101

Center for Information & Research on Civic Learning and Engagement (CIRCLE), 257, 299

character, in heroism, 203–5

Chen, K., 39

childhood, learning politics in, 25

Cilluffo, Anthony, 6

CIRCLE. *See* Center for Information & Research on Civic Learning and Engagement

citizens: college-educated, 247; democracy participation by, 287; engaged, 99–100, 300; foreign-born, 126; voting by less-educated, 246

city characteristics, *360–61*

civic engagement: from political science, 269–70; by presidential candidates, 265–66; in primary election, 273–80, *274–79*, 290n30; from rally experience, 280–81; with social media, 281; of young adults, 288n7

civic membership, 98

civics class, 252–53

civil disobedience, 222–23

Civil Rights Act (1964), 217, 223, 227

civil rights movement, 5; African Americans in, 216–17, 220, 371; campus protest tactics in, 223–24; civil disobedience used by, 222–23; climate similarities with, 214, 219–25; events of, 217; face-to-face planning in, 232; legislative reform in, 223–24; protests in, 195; race relations and, 153; racial issues in, 225–26; supportive network for, 216, 226–29, 232–33

Cleaver, Eldridge, 227

climate change, 166; Millennials Democrats on, 406; Millennials on, 358, 389, 406; in presidential election (2020), *342*; Republican's denying, 215–16; weather pattern changes in, 220; young adults on, 215–17

climate movement, 5; air quality agenda in, 218; Biden advancing, 218; civil rights similarities with, 214, 219–25; earth getting warmer in, 221; generational divide within, 231–32;

Gen Z on, 214; goals of, 217–18; legislative reform in, 224–25; Millennials on, 214, 221–22; racial issues in, 225–26; supportive network lacking for, 226–29; Trump causing setbacks in, 217; young adults in, 217

Clinton, Bill, 103–4

Clinton, Hillary: different generations exposure to, 166; Florida's young voters not energized by, 339–40; generations voting and, 309; Millennial voting behavior and, 319–20; presidential campaigns and, 286; women in politics and, 176

coal-burning power plants, 224

cocaine, 140

Coenders, M., 123

Cohen, Brett, 162

cohort effect, 134

cohort groupings, 42–44, 120–21

cohort replacement, 41

collective memory, 89

collective trauma, 86

collectivist worldview, 302

college: campaign visits to, 262–63; citizens educated through, 247; free tuition for, 264; political campaigns visiting, 262–63, 284–85; presidential campaign visits to, 266; Sanders visiting campuses of, 5, 261, 263–66; voter registration at, 245–46

college students: Obama helped by, 263; Sanders mobilizing, 284, 286

Colorado River Drought Contingency Plan Authorization Act., 407

Columbus, Christopher, 193, 195, 207n13

Community Action Agencies (CAAs), 225

Congress: African American woman in, 397; data collection from, 413n4; Democrats winning, 78n1; diversity term used by, 413n3; legislative behavior of, 7; Millennial legislators in, 392–93; Millennial members of, 6–7, 385–86, 409–10; Millennial political parties in, *395*; Millennial's

Congress (*continued*)
elected into, 414n15; Millennial's substantive representation in, 400–408; Millennial's underrepresented in, 410; party polarization in, 409–10; political parties and words of, 412; representation by, 387, 390–91; women in, 351n9

Congressional Future Caucus, 410

consciousness of self, 16

conservatism, aging prompting, 24, 40, 152, 206n3, 306

content analysis, 391

Controlled Substances Act, 142, 153–54

Converse, P. E., 14, 40

conviction, of Correia, 377n1

Cooper, Jim, 224

core persona, 6, 121, 126

Correia, Jasiel, II, 362–67, 370–71, 377n1

Corrigall-Brown, C., 123

cost-benefit terms, 248–51

Cournoyer, Caroline, 355–56

covariate values, 273–80

COVID-19 pandemic: ages influenced differently by, 341–43; Florida's in-migration from, 330–31; generations and, 92–93; Gen X and, 92; Gen Z and politics during, 86, 92–94; mental health during, 93, *93*; Millennial crisis of, 301; political campaigns influenced by, 287; in presidential election (2020), *342*; youth turnout influenced by, 346

Crenshaw, Dan, 385, 397

Crenshaw, Kimberlé Williams, 225

criminal approach, 156–57

criminal justice, 200

Cronkite, Walter, 243

cultures: Black Lives Matter and trauma of, 108; conflict of, 104; stories regenerating, 183–84

Cunningham, Joe, 414n15

DAG. *See* directed acyclic graph

Dalton, R., 99, 184, 245, 300

DARE. *See* Drug Abuse Resistance Education program

data: from ANES, 42–46; from Congress, 413n4; from content analysis, 391; controls for, 126–27; dependent variable as, 125; on generations term, 413n7; immigration policy collection of, 125–27; independent variable as, 125–26; intervals in, 289n22; from legislative bills, 391; matched, *282–83*, 359; from Meredith Poll, 166–68, 177; presidential elections using, 78n5; from press releases, 391; from research, 359; research methods and, 167–68, 268–71; sets, 413n10; survey, 205; from tweets, 391; from web scraping, 391–92

Davis, R. Carey, 369–70, 374, 377n5

Day, Tiana, 229–30

debates, on APC model, 134

democracy: citizens participation in, 287; Gen Z's responsibilities to, 108; January 6th Capitol attack on, *105*

Democratic Party: African American and Latino identification with, 100, 320; age cohorts leaning toward, *106*; aging influence on, 47, 47–48; in APC model, *71–72*; Biden campaign blamed for loss by, 345; on climate change, 406; demographic changes benefiting, 26–27; dominance erosion of, 35–36; elections and Congress won by, 78n1; Florida exit polls stunning, 345–46; generational replacement and, 66–68, 79n18; generations identifying with, 79n13, 100; in- and out-party ratings of, 79n20; in-party rating among, *60*; Millennials affiliation with, 306–8, 320; Millennials as leaning toward, 37; Millennials causing resurgence in, 63–64; Millennials in, 393; Millennials language used in, 408; non-Southerners identification in, *49*, 79n18; out-party ratings among, *61*; partisans identifying in, *46*; period influence on, 51, 63; in presidential elections, 108; press releases from, 406; Republicans compared to, 46–52; Republican's loss to, 34; Southerner's identification with, *49*, 79n18; Southern realignment and, 46–47; website platform of, 407

demographics: across-generations, 22–23; Democratic Party benefiting from, 26–27; education with variables of, 45; Florida's shifts in, 6, 328–29; of generation and age, *69–70*; of generations, 20–23, *69–70*; generations with variables of, 45; generations with words of, 411; Gen Z's composition of, 302–3; Millennial and non-Millennial characteristics, *394*; of Millennial's party status, *398–99*; population with shifts in, 41; Qualtrics quotas on, 304–5; Republicans benefiting from, 50–51; U.S. with changes in, 22–23; variables of, 78n10

Denison, Elli, 358

dependent variables, 125, 269

Desante, C. D., 13, 27

DeSantis, Ron, 340

descriptive representation, 387, 396–400

de-stabilization, 120

developmental psychological theory, 15

Diani, Mario, 219

Dickinson, Fairleigh, 205

digital age: day-to-day functioning in, 215; Millennials and Gen Z's in, 91, 214–15, 230–31, 233–34

Dinas, E., 248

directed acyclic graph (DAG), 289n15

discrete change coefficients, *132*, 132–33

discrimination: against women as political leaders, 166–67, 172; against women by voters, 164

distractions, in voting, 249–50, 254

diversity: Congress and term of, 413n3; in Florida, 331–33, 350, 351n1; of Florida's younger adults, 336–37; immigration policy and, 124; inclusion and, 390; of Millennials, 303–4, 375

Dixon, Jeffrey, 3, 124, 151

door-to-door canvassing, 346

Drug Abuse Awareness Campaigns, 142–45

Drug Abuse Resistance Education (DARE) program, 143

drug arrests, 154

drug policy: age group learning and, 145–47; generational attitudes on, 153–55; surveys on, 147–51

drug use: criminal approach to, 156–57; generational attitudes on, 146–47; generational divide on, 139–40, 147–52; generations on, 143, 157; Gen X on, 139, 144, 146–48, 154–55, 157; Gen Z on, 151–53; medical benefits of, 150; race and, 153–55; scare tactics used on, 143–44; in U.S., 140–42; zero-tolerance policy for, 141

Duffy, Bobby, 2, 19

Dylan, Bob, 213

earth, warming of, 221

economics: development in, 365–66, 372–73, 376; equality in, 243, 247; formative crisis in, 124; issues in, 388; recession in, 358

education: demographic variables and, 45; literacy in, 374; mayors on, 366–67, 373; party ratings based on, 80n22; population by rates of, *247*; Republican Party and, 80n23; voter turnout by level of, *246*; voting and levels of, 247

18@Second Vote, 254

Eisenhower, Dwight, 206n12

elections: Democratic wins in, 78n1; Florida's gubernatorial, 340–41; Gen Z engagement in, 104–8; gradual or revolutionary change in, 314–16, 321–22; midterm, *242*; Millennial and non-Millennial characteristics, *394*; primary, 271, 273–80, *274–79*, 280, 284–85, 290n30, 319; technology used in, 391; 26th Amendment and, 243–47; voter turnout for, 86. *See also* presidential elections

electoral process, 251
eligibility, for voting, 250
Ender, Morton, 13
End-of-Year Fiscal Responsibility Act, 397
enemy symbol, 102–3
engaged citizenship, 99–100, 300
Engels, Friedrich, 18
Environmental Protection Agency (EPA), 217, 224
Erikson, Erik, 25
Espenshade, T. J., 122
ethnic conflict theory, 123
ethnicity: in Florida, 330, 331–33, 332; Florida's presidential election by, 348; by generation in U.S., 23; race and, 303
Europe, 119
events: age cohorts and remembered, 98; of civil rights movement, 217; generations with defining, 21, 21–22; national, 244, 335, 336; trigger, 98, 107, 121
exit polls, in Florida, 345–46

face-to-face planning, 232
Feminine Mystique (Friedan), 11
Ferrari, Giuseppe, 14–16, 27
Finkinauer, Abby, 414n15
Firebaugh, G., 39
Fisher, Dana, 221
Florida: Baby Boomers in, 330–31, 350; Clinton, H., not energizing young voters in, 339–40; COVID-19 causing in-migration in, 330–31; Democrats stunned by exit polls in, 345–46; demographic shifts in, 6, 328–29; diversity in, 331–33, 350, 351n1; diversity of younger adults in, 336–37; generational replacement in, 332–33, 350–51; generations in, 329–31; Gen X and Gen Z in, 330; Gen Z voters in, 332; gubernatorial election in, 340–41; Hispanics in, 329, 351n1; Hispanic turnout in, 348; important issues in, 343; Latinos in, 331–32; Millennials in, 330; non-white voter

registration in, 333; Obama wins in, 337–39; older generations in, 337; party preferences by generation in, 333–35; population growth in, 329; presidential election by ethnicity in, 348; presidential election by gender in, 348–49; presidential election by race in, 348; race and ethnicity in, 330, 331–33, 332; Trump winning, 339; 2020 election turnout in, 347; voter registration by generation in, 331–33, 335; voter registration by party in, 334–35; voter turnout by generation, 344; young adults in, 337, 344–45; young adults voter registration in, 334–35; young vs. old in, 337
Floyd, George, 343; Black Lives Matter after death of, 193, 229, 351n10; civil rights protests and, 195; generational divide on, 193; racial justice protests from, 202, 343
foreign-born citizens, 126
foreign policy, Millennials on, 388–89
Fosse, E., 42, 126, 128
Franklin, M. N., 251
free tuition, for college, 264
Friedan, Betty, 11
Friedman, Sally, 6
Fullerton, Andrew, 3, 124, 151

Gallego, A., 245, 251
Gandhi, Mahatma, 222
Garcia-Rios, S., 303
Gelman, Andrew, 101
gender: balance laws by, 174–76, 175; Florida's presidential election by, 348–49; Gen Z and political leaders by, 171; heroism traits by race and, 197; parity, 163–64; political leaders by generation and, 169–71, 173, 175; stereotypes, 165; young adult's turnout rate by, 348–49
General Social Survey (GSS), 118, 125
generational attitudes: on drug policy, 153–55; on drug use, 146–47; toward heroism, 185–86, 200–203
generational divide: within climate

movement, 231–32; on drug use, 139–40, 147–52; on Floyd, 193; on immigration policy, 117–18, 122–23; Millennial's attitudes in, 121–22

generational replacement, 85, 145; Democratic Party and, 66–68, 79n18; in Florida, 332–33, 350–51; with Gen X, 41; political parties influenced by, 59–63; in politics, 202–3; Republican Party influenced by, 63, 66–68

generational studies: on individual and macro-level, 36, 65, 68; methodological issues in, 16–19; partisanship differences in, 49; political parties differences in, 48, 63–64; political science on, 25–26; pulse-rate *versus* imprint approaches in, 94–98

generations: affective polarization differences by, 57–59; attitudes across, 26; on Biden and Trump, 198; Biden on feeling thermometer by, 102; bonds through de-stabilization of, 120; characteristics of, 15–16; Clinton, H., different exposures by, 166; cohort groupings in, 42–44; concept of, 14–16, 18, 27; concrete groups in, 15; constant interaction of, 152; COVID-19 and, 92–93; cycle of, 17; data and use of term, 413n7; defining, 19–20, 88; defining events for, 21, 21–22; Democrats identified by, 79n13, 100; demographics of, 20–23, 69–70; demographic variables of, 45; demographic words and, 411; digital day-to-day functioning, 215; on drug use, 143, 157; eras of, 39–40; ethnicity and religion in U.S. by, 23; in Florida, 329–31; Florida 2020 election turnout by, 347; Florida's party preferences by, 333–35; Florida's presidential election by, 348–49; Florida's voter registration by, 331–33, 335; Florida's voter turnout by, 344; greenest of, 389; on heroism characteristics, 189; heroism of, 195–96; heroism's recognition across, 201–2; how things are going by, 99; hypothesis about, 188–89; identity, 26;

Independent party and, 53–54, 55, 64–65; Independents differences by, 53–54, 55; issues in presidential elections by, 265, 265–66; January 6th Capitol attack by, 105; legislators use of term, 413n8; Mannheim on influence of younger, 156; marijuana bonding across, 150–51; Millennials not focused on, 397–400; Millennials role in, 357–59; outreach strategies for, 335–37; party identification by, 100; Pew Research on, 168; political, 38–40; political activities drop-off by, 245; political campaigns and differences of, 337; political identity groups by, 187; political identity of, 95–96; political leaders by gender and, 169–71, 173, 175; political science analysis of, 12; political science influence of, 7; political science on changes in, 28; in politics, 1–2, 4–5; population estimates of, 22–23; replacement influence of, 54–55; Republican feelings differences by, 80n21; Republican Party and, 37; shared experiences of, 264–65; Stoker on concept of, 14, 24; Stoker's characterization of, 186–87; studies of, 2; Trump and feeling thermometer by, 103; in U.S. politics, 20; values impacted by, 4, 26; voter responses by, 177–79; Votes@18 in, 239–40; voting by, 157, 309; on women as leaders, 168–70. See also age cohorts

Generations (Strauss and Howe), 12, 17–19

Generations and Politics (Jennings and Niemi), 95

Gen X: Baby Boomers eclipsed by, 45; COVID-19 and, 92; on drug use, 139, 144, 146–48, 154–55, 157; in Florida, 330; generational replacement with, 41; on heroism, 198; as Independents, 53–54; party identification of, 64–65; Republican affiliation of, 59, 63, 67, 79n14, 101; on socialization, 231; Southern realignment and, 48; timeframe of, 39, 213

Gen Z, 39; in age cohorts, 90–91; Biden support by, 102, 343; Black Lives Matter and, 86; on climate movement, 214; collective trauma of, 86; COVID-19 and politics of, 86, 92–94; democracy responsibilities of, 108; demographic composition of, 302–3; in digital age, 91, 214–15, 230–31, 233–34; on drug use, 151–53; election engagement of, 104–8; in Florida, 330; Florida voters as, 332; historical experience of, 153; Millennial's attitudes similar to, 93–94; as NPA, 333–34; political causes motivating, 220–21; political leader by gender, 171; on political leadership, 169; political parties influenced by, 87–88; political significance of, 85–86; as post-Millennials, 90–91; social media used by, 219, 267–68; trigger events of, 107; Trump and, 99–104; 2020 elections engagement by, 107–8; 2022 elections and, 104–8; as voting generations, 157; on women in politics, 172

Ghitza, Yair, 101

Gibson, J. L., 38

Gillum, Andrew, 340

Gingrich, Newt, 206n11

Glenn, N. D., 20

globalization, 318, 388–89

Goldwater, Barry, 34

Gonzalez, 408

Gore, Al, 224

government: green, 407; Millennial mayors and, 6, 356–57; technology modernized by, 374; trust in, 243, 244, 247

gradual change, in elections, 314–16, 321–22

Great Depression, 87, 260

Great Emancipator, 196

Greatest generation, 39, 121, 260, 330

Great Recession, 301, 303

Great Society, 228

Green, D. P., 79n14, 250

greenest generation, 389

green government, 407

Grimmer, Justin Ryan, 391

group threat theory, 119

GSS. See General Social Survey

gubernatorial election, 340–41

Guizot, François, 24

gun laws, 166, 343

habitual behavior, 248

Hamilton, John, 372–74, 376, 377n5

Hampton, Fred, 227

Hansen, J. M., 263

HAPC models. See hierarchical age-period-cohort models

Harris, Kamala, 162

Harrison Act, 140–41

Hart-Brinson, P., 98

Harvard Youth Poll, 94

Head Start, 228

Hempstead, K., 122

Herbert, Gary, 224

heroism, 182–83; age correlations with, 206n6; Baby Boomers on, 200; character in, 203–5; characteristics in, 189; classes of, 204–5; Columbus in, 207n13; cross-generational recognition of, 201–2; dimensions of, 188; era of national, 202; generational attitudes toward, 185–86, 200–203; of generations, 195–96; Gen X on, 198; headline heroes in, 186; hypothesis about, 188–89; identification in, 190; individual actions of, 206n2; individual's identification with, 190; Jesus in, 206n5; military, 198; national, 202; nonpartisan, 194–95, 199–200; of older generations, 191–93; particular figures and, 185; personalities and qualities in, 199; political candidates in, 193, 194; political parties identifying, 198–99, 199; within Republican Party, 195; society role of, 184, 192, 194–95; traits by gender and race in, 197; traits of, 206n8; U.S. values reflected in, 191; of young adults, 195–96

Hess, A. J., 157

hierarchical age-period-cohort (HAPC) models, 122–23, 128
Highton, B., 285
Hill, Katie, 397
Hillygus, D. S., 250, 255
Hispanics: Democratic identification by, 100; in Florida, 329, 351n1; Florida's turnout of, 348
historical experience, of Gen Z, 153
Holbein, J. B., 250, 255
Hopkins, D. J., 119
House of Representatives, 397
Hout, M., 48
Howe, Neil, 12, 17–19, 94, 96
how things are going, by generation, 99
Hutton Blumenfeld, Leah, 3–4
hypermasculinity, 176

identification problem, 118
identity politics, 409
identity portfolio, 303
ideological words, 413n2
Imbens, G. W., 271, 273, 281, 289n22
immigration, 3; age and families here through, 78n4; attitudes toward, 119–20; Europe's prejudice against, 119; independent variables on, 127–28; in-migration in, 332–33; Millennials as children from, 264; Millennial's tolerance of, 122–25, 133–34; multinomial logit models of, 129–30, 131–32
immigration policy: data collected on, 125–27; diversity and, 124; generational divide on, 117–18, 122–23; HAPC used on, 123; study methods on, 128–29; study results on, 129–33
impressionable years, 213–14
imprint approach, 94–98, 101
incarceration, from marijuana, 154
Inciardi, J. A., 141
inclusion, diversity and, 390
income inequality, 388
Independent party: aging influences on, 52–53, 54; anti-party sentiment and, 67; APC model on, 73, 79n16; generational differences in, 53–54, 55, 64–65; Gen X as, 53–54; partisan

dealignment and, 34–35; period effects on, 54–55; trends of, 52, 53, 56
independent variables, 127–28
individualism, in U.S., 119
individual-level generational studies, 36, 65, 68
individuals: accumulated heritage of, 146; actions of heroes as, 206n2; heroism identification of, 190
in-migration, 332–33
in-party ratings: by aging, 56–57, 58; APC model with thermometer of, 74–75; of Democrats and Republicans, 60, 79n20; trends in, 57, 62
in-person contact, 346
institutional change, 124
Institutional Review Board, 288n5
international politics, 28–29
intervals, in data, 289n22
issue words, 411–12

Jackman, S., 96, 165–66
Jacobson, G. C., 101, 166
Jaeger, Hans, 96
January 6th Capitol attack, 104–5, 105
Jennings, K., 95
Jennings, M. K., 39
Jervis, R., 14
Jesus, 198, 206n5
Jim Crow laws, 216
job opportunities, 373
Johnson, Lyndon, 34, 141, 202, 227–28
Jones, J. M., 150
Journal of Politics, 12
Just Say No slogan, 143

Kanter, Rosabeth Moss, 410
Kaplan, Thomas, 328
Kemp, Jack, 206n11
Kennedy, C., 305
Kennedy, John F., 202, 227
Kennedy, Robert, 284
Key, V. O., Jr., 14
Kim, Andy, 401, 407, 413n8
King, G. C., 270
King, Martin Luther, Jr., 198, 200, 217, 221

Klas, Mary Ellen, 328
Knoke, D., 48
Krosnick, J. A., 146
Kruzan, Mark, 372, 374, 377n5

Lamb, Conor, 413n4
Land, K. C., 126
language: Democratic Millennials use
    of, 408; of Millennial legislators, 386;
    political parties differences of, 401–
    6, *402–3*; political parties issue words
    and, *404–5*. *See also* word use
Latinos, 64, 303; antisocial rallying cry
    of, 345; Democratic identification by,
    320; in Florida, 331–32; Millennial,
    306–8; on political change, 314–17;
    political system rigged and, 322; vot-
    ing by, 308–10. *See also* Hispanics
law review article, 255
learning: age group, 145–47; childhood
    political, 25; from social media, 155–
    56; two stage model of, 17
Lee, Susie, 406–7
legalization, of marijuana, 147–50, *148*,
    154–55
legislative behavior, 7
legislative bills, 391, 404–5, 413n7
legislative reform, 223–25
Leighley, J. E., 246, 285
Level Importance method, 51–52
liberal politics, 3, 118, 206n3, 305–10,
    389
life cycle theories, 260–61, 306
Lincoln, Abraham, 195–98, 200, 205
literacy, in education, 374
literature, sexism in, 163–64
livestreaming, 268, 270–72, *278–79*;
    political campaign's website, 291n32;
    rally attendance and, 291n31

MacManus, Susan, 6, 20
macro-level generational studies, 36,
    65, 68
macro-political changes, 44
macro-political trends, 41
Mannheim, Karl, 2, 27, 38; on institu-
    tional change, 124; political disrup-

tions from, 87–88; political genera-
    tions theory of, 85–86, 89, 96–97;
    "The Sociological Problem of Gener-
    ations" by, 15–16; younger genera-
    tions influence from, 156
Manzo, Whitney Ross, 4
March of Our Lives, 221, 343
marginalized groups, 375–76
Margolin, Jamie, 224, 231
Marihuana Tax Act, 141
marijuana, 139, 141; age cohort support
    of, *149*; intergenerational ties on,
    150–51; legalization of, 147–50, *148*,
    154–55; mass incarceration from,
    154; tamer status of, 151
marijuana legalization organization,
    142
Marx, Karl, 18
matched data, *282–83*, 359
Matching Frontier technique, 270–71,
    273, 289n15, 289n19, 290n30
Matott, Emily, 6–7
Matthews, Michael, 13
mayors: activities of, *369*; Buttigieg as,
    363, 365–68, 372, 377n1; city charac-
    teristics and, *360–61*; Correia as,
    362–67, 370–71, 377n1; Davis as, 369–
    70, 374, 377n5; on economic develop-
    ment, 365–66, 372–73, 376; on educa-
    tion, 366–67, 373; government and
    Millennial, 6, 356–57; Hamilton as,
    372–74, 376; marginalized groups
    represented by, 375–76; Millennial's
    activities as, *369*, 376–77; Millennials
    as, 6, 356–59, 362–68; Mitchell as,
    370–71, 374, 377nn4–5; non-
    Millennial, 368–75, *369*, 377n5; Price
    as, 371–72, 374–75, 377n5; stereo-
    types of, 364–65; Stoney as, 363–67,
    371–72; Tubbs as, 363–69, 376, 377n1;
    young adults reached out to by,
    367–68
Mazzei, Patricia, 328
McBath, Lucy, 407
McCain, John, 337
McCarthy, Eugene, 284
McCarthy, Joe, 104

McLaren, L. M., 119
McLean, Scott, 3, 187, 285
McLennan, David, 4
McMahon, Andrew, 7
mean probability, *274–79*
medical benefits, of drugs, 150
Medicare, 343
mental health, 93, *98*
mentoring programs, 367
Meredith Poll data, 166–68, 177
Michelsen, Niall, 5, 285
midterm elections, *242*
military heroes, 198
The Millennial Generation and National Defense (Ender, Rohall and Matthews), 13
Millennials, 39; African American and Latinos as, 306–8; age cohorts within, 129–32, *130*; for Biden, 309, 320; Biden support of, 343; on climate change, 358, 389, 406; on climate movement, 214, 221–22; cohort effect and, 134; congressional activities of, *395*, 409–10; as congressional legislators, 392–93; congressional members as, 6–7, 385–86, 409–10; Congress with elected, 414n15; Congress with underrepresented, 410; core persona of, 6, 121, 126; COVID-19 crisis for, 301; in Democratic Party, 393; Democratic Party affiliation by, 306–8, 320; Democratic resurgence by, 63–64; demographics and characteristics of, *394*, *398–99*; descriptive representation by, 396–400; as different, 395–96; in digital age, 214–15, 230–31, 233–34; discrete change coefficients for, *132*, 132–33; diversity of, 303–4; economic issues faced by, 388; in Florida, 330; on foreign policy, 388–89; generational divides in attitudes of, 121–22; generational role of, 357–59; generations not focus of, 397–400; Gen Z's attitudes similar to, 93–94; identity politics of, 409; as immigrant children, 264; immigrant tolerance by, 122, 133–34; issue categories of, 406–

7; on issues, 389; legislator language of, 386; legislators as, 414n15; legislator's press release words used by, *396*, *398–99*; liberal politics of, 3, 118, 305–10, 389; as mayors, 6, 356–59, 362–68; mayor's activities as, *369*, 376–77; as more democratic, 37; as NPA, 333–34; Obama supported by, 99–101; partisanship valued by, 390; political attitudes of, 304–5, 319–20; political changes sought by, 314–18, *315*; political dissatisfaction of, 300; political engagement by, 301–4, 310–11, *311*, 321–23; political ideology of, *307*, 308–10; political parties identification of, 107, 308–10, *309*, 319–21; political parties issue words of, *404–5*; on political system, *316*, 316–18; post-, 90–91; presidential elections voting by, 313; pro-immigration attitudes of, 123–25, 133–34; racial attitudes of, 13; in Republican Party, 59, 393; shared experiences of, 318–19; slacktivism of, 310; socializing experiences of, 414n16; social media used by, 219, 267–68; style diversity of, 375; substantive representation by, 400–408; technology proliferation for, 302; trigger events of, 121; trust important to, 313; voter turnout of, 311–14, *312*; voting as choice by, 99; voting behavior of, 319–20; as voting generations, 157; web biographies word use by, 396–97
Miller, W. E., 255
minimum age, for voting, 239, 251–53
minority groups, by race, 264
minority youth, 87–88
Mississippi Freedom Summer (1964), 227
Mitchell, Jon, 370–71, 374, 377nn4–5
mobilization, of young adults, 344–45
Moffett, Kenneth, 5, 290n29
Montgomery bus boycott, 226, 228
morphine, 140
Morris, S., 155
Morse, Alex, 356

motivated reasoning, 38
Mount Rushmore, 182–83
Muir, John, 225
multinomial logit models, 129–30, 131–32
multistage sampling, 125
Musto, D. F., 141
"My Generation" (song), 11

NAACP. See National Association for the Advancement of Colored People
Nagler, J., 246
Nakate, Vanessa, 225
Nash, Victoria, 3
National Association for the Advancement of Colored People (NAACP), 216
national events, 244, 335, 336
national heroism, 202
National Student Association, 228
National Study of Learning, Voting, and Elections (NSLVE), 266
National Voter Registration Act, 254–55
Nation's Report Card, 92
negative partisanship, 35
Neguse, Joe, 397, 407, 413n8
Netherlands, 123
netizens, 245
Neundorf, A., 42
neuroplasticity, 215
New Jersey, 203–5
Newton, Huey, 227
NextGen group, 334
Niemi, R. G., 42, 95
9/11 Generation of heroes, 183
Nixon, Richard, 103–4, 141–43
nobody asks problem, 263, 267, 285
non-Millennials: demographics and characteristics of, 394; issue categories of, 406; mayors, 368–75, 369, 377n5
nonpartisanship, 194–95, 199–200
non-Southerners, 49
nonsystematic biases, 288n9
No Party Affiliation (NPA), 329, 333–34
NORML (marijuana legalization organization), 142
North Carolina, 167, 177

NPA. See No Party Affiliation
NSLVE. See National Study of Learning, Voting, and Elections

Obama, Barack, 91; college students helping, 263; Florida win of, 337–39; Millennial support of, 99–102; 9/11 Generation of heroes hailed by, 183; party identification and, 107; presidential elections of, 311–12; Republican's approval of, 206n12; Tubbs meeting, 363; young adults influenced by, 166, 241
Obama administration, 89–90
Ocasio-Cortez, Alexandria, 224, 300, 385
Occupy Wall Street (OWS), 232
odds ratios, 131–32
older generations: Biden's support from, 341; in Florida, 337; hero's of, 191–93; on leadership by women, 175–76; political engagement by, 321; on political leadership, 175–76; in presidential elections, 240–43, 241–42; voting by, 255; voting patterns of, 343–44
OLS regression, 79n17
Omar, Ilhan, 385, 401, 406, 409
oppositional voting, 313
Ossoff, Jon, 414n15
out-party ratings: by aging, 56–57, 58; APC model with thermometer of, 76–77; among Democrats and Republicans, 61; of Democrats and Republicans, 79n20; hostility in, 85; trends in, 57, 62
outreach strategies, 335–37
OWS. See Occupy Wall Street
Oxley, Zoe, 164

Palmquist, B., 79n14
Panning, Jennifer, 92
parents, political regimes transmitted by, 95
Paris Agreement, 218
Parkland shooting, 221, 257
Parks, Rosa, 216, 233

partisan dealignment, 34–35
partisanship: age cohorts and, 193–94; Democratic Party identifying in, *46*; generational differences in, *49*; ideological words and, 413n2; legislative behavior influenced by, 7; Millennials valuing, 390; negative, 35; nonpartisanship and, 194–95, 199–200; polarization, 35, 184–85; political parties trends of, *50*; U.S. landscape of, 66–68
Partnership for a Drug-Free America, 143
Partnership to End Addiction, 143–44
Peabody, Bruce, 4
Pearl Harbor, 87
peer personality, 17
People's Climate March, 222, 224
period effects, 41; in affective polarization, 59, 65; on Democratic Party, 51, 63; on Independent party, 54–55; on political parties, 50–51
personal characteristics, 269
personalities, in heroism, *199*
Pew Research, 166, 264–65; age variables from, 78n8; on generations, 168
phrases, 410–11
Pitkin, Hanna, 198
Plutzer, E., 250
police reforms, 200, 301
political campaigns: colleges visited by, 262–63, 284–85; COVID-19 influencing, 287; generational differences and, 337; presidential campaigns as, 266, 269–70, 286, 288; Sanders issues of, 407; website livestreaming by, 291n32
political candidates, 193, *194*
political engagement: by Millennials, 301–4, 310–11, *311*, 321–23; Millennials attitudes and, 304–5, 319–20; by older generations, 321
political generations, 38–40; Baby Boomers as, 97; Mannheim's theory of, 85–86, 89, 96–97
political identity: generational groups

with, 187; of generations, 95–96; of Millennials, *307*, 308–10; parents transmitting, 95; socialization and events for, 96
political knowledge, 250
political leaders: APC model on women as, 165–66; Black Lives Matter and, 195–96; discrimination against women as, 166–67, 172; by gender and generation, *169–71, 173, 175*; generations on women as, 168–70; Gen Z on, 169; Gen Z on gender of, 171; older generations on, 175–76; women and characteristics of, 164; women as, 162–63, 166–70; women facing barriers to be, 167–68, 170–73; young adults readiness as, 367–68
political parties: affective polarization hostility toward, 67–68; APC model with identification of, 44; Baby Boomers identity with, 188; congressional words and, 412; education based ratings of, 80n22; Florida 2020 election turnout by, *347*; in Florida by generation, 333–35; Florida voter registration by, *334–35*; generational differences toward, 48, 63–64; generational replacement influencing, 59–63; generation's identification of, *100*; Gen X's identification with, 64–65; Gen Z influence on, 87–88; heroes identified by, 198–99, *199*; issue words used by, *404–5*; language and words by, *404–5*; language differences of, 401–6, *402–3*; Millennial's congressional activities of, *395*; Millennial's demographic words and, 396, *398–99*; Millennial's identification of, 107, 308–10, *309*, 319–21; negative partisanship of, 35; Obama and identification of, 107; partisanship trends of, *50*; periods influence on, 50–51; polarization in Congress of, 409–10; recruitment practices of, 409; thermometer ratings of, 44–45; trends of, 46–47; young adult's turnout rate of, 347. *See also* in-party ratings; out-party ratings

political science: civic engagement from, 269–70; generational analysis in, 12; generational change in, 28; generational influence in, 7; on generational studies, 25–26; research in, 27

politicized places hypothesis, 119–20

politics: age cohorts distinction in, 89; change after Trump in, 322; children learning, 25; COVID-19 and Gen Z, 86, 92–94; generational replacement in, 202–3; generations drop-off in activities in, 245; generations in, 1–2, 4–5, *20*; Gen Z motivated by, 220–21; Gen Z on women in, 172; Gen Z's significance in, 85–86; identity, 409; international, 28–29; liberal, 3, 118, 206n3, 305–10, 389; Mannheim on disruptions in, 87–88; Millennial's dissatisfaction with, 300; Millennials on system of, *316*, 316–18; Millennials seeking changes in, 314–18, *315*; reforms in, 238–39; Sanders influencing young adults in, 267–68; socialization of attitudes on, 24–27, 176; voting for change in, 312–13; women in, 4, 174–76, 289n10; younger adults knowledge of, 256–57; young voters views on women in, 162–63

The Politics of Millennials (Rouse and Ross), 310

polling booths, 245

population: demographic shifts in, 41; education rates of, *247*; Florida's growth in, 329; generational estimates of, *22–23*; Southern realignment with changes in, 51

post-Millennials, 90–91

prescription drugs, 144

presidential campaigns, 266, 269–70, 286, 388

presidential candidates, 5; civic engagement by, 265–66; visits from, 261–62; voter turnout rates for, 288n3; younger adults targeted by, 262–63

Presidential Character (Barber), 25

presidential election (2020): candidates

age and race in, 341–47; Florida by gender in, *348–49*; Florida by generation, race and ethnicity in, *348*; Florida's voter turnout in, *347*; important issues in, *342*; voter turnout during, 162

presidential elections: ANES data used on, 78n5; Biden not recognized as winning, 313–14; Democratic and Republican Parties in, 108; Democrats winning, 78n1; issues by generation in, *265*, 265–66; Millennials voting in, 313; of Obama, 311–12; older generations in, 240–43, *241–42*; study of year and age in, *43*; voter fraud concerns in, 313–14; voters age gap in, *338*; voting rates by age in, *240*; youngest to oldest in, 240–43, *241–42*

presidents, 333, *336*

press releases: in data set, 391; from Democratic Party, 406; legislators using generation in, 413n7; Millennial legislator's words used in, 396, *398–99*; Millennials and party status in, *404–5*; social issues words in, 411–12, 414n14

Price, McKinley, 371–72, 374–75, 377n5

primary election: ATT for voting in, 271; civic engagement in, 273–80, *274–79*, 290n30; Sanders losing in, 280, 319; voters mobilized for, 284–85; voting in, 271, 280, 319

Progressive Labor Party, 227

protesters, 232; civil rights, 195; racial justice, 202, 343; tactics of campus, 223–24

pruned observations, *272*, *274–79*

pulse-rate approach, 94–98, 101

Qualtrics, 304–5

Quillian, L., 119

race: bias based on, 154; civil rights and, 153; in climate and civil rights movement, 225–26; Controlled Substances Act and, 153–54; drug use and role of, 153–55; ethnicity and,

303; in Florida, *330*, 331–33, *332*; Florida's presidential election by, *348*; Floyd and protests about, 202, 343; by generations in U.S., *23*; heroism traits by gender and, *197*; inequality by, 343; injustice by, 301; justice and, 154–55; marijuana incarceration and, 154; Millennial's attitudes on, 13; minority groups by, 264; presidential candidates age and, 341–47; racism against, 153; in 2020 presidential election, *342*; young adults turnout rate by, 347–48

rally attendance: ATT plots of, *272*; civic engagement from, 280–81; livestreaming and, 291n31; mean probability of voting from, *274–75*; Sanders impact on, *282–83*; Sanders with livestream and, 273; social desirability bias and, 288n8

Reagan, Ronald, 59, 101, 141, 143, 183

rebalancing routines, 289n17

recruitment practices, 409

Reefer Madness (film), 141, 143–44

religion, by generation in U.S., *23*, *23*

representation, by Congress, 387, 390–91

Republican Party: age and generations in, 37; antisocialism rallying cry of, 345, 348; in APC model, *71–72*; climate change denied by, 215–16; Democrats beating, 34; Democrats compared to, 46–52; demographic changes favoring, 50–51; door-to-door canvassing by, 346; education and, 80n23; generational differences and, 80n21; generational replacement and, 63, 66–68; Gen X affiliation with, 59, 63, 67, 79n14, 101; heroes within, 195; in- and out-party ratings of, 79n20; in-party rating among, *60*; Millennials in, 59, 393; Obama not approved by, 206n12; out-party ratings among, *61*; in presidential elections, 108; Southerners benefiting, 59–63; Southern realignment with, 48; white men in, 413n10

research: content analysis in, 391; data and methods for, 167–68, 268–71; data in, 359; design of, 359–62, 390–400, 410–12; Matching Frontier technique in, 270–71; methodological issues in, 16–19; in political science, 27; results from, 271–73; surveys and results of, 189–96

"Revolution" (song), 11

revolutionary change, in elections, 314–16, 321–22

Rice, Laurie, 5, 290n29

Robinson, Jo Ann, 216

Roessner, Amber, 183

Roe v. Wade, 108

Rohall, David, 13

Romney, Mitt, 337

Rose, Max, 409, 414n15

Rosenstone, S., 263

Ross, Ashley: COVID-19 influence from, 287; economic crisis as formative from, 124; generational identity from, 26; Millennial persona from, 6, 121, 126; Millennial's generational divides in attitudes from, 121–22; Millennials on issues from, 389; *The Politics of Millennials* by, 310

Rouse, Stella: COVID-19 influence from, 287; economic crisis as formative from, 124; generational identity from, 26; Millennial persona from, 6, 121, 126; Millennial's generational divides in attitudes from, 121–22; Millennials on issues from, 389; *The Politics of Millennials* by, 310

R-studio, 392

Rubio, Marco, 286, 339

Ryder, N. B., 120

Sabato, Larry, 167

Sanders, Bernie: campaign issues of, 407; college campuses visited by, 5, 261, 263–66; college students mobilized by, 284, 286; in presidential campaigns, 388; primary election voting and, 280, 319; rally activities impact of, *282–83*; rally or livestreaming of,

Sanders, Bernie (*continued*)
273; time between visits of, 288n9;
young adult's political participation
and, 267–68; young adult's support
for, 341
scare tactics, 143–44
Schaller, M., 141
Scheepers, P., 123
Schickler, E., 79n14
Schultz, David, 2, 95, 219
SCLC. *See* Southern Christian Leadership Conference
Seale, Bobby, 227–28
Seal Team 6, 188
secular realignment, 34
segregation, 153
service announcements, 143–44
SES. *See* socioeconomic status
Sessions, Jeff, 141
sexism: in literature, 163–64; socialization passing on, 164; of voters, 162–63
Shachar, R., 250
Shanks, J. M., 255
shared experiences: of generations,
264–65; of Millennials, 318–19
Sigel, Roberta A., 24, 27, 164
Silent generation, 39, 157, 170, 172, 330
Silent Spring (Carson), 11
single-payer health care, 264
sit-ins, 216–17, 220, 222, 230
16@First Vote, 252–54
slacktivism, 310
slavery, 196, 203
smartphones, 91, 155, 231, 233, 336
Smith, C. W., 13, 27
SNCC. *See* Student Nonviolent Coordinating Committee
social desirability bias, 288n8
social issues, 39, 414n14
socialization: age and political, 38; in
age cohorts, 145–46; of Boomers and
Gen Xers, 231; Millennials experiences of, 414n16; of political attitudes, 24–27, 176; political events for,
96; sexism passed on through, 164;
theories of, 4; young adults with different, 163

social justice, 231, 343
social media: Baby Boomers on, 156;
Black Lives Matter using, 229–30;
civic engagement with, 281; Gen Z
using, 219, 267–68; in-person contact
and, 346; learning from, 155–56; Millennials and Gen Z using, 219, 267–
68; Thunberg's reliance on, 223
social movements, 5, 216
social security, 343
society, heroism in, 184, *192*, 194–95
socioeconomic status (SES), 303
"The Sociological Problem of Generations" (Mannheim), 15, 38
Souls to the Polls, 348
Southern Christian Leadership Conference (SCLC), 226–28
Southerners: Democratic identification
by, *49*, 79n18; non-Southerners and,
49; Republicans benefiting from,
59–63
Southern realignment: Democratic
Party and, 46–47; Gen X and, 48; population changes in, 51; with Republicans, 48
Special Action Office for Drug Abuse
Prevention, 143
Steil, Bryan, 401, 408
stereotypes, 165, 364–65
Stoker, Laura: APC laid out by, 2, 87;
concept of generations from, 14, 24;
generations characterized by, 186–
87; identity and evaluation shifts
from, 151; on impressionable years,
213–14; partisan polarization from,
184–85; on party alignment, 85;
social issue divergence from, 39
Stoney, Levar, 363–67, 371–72
Strauss, William, 12, 17–19, 94, 96
student loan debt, 264, 388, 406
Student Nonviolent Coordinating Committee (SNCC), 218
subgroups, 78n9
substantive representation, 387,
400–408
suffrage movement, of women, 346
Sundquist, J. L., 14

Sunrise Movement, 222, 224, 226
supportive networks, 216, 226–29, 232–33
Supreme Court, 223
survey data, 205

Taylor, P., 26
technology: elections using, 391; globalization and, 318; government modernizing, 374; Millennials with proliferation of, 302; young adults getting news from, 336–37
terrorism, 414n14
thermometer, feeling and rating: APC model for in-party, 74–75; APC model for out-party, 76–77; Biden on, 102; men and women on, 103; of political parties, 44–45; on Trump, 102–4
Thomas, Leah, 225–26
Thomas, Zee, 229
Thunberg, Greta, 217, 221, 223–25, 257
Thurmond, Strom, 206n11
TikTok, 230
Till, Emmett, 216
Timmons, William, 401, 408
Tocqueville, Alexis de, 206n8
Torres-Small, Xochitl, 414n15
trait stereotypes, 165
Transform Student Debt to Home Equity Act, 406
trends: in affective polarization, 55–56, 56; in- and out-party ratings, 57, 62; with Independent party, 52, 53, 56; macro-political, 41; of political parties, 46–47, 50
The Trial of the Chicago 7 (film), 228
trigger events, 98; of Gen Z, 107; of Millennials, 121
Tripp, Jim, 231
Truman, Harry, 101, 261
Trump, Donald, 86, 320; climate movement setbacks from, 217; as cultural conflict symbol, 104; as enemy symbol, 102–3; on feeling thermometer, 102–4; Florida won by, 339; generational split on, 198; Gen Z and, 99–

104; as heroic, 193; men and women on thermometer for, 103; Mount Rushmore visit of, 182–83; political change after, 322; rallies held by, 287; voter gains by, 308–9; white voters favoring, 87–88; young adults alienated by, 101
Trump Anxiety Disorder, 92
trust: in government, 243, 244, 247; Millennial's importance of, 313
Tubbs, Michael, 363–69, 376, 377n1
Tubman, Harriet, 186
Twenge, J. M., 48, 231
26th Amendment: elections and, 243–47; minimum voting age dropped in, 239, 251–53; young adults and, 254–55
Twitter, 230, 391, 402–3, 413n7

undergraduate students, 268
Underwood, Lauren, 385, 387, 396, 408–9
United Nations, 221, 257
United States (U.S.): demographic changes in, 22–23; drug use in, 140–42; ethnicity by generations in, 23; generations in politics of, 20; heroism reflecting values of, 191; individualism in, 119; law review article in, 255; macro-political changes in, 44; partisan landscape of, 66–68; religion by generation in, 23, 23; voting costs in, 248–49

Valdivia, John, 369–70
values: covariate, 273–80; generations impacting, 4, 26; heroism reflecting, 191
variables: of age, 78n8; of demographics, 45, 78n10; dependent, 125, 269; independent, 125–26, 127–28
Vietnam War, 88, 239, 244
volunteering attendance, 272, 276–77
voter registration: at colleges, 245–46; in Florida by generation, 331–33, 335; in Florida by party, 334–35; Florida's non-white, 333; of Florida's young adults, 334–35

voters: colleges registering, 245–46; discrimination against women by, 164; election turnout of, 86; Florida's Gen Z, *332*; generational responses from, 177–79; from North Carolina, 167; Obama winning younger adults as, 337–39; presidential elections age gap of, *338*; primary election mobilized for, 284–85; sexism of, 162–63; Trump favored by white, 87–88; Trump's gains of, 308–9; 2020 presidential elections turnout of, 162; types of, 253–54; Votes@18 as, 239–40; white, 87–88; young adults as, 166

voter turnout: by age, 251–53; COVID-19 influencing young adults, 346; by education level, *246*; for elections, 86; in Florida 2020 presidential election, *347*; in Florida by generation, *344*; Florida's Hispanic, 348; gender of young adults in, 348–49; of Millennials, 311–14, *312*; national events impacting, 244; personal characteristics in, 269; presidential campaign visits impacting, 266, 269–70; presidential candidates and rates of, 288n3; during presidential election (2020), 162; reform goals for, 255–57; young adults by race in, 347–48; young adults in political parties, 347

Votes@16, 252–54, 256

Votes@18, 239–40, 243–44, 247

voting: by African Americans and Latinos, 308–10; age, 78n6; age lowered for, 243, 254–57; cost-benefit terms in, 248–51; covariate values for, 273–80; distractions in, 249–50, 254; economic equality in, 243, 247; education levels and, 247; eligibility for, 250; energy and time in, 249; factors of, *249*, 252; by generations, 157, 309; Gen Z, 157; as habitual behavior, 248; by Latinos, 308–10; less-educated citizens, 246; mean probability of, *274–79*; midterm elections, *242*; Millennial's behavior in, 319–20; Millennial's choice of, 99; Millennial's presiden-

tial election, 313; minimum age for, 251–53; by older generations, 255; older generation's patterns of, 343–44; opposition, 313; for political change, 312–13; political knowledge and, 250; political system rigged and, 316–18, 322; in presidential elections by age, *240*; presidential elections fraud concerns in, 313–14; in primary election, 271, 280, 319; rally attendance and mean probability of, *274–75*; rates dropped in, 246–47; 16@First Vote in, 252–54; trust in government in, 243, *244*, 247; 26th Amendment dropping minimum age for, 239; U.S. costs of, 248–49; young adult issues in, 349–50; young adults first time, 250–51, 253–54

Voting Rights Act (1965), 217, 223, 227

War on Drugs, 141–42

Warren, Earl, 39

Washington, George, 193, 195–98, 200, 203, 205

Wattenberg, M., 240

weather pattern changes, 220

websites: biographies, 396–97, *398–99*, 400–406, *402–3*, 408–9, 413n7; data scraped from, 391–92; Democratic Party platform on, 407

whistle-stop campaign, 261

white voters, 87–88, 162, 340

the Who, 11

Wilkes, R., 123

Winship, C., 42, 126, 128

Wolfinger, R. E., 285

women: African American congressional, 397; APC model on political leaders as, 165–66; in Congress, 351n9; discrimination of political leaders as, 166–67, 172; on feeling thermometer, *103*; Gen Z on politics for, 172; as leaders by generations, 168–70; older generations on leadership by, 175–76; as political leaders, 162–63, 166–70; political leadership barriers faced by, 167–68, 170–73;

political leadership characteristics and, 164; political participation by, 174–75, 289n10; in politics, 4, 174–76, 289n10; suffrage movement of, 346; voters discriminating against, 164; young voters views on politics for, 162–63

word use: of Congress, 412; in demographics, 411; ideological, 413n2; Millennial legislators, 396, *398–99*; by Millennials, 396–97; political parties issue, *404–5*; social issue, 411–12, 414n14; web biographies, 396–97

World War II, 200, 206n10

Yang, Y., 126

Yeampierre, Elizabeth, 226

Young, Andrew, 213, 229, 232

young adults, 20; civic engagement by, 288n7; on climate change, 215–17; in climate movement, 217; COVID-19 influencing turnout of, 346; first time voting for, 250–51, 253–54; in Florida, 337, 344–45; Florida's diversity of, 336–37; Florida's voter registration of, 334–35; heroism of, 195–96; impressionable years of, 213–14; leadership readiness of, 367–68; life cycle theories and, 260–61; mayors reaching out to, 367–68; mobilization of, 344–45; Obama's influence on, 166, 241; Obama winning votes of, 337–39; political parties turnout rate of, 347; politics knowledge by, 256–57; presidential candidates targeting, 262–63; Sanders influence on political participation by, 267–68; Sanders support from, 341; smartphones reliance of, 233; socialization different for, 163; technology for news by, 336–37; Trump alienating, 101; turnout rate by gender of, 348–49; turnout rate by race of, 347–48; 26th Amendment and, 254–55; vote by issues of, 349–50; as voters, 166

Young Man Luther (Erikson), 25

young voters: Biden victory importance of, 162; Clinton, H., not energizing, 339–40; in Florida gubernatorial election, 340–41; in presidential elections, 240–43, *241–42*; women in politics views of, 162–63

Young Voters of Color Get Out the Vote campaign, 345

youth Bill of Rights, 362

Zero Hour, 224

zero overall slope, 128

zero-tolerance policy, 141

Zukin, Cliff, 26, 202